Choral Music on Record

Choral Music on Record

edited by
ALAN BLYTH

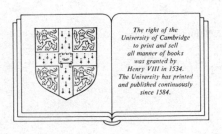

The right of the
University of Cambridge
to print and sell
all manner of books
was granted by
Henry VIII in 1534.
The University has printed
and published continuously
since 1584.

CAMBRIDGE UNIVERSITY PRESS
Cambridge
New York   Port Chester
Melbourne   Sydney

Published by the Press Syndicate of the University of Cambridge
The Pitt Building, Trumpington Street, Cambridge CB2 1RP
40 West 20th Street, New York, NY 10011, USA
10 Stamford Road, Oakleigh, Melbourne 3166, Australia

First published 1991

Printed in Great Britain at the University Press, Cambridge

British Library cataloguing in publication data
Choral music on record.
1. Choral music. Sound recordings
I. Blyth, Alan, *1929–*
780.266

Library of Congress cataloguing in publication data
Choral music on record/edited by Alan Blyth.
    p.   cm.
ISBN 0-521-36309-8
1. Choral music – Discography.   2. Sound recordings – Reviews.
I. Blyth, Alan.
ML 156.4.V7C54 1990
016.7825'026'6 – dc20   90-1638   CIP   MN

ISBN 0 521 36309 8 hardback

WG

Contents

v

Contents

vi

Preface

In compiling this volume, we have endeavoured to cover the major choral works that a music lover is likely to encounter in the concert hall or to sing in a choral society. I am well aware that there are omissions. To keep the book within reasonable bounds I have had to exclude, for instance, Tudor and Renaissance works, Haydn's, Schubert's and Bruckner's Masses, and a number of more recent works on the margin of popularity. The most frequently recorded pieces are included, however, and most recordings up to the end of March 1990 have been considered. As has been my practice in earlier volumes in the 'On Record' series, I have let the work and the author dictate the format of each chapter. For instance, it was essential in the case of *Messiah* to let Teri Noel Towe have the freedom to describe in detail the various performing editions and to indicate anomalies in their performance.

We have endeavoured to make each chapter as comprehensive as possible in its coverage of the work in hand, but inevitably, even with the help of several collectors and libraries, certain sets have eluded us. As in previous volumes, it has amazed me how, without any collusion, different authors have come to similar conclusions about certain artists. There is also an astonishing uniformity in the adverse criticism of conductors and singers in ignoring composers' wishes, in particular as regards tempo. In most cases this criticism is aimed at slow speeds: too many performers today seem to equate a deliberate tempo with deep meaning. Important interpreters of the past seldom make that mistake. Another marked tendency evident throughout is one away from individuality of utterance to a more generalised approach, mostly occasioned by the internationalisation of musical performance. It is a habit to be deplored. In spite of these strictures, enough great performances are chronicled here to make the effort of listening to so many recordings well worthwhile. At least I hope my hard-working contributors feel that way. I am sure that they, like me, are also fascinated by the study of the history of performance throughout some seventy years, which is now available on disc.

Once again thanks are due to fellow-authors for their many hours of fruitful labour, and also to John T. Hughes for his inestimable help in compiling and editing the discographies, and in proof-reading. He has also helped authors through the loan of rare records, as have Brian Gould, Peter Lack and Christopher Norton-Welsh. Derek Lewis, BBC Record Librarian, has again given considerable assistance. Penny Souster, as publisher's editor, has given constant encouragement.

Teri Noel Towe's chapter on Handel's *Messiah*, though heavily revised, is derived from articles previously published in *American Record Guide*, *High Fidelity*, *Opus*, and *The American Organist*. Thanks are due to the Editors of these journals for permission to use those materials. My own chapter on Verdi's Requiem is a revised version of a chapter which first appeared in *Opera on Record 3*, Hutchinson (1984). Thanks are due to the publisher for permission to use this chapter.

Alan Blyth

Discographies for all chapters have been placed at the end of the volume.

Monteverdi: Vespers (1610)

DAVID FALLOWS

Ideas about the performance of early music have changed radically over the past forty years. There has been considerable research on the vocal and instrumental forces Monteverdi is likely to have had in mind. For most baroque music, we now prefer an athletic and transparent texture to the lush, full sound of yesteryear. Different views of tempo go hand in hand with these ideas; in fact, in some ways they flow almost inevitably from them. Those in their turn lead to a questioning of earlier assumptions about form and design. Pitch, pitch-standards and intonation have similarly been examined exhaustively in a historical context, with results that have a fundamental impact on the performer's approach. In the particular case of Monteverdi's 1610 Vespers there has been enormous discussion of how far it is really to be seen as a single work, whether liturgical material needs adding, and if so how much. Few of these areas of discussion have led to unanimously accepted conclusions: that is often the way with historical investigation, in music as much as in anything else. And not all conductors have shown themselves equally informed or equally prepared to accept the latest conclusions at any one time. But the range of areas in which attitudes have changed means that each performance is to some extent a child of its time. The date of a recording is important.

Not that the date of itself says much about the quantity of musical pleasure to be derived from a particular recording. Most musicians would accept that there are qualities of musicianship which retain their power irrespective of historical purity. Nadia Boulanger's pre-war recordings of Monteverdi madrigals with piano accompaniment are particular favourites because they do manage to touch on something vital in Monteverdi's genius; sadly, she seems never to have approached the 1610 Vespers. A moving performance of baroque music with a band of saxophones remains a moving performance. And it would be easy to argue that the best record of the Monteverdi Vespers is one of the earliest, that conducted by Anthony Lewis – vivacious, exciting, teeming with conviction and above all constantly dancing. It is also, despite its date, recorded with extraordinary clarity. Every detail is audible.

1

DAVID FALLOWS

The search for better informed performances has one main justification: that the correct forces and an appropriate attitude to performance should make it easier to achieve the effect the composer had in mind. Quite often they seem not to do so. The reasons can include the unfamiliarity of the techniques, the insufficiency of the research (which by its nature must always remain insufficient) and the individual qualities of the performers. But the available recordings of the Monteverdi Vespers do show changing attitudes and evolving solutions to the music's problems. They also point the way to the future.

Monteverdi's publication of 1610 has a long and elaborate title that has in itself raised much discussion. It opens, in large letters, with the words 'Mass for the Virgin in six voices for church choirs'. After that comes, in very small type, 'and Vespers for several voices to sing', followed by slightly larger type for 'with some sacred concerti (*sacris concentibus*) suitable for chapels or princely apartments'. The Mass that opens the volume and furnishes its main title is the rarely performed parody-Mass on Nicholas Gombert's motet *In illo tempore*. Only after that comes the music that we think of as the '1610 Vespers'. But at the end of the volume, alongside the seven-voice Magnificat normally used, there is another Magnificat, in six voices – a relatively slight work, sharing some musical material with its grander and more famous companion, but nonetheless a masterpiece. (Some believe it may be appropriate for a performance without instruments or for the 'first' Vespers of the feast.) The Mass and the six-voice Magnificat have occasionally been recorded separately, but the only version of the entire volume is Schneidt's on three records (1975). This is a most impressive set, not least for the wonderfully spirited singing of the Regensburg Cathedral Choir, though the ideals of historical veracity represented by Archiv make it sometimes tend towards the drab and dutiful. It is, however, one of the few recordings to confine itself to the voices Monteverdi is likely to have used, specifically excluding women. (The other is Segarra (1976), in many ways Harmonia Mundi's answer to the Archiv challenge, and curiously similar in its musical effect.)

There are several good reasons why nobody else has attempted to record the entire collection. The Mass is widely regarded as well below the inspirational level of the remaining music; and it certainly inhabits an entirely different world, that of the Roman *stile antico* rather than the new north Italian dramatic style with voices and instruments. In any case the 1610 publication was probably not intended to record a particular performance. There is no clear evidence that it was ever performed as a unit, though there are a couple of conceivably appropriate events at Mantua within the four years before it was published. Several of the pieces may have been composed much earlier. The publication's main aim was probably to display the range of Monteverdi's skill in composing church music. At the age of just over forty, he was beginning to look for a new job. His fame so far was mainly as a composer of madrigals; and this was in a sense his portfolio for a church position. The Mass is in the

2

Roman style, and the whole volume was dedicated to the Pope. But much of the Vespers music is in the new style most famously associated with Venice, and three years later it was in Venice that Monteverdi eventually received the post of *maestro* at St Mark's, which he was to hold for the rest of his life.

But once the 1610 collection is seen from that angle, further questions obviously arise. After the Mass, the remaining music is as follows:

EXORDIUM: Deus in adjutorium (6 voices, 6 instruments)

PSALM 109: Dixit Dominus (6 voices, with optional interludes for 6 instruments)
    CONCERTO: Nigra sum (Tenor solo)

PSALM 112: Laudate pueri (8 voices with organ)
    CONCERTO: Pulchra es (2 Sopranos)

PSALM 121: Laetatus sum (6 voices)
    CONCERTO: Duo seraphim (3 Tenors)

PSALM 126: Nisi Dominus (2 groups of 5 voices each)
    CONCERTO: Audi coelum (2 Tenors with 6-voice close)

PSALM 147: Lauda, Jerusalem (7 voices)
    CONCERTO: Sonata sopra Sancta Maria (Soprano with 8 instruments)

HYMN: Ave maris stella (2 choirs of 4 voices with ritornellos for 5 instruments)

CANTICLE: Magnificat (7 voices and 6 instruments)

CANTICLE: Magnificat (6 voices and organ)

While the psalms, hymn and one Magnificat are part of the Marian vespers liturgy, the concerti are not and never have been. That could suggest that Monteverdi's Venetian publisher simply put the music in a convenient order that has nothing to do with any intended performing sequence. So Hans Redlich's edition of 1935 reshuffles the music and omits two psalms ('thus the whole work is kept within the limits of a two-hour performance'); that edition was used by Hans Grischkat (1953), in a mistily romantic recording that is very much a child of its time and place. Grischkat's main principle seems to be that sacred music must, above all, not dance. Thus anything that could lilt along is slowed down to the nature of a cortège, very much to the discomfort of the chorus. Its general effect now seems unpleasant and puddingy.

Robert Craft (1967) also resequences the pieces 'according to their individual characters and the "sense" of a concert-hall performance'. But his performing order does in fact work rather well. His chorus is bright and responsive, working against a heavy orchestra.

Another view was that the way the five concerti are described on the title page suggests that they are quite separate from the piece that could be described as Monteverdi's 'Vespers of 1610'. So Denis Stevens's recording (1967) omitted them entirely. On the other hand, he added the appropriate plainchant antiphons before and after each psalm, thereby creating something rather closer to a liturgical vespers service. His chorus is less vital than those of Lewis or Craft, and often somewhat wobbly; and for Monteverdi's cornetti he uses oboes, with extremely uneven results. But the general sound is more convincingly Italian than anything offered so far: the consonants, the vowels and the moods represent what at the time was a significant novelty in 'authentic' performance.

In the same year Jürgen Jürgens inserted plainchant antiphons but otherwise retained Monteverdi's sequence. And Harnoncourt did the same in what was evidently intended as Teldec's replacement for Jürgens in 1987.

Others have continued to omit the antiphons, on the surely valid principle that such a grand conception need not doggedly follow the liturgy. The versions of Schneidt, Segarra and Corboz gain considerable power from the way each piece follows directly on from the last.

But Andrew Parrott (1984) makes a comprehensive and radical attempt to reconstruct a festal Vespers service on the basis of recent research. His first principle is that there seems to have been a tradition of replacing the repeat of the antiphon after the psalm with a sacred concerto or instrumental piece. This 'explains' all but one of the concerti: they are simply antiphon substitutes. But the exception – 'Duo seraphim' – has no explicit Marian connections; so it must be treated as a substitute for the 'Benedicamus Domino' and shunted away to the end of the service. Moreover, the 'Sonata sopra Sancta Maria' is put in what seemed musically a more appropriate position, after the Magnificat. There are therefore two psalms that lack adequate antiphon-substitutes to follow them; and here he puts instrumental sonatas (by Giovanni Paolo Cima) in their place.

Another approach comes from Harry Christophers (1989) who, on the advice of Graham Dixon, proposes that the whole volume is a massive palimpsest and that the music was originally a second vespers for the feast of St Barbara. In the 'Sonata sopra Sancta Maria' the words are changed. And, again, the sequence of movements is juggled round in line with what can be discerned from surviving service-books of the time, with inserted instrumental pieces, a Palestrina motet and, to end the work, the 'Sonata' followed by 'Ave maris stella'.

All this is obviously distressing for those who hear the old-style Monteverdi Vespers as reaching an awesome climax in the Magnificat and particularly in its wonderfully conclusive 'Gloria Patri': the way Parrott's performance tails off with 'Duo seraphim' followed by a few gentle pieces of plainchant may be in line with current awareness that baroque 'form' did not work to an inevitable conclusion in the Wagnerian sense, but it is nonetheless disappointing to those brought up on the more common sequence of events. (Harry Christophers's ending is perhaps more satisfactory in its own way

4

for those who hear the work in the received manner.) It is also distressing for those who see a musical logic in the pattern of the concerti: solo voice, two voices, three voices, six voices and finally the massive 'Sonata sopra Sancta Maria' before the serene hymn and the Magnificat. Moreover, those who are puzzled that this research can explain the position of all but two works in Monteverdi's collection may wish to reflect on four matters. First, while we know quite a lot about Venetian liturgies during those years we know rather less about the liturgy of Mantua, where Monteverdi composed the music. Second, we know nothing for certain about the event or events for which the music may have been composed. Third, composers throughout the ages have occasionally done strange things with liturgy for their own purposes. Fourth, there is in any case a clear principle going back to the twelfth century that the service had, in Stephen Bonta's words, 'two levels, liturgical and musical, that run along concurrently'; that is to say, liturgical fundamentalism may not be the clearest guide to Monteverdi's intentions. Among scholars who have discussed the matter Denis Arnold, Stephen Bonta and Andreas Holschneider have agreed that Monteverdi's print includes – after the opening Mass – everything necessary for both a first and a second vespers for the Virgin; their view has not been universally accepted, but it seems tenable. That is presumably why the two recordings of 1987 simply follow the printed order. (It may or may not be relevant here that the 11th movement in Monteverdi's sequence contains just eleven statements of the melody 'Sancta Maria ora pro nobis'.)

Another distressing change of attitudes came from a closer examination of the original partbooks. This showed that the last psalm, 'Lauda Jerusalem', and the Magnificat are written in what are known as 'high clefs' and need to be transposed down a fourth to bring them in line with the other movements. The arguments for that were first fully laid out by Andrew Parrott in an article for *Early Music* (November 1984). Here is not the place to justify it except to observe that its history goes back to Gregorian chant. You wrote chant down at the pitch that put the tones and semitones in the right places; and you simply sang it at the pitch that felt comfortable. So for several centuries there were two concurrent ways of thinking about, for example, middle C: as an appropriate frequency obtained from the organ (which itself varied from church to church) and as a step within a tonal, or rather modal, framework. Quite often in a collection of motets from the sixteenth or seventeenth centuries there is a sudden change of clefs and ranges. Monteverdi's 1610 collection is as clear a case as any. The Mass, the psalm 'Lauda Jerusalem' and the two Magnificat settings are in high clefs, consistently; the rest is in low clefs which are equally consistent. The voice ranges are higher in the 'high clef' movements. Briefly, the historical and logical arguments for transposing those sections down a fourth in relation to the remaining music seem unassailable.

Of the recordings available so far, only those of Andrew Parrott (1984)

5

and Philippe Herreweghe (1987) follow that transposition pattern. Nikolaus Harnoncourt (1987), for example, studiously ignores it even though he must surely have known the arguments. But in the event neither Parrott nor Herreweghe entirely justifies the procedure. Certainly the 'Lauda Jerusalem' sounds considerably better in both. Previously it had always seemed a mess, largely because the tenor line carrying the chant goes uncomfortably high: my notes on these recordings nearly all read either 'tenors ugly' or 'tenors inaudible' (with the significant exceptions being Lewis and Gardiner), though a couple solve the problem by scoring the line for trombones. Moreover the cruelly high cornett parts in the Magnificat become infinitely more comfortable and secure in the transposed version. On the other hand, transposition causes some major problems in the Magnificat. The section 'Et misericordia' lies unusually low, with the basses descending to bottom G. Put that down a fourth and you have something rather freakish, even though David Thomas sings them (for both Parrott and Herreweghe) with miraculous clarity; and Herreweghe goes some way towards resolving the problem by adopting a much slower tempo. Anyone who has done research on performance practice knows that you must suspend value judgements and that ideas contrary to a particular musical reaction are the ones that are most difficult to accept. But the passage is astonishingly low, and makes one begin to wonder whether there isn't some way of softening Parrott's conclusions.

The other problem is even more subjective, though it is likely to be shared by most listeners. As we have come to know it in the concert hall, the Vespers leads inexorably towards its conclusion with masterly pacing. The fifth and last psalm, 'Lauda Jerusalem', is in an audibly higher register, audibly more of a strain on the singers, and audibly a culmination to the group of psalms. Then comes for the first time an almost entirely instrumental piece, the 'Sonata sopra Sancta Maria', after which comes the ineffably gentle and luminous hymn setting, 'Ave maris stella', before we launch into the concluding Magnificat, itself bright and colourful, not merely because of its slightly higher pitch but also because of the elaborate instrumental participation. And then at the end of the Magnificat comes the moment that so many listeners have found themselves subconsciously waiting for all evening, those wonderful tenor runs down from the high G in the closing 'Gloria Patri' section. Inevitably these runs lose their steam if they begin only on a D and run down well below the comfortable range of most tenor soloists.

What can be done about this? First, it must sadly be accepted that part of the singular success of the Vespers in the order printed by Monteverdi may be just the chance result of modern misunderstanding of Monteverdi's notation. Second, however, while there can really be no serious argument about the relative pitch of the various movements, there is room for considerable discussion of the actual pitch standard within which these relationships exist. Much baroque music nowadays is performed at a pitch-standard a semitone below modern concert pitch; but the available information clearly shows that there was a whole range of pitch-standards used in various places and at various times in the seventeenth and eighteenth centuries. There is in fact some evidence that Monteverdi was here using a pitch-standard somewhat higher than ours. A glance at the voice-ranges throughout the work suggests that much of the music lies uncomfortably low. The beautiful tenor solo concerto 'Nigra sum', for example, makes extensive use of the low D and rises as far as top G just once and almost in passing. It would surely work better at least a tone higher. In 'Audi coelum' the tenor must go down to low A: the most convincing performance of this, incidentally, is in Corboz (1983) where – contrary to the sleeve information – he uses the baritone Philippe Huttenlocher for that solo. For these and other reasons, it seems likely that Monteverdi's pitch-standard here was between a tone and a minor third higher than ours. That would bring all the voices into a more comfortable, brighter, range. It would solve the problem of the low notes just mentioned. And it would particularly restore some brilliance to the evidently brilliant runs at the end of the Magnificat.

So far, all recordings of the Vespers are at modern concert pitch (though Schneidt comes down a tone for the high-clef Mass, thereby bringing that work, at least, to what I would consider the appropriate pitch). To record it at a higher pitch would involve restringing stringed instruments, radically retuning organs and making new sackbuts – all of which at the moment seems disproportionately expensive. But until that is done we are unlikely to hear a fully convincing performance that follows the inevitable conclusions from Monteverdi's clefs. Returning to the points made at the beginning of this chapter: a further new insight into the nature of the Vespers has solved some problems but created new difficulties which will be resolved only gradually.

Scoring has inevitably varied over the years. Only recently has it been agreed that the psalms mainly demand organ continuo whereas the smaller concerted numbers are more in the chamber style (as the title-page indicates) and would be better accompanied by plucked string instruments, probably without even a melodic bass instrument. In 'Nigra sum', for example, the solo chitarrone used by Segarra (1976), Parrott (1984) and Christophers (1989) seems by far the most satisfactory solution. For the larger concerti and the 'Sonata sopra Sancta Maria' there would be a case for a more substantial group of plucked instruments: recent experience with other Italian soloistic music of the time suggests that several lutes, several chitarrones and several harps would be appropriate, though financial considerations have meant that such a solution is still extremely rare. What does need saying is that the earlier approaches with harpsichord and a heavy melodic bass instrument now seem hopelessly unstylistic for this music.

That raises the broader question of 'orchestration'. Jürgens (1967) and Harnoncourt (1987) offer the boldest recent solutions, with a wide range of wind instruments and constantly varying instrumentation, based largely on the writings of Michael Praetorius (1619). Certainly Praetorius gives us the fullest and most detailed information about the inclusion of instruments in concerted polyphony; but it is surely dangerous to use a north German writer to tell us about Italian music. Moreover, theirs is merely an extreme case of an issue that has existed as long as the Vespers has been performed. The decision to use a large body of instruments throughout brings with it the need to make the most elaborate reconstructions – indeed, orchestrations – which effectively make Monteverdi's original partbooks entirely inadequate for any performing purposes. Harnoncourt apart, recordings over the years have represented an increasing search for simplicity. They have moved to a position where the cornetti, for example, are used only in the opening 'Deus in adiutorium' and in the later passages where they are specified, namely in the 'Sonata sopra Sancta Maria' and the Magnificat. And other instruments are used only when specified and absolutely necessary. The single exception to this, of course, is in the continuo group: there seems every evidence that such groups were accustomed to devising the most elaborate patterns on the basis of the written bass line. Recent recordings, such as those of Parrott and Herreweghe, more or less follow those principles. In some ways they make the work less colourful; but at the same time they undeniably clarify the texture and focus the ear on the notes that Monteverdi actually wrote.

Which in its turn brings us to the use of the chorus. Was Monteverdi writing for massed choirs or for an ensemble of soloists? The available evidence increasingly favours relatively small forces. A crux can be heard at the end of the second psalm, *Laudate pueri*, where a grand doxology gives way to an 'Amen' section in which the voices drop out one by one and the movement ends with two tenors intertwining with increasingly florid melismas of a kind that surely demand soloists. To perform the main body of the movement with a large chorus involves intricate decisions about where the soloists take over; and albeit less severely, the same problem arises innumerable times in the course of the Vespers. Whatever the specific virtues of Joshua Rifkin's arguments about the appropriate vocal ensemble for Bach's choral works, they draw attention to the enormous body of evidence that much of what used to be thought of as early choral music was designed for an ensemble with just one singer on each line. Here again it is Parrott who adopts the most extreme solution. He does have a chorus; but he uses it very sparingly indeed. Mostly he eliminates the need for painful pragmatic decisions about where soloists take over by allocating everything to solo voices. His results are often highly convincing, though they occasionally underline the fact that much of the homophonic writing does seem to demand a fuller choral sound. At the opening of 'Laudate pueri' one longs for the massive climax produced by Gardiner and Corboz.

Tempo is a matter that in some ways follows directly from the size of forces used. With a few solo voices there is little scope for a massive choral climax; but then many of the developments in baroque music over the last few years have been towards eliminating the need for such grand late-Romantic gestures. Parrott and Herreweghe are happy to let the music take its course and prefer to establish a tempo that can be retained throughout a movement. In some ways Schneidt and Segarra are even more cautious: when Monteverdi inserts passages in triple time they interpret it precisely according to the theorists, with results that can be numbingly dull. Others take what could be seen as a more old-fashioned view of Monteverdi as an essentially dramatic composer who strove for effects at every possible point. Here the extreme cases are Gardiner (1974) and Corboz (1983): both seem happy to halve or double the tempo on a whim; they will draw out what seems a significant cadence, insert massive pauses to clarify a textural articulation and rush at a passage that seems geared to generating excitement. I much prefer this approach. Both seem to me to succeed magnificently, not least because of the evident commitment they thereby gain from their choirs. Of the two, perhaps Corboz gains in that he can be gentler, creating large areas of space that contrast even more strikingly with the high-energy passages – though it is easy to predict that Gardiner's forthcoming second attempt will challenge Corboz in precisely that respect. But, then, much depends on whether one believes that Monteverdi's 'Vespers of 1610' is a single work, correctly published, or something of a mixed bag.

J.S. Bach: St John Passion

TERI NOEL TOWE

(Numbers in brackets refer to corresponding numbers in the discography)

The history of the *St John Passion* is more complex than that of Bach's other surviving setting of the Passion story, the *St Matthew Passion (qv)*. First performed in 1724, three years before the first version of the Matthew, this direct and deceptively 'simple' oratorio was subjected to a revision the following year that resulted in the substitution of new choruses for the opening and concluding ones, and the insertion of three alternate arias in the body of the work. All of the music for this first revision survives.

In the early 1730s, Bach returned, in essence, to the 1724 sequence, but with a few modifications. In the intervening years, the 'new' opening chorus, 'O Mensch, bewein' dein Sünde gross', became the concluding chorus of Part One of the *St Matthew Passion,* and thus was no longer available for use in the St John. Furthermore, ecclesiastical authorities in Leipzig had evidently objected to Bach's insertion of two intensely dramatic sequences from the Gospel according to St Matthew into the *St John Passion* (hereinafter *SJP*), and he removed them. Bach provided no replacement for the first of these excised interpolations, the passage describing Peter's remorse at his denial of Christ; but for the second, the earthquake episode after the Crucifixion, he substituted an instrumental sinfonia that has not come down to us. The aria that he wrote to replace 'Ach mein Sinn' in this third form of the *SJP* has also not been preserved. Finally, this third version did not have the chorale that follows the concluding chorus in the first version.

In the very last years of his life, Bach returned to the *SJP* and confirmed the sequence of the original version, restoring both the final chorale and the interpolations from the Gospel according to St Matthew that he had omitted from the third version. On Good Friday 1749, Bach gave a performance of the *SJP* that turned out to be the last performance of a Passion setting that he himself directed, for the following year he was unwell and he died on 28 July. This last performance was indeed a grand one; it called for a larger ensemble than he had used in previous productions, and it must have been a worthy valedictory to this important facet of Bach's musical life. This

10

'final' version contains a puzzling doubling continuo part for 'bassono grosso'; what kind of an instrument Bach intended this part to be played on is still a subject of controversy and uncertainty among Bach scholars. Of greater significance, however, at least to those who are interested in recordings of the *SJP*, is Bach's reinstrumentation of the arioso 'Betrachte meine Seel' and the following aria, 'Erwäge'. During the twenty-five years that had elapsed since the premiere performance, the lute, which Bach specifically calls for as a continuo instrument in the arioso, had become a very rare bird indeed, and the two viole d'amore appear to have been unavailable, too. Accordingly, Bach rescored these numbers for two muted violins and harpsichord. One of the many oddities involving the *SJP* on records is the infrequency with which one encounters the revised version of these numbers. Since the first complete recordings, the early version calling for the 'obsolete' instruments has been the one preferred by all and sundry.

The *SJP* was one of the first major compositions by Bach to be revived in the years following Mendelssohn's seminal performance of the *St Matthew Passion* on Good Friday, 1829. The first 'modern' performance of the *SJP* was given by the Singakademie in Berlin 1833; the first American performance took place in 1888, in Bethlehem, Pennsylvania, under the baton of Dr J. Fred Wolle, who twelve years later inaugurated the annual Bethlehem Bach Festival with the first complete performance of the B Minor Mass in the United States and perhaps only the second complete performance anywhere.

Of the three major choral works of Sebastian Bach, the *SJP* was the last to be accorded a complete recording. During the 78 era, precious little from this magnificent setting of the Passion story was available to the record collector. This sad state of affairs seems, at least in part, to have been a by-product of the common perception of the work as 'inferior' to the *St Matthew Passion* in some intangible and indescribable way.

It is, therefore, something of an irony to discover that among the handful of excerpts that were available on 78s was a disc devoted to the first of the three alternative arias that Bach composed for the second, 1725, version of the work. Sung by the querulous Jacques Bastard, who is accompanied by the members of the original Ars Rediviva Ensemble, which made a number of important pioneer recordings of the baroque repertory, this performance of 'Himmel, reise', BWV 245a, is, understandably, something of a collector's item, if only because of its novelty and scarcity (DA 4933). This performance, however, is one of only two on record in which the chorale *cantus firmus* is intoned correctly by a solo soprano, rather than the soprano section of the choir.

Little else was available to those interested in the work. In the early 1930s, French Columbia published four twelve-inch sides that contain abridged versions of the opening and concluding choruses, one 'turba' chorus, and two chorales (Fr. Col. D 15015/6). Performed in French by the 300-member Chorus and Orchestra of the Brussels Royal Conservatory under the direction of the

Belgian conductor Désiré Defauw, later Frederick Stock's su~~~~~~ ~~ M~~~~
Director of the Chicago Symphony Orchestra, these conser~
dimly recorded interpretations are of limited interest. A sing
excerpts from the 'Condemnation' section, followed by the co~
sung by the Choir of the Eglise St Guillaume of Strasbourg,
and organ accompaniment, under the baton of Charles Munc~
Fritz, appeared at about the same time (Parlo. E 10917). O~
today are two 78s of excerpts conducted by the Bach schol~
(EH 1062 and EG 6010). The concluding chorus, the conclud~
one other chorale are performed with sensitivity and with u~
a small chorus and orchestra led by a musician who was in ~
the revival of interest in the stylistically correct performance o~

Incredibly, there were only three 78rpm recordings of t~
number, the alto aria 'Es ist vollbracht'. Leopold Stokowski r~
orchestral arrangement with the Philadelphia Orchestra (Vic~
sung in French, the performance by Lina Falk, with the g~
played by Clerget and organ accompaniment by Noëlie Pierron~
over half a century, one of the more satisfying accounts of t~
3.20.006). The same may be said of Marian Anderson's heartr~~~~~~~ ~~~~~~~
in English, which was recorded in 1941, and was subsequently transferred to
LP in the early 1950s (ED 318; Vic. LCT 1111).

Apart from 'Es ist vollbracht' and 'Himmel, reise', only two arias seem
to have found their way to record during the 78 era. Both discs are justly sought
after by vocal collectors. One is a poignant performance of 'Ach mein Sinn'
sung by Julius Patzak (Pol. 62791; EPL 30191); the other is a recording of
'Ich folge dir gleichfalls' sung by Margherita Perras (DB 10094).

The first 'complete' recording of the *SJP* (1) was not made until the late
summer of 1950 (the bicentenary of the death of Bach), twelve years after the
first complete recording of the *St Matthew Passion* and thirty years after the
first recording of the *B Minor Mass*. Even then, it was not truly complete,
because the conductor, Ferdinand Grossmann, cut the reprise of the initial
ritornello in the opening and the concluding choruses, both of which are strict
da capos. The recording has little to recommend it in any case. The instrumental intonation leaves much to be desired; the winds are especially painful
to the ear. The chorus is not far enough forward within the ensemble. Apart
from bass Walter Berry, then at the beginning of his long career, none of the
soloists is worthy of special mention: Ferry Gruber, the Evangelist, sounds
a touch querulous; the rest are merely adequate.

As is the case with the *St Matthew Passion*, the first complete recording
was sung in English and was made in the United States (2). An aggregation
of New York's best freelance instrumentalists, a distinguished group of
soloists, a superb professional chorus and a remarkable amateur chorus came
together to record the *SJP* in the autumn of 1950 under the direction of

Robert Shaw, then as now America's greatest choral conductor. Blanche Thebom is especially affecting in the alto solos. All of the soloists sing with sharp diction and a focused tone. Apart from an excessively slow reading of 'Ach mein Sinn', Shaw's is a finely paced recording, and the interpretation is taut, dramatic and devoid of emotional excess. It was and still is a particularly distinguished account, despite the translated text, which the conductor himself adapted from the King James version of the Gospel and the Henry S. Drinker translation of the poetry.

The abridged recording conducted by Gottfried Preinfalk (3) that appeared in 1952, on the other hand, is unabashed in its emotional expression. With exaggerated ritards, much rubato, and extremes of dynamics, the performance can accurately be described as a Mengelbergesque account. The disc is not a selection of excerpts. It is a true abridgement: only a shortened version of the 'A' section of the opening chorus is presented, for instance. One rather regrets that Preinfalk was not given the chance to record the Passion in its entirety, because his reading has a conviction and spark that is lacking from most of the others made in the early 1950s, especially the Grossmann.

Recorded in the Thomaskirche in Leipzig in the summer of 1954, the legendary Günther Ramin account (4) is the first of a series that reflects the neo-baroque tradition that is less the outgrowth of the early nineteenth-century classical tradition established by Mendelssohn than the 'scholarly' refinement of that approach initiated by the Thomascantor Karl Straube (1873–1953), one of the pioneers of the return to musicologically accurate performances of early music. Straube's pupil and eventual successor as Thomascantor, Ramin, leads the Thomanerchor, an ensemble of eighty boys' and men's voices, and thirty-eight members of the Leipzig Gewandhaus Orchestra in a performance that, while it may have seemed revelatory thirty-five years ago, sounds dated today. Quite simply, the interpretation, unlike Ramin's severely abridged account of the *St Matthew Passion*, lacks the charisma needed to make it timeless. Matters are not helped by the pounding realisation of the figured bass on a clangorous metal-framed harpsichord. The quality of the solo singing, however, is very high, the contributions of Marga Höffgen and Ernst Haefliger being especially noteworthy. Though obviously large, the chorus does not sound as big as it clearly is, judging from the annotations.

The pseudonymous recording by the 'Bach Society of Berlin and Cathedral Choir' conducted by Hans Burckhardt (5) also evidently dates from 1954; it appears to be a performance recorded off the air. There are mindless 'cuts', often snippets of movements, that may indicate enforced tape or acetate changes. It is impossible at this late date to hazard a guess as to the true identities of the conductor and the performers, except to say that the Evangelist sounds like Helmut Krebs, whose interpretation of the tenor part, fortunately, was properly documented in a studio recording.

In the late 1950s, shortly before he left East Germany and settled in the

West, Kurt Thomas, Ramin's successor as Thomascantor, recorded the work with a large orchestra and chorus (6). Contemplative but not well focused, respectful rather than reverent, the performance is not a particularly successful one, and matters are not helped by the rather muddy sound. Thomas's recording, however, is one of the tiny handful to adopt the late form of 'Betrachte meine Seel' and 'Erwäge'. Of the soloists, only Sibylla Plate need be singled out: her solid, clear voice sounds, paradoxically, almost boyish at times; she sings the alto solos with affection and understanding.

Although it was not recorded until 1975, the Hans Joachim Rotzsch account is best discussed here, because his is the third, and most recent, recording conducted by a Thomascantor (7). It is also the most successful of the three, and, in its quiet way, one of the most satisfying recordings of the oratorio overall. Rotzsch, who was himself a fine tenor and who appears as a soloist in many of Ramin's recordings of Bach Cantatas, also uses a large chorus and orchestra. Peter Schreier here makes his debut on record as the Evangelist and acquits himself nobly, bringing a special dignity and keenness to the narration of the story. Theo Adam's voice had grown a little woolly by the time he made this recording, and that makes him sound rather 'old' as Jesus, but he sings the role with great understanding. Of the remaining soloists, including a radiant Arleen Augér at the dawn of her career, Heidi Reiss is the most notable. Her 'Es ist vollbracht' is a particular joy.

In 1988, Peter Schreier made his own recording of the *SJP* (8); he directs the performance and sings the role of the Evangelist as well as the tenor arias. As seems so often to be the case with those who sing Bach's Evangelist parts, Schreier is even better second time around, and he may well be the pre-eminent interpreter of these roles today. Robert Holl is an excellent, impassioned Jesus. While Olaf Bär interprets the bass arias sensitively, his voice is marred by a tight, rather bleaty vibrato. The other soloists are more than adequate. A mixed choir of some fifty voices and modern instruments are used.

Schreier's interpretation is straightforward in the main, but it is not without its eccentricities. The opening chorus, for instance, is marred by a curious stressing and lengthening of the strong beats that interferes with the relentless foreboding implicit in this highly charged music. On dubious musicological grounds, the running eighth-note bass line in 'Lasset uns den nicht zerteilen' is given to a solo bassoon. Schreier's reading is, however, one of the four so far made to include as an appendix the three alternative arias from the 1725 version; unfortunately the alternative opening and concluding choruses are omitted.

Had he not elected to emigrate from East Germany, Karl Richter probably would have succeeded his teacher Günther Ramin as Thomascantor. Instead, he moved to Bavaria and founded the Munich Bach Choir, which he built into what was, in the 1960s and 1970s at least, the most famous ensemble in the world specialising in the performance of Bach's sacred music. Though some of them are now thirty or more years old, many of Richter's recordings are still in the catalogue, and with good reason. His account of the *SJP* (9), recorded in 1964, is taut, incisive, intense, and charismatic; stylistically, his dramatic, at times operatically paced reading is a curious but successful marriage of the neo-baroque and the post-Romantic. The chorus of ninety and the rather large orchestra perform with precision and total commitment both to the music and to Richter's view of it. Haefliger shines once more in the tenor parts, singing with even greater beauty and profundity for Richter than he did for Ramin. Evelyn Lear's voice is perhaps too 'dramatic' in character for this music; her diction is muddy, and the text, therefore, is often unintelligible. Hermann Prey is an effective, youthful Jesus.

Recorded at about the same time as Richter's, Fritz Werner's interpretation (10) is a contemplative one. He adopts a slow tactus throughout, which emphasises his reverent view of the music. Krebs is a heavenly Evangelist: his clear and distinctive voice combines with an innate sensitivity for both music and text to produce one of the truly memorable accounts of the rôle. With like understanding and a clear, solid tone, Marga Höffgen excels in the alto solos, as she does for Ramin. As Jesus, Franz Kelch is empathetic, but his voice is covered, dry, and strained; alas, it had deteriorated a great deal since he recorded the part so effectively for Ramin a decade earlier.

While not as inspired as Werner's, Karl Forster's reading (11), taped in 1961 in Berlin, is similar in tone; the distinguished German choral conductor is earnest if rarely inspiring. What makes his recording special, however, is the presence of the aptly named Fritz Wunderlich. The white heat and searing clarity of his voice and the keen sincerity of his interpretation make his Evangelist a particularly special one; one regrets that he was not assigned the tenor arias as well, for Josef Traxel's vocal production is tight and strained. Karl Christian Kohn is equally disappointing in the bass arias and in the parts of Peter and Pilate; his is a big voice, but pressed at the top and marred by an unpleasant, narrow vibrato. Since a radiant-voiced Dietrich Fischer-Dieskau sings Jesus with dignity and understanding, one regrets Kohn's weaknesses all the more. Both Elisabeth Grümmer and Christa Ludwig, however, handle their assignments admirably in this oddly uneven recording.

The year before the Forster interpretation was taped, the first of the two English-language recordings made in England was released. Both of these performances feature the incomparable Peter Pears as the Evangelist. In the earlier of the two (12), an English text by Peter Pears and Andrew Raeburn that was based on the 1872 Troutbeck translation is used. The translation of the Gospel for the recitatives was Pears's primary responsibility, and it was his goal to make the words fit Bach's notes as closely as possible, rather than the other way around. David Willcocks leads the Choir of King's College Cambridge and the Philomusica of London in the recording made in the brightly resonant and richly reverberant acoustics of King's College Chapel.

15

A galaxy of the best oratorio singers then active in Britain was assembled for this recording (Robert Tear, then at the beginning of his career, sings the 'bit' part of the Servant), but the performance lacks spark; it is dutiful and lacking in intensity.

The Benjamin Britten recording (13), on the other hand, has all the life and depth that the Willcocks account lacks. A composer-performer with an innate sense of drama, Britten, who prepared the performing edition himself, turns the work into a sacred opera in the best sense of the term. There is no interpretative excess, however. All that is in evidence is Britten's exquisite sense of drama, tension, and pacing. Although Pears is not in quite as good voice as he was in the Willcocks recording a dozen years earlier, every one of the soloists is excellent. The chorus, however, is very large, and its diction is muddy. The translation was prepared by Pears and Imogen Holst, but in this version, the words are viewed as more important than the note values in the Evangelist's recitatives; none of Bach's harmonic progressions is altered, however.

In 1968, as a part of its invaluable 'Das Alte Werk' series, Telefunken released the first recording in which period instruments were employed (14). It features the Vienna Boys' Choir, the Chorus Viennensis, and Nikolaus Harnoncourt's Concentus Musicus Wien. More than twenty years after its initial release, this performance is still unsurpassed among the 'authentic' accounts, and, overall, is certainly one of the handful of sets from among which those seriously interested in the work should pick. From first to last, sinew, incisiveness, emotional commitment, profound understanding, and a desire to communicate the power of the score on every level are in evidence.

The soprano and alto solos are sung with surprising maturity and accuracy of intonation by anonymous members of the Vienna Boys' Choir. One of Peter Schreier's few rivals for pre-eminence among recent Evangelists, Kurt Equiluz stresses the dramatic rather than the narrative aspects of the Gospel text; his is an intensely colourful reading that is matched perfectly by Max van Egmond's powerful, larger-than-life conception of Jesus.

When this remarkable version was first published in 1968, Dr Hans Gillesberger, then the director of the Vienna Boys' Choir, was credited as the conductor. Surely the development of the interpretation was a communal effort in which both Nikolaus Harnoncourt and Gustav Leonhardt, who played keyboard continuo, were influential, but the many session photos included in the booklet that accompanied the original LP release make it quite clear that Dr Gillesberger conducted. It is lamentable, therefore, that the direction of the performance is now ascribed to Harnoncourt, Gillesberger being credited, in essence, only with the preparation of the choir. One can understand Teldec's desire to capitalise on the value of Harnoncourt's now more widely known name, but this apparent distortion of the historical record must nonetheless be deplored.

16

The Gillesberger recording was the first of what is now a substantial number of period instrument readings. It struck all who heard it at the time of its release as a revelation; it was the musical equivalent of the Rembrandt 'Night Watch' after all the Stygian varnish had been removed. Still, almost inexplicably, it stood alone for ten years until the advent of the Schneidt recording in 1979. During that decade, however, several 'modern instrument' performances were released.

Recorded at about the same time as the Gillesberger but not published until the spring of 1971, the Eugene Ormandy account (15) is a Central European, late nineteenth-century view of Bach and his sacred music. While there is nothing extreme about the interpretation, it is tinged liberally but tastefully with Romantic flourishes and exaggerations. Richard Lewis is a patrician and somewhat reserved Evangelist; George Shirley evinces strain in the tenor arias. Maureen Forrester's solid, plummy voice is particularly compatible with Ormandy's interpretation; she sings 'Es ist vollbracht' with great affection and conviction. The two bass soloists are adequate, but neither is outstanding. The chorus is a large one. Modern instruments, of course, are used but, while Ormandy chose to record the early version of 'Betrachte meine Seel', he nonetheless assigned the gamba obbligato in 'Es ist vollbracht' to the cello.

Eugen Jochum's 1967 *SJP* (16) also features a large chorus and orchestra, and, like Ormandy's, is liberally tinged with Romantic touches. The introspective but urgent opening chorus sets the tone for the whole performance. The mild tenderness at the upper end of his vocal range only heightens the keenness and dignity of Ernst Haefliger's interpretation of the Evangelist's recitatives. Agnes Giebel and Marga Höffgen are pure, solid, and reliable, as always, but Alexander Young's voice sounds a little worn. Walter Berry sounds stuffy as Jesus, but that's not entirely his fault; Jochum is one of those conductors who slows down for the words of the Saviour.

The Akkerhuis recording (17), released in the Netherlands in 1974, preserves a 'stylistically correct' interpretation using modern instruments. There is little of the unusual or exciting about it, and one might quickly dismiss it as ordinary were it not for Marius van Altena, whose crisp, clear, warm voice is well suited to the Evangelist's role, even if he is somewhat tentative and tender towards the top. Akkerhuis, incidentally, seems to anticipate Schreier's reading of the chorus 'Lasset uns den nicht zerteilen'; he, too, apparently gives the continuo line to a solo bassoon.

Of much greater significance is the György Lehel performance, recorded in Hungary in 1976 (18). A reflective but intensely colourful reading of the opening chorus sets the tone for an especially rewarding performance that is remarkable for its overall consistency of interpretation and execution. Lehel achieves an almost perfect blend of poignancy and reverence. Every soloist is first rate; all sing with crisp diction and clear tone, but it is Julia Hamari who is particularly pleasing. The tawny, rich quality of her voice is entirely congruent with Lehel's passionate but dignified approach to the score.

Michel Corboz's 1977 recording (19) is also remarkable for its overall interpretative and technical consistency. He stresses and conveys the disquieting inevitability, the urgent sense of the predestined, that is so deeply embedded in Bach's setting of the story. In addition to a first-rate mixed chorus of about fifty voices and excellent instrumental support, Corboz is blessed by a stellar group of soloists for his superbly paced interpretation. Equiluz once again sings the role of the Evangelist with security and innate understanding of the drama. Birgit Finnilä imbues the alto arias with an extraordinary colour; the burnished gold of her unique voice is oddly reminiscent of Rosa Ponselle's.

When it appeared in 1979, Hanns-Martin Schneidt's period instrument 'authentic' account (20) provided stiff competition for Gillesberger's. To begin with, Schneidt included the five alternative numbers from the 1725 version of the oratorio to fill the sixth side of the three-record set. Gillesberger offered no such bonus. Both performances featured a boys' choir and boy soloists (identified this time). The two youths sing well enough – Soprano Frank Sahesch-Pur is a bit wavery; alto Roman Hankeln is somewhat breathy – but both are victims of that peculiarly insecure intonation that seems endemic to boys' voices. Furthermore, both are too busy working their way through the music to show much interpretative commitment. Aldo Baldin's magnificent voice and compelling interpretative sense combine to make the tenor solos especially moving and rewarding listening experiences.

In many ways, the Schneidt and the Gillesberger performances complement each other neatly. For example, Heiner Hopfner evinces strong emotional commitment as the Evangelist, but his is an intimate view of the role that emphasises the narrative aspects more than the dramatic ones. In that sense Hofner's Evangelist mirrors Equiluz's perfectly. Similarly, Nikolaus Hillebrand gives the part of Jesus an aura of calm resignation that contrasts sharply with Max van Egmond's heroic and dramatic conception of the part.

The singing of the twenty-five members of the Regensburger Domspatzen and the playing of the Collegium St Emmeran are of high standard, but it has to be said that Josef Ulsamer's playing of the viola da gamba obbligato in 'Es ist vollbracht' is appallingly stiff and perfunctory; when his interpretation is compared to Harnoncourt's radiant reading in the Gillesberger set, the unpleasantness is emphasised.

What made the Schneidt set peculiarly valuable to all who are interested in the work, however, was the five alternative numbers from the 1725 version. Until the arrival of the superb Slowik account (see below) these alternatives had not otherwise been gathered together in one place in a period instrument performance, and the three arias have still not been better interpreted elsewhere. Baldin's account of the sinuously onomatopoeic 'Ach windet euch nicht so, verplagte Seele', BWV 245c, will give the listener goose bumps, and it has been equalled only by Jeffrey Thomas's reading in the Slowik set.

In addition to the Schreier set, a number of modern instrument sets have appeared since the release of the Schneidt performance in 1979. One of these is perhaps the single most satisfactory account of the oratorio so far made (21). Recorded in the Kirche St Mariä Himmelfahrt in Cologne on 3 February 1980, this performance is a remarkable case of the whole being worth infinitely more than the sum of the parts. Peter Neumann leads the Kölner Kammerchor, a mixed choir of around thirty voices that he founded in 1970, and the Kölner Bach-Collegium, whose members play with verve and sensitivity, in an interpretation that is marked by thoughtful, crisp, yet natural articulation and that is suffused by a halo of compassion and empathy that can be found in no other recording. After a somewhat rocky start, Lutz Michael Harder proves equal to the demands of not only the Evangelist's role, which he sings with great drama, but also the tenor arias. The other soloists all are restrained but effective, although soprano Ute Frühaber's voice is admittedly somewhat strained at the top and more than a wee bit dry. Neumann, incidentally, opts for the revised version of 'Betrachte meine Seel' and 'Erwäge', with muted violins rather than viole d'amore.

On the other hand, the Karl-Friedrich Beringer account (22), recorded in April 1979, has little besides Michel Brodard's quiet and sensitive Jesus to recommend it (he sings Pilate and the bass arias in the Neumann performance). Alejandro Ramírez, the Evangelist, has a hideous, thin voice, that is suffused by a tight, bleaty vibrato; the sound is so ugly that it is impossible to judge his interpretation fairly. The Amadeus Chor, some sixty or seventy strong, and the Amadeus Orchester do their best, but Beringer leads a performance that can best be described as listless.

The Theo Loosli recording (23) is nearly as bad. Apparently a production of primarily local interest, it is bland, flabby, and uncharismatic. Adalbert Kraus proves to be a mediocre Evangelist; his voice is tender at the top, and his difficulties are exacerbated by the slow pace that the conductor sets for the narrative. Loosli's brother, Arthur, is a tired-sounding Jesus. Harder is satisfactory in the tenor arias, but he does not rise to the occasion as he did in the inspired Neumann concert recording. Augér must have wondered what she was doing caught up in this muddle. Matters are not helped by the engineering; the sound is dull, and the large mixed chorus sounds muffled. That the recording happens to include the five alternate numbers from the 1725 version is no bonus. The tenor aria 'Ach windet euch nicht so' is painfully slow, and all of this music is performed to much greater effect by both Slowik and Schneidt and their colleagues.

Armin Brunner's recording (24) was conceived as the soundtrack for Werner Düggelin's visually free interpretation of the *SJP*, filmed on location in Switzerland and Italy in 1984. Brunner had learned all the fashionable

19

authentic performance practice tricks, and he applies them carefully throughout the recording, indulging, for instance, in the voguish device of stressing the strong beats in the opening chorus. Vandersteene is a fine Evangelist, the other soloists are more than adequate, and the chorus and orchestra are responsive to the conductor's direction, but Brunner's is not a memorable or inspiring interpretation. It is of value only to those who want the soundtrack to the movie.

A more intriguing curiosity, however, is a complete set recorded in Leningrad in the late 1970s or early 1980s (25). The first complete recording of a major Bach choral work made in the Soviet Union, this performance, conducted by Arkady Steinlucht, is sung and played in a style far more appropriate to Russian sacred music — or even the Kirov Opera. The pace of the narrative is almost painfully slow, and the tenor (which one of the two sings the Evangelist is not specified in the literature that accompanies the discs) declaims the text in heavily accented German. Tempi throughout are slow, the playing and singing lush. The imaginative listener can easily close his eyes and pretend that he is attending a performance of the work under the direction of Rimsky-Korsakov.

A more recent complete *SJP* from Leningrad is similar in character, even though it is somewhat more stylish (26). Under the direction of Eduard Serov, who, incidentally, opts for the revised versions of 'Betrachte meine Seel' and 'Erwäge', with muted violins rather than viole d'amore, this recording features the Soviet Union's most famous boys' choir. Unfortunately the Boys' Chorus of the Moscow Choral School is often shrill, hooty, and off-pitch. The soloists are adequate and committed but, like their confrères in the Steinlucht recording, have little understanding of the tradition of which the Bach Passions are a part.

Less extreme interpretatively, and therefore less interesting than either of the two Soviet sets, is an abridged recording of a complete performance of the *SJP* that was given at the final concert of the 12th Meeting of the Yugoslav Music Academies and Faculties in Zagreb on 15 May 1985 (27). Igor Gjadrov conducts an enormous chorus and an orchestra of 'symphonic' proportions; Branko Robinsak is an acidulous Evangelist; and the seemingly mindless cuts made, evidently, to fit the performance onto two black discs result in the loss of a substantial number of arias and ariosos, including 'Betrachte meine Seel', 'Erwäge', 'Eilt, ihr angefocht'nen Seelen' and 'Mein teurer Heiland'.

At least seven complete recordings of the *SJP* in which period instruments are used have appeared since the celebration of the tercentenary of the birth of Sebastian Bach in 1985. John Eliot Gardiner's was the first to be released (28). A mixed chorus of sixteen is accompanied by an instrumental ensemble slightly larger in size. A larger than usual complement of soloists is employed, occasionally to the performance's detriment. For instance, Nancy Argenta, who sings 'Zerfliesse, mein Herze', has both a warmer voice and a more profound interpretative sense than the white-voiced, boyish sounding Ruth Holton whose

20

'Ich folge dir gleichfalls' is cool to say the least. Anthony Rolfe Johnson is a good if not memorable Evangelist. Michael Chance is the best of the soloists: his excellent interpretation of 'Es ist vollbracht' is made even more remarkable by Gardiner's decision to use the lute as a continuo instrument. The performance starts off coolly, but it gathers momentum as it goes along, gaining in commitment and focus as it proceeds.

Despite fine playing by the members of La Petite Bande, despite sensitive and sturdy singing by the sixteen members of the mixed voice choir assembled for the performance, and despite the valuable contributions of several excellent vocal soloists, Sigiswald Kuijken's recording (29) is quite ordinary. It is a bland and uninspiring interpretation that lacks fervour or compassion. Almost twenty years after he sang for Gillesberger in the first period instrument recording, Max van Egmond is still superb, René Jacobs sings 'Es ist vollbracht' with profound beauty and sincerity, and Nico van der Meel has a gorgeous tenor voice, but Harry van der Kamp, alas, is a singularly dry-voiced Jesus, and his vocal weakness is emphasised by his application of the essentially vibrato-less technique that is correct for the authentic performance.

Although not without its brilliant moments, Philippe Herreweghe's reading (30) is also cool and strangely lacking in emotional commitment. He is the only conductor of a period instrument recording to opt for a female alto soloist throughout. He feels that the alto numbers, 'especially "Es ist vollbracht", are infused with a greater degree of the sonorities of nocturnal affliction when sung by a boy alto or by a certain type of female alto, which are lower registers, than by a falsetto voice'. Catherine Patriasz certainly makes an excellent case for the validity of his decision. Like Gardiner, by the way, Herreweghe also uses a lute as a continuo instrument in 'Es ist vollbracht'. A very fast, almost flippant 'Ach mein Sinn' is compensated for by a lovely, contemplative, and especially affecting 'Betrachte meine Seel'. Howard Crook makes a fine Evangelist, and, in fact, the soloists overall are of equally high quality.

There is nothing cool or detached, however, about Anthony Newman's interpretation (31). In fact, his is without question the most extroverted and operatic account of the oratorio ever recorded. The tempi are brisk without ever sounding rushed. The thorough bass realisations are florid; there is even a harpsichord flourish linking the end of the 'B' section to the reprise of the 'A' section in the opening chorus! Some will dismiss this white-hot, overtly dramatic performance as irreverent, if not downright disrespectful, but it is anything but that. Newman understands the link between the German Passion and baroque opera and oratorio; he understands that the Bach Passions and the Handel oratorios are more closely related than many musicologists would like us to believe. In short, Anthony Newman gives us the *St John Passion* as it might have sounded under Handel's direction had he included it in the repertory of one of his Lenten oratorio seasons at the Theatre Royal in Covent Garden in the late 1740s.

For his recording, Newman assembled an excellent battery of soloists, all but one of whom (the Evangelist) sing in the choruses, as Bach's *concertisten* did. Jeffrey Dooley possesses a countertenor voice that is particularly warm and pure, and he knows how to use vibrato as an embellishment. William Sharp is one of the best interpreters of the role of Jesus in the United States, and Jeffrey Thomas is one of the best Evangelists. The clear-voiced Julianne Baird gives an evocative performance of 'Zerfliesse, mein Herze' that even includes a short interpolated cadenza! Newman's, by the way, is the only one of the period-instrument recordings in which the later version of 'Betrachte meine Seel' and 'Erwäge', with muted violins and harpsichord, is used.

In the spring of 1990 two new period instrument recordings of the *St. John Passion* appeared. One of these can be recommended unequivocally as the best of the period instrument performances overall. Recorded in the rich but not overly reverberant acoustic of the Renwick Gallery in Washington, D.C., by the Smithsonian Chamber Players under the direction of the cellist and gambist Kenneth Slowik (36), this recording features a chorus of twelve (one singer more per vocal line than Bach used in the choruses), from whom are drawn all of the soloists. The solos are not, however, allocated among the members of the chorus in the same manner that the original performing parts indicate that Bach assigned them.

The 1749 version of the score, complete with a double bassoon playing the bassono grosso part, is followed in the main, although the 1724 versions of 'Betrachte meine Seel' and 'Erwäge', with lute and viole d'amore, are used. One regrets that the later versions were not included in the appendices, along with the five alternative numbers from the 1725 version which are a part of the compact disc, but not the LP or cassette formats, of the recording. The discs are cued in such a way that the listener can easily programme his player for either the 1724/49 or the 1725 form of the Passion.

Interpretatively, Slowik's is an especially satisfying recording. There is nothing extreme about this thoughtful and compelling reading, and he and his colleagues evince a particular sensitivity to detail without ever losing sight of the meaning of the whole. As might be expected from a performance directed by a cellist and gambist of international stature, the realisation of the continuo lines is remarkable, and Slowik's handling of the gamba solo in 'Es ist vollbracht' and the cello obbligato in 'Himmel, reise' is unsurpassed in warmth, passion, and security. The instrumental playing and the singing are of an equally high stature, although Jeffrey Thomas's clear-voiced Evangelist and Jennifer Lane's poignant, introspective reading of 'Es ist vollbracht' are worthy of special mention.

Harry Christophers's account, with The Sixteen Choir and Orchestra (37), also appeared in the spring of 1990; it was recorded live in the rich acoustic of St John's Smith Square, London, in March 1989, with a chorus of eighteen and a period instrument band of twenty-one. Christophers leads a solid, warm, and

22

effective account of the 1724 version. Ian Partridge is a distinctive and compassionate Evangelist; the unusual timbre of his elegant, mature voice often calls to mind that of Aksel Schiøtz. Once again, the singing and the playing are of a particularly high quality. Having opted for the original versions of 'Betrachte meine Seel' and 'Erwäge', Christophers makes extensive use of the lute as a continuo instrument in other portions of the Passion.

SUMMARY

Those who want an 'authentic' recording of the *St John Passion* in which period instruments are used will find the Slowik to be the best choice, although the Newman, the Gillesberger, the Christophers and the Schneidt recordings all have their special virtues; while marginally less powerful than the Gillesberger, the Christophers, or the Newman, the Schneidt does, like the Slowik, include the bonus of excellent interpretations of the five alternative numbers from the 1725 version of the Passion.

Those who prefer a performance in which 'modern' instruments are used should choose from the Neumann, the Rotzsch, and the Richter versions. None of these, however, includes the alternative numbers from the 1725 version; the three arias are included as an appendix to the Peter Schreier recording.

Those who wish the *SJP* work sung in English are advised to track down a copy of either the Shaw or the Britten recording.

J.S. Bach: St Matthew Passion

TERI NOEL TOWE

The *St Matthew Passion* is the penultimate Passion of five that Bach's sons recalled their father having written, and it is the second of the three of which we have certain knowledge. The first of the three is the *St John Passion*, BWV 245, which is discussed in the previous chapter, and the third is the *St Mark Passion*, written in 1731, for which only the text has been preserved. Very early on in the nineteenth-century Bach Revival, however, scholars realised that the *St Mark Passion* contained many reworkings of music used elsewhere, and several conjectural recoveries of lost choruses and arias have been made. There is even a recording of a completely reconstructed setting!

The *St Matthew Passion* (hereinafter *SMP*), on the other hand, contains little that is borrowed and almost certainly nothing that has been reworked from pre-existing music. In fact, as Joshua Rifkin has cogently argued, the *SMP* may have been composed for 'essentially private reasons' and was also 'the first vocal contribution to that remarkable, and evidently self-motivated, series of "exemplary" works so strikingly characteristic of his output; and it stands, too, as the piece that marked his inward resignation from his job as Thomaskantor'.

The first version was given its first performance in the Thomaskirche, Leipzig, on 11 April 1727. Originally, there was but one continuo line that accompanied the two four-voice choirs rather than two independent ones, and the obbligato instrument in the aria 'Komm süsses Kreuz' and the preceding arioso [Nos. 65 and 66] was a lute rather than a viola da gamba. The First Part lacked the chorale 'Ich will hier bei dir sterben' [No. 23], and, more importantly, ended not with the remarkable and monumental chorale fantasia 'O Mensch, bewein' dein Sünde gross', which Bach originally composed to open the 1725 version of the *St John Passion*, but with a simple four-voice chorale setting. This first version, which has survived only in a copy made by Bach's son-in-law Johann Christoph Altnickol in the mid-1740s, has *never* been recorded.

Almost two years later, early in 1729, Bach used the work as a quarry for

24

nine arias as well as for the final chorus of the funeral cantata he performed at the interment service for his one-time employer and friend, Prince Leopold of Anhalt-Cöthen. In 1736, Bach came back to the *SMP* and prepared a beautiful 'fair copy' of the revised version that is familiar to audiences today and presented it, in the Thomaskirche, on Good Friday of that year.

The original performing materials for this 'definitive' 1736 version have been preserved, and, as Joshua Rifkin has convincingly demonstrated, an open-minded examination of those parts and their implications yields some startling results. There are twelve vocal parts in all, one for each of twelve singers; no part was shared by more than one performer. There are eight 'basic' parts, containing both the 'choral' and 'solo' music for the soprano, alto, tenor and bass of each of the two 'choruses'. The remaining four parts are not doubling parts. They contain only 'extra' music not assigned to the members of the two 'choral' quartets. There is a part for the lone soprano who intones the chorale *cantus firmus* in the opening and concluding choruses of Part One; there is another soprano part that contains only the music for the First Maid, the Second Maid and Pilate's Wife. Lastly, there are two bass parts; one contains the music for Judas and the First Priest, and the other contains the music for Peter, The High Priest, the Second Priest, and Pilate. None of these 'subsidiary' parts contains any of the music for any of the choruses or chorales. Furthermore, the parts for the tenor and the bass of Chorus One are marked 'Evangelist' and 'Jesus' respectively, but they are devoid of any 'cues' for any doubling singers in the 'choral' numbers. The conclusion is as inescapable as it is obvious. Bach performed the *SMP* with a total of eight singers in the double choruses.

The instrumental complement, Rifkin claims, was similarly intimate: a solo violin in each of the two bands, one of which accompanies Chorus One and the other of which accompanies Chorus Two, two ripieno first violins, two second violins, one viola, one cello, a violone and − in 1736, at least − two continuo organs. None of the winds was doubled.

That Bach could successfully have brought off a work as lengthy, as demanding and as monumental as the *SMP* with such intimate forces seems impossible to us nowadays, particularly since we know how vociferously he complained about the inadequacies of the performing forces available to him. But the *SMP* is a remarkably carefully balanced work. The allocation of ariosos and arias between the members of the two choruses assures that each *concertist*, as he was called, got ample time to rest; furthermore, the two Parts were separated by the preaching of the Good Friday sermon, an especially long-winded affair lasting some two hours or so. The performers, therefore, had an adequate chance to recover their stamina before they had to come back to sing and play Part Two.

The two instrumental and vocal choruses were split between the two organ lofts, nearly 100 feet apart, but the then favourable acoustics of the

Thomaskirche made it possible to keep the two ensembles together. By the time Bach revived the work in the early 1740s, however, the organ had been removed from the second loft and Bach was forced to substitute a harpsichord for the continuo of Chorus Two. It is something of an irony, then, that, when harpsichord and organ are used together in 'modern' performances of the *SMP*, the harpsichord almost always accompanies the Evangelist, who is a member of Chorus One. To compensate for the disappearance of this second organ, Bach added a second ripieno soprano to the opening and concluding choruses of Part One. In all other respects, the vocal parts that Bach used in the early 1740s (almost certainly 1741) are the same ones that he used in 1736, and there is no evidence to support the contention that Bach used additional singers for the 'choral' numbers in this, most likely the last, performance of the work that he presented.

The other significant change that Bach made in the score of the *SMP* for the 1741 revival is the addition of the chordal part for the viola da gamba in the arioso 'Mein Jesus schweigt' [No. 40]; the viola da gamba also plays the obbligato in the following aria 'Geduld, Geduld'. This alternative version is occasionally, though infrequently, used; unless otherwise specifically mentioned, the reader may assume that the 1736 versions of these numbers have been followed in the recordings discussed in this essay.

Needless to say, there has so far not been a commercial recording of the *SMP* reflecting this 'radical' but as yet unrefuted analysis of the evidence, but those of us who had the good fortune to be in the audience at the University of North Carolina in 1985, for the concert performance of the 1736 version given by Joshua Rifkin, The Bach Ensemble, and a first-rate cast of the best early music singers in America, including Ann Monoyios and William Sharp, vividly recall that it was as though we were hearing this familiar and beloved masterpiece for the first time. The searing clarity, the poignancy, the emotional intensity, and the relentless, heartrending drama of both score and text were conveyed with a power and sincerity surpassed by no other approach to this music and equalled by few. It is fortunate for all who are interested in how Bach heard his music performed that this incredible performance was recorded for later broadcast on North Carolina Public Radio and has been circulated privately (1).

Of all the recorded performances, whether with period instruments or modern ones, whether 'authentic' or 'Romantic', there are but two in which the distinction that Bach draws between the singers of Chorus One and the singers of Chorus Two is followed at all consistently through the 'solos' and the 'choruses'. Both of those recordings are conducted by Nikolaus Harnoncourt.

In the earlier of the two Harnoncourt sets, the first period-instrument set (2), the division of the solos between members of the two Choruses is adhered to almost exactly; apart from a substitute alto soloist in two numbers,

26

the only deviations are Harnoncourt's allocation of the part of Jesus and bass arias of Chorus One to separate singers and his apparent assignment of the subsidiary roles to the eight 'soloists'.

A modern double chorus, some forty strong, is used, of course, but it is made up of boys' and men's voices. The soprano solos are sung by two exemplary but anonymous soloists from the Wiener Sängerknaben, but their birdlike voices, clear and pure though they are, are simply not mature enough, emotionally or physically, for this music. Voices broke much later in Bach's day than they do now, and consequently the sound he and his contemporaries heard was fuller than any one might expect to hear from a prepubescent voice today. The use of a woman's voice of an appropriately boyish character is an inevitable compromise that must be made nowadays by those who seek to perform this music in an 'authentic' manner.

The adult soloists are all excellent. Particularly noteworthy are Paul Esswood and James Bowman, who bring emotional commitment, technical security, and distinctive timbre to the alto music. Kurt Equiluz is one of the great interpreters of the Evangelist. He sings the narration in a dramatic, but straightforward and conversational way; he 'reads' the part, if you will, in the manner of a great actor. Karl Ridderbusch is an excellent Jesus; he has a dark but natural voice, and his interpretation is suffused by a unique sense of vulnerability and resignation as to the inevitability of Christ's crucifixion.

The overall tactus is brisk. There is some stressing of strong beats, but this quirk of Harnoncourt's, which has developed into a most disquieting mannerism, is not pronounced, and here serves only to heighten the dance-like qualities that pervade so much of the music in the *SMP*. Although Harnoncourt was responsible for shaping the overall interpretation, David Willcocks, then the Director of the Choir of King's College, Cambridge, evidently conducted the choruses and chorales. As one might expect from a virtuoso gambist like Harnoncourt, the 1741 forms of 'Mein Jesus schweigt' and 'Geduld, Geduld' are used.

The bloom and freshness of this extraordinary recording, which startled and opened the eyes and ears of many of us when it first appeared in 1970, has not faded. It is still unsurpassed among the period instrument recordings, and it has only a handful of equals.

Harnoncourt's second version (3) was recorded at a concert in the Concertgebouw on 31 March 1985, at the tenth annual performance he had given with the Concertgebouw orchestra; all of the artists waived their royalties for this set, which is being sold to benefit the fund to restore the Concertgebouw, Amsterdam's magnificent and venerable concert hall. For a variety of reasons, the interpretation is unfortunately nowhere near as successful as Harnoncourt's first. For one thing, he uses a modern orchestra and chorus whom he has carefully schooled in copying period timbres; they sound 'modern' nonetheless. The natural but curious clarity and the innate but bizarre incisiveness of period instruments just cannot be duplicated by modern ones.

Matters are not helped by soloists who are accustomed to singing the 'modern' way. Harnoncourt, however, once again comes close to copying Bach's allocation of the "solos" among eight singers, but this time, Equiluz sings only the Evangelist, again with distinctive character, pure sound, and emotional clout. The tenor arias are over-interpreted by a rather wobbly Neil Rosenshein. Once again, all the subsidiary roles for which Bach provided parts for three additional singers are divided among the eight soloists. The part of Jesus is not sung by the bass in Chorus One, the rather dry and woolly Ruud van der Meer, who also sings Peter, Pilate, the High Priest, in addition to Judas, and, apparently, the First Priest. Anton Scharinger, who evidently sings only the Second Priest in addition to the arias assigned to the bass in Chorus Two, has a cleaner and more pleasing tone. Robert Holl is a fuzzy and posturing Jesus. The female soloists are fine in the main. The mixed chorus is medium in size, and is augmented in the opening and closing choruses of Part One by a boys' choir which sings the chorale cantus firmuses.

Surprisingly, there so far have been only three other period instrument recordings of the *SMP* released since Harnoncourt's appeared two decades ago. The most recent of these, featuring the Tölzer Knabenchor and La Petite Bande under the direction of Gustav Leonhardt (4), is also the third of the three accounts in which Bach's division of the solos between the two choruses is observed to any significant degree. The role of the Evangelist is eloquently and clearly declaimed by Christoph Prégardien, and Jesus is warmly and poignantly sung by Max van Egmond, a veteran of Harnoncourt's first recording. The remaining solos are divided among eight singers, four assigned to each chorus, but the annotations to the recording are silent about the allocation of the subsidiary roles, like Pilate and the First Maid.

The soprano solos are sung by boys from the Tölzer Knabenchor. Both sing with security and relative purity, but, as is almost always the case with child sopranos and altos, they lack the emotional maturity and the physical power to convey the meaning of the texts in a truly convincing fashion. The adult soloists are all superb. Though five years older than when he recorded the alto solos for Philippe Herreweghe, René Jacobs is still in top form in the alto solos in Chorus One. Each chorus is made up of sixteen singers, four for each line.

Leonhardt leads a performance that is convincing and sensitive, and it is only occasionally marred by the mannerisms that have scuttled too many of his otherwise worthy interpretations. His irritating habit of forcefully stressing strong beats and pushing and pulling the tactus, for instance, only infrequently rears its ugly head. Overall this worthy interpretation is characterized by elegance and reserve, but never at the expense of emotional commitment or directness.

28

Philippe Herreweghe's interpretation (5) is less extroverted, less brilliant than Harnoncourt's, and it does not emphasise the dance-like character of many of the movements to anywhere near the same degree; instead Herreweghe's reading is more reverent, more relaxed and, paradoxically, more relentless in character. It is imbued with a pervasive sense of gentleness, awe and faith that sets it apart from all the other recordings. The two ensembles that make up Choruses One and Two are both mixed choirs; the soprano soloist is a woman; the alto a man. (Whether Bach used boys or men for his altos has been the subject of some dispute; surely some of the more mature students at the Thomasschule were altos, and his son Carl Philipp Emanuel was apparently a gifted falsettist.) The 1741 versions of 'Mein Jesus schweigt' and 'Geduld, Geduld' are used.

René Jacobs's distinctive, plangent voice is perfectly suited to the alto solos; his exquisite account of 'Erbarme Dich, mein Gott' is among the most poignant on records. Like Ulrik Cold, the clear-voiced, straightforward Jesus, Howard Crook treats the Evangelist's role in a more conversational manner than most, and his quiet and natural unfolding of the narrative comports perfectly with Herreweghe's contemplative view of the score. In sum, this account of the *SMP* is every bit as satisfying as Harnoncourt's first one, but in a different way; the two sets complement each other neatly.

Although there are eight soloists in John Eliot Gardiner's recording (6), the division of responsibilities among them does not always follow Bach's allocation of the solos between Chorus One and Chorus Two; the assignment of the ariosos and arias among the various singers was apparently based primarily on vocal range and timbre. Anthony Rolfe Johnson is disappointing as the Evangelist; his voice is tattered and tender at the top, often painfully so, and his interpretation is quite mannered. Especially annoying is the sudden halving of the tactus of the narrative during the Crucifixion recitatives. Andreas Schmidt is a fine, straightforward Jesus. Of the remaining soloists, all of whom are first-rate, the sensitive and clear-voiced Ann Monoyios is particularly noteworthy. The relatively large mixed choirs and the mixed-voice children's chorus that intones the *cantus firmus* in the opening and concluding choruses of Part One all sing with assuredness and sensitivity.

Gardiner's approach to the *SMP* is a traditional, classical one. It is tempting to describe his interpretation as 'Mozartian' in feeling, but it is perhaps most accurate to say that Gardiner's interpretation is early nineteenth-century in character. This fine reading evinces many of the characteristics of the conservative, fleet and direct approach taken by Felix Mendelssohn and his followers.

The 1741 performance appears to have been the last that Bach himself presented. It was also the last performance given for nearly ninety years. The vagaries of the preservation − and loss − of many of Bach's scores and performing materials are too well known to warrant discussion here, but, by the 1820s, his music was well on its way to total rediscovery. Of course, Mendelssohn's revival irreversibly expanded Bach's audience to the world at large. Still, it is a common misconception that the performance that Mendelssohn gave with the Singakademie in Berlin on 11 March 1829, was complete and uncut. It was no such thing. Four ariosos, ten arias, six chorales and substantial portions of seven of the Evangelist's recitatives were excised, to reduce the length of the work by more than an hour.

Among the numbers cut were such famous solos as 'Aus Liebe will mein Heiland sterben' and 'Mache dich, mein Herze, rein'. Mendelssohn was also responsible for the custom of singing 'Wenn ich einmal soll scheiden' *a capella*, a practice still frequently encountered today, and of strengthening Bach's economical instrumentation of the 'Earthquake' recitatives, another practice that lingered well into this century; such shenanigans can be heard in the notorious Furtwängler concert recording, for instance. In addition, Mendelssohn was compelled to adjust the instrumentation by substituting currently available instruments for those that had become 'obsolete' since Bach's day; clarinets, for instance, replaced oboes d'amore and oboes da caccia.

Whatever Mendelssohn's motives may have been, his abbreviation sanctioned the practice for all and sundry and, as others performed it throughout Germany, then England, and ultimately the world at large, the work made its 'modern' début in a truncated form. It was not until 1912 that an audience finally heard this masterpiece complete and uncut. The conductor was Siegfried Ochs, the founder and director of the Berlin Philharmonic Choir. Ironically, notwithstanding his interest in Bach in particular and early music in general, Ochs was apparently a conservative interpreter. Through the violinist Joseph Joachim, he stood in a direct line of pedagogical descent from Mendelssohn himself, and his brisk urgent tempos and long legato phrases have their origins in the essentially late classical style in which both Mendelssohn and his colleagues in Berlin and Leipzig performed their own music and that of their antecedents. It comes, therefore, as a shock for those who hear it for the first time to discover that Ochs's recording of the opening chorus (HMV EJ 195) is the exact opposite of the ponderous and turgid interpretations that the well-known Mengelberg performance had previously misled them into assuming to have been the norm. Split over two sides of a 12-inch 78 with plenty of room to spare on the second side, 'Kommt, ihr Töchter' lasts five minutes and twenty-six seconds, less than half the time it takes Mengelberg to make his stately and effusive progress through the same music.

Like Bach himself, and Mendelssohn too, evidently, Ochs liked his tempi fast. One cannot help but wonder, under the circumstances, if Hermann Scherchen's view of the *SMP* (7) was not strongly influenced by Ochs's. Scherchen was a native of Berlin and received his early training there.

His opening chorus is almost as fast as Ochs's, and his entire interpretation is notable for its exceedingly fleet pacing. Like Ochs, too, Scherchen favours the cleancut and the straightforward; his phrases are long and legato. Some of the contemplative movements may seem flippant at first, but the *turbae* choruses are especially dramatic at Scherchen's tempi; never have the crowd's fury and the priests' hatred of Christ been more vividly conveyed to the listener.

The distinctive timbre of Hugues Cuenod's voice makes his Evangelist seem almost unearthly and, despite the mildly dry character of his voice, Heinz Rehfuss makes Jesus seem both warm and vulnerable. The other soloists run from the acceptable to the good, but it is worth noting that Equiluz, one of the great Evangelists of our time, made his début as a soloist in *SMP* recordings as the Second Witness in the Scherchen set.

If Ochs's tempi represented something of an extreme, what represented the norm among traditional, classic nineteenth-century style performances in Germany? Who best represented the conservative Mendelssohnian, Leipzig–Berlin approach to the work? Gerhard Herz, the distinguished Bach scholar, recalls the conducting of Hans Weissbach as being the paradigm. As it happens, Weissbach was also a graduate of the Hochschule für Musik in Berlin, of which Joachim was the Director and where Ochs also had studied.

Fortuitously, a concert performance under Weissbach's leadership has survived (8). Recorded in the Altes Gewandhaus on 19 April 1935, his interpretation is characterised by the same classical legato phrases heard in Ochs's recording of the opening chorus, but the overall pulse, while brisk, is not as fast as those adopted by Ochs or by Scherchen. Another Mendelssohnism in evidence is the beefed-up instrumentation of the 'Earthquake' recitative. Koloman von Pataky is a thrilling Evangelist and tenor soloist: his positively ecstatic 'Ich will bei meinem Jesu wachen' is challenged only by the passionate full-voiced Walter Widdop's 1930 English-language version (D 1872; HQM 1114). Margaret Klose has a rather tight vibrato, but it is compensated for by a solid chest tone and an emotionally searing 'Erbarme Dich, mein Gott'. Rather detached emotionally at first, Paul Schoeffler, the Jesus, warms up as the performance progresses. Kurt Böhme's big, dark, stirring voice brings a special power to the bass arias, or at least those that are left in this cut performance. Also worthy of mention is Weissbach's particularly plastic and affecting account of the final chorus.

The conservative Mendelssohnian approach centred in Leipzig and Berlin survives to the present, despite the many subsequent and varying developments in Bach performance practice, including the Straube/Ramin style forged in Leipzig in the 1920s and 1930s. Several performances in this classic style have made their way to records since Ochs's and Weissbach's work was documented.

The earliest among them is an abridged performance recorded in Berlin in the mid 1930s by the Bruno Kittel Choir under the direction of its founder,

Bruno Kittel (9), Ochs's successor as the German capital's foremost choral conductor. Like Ochs and Weissbach, Kittel preferred brisk tempi in the main, legato phrases and relatively straightforward expression; despite occasional touches of Romantic colouration, there is little funny business here. Kittel's great reputation as a choral director was justified. Never has so large a choir sung 'Wenn ich einmal soll scheiden' (here again *a capella*, *à la* Mendelssohn) so softly and with such unearthly beauty, and these same voices are suitably venomous, but never ugly, in the crowd scenes.

Kittel is blessed by a particularly well-balanced group of soloists, all of whom have bright, firmly centred voices. Most remarkable is the trumpet-voiced Walther Ludwig, who sings the role of the Evangelist and the tenor solos with white-hot passion. Throughout, he is completely at ease with the wide range of the music and is one of the few who does not stab at or flinch from the high note to which the word 'laut' is set in the Crucifixion recitatives.

Incidentally, the two separately released discs of excerpts under Kittel's leadership (Poly. 66721) are not taken from the complete set and feature different soloists. The alto, the redoubtable Emmi Leisner, also made a splendid single disc of 'Erbarme Dich, mein Gott'. This especially poignant aria – Bach certainly wrote none better – appears to have been the most frequently recorded single excerpt during the 78 era.

Among the most worthy of such accounts are the dark-voiced Sigrid Onegin's acoustic disc (Poly. 72745), the Dutch contralto Maartje Offers's searing reading with the much under-appreciated Isolde Menges playing the violin obbligato (DB 907) and, from the post-Second World War era, the singular interpretation of Marian Anderson (Victor 11–9380; GD 87911). Although it is not of 78 origin, one of the most transcendent accounts of this heavenly aria was recorded by the mezzo-soprano Jennie Tourel at the 1951 Perpignan Festival, with Casals conducting (Am. Col. ML 4640).

More recent recordings in the classic, Mendelssohnian manner include Fritz Lehmann's 1949 concert performance, the first uncut recording in German (10). The two previous German commercial 'complete' recordings – the Kittel and the Günther Ramin (11) – were abridged, as is Weissbach's performance. Not identical but often congruent, these cuts are not identical to those made by Mendelssohn; they are, however, indicative of the cuts that were the standard throughout Germany as early as the last quarter of the nineteenth century and, in the case of the Ramin recording, are the cuts that had customarily been made in performances given by the Thomanerchor in Bach's 'own' Thomaskirche in Leipzig since the early years of the twentieth century at least. That the universal and 'standard' cuts of the type found in the Kittel and Ramin recordings happen to eliminate most, if not all, of the specific references to the Jews is a now unfortunate and distasteful coincidence. And, of course, it is thus more than mildly ironic that it was left to predominantly American soloists, American instrumentalists and American choristers, many of whom were

32

refugees from the Nazis, to record the first complete and uncut version in English in Boston on Good Friday, 26 March 1937, under the baton of a Soviet *émigré*, Serge Koussevitzky (12).

Recorded at a concert in a divided and devastated Berlin, the Lehmann performance is among the greatest performances of the *SMP* on disc. His potent reading is squarely in the classic, Mendelssohnian tradition – straightforward and relatively brisk overall, with long, legato phrases and rhythmic robustness. Helmut Krebs was one of the great interpreters of the Evangelist; his distinctive, pure and mildly nasal voice lends a particularly patrician quality to the narrative, and then he sings the tenor arias with nobility and commitment. The young Dietrich Fischer-Dieskau, then at the dawn of his career, is a magnificent, virile Jesus; he may have refined and polished his interpretation over the years, but he never again sang the part with such youthful freshness and naturalness. The other three soloists all possess solid, focused, round voices.

It is frustrating, therefore, to have to report that the recording is marred by occasional cuts. For example, a few measures are missing from the opening ritornello of 'Ich will bei meinem Jesu wachen'. The cause of these elisions is not clear, and a set of the Discophiles Français 78s was not available for consultation. All is not lost, however, for the so-called Joseph Balzer performance on the Royale label (13) is really the Lehmann, apparently taken off the air from the broadcast of the same performance that was recorded for commercial release. The 'Balzer' is, apparently, absolutely complete and not marred by these unexplained 'cuts'. The Gramophone set (14) (no relation to HMV!) featuring 'The Cathedral Choir and Symphony Orchestra' is identical to the 'Balzer'.

Choruses and chorales conducted by Karl Forster (15), who was for many years the choir director of St Hedwig's Cathedral, are also very Mendelssohnian in feeling. One wonders how the Passion in its entirety sounded under Forster's capable leadership.

Kurt Thomas, who studied at the Leipzig Conservatory with Karl Straube before Straube became interested in issues of authentic performance practice, made a recording in the 1950s that is very much in the conservative mould (16). His straightforward reading is the one truly inspired recording that Thomas made. It is also apparently the earliest to make use of the 1741 versions of 'Mein Jesus schweigt' and 'Geduld, Geduld'. A relatively small chorus and orchestra are employed. The soloists range from adequate to fine. As Jesus, Horst Günter is solid and direct and Helmut Kretschmar's fine account of the Evangelist and the tenor solos is marred only by his tendency to shriek at the top. At a relatively early point in her distinguished career, Agnes Giebel's voice is fresh, clear, and pure.

Heinz Markus Göttsche's recording (17) is much like Thomas's; direct and without pretension, a well-sung, high-quality provincial performance in the conservative tradition; it also features the gamba versions of 'Mein Jesus schweigt' and 'Geduld, Geduld'. The recording, however, leaves something to be desired. The soloists are right in the listeners' laps, but the chorus is in the next block. Of the reliable soloists, Ortrun Wenkel stands out: here is a big, tubby contralto voice with a potent, centred tone.

Much more impressive in every respect, however, is the Rudolf Mauersberger set, made in Dresden early in 1970 (18). It is the quintessential recorded performance in the Mendelssohn style and one of the best accounts of the *SMP* overall. Born in 1889, Mauersberger began his studies at the Leipzig Conservatory just a few months after the death of a long-time faculty member, the pianist Carl Reinecke, who had known Mendelssohn personally. From the first note to the last, this reading has a wonderful lilt. Mauersberger possessed an excellent sense of drama, and the performance is perfectly paced, with one number leading into the next, powerfully but never melodramatically.

The two boys' choirs – the Thomanerchor Leipzig, which was prepared by the then Thomascantor, Rudolf's younger brother Erhard, and Rudolf's own Dresdner Kreuzchor – sing with precision and with warmth. The soloists are at one with their octogenarian conductor. A youthful Peter Schreier, himself an alumnus of the Kreuzchor, sings the Evangelist with brilliance, conviction and empathy; tenor Hans-Joachim Rotzsch, who was to succeed Erhard Mauersberger as Thomascantor, has a pure light voice, but it is a little tender at the top. Theo Adam is a wonderfully dignified and forthright Jesus, but his voice is beginning to show the first signs of wear. The bass arias are sung by Günter Leib, whose light voice is precisely focused and pure of tone.

The most recent recording in the Mendelssohn tradition, and the most colourful in the genre, is, surprisingly, Sir Georg Solti's (19). Whether he did so consciously or not, Solti has given us another quintessential modern recording of a mid-nineteenth-century central German style reading of the score. Speeds tend to be brisk, the approach straightforward; there is no simpering or lingering here. Since both the Lehmann and the Mauersberger have been out of the catalogue for many years, this version is more readily available to those who are interested in this approach.

The relatively small orchestra, a chorus some eighty voices strong and the battery of top-flight soloists acquit themselves nobly, supporting Solti's interpretative goals to the fullest. Hans Peter Blochwitz, who sang the tenor arias in Herreweghe's period instrument recording, here proves to be a distinguished Evangelist, and Kiri Te Kanawa is equally impressive in the soprano solos. Organ continuo is used throughout and the gamba versions of 'Mein Jesus schweigt' and 'Geduld, Geduld' are employed.

Solti, however, is not the first 'big-name' conductor to record a great performance of the Mendelssohn type. That honour goes to Otto Klemperer, whose 1963 recording is justly revered (20). The tempi and overall beat are admittedly slow, which creates an intensity that heightens the inevitability of the course of the story almost unbearably, but there is no sentimentality.

J.S Bach: *St Matthew Passion*

Despite the deliberate pacing, the narrative recitatives never sound stodgy or didactic; they have a suitably conversational tone. The phrases are long and smooth, the pacing paradoxically urgent and relentless.

No conductor has been blessed by a more stellar constellation of soloists and all are in top form. In fact, it has to be noted that some of the tiniest roles are gladly taken by artists either at the peak (Geraint Evans – the Second Priest) or on the verge (Janet Baker – the Second Maid) of major international careers. Klemperer, incidentally, opted for the 1741 gamba versions of 'Mein Jesus schweigt' and 'Geduld, Geduld'. Peter Pears is The sovereign Evangelist, Fischer-Dieskau the authoritative Jesus. Elisabeth Schwarzkopf, Nicolai Gedda and Walter Berry are at their best in the solos.

Klemperer and Solti are the exceptions not the rule. Charismatic conductors of international stature are rarely musical conservatives either consciously or unconsciously intent on preserving established performance traditions, no matter how important they may be. Powerful creative or recreative personalities are usually egocentrics who seek to go their own ways and to create styles of their own. The performance traditions associated with this work are not immune from this reality.

As luck would have it, the first complete recording was made by just such a charismatic conductor, one who, furthermore, had no knowledge of the Mendelssohnian traditions. That man was Koussevitzky, the Russian-born double-bass virtuoso who conducted the Boston Symphony Orchestra for twenty-five years. His *SMP* is a free-wheeling affair to say the least, eccentric and Romantic in an almost Tchaikovskian sense. He may have had no more knowledge of 'correct' Bach performance practice than the Gilbertian novice in a nunnery, but hc had the sense to perform the work in its entirety. He engaged the services of the distinguished German *émigré* harpsichordist Ernst Victor Wolff to accompany the Evangelist and fill in the figured bass in many of the solos; he also hired the pioneer gambist Alfred Zighera to play the obbligato in 'Komm, süsses Kreuz' and the preceding arioso. But Koussevitzky couldn't stomach the notion of 'Geduld, Geduld' with a simple continuo accompaniment; the harmonies are realised in a fully written-out, through-composed setting for full string orchestra.

While all are more than adequate, none of the soloists other than the British Keith Falkner, however, is memorable, and Koussevitzky's recording is now valuable primarily as an extremely rare collector's item. But one singer who received no credit for his participation in this gargantuan under-taking went on to fame and fortune. He was a Harvard undergraduate and a member of the Glee Club at the time. He became a protégé of Koussevitzky's and a charismatic 'big name' conductor in his own right. His name is Leonard Bernstein, and he, too, has recorded the *SMP* in English (21).

Bernstein's, however, is a severely abridged, extroverted, sharp-edged, oper-atic account that is ultimately scuttled by inadequate soloists – a querulous,

35

bleaty Evangelist, a stentorian Jesus, a solid, clear-voiced soprano who approaches every note above the staff with fear and trepidation. Only the molten-voiced mezzo-soprano Betty Allen is truly enjoyable to hear and one wishes that Charles Bressler, though not in his best form, had sung the Evangelist's narrative, in addition to the two tenor solos that did not end up on the cutting room floor.

A performance of Part One by the New York Philharmonic under the direction of Bruno Walter, Bernstein's other great mentor, broadcast on 18 April 1943, has survived in dull and rather muddy sound and it circulated semi-privately in the early 1970s (22). (Part Two, which was broadcast the following week, is also rumoured to exist in the Philharmonic's archives, but it has not as yet surfaced.) Sung in the Henry S. Drinker translation, the performance is rather Mahlerian in tone, but it is not as extreme as Koussevitzky's or Mengelberg's. Walter makes no cuts, *per se*, but he does find it convenient to play only the reprise of the opening ritornellos of the four *da capo* arias in Part One.

Perhaps the greatest culprit among the 'big-name' conductors is Mengelberg, the brilliant and eccentric conductor of the Concertgebouw Orchestra of Amsterdam, whose abridged Palm Sunday, 1939, concert performance was one of the first to be released on LP (23). An effusive and 'Romantic' performance to say the least, Mengelberg's intensely personal view is replete with grand ritards, neo-Mahlerian plasticity, rubati within rubati and phrases within phrases and a fastidious attention to details of dynamics within phrases. The eccentricities, great and small, are legion. A description of a tiny one will suffice: nearly every chord in the recitatives is broken, strummed on the harpsichord as though it were a lute or a guitar. Needless to say a large chorus and orchestra are used.

The soloists are uneven. Louis van Tulder sounds pinched and pressed in the tenor arias, and Willem Ravelli, the Jesus, has a rather tight wobble, but his is a characterisation of great reserve, resignation and sensitivity. Karl Erb was in better voice in the Ramin 'studio' recording made two years later, but he was indisputably one of the finest Evangelists of all time, and more of the part can be heard here. Jo Vincent had a special soprano voice, radiant and burnished, pure and very tightly focused.

Piet van Egmond, who played organ continuo in the Mengelberg performance, recorded an uncut *SMP* in the early 1950s (24). Although he is nowhere near as effusive or idiosyncratic, Egmond was obviously heavily influenced by Mengelberg. Once again, a large chorus and orchestra are called into play. The singing, from chorus and soloists alike, is quite raw.

The large shadow that Mengelberg's approach to the work cast in the Netherlands can be felt in Anthon van der Horst's recording, which was made in concert in the Grote Kerk in Naarden in 1957 (25). The pulse is slow in this performance, in which the gamba versions of 'Mein Jesus schweigt' and

'Geduld, Geduld' are employed. Dr van der Horst was inclined to the scholarly, and he pays more than casual attention to the principles of 'correct' performance practice. Mengelberg's much-tempered influence can nonetheless still be felt in the careful highlighting of inner voices in choruses and arias alike. The soloists are uneven. Best is Tom Brand, a pure-voiced Evangelist with security and power at the top end of his register.

In its way, Furtwängler's concert performance of 14 April 1954 (26) is as eccentric and iconoclastic as Mengelberg's. That this recreative genius is beholden to no tradition, no matter how venerable and no matter how worthy, becomes apparent in the opening chorus. He inserts momentum-breaking caesuras between the Chorus One 'Sehet!' and the Chorus Two responses. A single-minded determination to create an intensely dramatic, operatic interpretation sweeps all before it. As Jesus, the clear-voiced, articulate Fischer-Dieskau knuckles under to Furtwängler's interpretative demands and so do all the other soloists, the chorus and the orchestra in this weird but often powerful reading. The score is disfigured by cuts that are almost as extreme as those made by Ramin, Kittel, and Mengelberg. Except for Fischer-Dieskau and the dramatic and tonally beautiful Elisabeth Grümmer, the soloists leave much to be desired. Höffgen is weak and wobbly; subsequent sterling performances leave no doubt that she was simply having an off day. Dermota tends to over-inflect and over-interpret, which works fine within the Furt-wänglerian context, but he strains at the top in the Evangelist's recitatives. The less said about Otto Edelmann's voice, which had deteriorated badly in the four years since he had sung in Karajan's uncut *SMP* in Vienna in 1950 (27), the better.

There are some wonderful moments, nonetheless: a hushed *a capella* 'Wenn ich einmal soll scheiden' of ethereal beauty and a 'Komm, süsses Kreuz' — with the gamba obbligato adjusted to suit the cello — taken at a tempo slow enough to make the onomatopoeic dragging of the cross especially vivid come immediately to mind. Still, Furtwängler's is a turgid *SMP* best left to his idolators.

Even in 1950, at the age of 42, Herbert von Karajan qualified as a charismatic 'big-name' conductor and his complete and uncut *SMP* from that year contrasts sharply with Furtwängler's. Karajan's is a powerful and dramatic reading, Michelangelesque in its monumentality; he often borders on the excessive but never crosses over the line into the maudlin or the self-indulgent. He has the benefit of an extraordinary cast. Though a bit less secure than he had been when he sang for Bruno Kittel more than a decade earlier, Walther Ludwig is still a passionate, committed tenor soloist, an Evangelist to be reckoned with; here, however, the listener gets the bonus of hearing his interpretation of the role complete and uncut. Irmgard Seefried is pure and impassioned in the soprano solos and it is wonderful to have a recording of the unique Kathleen Ferrier singing all of the alto's solos in German. The

37

balances, however, are poor and the dry sound varies from clear to muddy throughout this recording, which apparently was salvaged from a homemade 'off-the-air' tape.

Little changed in the nearly twenty-five years that elapsed before Karajan made his studio recording (28). The sound is rich-hued but oddly artificial, as seems to have been the conductor's preference. The reading is quite self-indulgent and idiosyncratic, but it remains powerful; in fact for those who prefer a heart-on-the-sleeve approach, this set is one of the two best choices. Once again, the overall tactus is slow, the approach colourful but restrained. Schreier is again a top-notch Evangelist, Fischer-Dieskau a forthright and unpretentious Jesus and Christa Ludwig powerful in the alto solos, but Berry's voice is now painfully tight above the staff, particularly in the exceedingly deliberately paced 'Gebt mir meinen Jesum wieder'. Karajan chose the 1741 version of 'Mein Jesus schweigt', but seems to have had the part played on the cello; he himself makes a cameo appearance as the organist in a maddeningly slow 'Geduld, Geduld'. 'Wenn ich einmal soll scheiden' is sung *a capella*, as it was in the 1950 Vienna performance.

Eugen Jochum's set (29) is the other good choice for those who prefer an emotionally extroverted interpretation. His is a loving, supple, dramatic and colourful reading, with much ebb and flow, and a full range of dynamics, *crescendi* and *diminuendi*. Another of the truly great Evangelists, Ernst Haefliger shows little vocal strain and yet greater emotional depth in this, his penultimate recording of this work. As Jesus, Berry proves dignified, solid and mature, but never stuffy. The sensitive John van Kesteren sounds a shade weary in the tenor arias.

Even more gorgeous but, alas, much more difficult to obtain is the Pablo Casals broadcast performance from June 1963 (30). The then 86-year-old Catalan cellist and conductor had a singular approach to music in general and Bach in particular. His compassionate interpretation is at once supple and incisive, emotional and restrained. The tonal and vocal colours are intense but subtle from the first moment to the last in this remarkable account. One regrets only that it is sung in English, particularly since Haefliger is the Evangelist! The other soloists are all of equally high calibre, and hearing the rich and pure soprano of Olga Iglesias makes the listener regret that this fine Puerto Rican vocalist chose not to pursue an international career. The instrumental playing is of an especially high order; in those days the Festival Casals de Puerto Rico Orchestra was the greatest 'pick-up' ensemble in the world; concertmasters from major orchestras gladly played at rear desks in the second violin section. The Cleveland Orchestra Chorus was prepared by Robert Shaw.

Certainly one of the more eccentric of the 'big-name' interpretations is Ralph Vaughan Williams's (31), recorded less than seven months before his death, on 5 March 1958, at the last of the twenty-three performances that he had conducted since 1931. RVW's is a very fluid, vibrantly coloured, highly Romantic interpretation, most notable for a flamboyant realisation of the basso continuo for the piano. (Like Beecham, Vaughan Williams hated the harpsichord with an almost religious fervour.) Liberally laced with sinuous and peculiar inner voices, this free-wheeling, through-composed part is anachronistic with a vengeance and not without some alterations of Bach's indicated harmonies; at especially dramatic moments there are thick, grace-noted chords that call to mind the concluding bars of the Bach–Busoni *Chaconne*.

The orchestra, a *mélange* of professionals and amateurs and the amateur chorus are adequate, the soloists rarely more than passable in this abridged English-language performance. The Evangelist, Eric Greene, was highly regarded in his day, but by this stage in his career his voice was in tatters; the straining for the high notes is painful and much more pronounced than in the nearly complete English-language set recorded nearly ten years before under the direction of Reginald Jacques (32).

Jacques's is an essentially Romantic performance that is valuable primarily as a souvenir of Kathleen Ferrier's distinctive voice, but she did better for Karajan in Vienna two years later. Of the other soloists, Elsie Suddaby is far and away the most satisfactory: her voice is light, fresh, and clear. Greene, as intimated earlier, is dry and timorous; so is Henry Cummings, who sings Jesus.

This kind of dry and querulous vocal production seems to have been prevalent in England if the few 78rpm records that were made can be taken as indicative. Silver-throated tenors like Walter Widdop seem to have been something of an anomaly in English Bach performances in those days. Two discs of excerpts recorded by a 'Special Choir' under the direction of Dr Ernest Bullock in Westminster Abbey about 1930 are a case in point (33). The unnamed soloists are hooty and shrill; their voices are constricted and bleaty. The Evangelist sounds like Eric Greene; if it is in fact he, his voice was dry and tight even then. The choir is vast, the interpretation soupy.

Even more sentimental, however, is a brutally truncated version of the *SMP*, newly arranged and edited by David McKinley Williams, who conducts from the organ. Recorded in St Bartholomew's Church in New York, this twelve-disc set was the first attempt at a 'complete' recording (34). A theatrical, sugar-coated disaster the interpretation is memorable only because of the participation of the tenor Allan Jones, who later went to Hollywood and played the Romantic male lead in the famous Marx Brothers comedy *A Night at the Opera*. Jones ranks among the most powerful and emotive Evangelists. His is a big, intense voice and his diction is superb. Hollywood's gain was classical music's loss.

In better taste but of similar limited interest is the single LP recorded in the early 1950s by the Handel Oratorio Society of Augustana College in

39

Rockford, Illinois (35). Billed as a 'Musical Digest' arranged by Lura Stover, the soprano in this English-language performance, the work is reduced to a simple narrative interspersed with excerpts from a handful of arias and choruses, with the instrumental ritornellos either abridged or cut altogether. The four better-than-average soloists and the 400-voice choir are accompanied on the organ.

From Canada in the early 1950s came a recording under the baton of Sir Ernest MacMillan (36). With a large chorus and orchestra, this somewhat abridged performance has little to recommend it. Edward Johnson has a rather tight wobble but has little difficulty with the range of the Evangelist's music. The bright spot is soprano Lois Marshall. Her distinctive, trumpet-like voice still has the bloom of youth on it and her interpretation evinces great sensitivity.

A more interesting recorded document from the same period is an LP side of excerpts from the first performance given in Moscow, under the direction of the Latvian choral conductor Janis Dumins (37). Recorded in the Great Hall of the Moscow Conservatory during the 1956 season, the performance is in no way eccentric; it is cast in the middle-of-the-road Eastern European legato style, but it eschews Romantic excess except for a big *decrescendo* at the end of the final chorus. The whole performance would certainly be worth hearing.

The ever-growing revival of interest in authentic performance practice and in old instruments that had begun at the turn of the century caused the influential organist and teacher, Karl Straube, Thomascantor from 1916 to 1938, to be 'born again' musicologically. He, who, in 1904, had published a performing edition of Bach organ works for the symphonic late-nineteenth-century Romantic organ, made an about turn in the 1920s and espoused the cause of the return to a more authentic performance practice for Bach's music. But, at heart, this close friend of Max Reger was still a late Romantic. The 'new' Leipzig style that he forged, and that he and his pupil Günther Ramin helped to popularise and disseminate, is, in essence, a thorough blending of the Mendelssohn tradition, Regeresque late Romanticism, and tenets of authentic performance practice.

A comparison of either the Weissbach or the Mauersberger set with the Ramin recording, for instance, will make the differences apparent. Straube's successor as Thomascantor, Ramin may have used smaller forces for his recording, made in the Thomaskirche in 1941, but his interpretation is much less straightforward. His version, the first 'complete' set issued in the UK, is rough-hewn from the opening bars, and it is neither as urgent nor as long-phrased as the Weissbach or the Mauersberger. Ramin strives for and achieves a craggy monumentality and consciously avoids sentimentality. Karl Erb is the distinguished Evangelist, and the extraordinary Gerhard Hüsch sounds appropriately fresh and youthful as Jesus. Friedel Beckmann is the solid, golden-voiced contralto. As mentioned earlier, the score is severely abridged, as was the practice in Thomaskirche performances in the early years of the twentieth century. Ramin's son, Dieter, however, recalls that his father battled hard with the recording's producers to prevent still further abridgements. A complete and uncut *SMP* with Ramin, dating from 1950, does, however, exist and it is to be hoped that it will soon be released commercially.

For better or for worse, the Straube–Ramin approach to the performance of Bach's vocal music, emphasising as it did smaller ensembles, crisper articulation and shorter phrases, seemed 'closer' to Bach's own practice and it was quickly espoused by a significant number of younger conductors. The most influential of these was Karl Richter, a student of Ramin's who emigrated to the West and established the Munich Bach Choir, a crack ensemble of upwards of ninety voices. His 1958 recording, made for the authenticity-minded Deutsche Grammophon Archiv label, had a tremendous impact on performers and listeners alike (38).

Somehow or other, Richter got the reputation for being the quintessential exponent of the modern German neo-baroque style. For that reason alone, what is most remarkable about Richter's approach, and there are three commercial recordings and a television film version of it, is its unabashed Romanticism. While his is essentially a more polished form of the granite-like Ramin interpretation, Richter proves to be more effusive than most conductors and he has a decided preference for slow speeds. The tempo of the opening chorus, for instance, is a little slower than Mengelberg's; and the overall beat is also slow.

Of Richter's three commercial recordings, the first is indisputably the most convincing. The interpretation is still fresh, and the soloists overall are the most satisfying. Haefliger, in his first Evangelist, is already one of the truly great interpreters. Fischer-Dieskau is also splendid in the bass arias. The second recording (39), which appeared only in Japan, was issued as a memorial to the conductor and documents a concert performance given in Tokyo on 29 May 1969. While both the chorus and orchestra seem tired at times, the opening chorus and many of the other movements sound more incisive. The tempi seem even slower than on the 1958 recording. Another significant difference is the injection of a much more prominent organ continuo. In fact, the continuo realisations in general have become more florid. Haefliger is once again the tenor soloist, and the alto is the ever-reliable Höffgen.

The third and final recording (40), made shortly before Richter's sudden and premature death, is, sadly, no credit to his memory. While his spectacular interpretation of the *B Minor Mass* (*qv*) stayed ever fresh, familiarity with the *SMP* bred stagnation. Richter's grand concept of this score, which he clearly loved deeply, is marred by over-interpretation and fussiness. The opening chorus is now not only slow but also disjointed. There is a curious slackness about the turgid overall tactus that stands in sharp contrast to both his previous recordings and to the relentless vigour of Klemperer's taut but deliberate pacing. And now, for the first time, the pulse and tempo of the narrative are pushed and pulled relentlessly. As disappointing as it is, Richter's valedictory recording of the work has many strong points. Schreier is a laudable successor to Haefliger as the tenor soloist and the special clear, molten warmth of Janet Baker's voice brings a unique beauty to both 'Buss und Reu' and 'Erbarme Dich, mein Gott'. Richter, incidentally, accompanies the Evangelist from the harpsichord.

Often thought of as the inheritor of Richter's mantle as the most prominent choral conductor in Germany, Helmuth Rilling, the founder of the Gächinger Kantorei of Stuttgart, is also very much an interpreter in the Straube–Ramin tradition. His version (41), however, has more of the Mendelssohn tradition in it than Richter's; it is brisker and more streamlined. The pacing is dramatic, almost operatic, but always tasteful. The solid group of soloists and impeccably trained chorus respond to Rilling's interpretative demands easily and gracefully. The 1741 gamba versions of 'Mein Jesus schweigt' and 'Geduld, Geduld' are used. Trivia buffs will be amused to note that David Thomas, now one of the foremost early-music singers in the world, sings the part of Judas in Rilling's recording.

A decade earlier, in 1965, Karl Münchinger, another conductor based in Stuttgart, made one of the few recordings in which a boys' choir is used (42). Like Richter, although not to the same degree, he opts for a slow pacing for his Raminesque account. All of the soloists are of high quality, yet it has to be said that Peter Pears is not in as good voice as he had been for Klemperer a couple of years before. Elly Ameling is radiant and bright in the soprano solos, but it is the indescribably beautiful singing of the tragically short-lived tenor Fritz Wunderlich that makes the Münchinger set worth having. The 1741 forms of 'Mein Jesus schweigt' and 'Geduld, Geduld' are used.

The recordings published since the bicentenary of Bach's death in 1950 that have not been previously discussed all represent, in varying degrees and proportions, blendings of the Mendelssohn tradition, the Ramin–Straube reaction to it, and the pressures brought to bear by the apostles of authentic performance practice. The collisions of these three contrasting approaches can have both positive and negative results.

There is no need to waste many words about Ferdinand Grossmann's undistinguished traditional account (43). A dull conductor, drab pacing, mediocre soloists and sound that is steely and muddy at the same time ensure that his recording is eminently forgettable. The Gönnenwein reading (44), which is largely of the Straube–Ramin variety, looks promising on paper, but proves a disaster on the turntable. The performance is drab *in toto*, but the major problem is the Evangelist, Theo Altmeyer, whose voice is tattered in the upper registers. He is simply not equal to the demands of the role. He declaims the recitatives at a plodding tempo that makes the narrative didactic and condescending, as if St Matthew is telling his listeners, 'I'll say this slowly so you'll be sure to understand me.' It puts a wet blanket on the proceedings, in which, by the way, 'Mein Jesus schweigt' and 'Geduld, Geduld' are presented in the 1741 versions. Only Julia Hamari's dignified, noble and committed account of the alto solos makes the Gönnenwein set worth keeping.

Warmer and more gripping are three recordings made outside of Germany. The earliest is a distinguished Swedish interpretation that was broadcast from the Englebrektskyrkan in Stockholm on 24 February 1963 (45). Under the direction of the highly respected choral conductor, Eric Ericson, the performance is remarkable for Kim Borg's dignified Jesus and John van Kesteren's Evangelist. Both men have big voices. Borg's tight, small vibrato is not annoying, and van Kesteren sails clearly and purely into the high registers without difficulty or tension. The chorus is large and somewhat distant within the reverberant acoustic.

The Frigyes Sándor account was also recorded in concert, on 23 May 1976, at the first performance in Budapest since 1928 (46). A medium-sized chorus is employed, but it has to be said that the intonation is often gamey. Sándor opts for a relaxed pacing, but his contemplative and dark-hued interpretation never flags, even if all the participants sound a little tired in Part Two. Vandersteene's thin and plangent voice is a bit tight in the upper registers, but his Evangelist is compelling and free of mannerisms. Hamari once again gives a sterling account of the alto solos. Sándor chose the 1741 versions of 'Mein Jesus schweigt' and 'Geduld, Geduld' and, for once, the gamba is correctly paired with a harpsichord.

Michel Corboz's 1982 recording (47) is very brisk overall: the interpretation is streamlined but dramatic, and is a most satisfactory, style-conscious, no-frills account. Gerhard Faulstich takes an unpretentious, conversational approach to the part of Jesus; he is direct and business-like. Philippe Huttenlocher shows himself to be a great singing actor and he injects much character into the various 'minor' roles that he sings with conviction. Laudably, none of this gift for characterisation intrudes into his straightforward interpretation of the bass arias. Equiluz, perhaps the finest Evangelist of the day, lives up to his well-earned reputation, and Anthony Rolfe Johnson is an impassioned and colourful tenor soloist.

Mogens Wöldike was one of the pioneers of the early-music movement and also one of the world's great choral conductors. A friend and colleague of the incomparable Aksel Schiøtz, with whom he made a stunning and emotionally draining 78 of 'Ich will bei meinem Jesu wachen' (DB 5267), Wöldike recorded the work more than a quarter of a century ago, but his graceful, contemplative, unpretentious and affectionate account still ranks among the most satisfying ever recorded (48). Uno Ebrelius is a dignified and poignant Evangelist, Hans Braun a no-nonsense, clean-voiced Jesus. The four distinguished artists who sing the arias are all in top form, but Max Welrich steals the show. He is the best Peter of all, the only interpreter of that crucial small part who makes audible the apostle's fear when challenged and questioned.

While Johannes Somary takes into account the many developments in Bach performance practice that have taken place over the years, his 1978 recording (49) is the best in the Straube–Ramin tradition; his speeds are well chosen, his pacing excellent. He also has an excellent group of soloists. This is Haefliger's most recent recording of the Evangelist. Not only does his voice seem warmer and more supple than it did twenty years before when he first recorded the part for Richter, but his interpretation has taken on a warmth, a colour and an emotional clout that it lacked two decades earlier. There is an innate pathos in Seth McCoy's unique voice that makes his singing of the tenor arias particularly affecting and Birgit Finnilä's molten tone is particularly well suited to the alto solos. The contributions of Elly Ameling, Benjamin Luxon and Barry McDaniel are also of the first order.

The two orchestras and the two choruses are laid out antiphonally, and the spatial effects have been effectively captured by the engineers. In addition to using the gamba versions of 'Mein Jesus schweigt' and 'Geduld, Geduld', Somary doubles the ripieno sopranos in the opening and closing choruses of Part One with organ, as Bach did in 1736. More conductors who use children to sing those ripieno parts should follow Bach's and Somary's lead, since such tender young amateur singers are often both off pitch and tonally acidulous.

The collision of the various performance traditions and conventions that have been – and are – applied to the *SMP* has also created havoc and brought about disaster. Peter Schreier's recording (50) is a witches' brew of Mendelssohn, Karl Richter, and the faddish trappings of 'authentic performance practice'. The opening chorus is taken at a good clip, but the momentum is eviscerated by 'chunka-chunka' articulation and mild *sforzandi* on strong beats; this unsettling opening is not a good omen. Schreier injects so much gratuitous articulation into the obbligato of 'Erbarme Dich, mein Gott' that all of the plaintive sinuousness is destroyed. The whole performance is fussy and finicky because of his misguided attempt to be 'with it' musicologically. In addition to conducting, Schreier sings the Evangelist; it is his only unsatisfactory account of the part – undisciplined and dramatic in the pejorative sense of the term. The patrician and poignant Evangelist that he called forth for Mauersberger, Richter and Karajan has evaporated completely. Adam is still a majestic Jesus, but his voice has developed a rather pronounced wobble. The 1741 versions of 'Mein Jesus schweigt' and 'Geduld, Geduld' are used.

Schreier's sins, however, are insignificant when compared to Raymond Leppard's (51). His self-indulgent, egocentric 'interpretation' is stuffed with every cheap authentic performance practice conjuror's trick imaginable, including but not limited to the application of inappropriate embellishments and performance conventions. For instance, what grounds does Leppard have for thinking that the appoggiatura convention was applicable to narrative recitatives in provincial Saxony in 1736? 'Blute nur' is disfigured by the bizarre intermittent slamming of strong beats. And the catalogue of atrocities goes on and on. The soloists don't help much. Jon Garrison produces an unpleasant constricted sound to begin with and exacerbates matters with a pretentious operatic over-interpretation of the role of the Evangelist; at least his approach is congruent with Leppard's flashy and fussy doings. This performance, in which the 1741 versions of 'Mein Jesus schweigt' and 'Geduld, Geduld' are used, can safely be said to be the only one on record that will arouse the righteous ire of all sensitive listeners who have the courage to confront it.

SUMMARY

Those who are truly interested in finding out how Bach heard the *St Matthew Passion* should try to find a copy of the tape of the Rifkin broadcast. The choice among the four commercial period instrument recordings available at the time this essay was finished — the first Harnoncourt, the Herreweghe, the Leonhardt and the Gardiner — will depend on the listener's preference for an extroverted interpretation, an inward approach, a reserved but elegant account, or a large-scaled, late-classical style reading.

Those who prefer the classic Mendelssohnian approach on modern instruments will find the Lehmann and the Mauersberger to be the most accurate and the most compelling, but both of these are out of print. That Solti and Klemperer are marginally less faithful to the true early nineteenth-century style is immaterial. Both sets rank among the greatest interpretations of the *SMP* on record.

The collector who prefers a charismatic, Romantic approach will want the 1950 Karajan performance if sound quality is not an important consideration. If it is, either the second Karajan or the Jochum set will prove eminently satisfactory. Those who want a 'modern' but relatively 'authentic' interpretation will want to choose from the Wöldike (the most conservative and Mendelssohnian), the Somary (the most Raminesque) and the Corboz (the fleetest and the most streamlined).

J.S. Bach: Mass in B Minor

TERI NOEL TOWE

The Mass in B Minor is best thought of as an anthology, a collection of his 'best' sacred music assembled by Bach in the last years of his life. During the 1730s and 1740s, Bach put together several such *Kunstbücher* (literally, books of art); the most widely known are *The Art of Fugue,* the four volumes of the *Clavier Übungen,* and the *17 Chorales of Different Kinds.* Some of these anthologies Bach either published or intended to publish; others, like the Mass, he did not. These less 'commercial' distillations he left to his heirs, physical and spiritual, to preserve and disseminate to those who were interested.

With the exception of the opening four measures of the first Kyrie, it seems that every movement of the Mass is a reworking of an existing vocal composition, either sacred or secular. At least one such movement, the Crucifixus, dates from the Weimar years. The Kyrie and Gloria were put together in 1733, as a presentation piece to the Elector of Saxony and King of Poland, from whom Bach sought, ultimately successfully, the professionally and socially invaluable position of Court Composer. The Sanctus is a careful and subtle revision of the setting of the text that he wrote for performance in Leipzig on Christmas Day, 1723. The Symbolum Nicenum [the Credo section] and the concluding movements of the Mass were added in the late 1740s, when both Bach's eyesight and his health were failing.

The Kyrie, the Gloria, and the Symbolum Nicenum are all in five voices; the texture expands to six voices in the Sanctus and eight in the Osanna. As Joshua Rifkin's controversial, but as yet unrefuted, findings have convincingly demonstrated, the Mass in B Minor, like almost all of Bach's concerted vocal music in fact, was meant to be sung by one singer to each line, even in the 'choruses'. The principle is a simple one: each performer got his own part, no matter how big or how small his role, and he shared that part with no one else.

The complement of five 'soloists' has caused numerous problems over the years. Who, for instance, sings the 'Laudamus te', which is assigned to the second soprano, in a performance for which only one soprano soloist has been

46

engaged? The soprano or the alto? Elly Ameling once remarked in a radio interview that it was the soloist who made the mistake of looking at the conductor first when the aria came up at rehearsal. Many conductors, however, assign the two bass solos to different soloists, when Bach calls for only one bass; the reason is simple: the 'Quoniam' lies lower in the main than the 'Et in spiritum sanctum'. While assembling the second half of the Mass some ten to fifteen years after he delivered the parts of the Kyrie and Gloria to the Court in Dresden, Bach was not concerned about making the compass of the two arias comport comfortably with one another.

Although many, if not all, of the components could have been, and were, performed as parts of the various Leipzig church services for which Bach provided the music, he gave no complete performance nor, apparently, did he ever intend to put one on. It is, therefore, supremely ironic that this, Bach's own distillation of his 'greatest' vocal music, apparently did not receive its first complete performance until more than 100 years after his death.

There was, however, interest in the work among the *cognoscenti* in the decades after Bach's death as well as in the years after the onset of the general revival of interest in his music that was spawned by Mendelssohn's seminal performance of the *St Matthew Passion* with the Berlin Singakademie in 1829. Carl Philipp Emanuel Bach put on a performance of the Symbolum Nicenum in Hamburg in 1786, preceding it with a short instrumental introduction of his own composition. (For this performance, as a guide to his copyists, Philipp Emanuel 'touched up' the orchestration a bit on his father's autograph score, which has also sustained some water damage, and his editorial changes went unnoticed until nearly ten years ago. As it happens, therefore, a couple of copies made before Philipp Emanuel's emendations provide a more accurate text than the autograph itself.)

Haydn owned a copy of the Mass. Beethoven unsuccessfully sought to obtain one. Spontini put on a performance of the Symbolum Nicenum, through the 'Et resurrexit', in Berlin in 1828, with ninety-two in the chorus, fifty-six strings, clarinets, horns and bassoons, but no trumpets or oboes. Under the direction of Carl Friedrich Rungenhagen, the Berlin Singakademie gave the Kyrie and Gloria in 1834, and the balance of the work the following year. Portions of the Mass were performed at the Birmingham Festival as early as 1837, and the Mass was among the works regularly performed by the London Bach Choir, which was founded in 1876.

The first complete performance in the United States was given in Bethlehem, Pennsylvania, by the Bach Choir of Bethlehem, under the direction of its founder, Dr J. Fred Wolle, in 1900. This first public presentation of the Mass in America inaugurated an annual series of festival performances of the work that continues in Bethlehem to this day.

For three decades, from 1939 – seven years after Dr Wolle's death – until 1969, the Bach Choir was directed by the distinguished Welsh choral

47

conductor, Ifor Jones. His forthright, Romantic reading of the score — chock-full of rubati and ritards — was recorded in 1960 (1). Even though it is clearly his own interpretative handiwork, Jones's performance preserves many of the traditions and conventions that had been established by Dr Wolle in his thirty-two years at the helm of the Choir, traditions and quirks that have been almost completely expunged, alas, in recent years. The first Kyrie, for instance, is preceded by a Moravian chorale. Intoned softly off-stage by a brass choir, the hymn setting gives the pitch to the chorus, which comes in, *forte*, on the chorale's final chord. Un-Bachian though it may be, the effect is undeniably overwhelming.

A very large but exceptionally well-trained amateur chorus — more than 175 singers — is balanced against a smallish orchestra made up largely of members of the Philadelphia Orchestra, including such distinguished instrumentalists as horn player Mason Jones and oboist John DeLancie. The vocal soloists are average; only the golden trumpet of soprano Lois Marshall stands out. In better voice than she was three years earlier when she sang the soprano part for Eugen Jochum, she is assigned the 'Laudamus te' in addition to the music normally given to the first soprano. This important documentation of the Bach Choir of Bethlehem's approach to the Mass before it was diluted by a much more recent director's preference for 'authenticity' rather than local tradition is also a satisfying reading, one that will prove particularly appealing to those who like Bach played 'with the heart on the sleeve', as the old saying goes.

The earliest recordings of any portion of the Mass appear to be a group of four 12-inch 78s recorded by His Master's Voice at a Royal Albert Hall concert in 1926 (D 1113, 1114, 1123, 1127). The Royal Choral Society, a massive choir, under the direction of the highly regarded organist and choir-master Dr Edward Bairstow, sings with gusto and with surprising subtlety in the handful of choruses that were rather inexpertly recorded by a pioneer mobile recording team. One cannot help but wonder what the solos in this concert performance of the Mass were like, but these eight sides give the curious listener a fascinating glimpse into Bach as his music was understood in England before the Second World War and before the revival of interest in the 'correct' performance of early music took hold.

Of greater importance, particularly to those who are interested in the history of performance practice as it is documented on records, is a recording of the 'Cum sancto spiritu' by the Berlin Philharmonic Choir under the direction of its founder, Siegfried Ochs (1858–1929) (EJ 250), a distinguished choral conductor who stood in a direct line of pedagogical descent from Mendelssohn. His fleet, broadly phrased, urgent and dramatic account of the final chorus of the Gloria provides an important, invaluable and tantalising hint of what the true Mendelssohnian Bach style must have been like.

The first complete recording of the Mass was made in 1929; there were seven sessions over a ten-week period, beginning 18 March and ending 31 May. Under the direction of Albert Coates (2), this wildly uneven production contains many marvellous moments. Among them are the contributions of the stellar vocal quartet: radiant singing from Elisabeth Schumann in the duets, a suitably brisk 'Laudamus te' from the underestimated alto Margaret Balfour, a moving 'Benedictus' from the silver-throated Walter Widdop, and a warm, expressive 'Quoniam' and 'Et in spiritum sanctum' from the remarkable Friedrich Schorr, a great Wagnerian bass who nonetheless could sing early music with emotion, empathy, a clear, full tone and exemplary diction. In fact, it can safely be said that neither of these two arias has ever been better sung on records.

Among the negatives are the crazy balances between chorus and orchestra, Coates's penchant for massive ritards before side breaks, the panoply of continuo instruments (some of the arias have piano, others the harpsichord; organ is used in the choruses) and some simply horrendous intonation. (How the two English horns managed to stay so consistently out of tune with one another in the 'Et in spiritum sanctum' is an enigma for the ages!) Clearly, recording the Mass was a challenge to all concerned, performers and engineers alike; they accepted it eagerly, and, uneven though the results may be, this important and unjustly forgotten recording stood alone in the catalogue for nearly two decades.

With a 'correct' complement of five soloists, a superbly prepared small chorus, and a crack 'pick-up' orchestra, Robert Shaw made a recording of the Mass early in 1947 that must have struck those familiar only with the Coates performance as a radical departure from the norm (3). In this, one of the last major recordings made on 78rpm discs (16-inch acetates), Shaw, like Coates, indulges in ritards before side breaks from time to time, but his interpretation, unlike Coates's, is remarkably streamlined and straightforward. The vocal soloists, among the best oratorio singers then active in New York, are all more than adequate, but it is the instrumental soloists who are particularly impressive. Some of the finest freelance musicians in the United States participated in the recording and the instrumental obbligatos played by the likes of violinist Oscar Shumsky, Robert Bloom (oboe d'amore) and John Barrows (horn) make for especially rewarding listening.

Again with a 'correct' complement of five soloists, a superbly prepared small chorus, and a crack 'pick-up' orchestra, Shaw recorded the Mass a second time in June 1960 (4). His basic interpretation may have changed little in the intervening years, but the recording was both radical and musicologically significant at the time of its release three decades ago. Shaw heeded the advice of the distinguished musicologist and Bach scholar Gerhard Herz and applied the principle of *concertino* and *ripieno* to many of the choruses. In the especially florid choruses like the 'Gloria', the 'Cum sancto

49

spiritu', and the 'Et resurrexit', for example, the exposed, sparsely accompanied contrapuntal sections are sung by a group of nine *Concertisten*.

While Herz's analysis of the significance of Bach's *solo* and *tutti* markings in his vocal music now seems to be incorrect in light of Joshua Rifkin's discoveries, Shaw's application of the *solo/tutti* principle to the choruses in this recording represented a startling and seminal departure from the standard practice that proved especially refreshing at the time. Its renown in the 1960s and 1970s was so widespread that an unauthorised single disc of excerpts was even published by Melodiya in the USSR!

Ironically, however, Shaw's interpretation now sounds dated, because of the surprisingly slow tempi and an approach to the score that seems rather Romantic even though there are hardly any interpretative excesses in evidence. As in the 1947 set, the singing and playing are of a very high standard and it is to be regretted that this important recording of the Mass has been unavailable for so long; it is a justifiably sought-after collector's item.

In 1950, the bicentenary of the death of Bach was commemorated by a divided Germany and by a world just beginning to recover from the horrors and devastation of the Second World War. Two live performances of the Mass from that historic year have found their way on to commercial recordings.

The first of these performances was given in the Musikvereinsaal in Vienna (5). It is the first, and the most exhilarating, of four recorded performances of the Mass under the direction of Herbert von Karajan that have so far been released commercially. While by no means competitive with the studio recordings, this fascinating document preserves Karajan's view of the Mass at its most colourful and operatic. Grand ritards, rich dynamics and expression, powerful interpretations from five world-class soloists (including Kathleen Ferrier, who otherwise never recorded the alto solos and duets from the Mass in their entirety), and complete commitment from chorus and orchestra (except for a tentative hornist who sounds absolutely terrified in the 'Quoniam'!) make this dramatic 'Furtwängleresque' reading of the Mass a thrilling listening experience, the wildly variable and often muddy sound notwithstanding.

Five years later, Karajan made the first of his two commercial recordings of the Mass (6). Once again, the locale was Vienna, but the only 'repeater' from the 1950 concert performance is Elisabeth Schwarzkopf, who once more acquits herself magnificently in the first soprano's three duets. Marga Höffgen is cool and clear in the alto solos, including a particularly slow 'Agnus Dei', but Nicolai Gedda sounds strangely uninvolved in the painfully languid 'Benedictus'. Karajan's interpretation is less operatic and less dramatic than it was five years earlier, but this incisive and persuasive reading remains a satisfying one, one of the best in the 'modern' style. Although a monaural recording, the sound is more natural and better focused than in the later DG stereo version.

J.S Bach: Mass in B Minor

Karajan presented the B Minor Mass at the Salzburg Festival in 1961, and the performance recorded on 20 August of that year for later broadcast was released commercially in Italy in the mid-1980s (7). Again available only in monaural sound, the performance features an especially fine battalion of soloists. Leontyne Price sings the first soprano's music with the power and conviction of a Verdi heroine (or, at least, a soloist in the 'Manzoni' Requiem!); Christa Ludwig's molten sound is powerful in the second soprano and alto parts; and Gedda is this time radiant, sensitive and effortless in all of the tenor solos, including the 'Benedictus'. Walter Berry, alas, did not have one of his best days; his singing in the 'Quoniam' is mildly tentative and uncommitted; Gérard Souzay's glistening, light baritone is perfect for the 'Et in spiritum sanctum', but his diction is at times unpardonably mushy for a Lieder singer of his stature. Particularly in the arias and duets, Karajan's tempi tend to be brisker than in either of the two commercial recordings.

In his second commercial recording of the Mass, published in 1974, Karajan coddles and over-interprets the music (8). It is not, however, a case of familiarity breeding contempt; rather, it is a case of sparing the rod and spoiling the child. Karajan's genuine affection and profound empathy for the Mass has begotten an interpretation that is too solicitous, too respectful and too loving. This impression is reinforced by the sonic aura of the recording, which is blemished by the bizarre artificial sound and balances that infect so many of his later recordings; the chorus is distant within the ensemble and the strings are peculiarly louder than the brass. The arias are very slow in the main. Christa Ludwig sings with a reserved drama and wonderful secure tone, particularly in the 'Agnus Dei', and Peter Schreier responds marvellously to the challenge posed by an incredibly slow tempo in the 'Benedictus'.

The second of the 1950 commemorative performances to be released commercially is a group of excerpts from a complete performance in the Thomaskirche in Leipzig that was issued in the West by Cantate in the early 1960s (9). Günther Ramin, then the incumbent of the Thomascantorate that Bach had held more than two centuries before, employed large forces, including two boys' choirs, in bringing forth his singular conception of the Mass: granitic yet not forbidding, monumental yet never stolid. A disciple of his immediate predecessor, Karl Straube (1873–1953), who had fused the neo-Classical Mendelssohnian Bach style prevalent in Leipzig and in Germany at the time of the First World War with both tenets of authentic performance practice and Regerian Germanic post-Romanticism, Ramin strives for and achieves powerful and grand effects; the extreme ritard at the end of the concluding 'Dona nobis pacem', for example, is mind-boggling. A recording of the complete performance exists. One hopes that it will soon be issued in its entirety.

That the performance would be worth releasing complete is confirmed by the commercial recording that Ramin made of the Mass shortly before

51

he died (10). A scrappy orchestra, a coarse chorus, by and large indifferent soloists and the pressures of working with unfamiliar forces under severe time constraints all apparently combined to defeat Ramin's attempt successfully to preserve his unique and powerful interpretation on a commercial recording.

Ramin's immediate successor at the Thomaskirche, Kurt Thomas, recorded the Mass in the late 1950s, shortly before he emigrated to the West (11). His drab, flaccid account, leaden rather than majestic, is marred by acidulous instrumental playing. A little better is the recording made in the late 1950s by Rudolf Mauersberger, the then director of the Dresdner Kreuzchor — one of the two boys' choirs that participated in Ramin's 1950 performance in the Thomaskirche (12). The choruses are crisply sung, with chiselled articulation, by the well-trained choir and the solo quartet is both sensitive and well-matched, but the performance as a whole sounds clinical and lacks both warmth and subtlety.

The harpsichord continuo in the 1950 Ramin performance was played by Karl Richter, who, like Kurt Thomas, settled in the West. In 1961, with his ninety-voice Munich Bach Choir and Orchestra and a distinguished quintet of soloists, Richter made the quintessential recording of the Mass in the modern neo-baroque Leipzig style (13). Now three decades old, this extraordinary performance remains unchallenged as the recording of choice for those who want a 'modern' reading of the work that is at the same time mindful of stylistic issues. Richter's charismatic, passionate, incisive and pulse-quickening reading is the logical extension of the Ramin approach, but it is more polished, less rough-hewn. This vividly recorded account remains the paradigm against which all 'modern instrument' performances of the Mass in B Minor must be measured.

Several years ago, as a memorial to Richter, Deutsche Grammophon Archiv issued, in Japan only, a recording of a performance of the Mass that Richter had given in Tokyo in 1969 while on tour with the Munich Bach Choir (14). Cut off the same bolt of interpretative cloth as the studio recording, this fascinating document does not, however, quite measure up to its precursor either sonically or technically. Both the recording and the television film of the Mass that Richter made in the early 1970s (will that performance, recorded in a magnificent baroque pilgrimage church in Bavaria, never appear on video cassette or video disc?) show, however, that not only did he adhere to his interpretation throughout his career but also that he never became glib or facile. The interpretation always sounds fresh.

Richter, by the way, is one of the handful of conductors who elected not to follow the text of Friedrich Smend's scholarly edition of the Mass, published by the Neue Bach Ausgabe in 1955, in one important particular. The autograph does not specify the obbligato instrument in the 'Benedictus'. The Bach Gesellschaft edition and all other editions prior to that published by the NBA give the part to the violin. Smend shows convincingly that, on

52

the basis of its compass and the absence of double stops, this instrumental solo was meant for the flute. Richter and a few others, like Herbert von Karajan, stuck by the violin through interpretative thick and scholarly thin. Unless specified to the contrary, however, the reader may assume that for all recordings made after the appearance of the Neue Bach Ausgabe Edition, the obbligato in the 'Benedictus' is assigned to the flute.

For many, the inheritor of Richter's mantle as the great interpreter of the Bach sacred vocal music in the modern German neo-baroque tradition is Helmuth Rilling. With his Gächinger Kantorei Stuttgart, he has recorded the B Minor Mass twice. Of the two sets, the first, which was published in 1977, is far and away the better (15). Often searingly clear but never clinical choral singing and instrumental playing and exemplary contributions from the five soloists are the most important hallmarks of this interpretation. Rilling's tempi are brisk but never overly so, and the interpretation has a grandeur and an incisiveness that evokes Richter's.

In the second half, at least, Rilling's 1988 recording of the Mass (16) has many of the same qualities as his first. His choice of brisker tempi in the Gloria, particularly, has resulted in an interpretation that sounds oddly glib and facile; it lacks the profundity and incisiveness so much in evidence in the earlier account. While commendable, the soloists are not, with the exception of tenor Howard Crook, up to the same high standard set by those in the 1977 recording.

Rilling's were not the first recordings of the Mass to be made by a Stuttgart ensemble. In 1971, Karl Münchinger, the founder of the Stuttgart Chamber Orchestra, committed his interpretation of the work to disc (17). It is much in the same vein as the Ramin, Richter and Rilling accounts; in the high neo-baroque German style, the reading is warm and earnest, solid but always plastic. The chorus, however, is muddy sounding from time to time, and there are some patches of gamey intonation. There are five first-rate soloists, including two sopranos, so Elly Ameling, who sings the first soprano part with great beauty, did not have to worry about being the first to look at the conductor at the first rehearsal for the 'Laudamus te'.

The most recent of the neo-baroque 'modern' instrument accounts in the Straube–Ramin vein to emanate from the then German Democratic Republic is Peter Schreier's, recorded in 1981-2 (18). Schreier unfortunately allowed himself to be seduced by some of the musicological fads that were voguish in the 1970s. He often stresses strong beats with swells and *sforzandi*, and he assigns the *corno da caccia* obbligato in the 'Quoniam' to a curious modern hybrid brass instrument of the same name that was invented to respond to some highly dubious findings that purportedly 'proved' that the *corno da caccia* part in the Mass was meant to be transposed up, rather than down. Ludwig Güttler plays the part superbly on this bastard brass instrument, but for the discerning listener the obtrusiveness of the repeated pedal tones as

53

played up rather than down, and the failure of the instrument to blend at all with the two bassoons, effectively puts the kibosh on the purported 'authentic' new 'old' brass instrument. On the plus side are a fine group of soloists, just tempi, and enthusiastic singing and playing from chorus and orchestra alike.

During the decade following the commemoration of the bicentenary of Bach's death in 1950, a number of other recordings of the Mass, in addition to those previously discussed, were released. Among the first was Hermann Scherchen's (19). Predictably quirky and iconoclastic, his recording features what is undoubtedly the slowest first 'Kyrie' of all. Scherchen takes Bach's marking – 'Largo' – absolutely at face value; the second 'Kyrie' is also very slow. The 'Benedictus', sung *sotto voce* by Anton Dermota, is weird: gummy with regard to both tempo and interpretation. Gertrud Burgsthaler-Schuster, the contralto, sings the 'Agnus Dei' particularly beautifully: she is emotive but never maudlin.

The distinguished German conductor Fritz Lehmann recorded the Mass shortly before his premature death. His is a powerful and assertive if somewhat brusque reading that calls to mind the famous description of Wagner's *Symphony in C*: 'The road may be more than a little bumpy, but he reaches his destination.' Lehmann employs a relatively large chorus and orchestra, and the basic tactus is measured but never turgid; in short, it is a grandiose interpretation of the Ramin type. The soloists are uneven: Margherita Di Landi is a rather unsubtle contralto, but Helmut Krebs's distinctive, pure, patrician tenor voice lends dignity and pathos to the 'Benedictus' particularly. Lehmann's interpretation, which was recorded in concert, if the less than accurate trumpet playing and some acerbic instrumental intonation can be taken as evidence, appeared in at least four different incarnations during the 1950s and 1960s, always with the same soloists listed but not always with the same orchestra and chorus receiving credit. Suffice it to say that all three issues listed in the discography are the same performance, note for note, and the Berlin Radio forces most likely the correct ones (20).

The greatest question mark in the discography of the Mass in B Minor is the anonymous recording that appeared in the United States in the mid-1950s on the Gramophone (no relation to His Master's Voice) label (21). Neither the conductor nor the soloists are identified; the performance is ascribed simply to The Cathedral Choir and Symphony Orchestra. On the basis of the pronunciation of words like 'coeli', one would surmise that the performance is German in origin, and it is almost certainly a recording of a radio broadcast. Normally, recordings like this can be given short shrift in a survey of this kind, but this set is the exception that proves the rule, for it fortuitously preserves an excellent, majestically paced 'Romantic' interpretation of singular vision, commitment and individuality, performed by a large chorus and orchestra and an exceptionally fine quintet of soloists. (There are two basses, and the soprano sounds extremely like Erna Berger.) Who was responsible

54

for this magnificent reading is anybody's educated guess, but is it possible that this is a recording of an otherwise undocumented broadcast of the B Minor Mass conducted by Wilhelm Furtwängler? One thing is certain; it does not closely resemble the interpretations of any of the conductors who made commercial recordings of the Mass during this period.

Another live recording from the same period was made at the International Music Festival in Strasbourg in 1958 (22). Under the direction of Fritz Münch, the elder brother of the distinguished conductor Charles Münch, this poorly balanced recording, in which the chorus is dim in relation to the orchestra, is an interesting souvenir of a worthy, earnest and somewhat Debussyian provincial interpretation of the Mass, which is characterised by sluggish tempi and acidulous trumpet playing.

Eugen Jochum conducted his first recording of the Mass that same year (23). His is a soft, gentle and dignified approach to the score that stresses its contemplative aspects. Lois Marshall is not in as good form as she was three years later for Ifor Jones, and a tentative and somewhat querulous Peter Pears is not up to his usual high standard either. Jochum's second recording of the Mass, made nearly twenty-five years later, is little different from his first (24). Overall, the soloists are marginally better, but Robert Holl is the only one who really stands out. He sings the 'Et in spiritum sanctum' clearly and warmly, with excellent breath control.

Anthon van der Horst's interpretation was recorded in concert in the Grote Kerk in Naarden, the Netherlands, in the early 1960s (25). The sound of the very large chorus is rough, and the recording is both badly balanced and muffled. Van der Horst was a musician much interested in questions of style, and his is one of the first recordings in which the implied, snappy Lombard rhythm is applied to the flute obbligato in the 'Domine Deus'. Its many virtues notwithstanding, however, the van der Horst recording, like the Fritz Münch, is valuable primarily as a souvenir of an important and interesting provincial performance.

Hermann Achenbach's recording (26), which dates from the early 1970s, is another worthy provincial performance; it is solid, sensitive and devoid of pretence or artifice. With reliable soloists and a good medium-sized choir and orchestra, this recording is more satisfying than many of those that have been inflicted on unwary listeners by more renowned artists.

Like van der Horst's, Walter Goehr's account of the Mass is also of Dutch origin; it dates from the mid-1960s, and is something of a mixed bag (27). A good medium-sized chorus and a decent orchestra are sabotaged by poor sound; the balance is unnatural. The solo quintet is better than average. Pierrette Alarie is cool and detached; Catherine Delfosse's 'Laudamus te' is wrecked by Goehr's painfully slow tempo and sentimental interpretation. Grace Hoffman is a fine, plummy alto, and Léopold Simoneau's distinctive, clear French tenor, so easy and unforced at the upper end, lends particular beauty to the 'Benedictus'. While he never forces and can reach all the notes, Heinz Rehfuss sings with a woolly tone and a tight wobble; he was much better in Karajan's first commercial recording nearly ten years before.

Eugene Ormandy's solid, Central European-style reading, which he recorded in 1962 with a large chorus and orchestra (28), is relatively straight-forward, though by no means devoid of Romantic flourishes. Yet his sincere, no nonsense, modern 'symphony orchestra' approach, which is as appropriate to the Beethoven *Missa Solemnis* as it is to the B Minor Mass, is always tasteful and is sullied by no interpretative excesses. The male soloists both have clear, well-focused voices that betray no strain at the top. Rosalind Elias's contralto is big, with much vibrato. Both she and Eleanor Steber, however, sound comfortable and at home in this unabashedly twentieth-century interpretation of the Mass.

Lorin Maazel's recording (29), which dates from the early 1970s, is neither particularly subtle nor stylish, but his is an enthusiastic, at times iconoclastic reading. The heavily aspirated and overtly articulated 'Laudamus te', for instance, is simply perverse, and the plodding 'Sanctus' is sung with finicky fastidiousness by the well-trained medium-sized chorus.

Remakes, as a rule, are rarely as good as or better than first recordings, and that truism proves accurate with respect to the many instances in which a conductor has tackled the Mass in B Minor twice. One of the few exceptions is Michel Corboz's second recording (30). His first account (31), which features a large chorus, is majestic and patrician, enthusiastic and sensitive as the mood requires, but the soloists, though adequate, are simply not the equal of those in the later version. While the Gloria may not have quite the same majesty the second time around, it is every bit as colourful, and the Ensemble Vocal de Lausanne turns in exceptionally fine and beautifully shaded choral work in the 'Et incarnatus est' and the 'Crucifixus', which are lusciously atmos-pheric. The distinctive, well-focused, golden voice of Birgit Finnilä is par-ticularly effective in the 'Qui sedes' and the 'Agnus Dei', but José van Dam is a little somnolent in the 'Quoniam'.

Otto Klemperer's is an often overlooked and much undervalued interpre-tation of the Mass in B Minor (32); it ranks with the 1961 Richter set as the best of the modern-style recordings. Klemperer's is a reading of true grandeur and majesty, of Michelangelesque monumentality. The paradoxical, taut relaxation of the tempi contributes significantly to the aura of radiance and nobility that pervades this dramatic and emotionally intense account. A top-flight chorus, a superb orchestra and an excellent solo quintet are at one with their conductor. Gedda is still excellent in the tenor part and is arguably more comfortable singing for Klemperer than he was performing for Karajan nearly fifteen years earlier. Janet Baker sings a forthright, firm and warm 'Laudamus te'.

Dame Janet, alas, was in nowhere near as good vocal estate almost a decade

56

later when she sang the same music for Neville Marriner (33). In fact, of the four soloists, only soprano Margaret Marshall is in top form. Robert Tear's strained tenor voice makes for an unpleasant 'Benedictus' and Samuel Ramey is uncharacteristically woolly and wobbly. Vocal problems are not restricted to the soloists; there are some insecure and rough passages in the choruses as well. The whole production seems slightly out of focus, as if the performers and the conductor were suffering from a collective artistic hangover.

By the time of its release, however, Marriner's recording, like other modern instrument accounts, was no longer the rule but the exception. The explosion of interest in period instruments and authentic performance practice had assured that. The first 'authentic' recording was Nikolaus Harnoncourt (34). It exploded on the Bach world like a bombshell in 1968; depending on one's point of view, it came as a revelation or a shock, to all who heard it. Five sterling soloists, a crack ensemble of 'original' instruments and a superbly trained chorus of men and boys that fluctuates in size from forty-two to sixteen, participate in this streamlined, fleet, but sincerely felt performance. If the illustrations in the booklet that accompanied the original LP release of this recording may be taken as an accurate indication, the actual conducting was shared by Harnoncourt, who was in charge in the arias and the duets, and Dr Hans Gillesberger, the director of the Wiener Sängerknaben, who led the ensemble in the choral numbers.

Via this inestimably valuable recording, which remains the only period-instrument account in which a boys' choir is used, Harnoncourt and his colleagues revealed facets of the Mass not clearly apparent before. Counter-point and tone colours obscured to some degree by the different characteristics of modern instruments, characteristics that Bach's internal musical ear could never have anticipated, now began to come out of the mists; all of a sudden, the Mass could be heard with a clarity akin to that of a sunny alpine morning. But Harnoncourt's is neither a clinical nor a scholarly performance in the pejorative sense of the term. It has life, it has fizz, it has verve.

Harnoncourt re-recorded the Mass, still with a period-instrument ensemble but with a mixed choir, in 1985 (35). Though the soloists are all first-rate (only Kurt Equiluz returned from the 1968 cast), the larger chorus of female and male voices combine with marginally, but noticeably, slower tempi to make this second version less exciting, less emotionally compelling, and less transparent than the first.

Joshua Rifkin's 1982, *Gramophone* Award-winning, recording of the Mass (36) was every bit as important a trailblazer as Harnoncourt's 1968 set had been fourteen years earlier. Rifkin's intensely powerful, revelatory reading reflects the iconoclastic results of his painstaking and open-minded resear-ches into Bach's performance practices. In seeking to understand the documen-tary evidence in light of the philological evidence of Bach's original performing parts, rather than the other way round, Rifkin arrived at the startling, but obvious – at least, to the open-minded – conclusion that every performer got his own part from which to sing or play, which means that, unless doubling parts are present, the vocal lines are meant to be sung by but one singer, even in the choruses. With a superb complement of vocalists and musicians, Rifkin put his conclusions into practice, and the resulting recording establishes the criteria, both scholarly and interpretative, by which all purportedly authentic recorded performances of the Mass in B Minor must be judged.

Rifkin was fortunate in being able to assemble a group of top-drawer singers and instrumentalists as committed to his radical conclusions as he is. Collectively, they had the guts to sing and play with vigour and sensitivity, warmth and understanding, confronting the listener and the Bach scholarly establishment with vibrant, musical proof of the accuracy of Rifkin's conclusions. Never have the instrumental and vocal lines of the Mass sounded so clear and so well balanced. Never has the first 'Kyrie' sounded so baldly plangent. Never have the fugal episodes in the 'Cum sancto spiritu' and the 'Et resurrexit' unfolded with such exhilarating clarity. Never has the 'Confiteor' glided into the 'Et expecto' so intimately, so personally.

The Bach scholarly community, of course, does not like to be told that its analysis of the documentary and philological evidence is wrong, and has been wrong, for decades. The traditionalists and vested interests, therefore, have fought a valiant rearguard action in defence of the status quo. Few have so far had the courage to follow Rifkin's lead and dispense with the customary choral complement. One of those is Andrew Parrott, who forthrightly acknowledges his debt to Rifkin in the annotations to his recording of the Mass (37). Even Parrott does not follow Rifkin's lead entirely, for in some of the choruses he allots two singers to each line. His decision to do so is defensible in theory, for, the year before he died, shortly after he had finished assembling the second half of the Mass, Bach put on a final performance of the *St John Passion* in which there were two singers to each vocal line in the choruses.

Parrott's is an exciting, if too often breathless, reading of the Mass; the 'Benedictus', for instance, is so brisk that it borders on the flippant. But this interpretation has a clout and a character that put it in the same league as Rifkin's, head and shoulders above the other, more traditional authentic accounts that have been made in recent years. And, like Rifkin, Parrott is blessed with excellent singers (including three fine boy altos from the Tölzer Knabenchor) and instrumentalists.

In comparison to the Rifkin and the Parrott sets, almost all of the other recent authentic recordings seem remarkably old-fashioned and, in one or two instances, downright stodgy. Gustav Leonhardt's account (38), with La Petite Bande and the Chamber Chorus of the Nederlandse Bach Vereiniging, is perhaps the drabbest overall. Almost completely devoid of excitement, it is fussy, colourless and puritanical, a desiccated interpretation preserved in the musical equivalent of the natron used to dry out mummies in pharaonic Egypt. The technically unimpeachable singing and playing of the majority of the participants cannot save this performance, and matters are not helped by the dry-as-desert-sand tone of bass Harry van der Kamp. About the only bright spot in the whole production is Max van Egmond's reliably warm, clear and wonderful singing in 'Et in spiritum sanctum', but even that is a mixed blessing, for Leonhardt's insistent stressing of the strong beats makes the aria sound sing-songy. Nearly as dull is the Joachim Martini set (39), a provincial production featuring four respected soloists and first-class period instrumentalists. The Mass is sung and played with journeyman precision; this dry-as-dust reading is a superfluity.

Philippe Herreweghe's recent recording of the Mass (40), on the other hand, is joy to the ear. It is the gentlest and most introspective interpretation on records, magnificently paced, and both taut and exciting when the mood requires. His twenty-one member Collegium Vocale, Ghent, sings the choruses with an enthusiastic and energetic accuracy, and his quintet of soloists is also first-rate, particularly male alto Charles Brett and tenor Howard Crook.

John Eliot Gardiner's 1985 recording (41) is in some ways a traditionalist scholar's reaction to the Rifkin approach; he makes use of *Concertisten* in the first 'Kyrie', the Gloria, and the '*Crucifixus*' (which is sung entirely by soloists, à la Rifkin), but his application of the *solo/tutti* principle is much more conservative than Robert Shaw's had been a quarter of a century earlier. Gardiner parcels the solos out among numerous members of his Monteverdi Choir; the quality of the singing and the ensemble is very high indeed. Gardiner's crisp and energetic reading is a performance of the Mass that will give much pleasure to those who want an authentic performance with a chorus in the modern sense of the term.

Shortly before this book went to press, Philips published a recording of a 1989 concert performance of the Mass featuring members of the Netherlands Chamber Choir and the Orchestra of the 18th Century conducted by Frans Brüggen (44). Warm but especially fleet without ever seeming rushed, Brüggen's is a particularly rewarding interpretation that ranks among the best period instrument accounts of a 'standard' character; soloists intrude into the choruses only in the 'Et in terra pax' and in the 'Et resurrexit'. The choir is made up of ten sopranos, six altos, six tenors, and six basses. There are four soloists, all of whom are of a high order; even Harry van der Kamp sings with a warm tone. The pure voiced Jennifer Smith sings the 'Laudamus te' in addition to all the solos allocated to Soprano One. Michael Chance is particularly effective in the alto solos. His voice is full, rich, and natural, and he imbues the 'Qui sedes' and the 'Agnus Dei' with a special poignance. Both choir and orchestra perform with verve and aplomb, and the security and flair with which the tromba players execute the florid fioriture at the brisk tempos that Brüggen sets is positively breathtaking.

TERI NOEL TOWE

SUMMARY

Collectors who wish a traditional account of the Mass played on modern instruments and sung by a chorus of substantial size can do no better than Richter's stirring 1961 recording or Klemperer's monumental and intense interpretation. Those who wish an especially romantic view of the Mass should initiate a search for either the I for Jones or the anonymous Gramophone set.

Those with an unswervingly authentic turn of mind will want to acquire Rifkin's recording, a marvellous partnership of exacting scholarship and enthusiastic music making; Andrew Parrott's set is a good second choice.

Those who find themselves seeking a middle ground will find the 1968 Harnoncourt recording the best choice if they want period instruments, with the John Eliot Gardiner, the Philippe Herreweghe or the Frans Brüggen a suitable alternative. Those who prefer a modern-instrument performance of an authentic character should select the first Rilling version.

***

After this article was sent to the printer, a B Minor Mass, recorded live in the Soviet Union, became available for review. Besides the unauthorised disc of excerpts from Robert Shaw's 1960 RCA recording, the Soviet state record label, Melodiya, has issued a recording of a live performance of the *Mass* that was given by the Robert Shaw Chorale in the Great Hall of The Moscow Conservatory on 27 November 1962, during the Chorale's historic tour of the Soviet Union (45). No soloists are listed on the recording, and at this late date it has proven difficult to determine who the soloists were at this performance, particularly since most of the solos were rotated among several singers during the course of the tour. As this article went to press, it was certain only that Florence Kopleff was the full-throated and remarkable contralto and Seth McCoy the praiseworthy clear-voiced tenor in the Moscow performance. Interpretatively, the reading is the twin of the second commercial account, except that it is yet warmer and more plastic.

60

Handel: *Messiah*

TERI NOEL TOWE

A keyboard virtuoso and composer of the highest calibre, George Frideric Handel was also a practical musician and entrepreneur. He owned at least an interest in the production companies that presented his operas and oratorios and he also frequently acted as an impresario, organising and promoting his own concerts. None of his compositions was graven on stone; he considered them all subject to revision, not only to improve them, but also to meet the practical requirements of particular performances. He often altered works to suit the capabilities of available performers.

In the case of *Messiah*, these observations are especially pertinent. Contrary to popular belief, the oratorio was not an immediate hit in England. After its initial success in Dublin, Handel took it back to London, where it met with indifference from the general public and outright hostility from those who – with the tacit support of Edmund Gibson, the then Bishop of London – considered it a sacrilege to perform a setting of biblical texts in a theatre, with popular stars as soloists.

In its first three seasons in London – 1743, 1745 and 1749 – *Messiah* was a dismal failure. Not until 1750, a couple of years after Thomas Sherlock had succeeded Gibson as bishop, did it catch on; Handel gave two benefit performances – the second by popular demand – in the Chapel of the Foundling Hospital, an orphanage of which he was a trustee. Thereafter, for the rest of Handel's life, *Messiah* was a staple of his annual spring season of oratorios.

Practically every year that he presented it, Handel made changes, rewriting, transposing or replacing individual numbers. Building on the foundations laid by such *Messiah* sleuths as Watkins Shaw and John Tobin and using annotated wordbooks and the composer's notes in his conducting score as his primary guides, the distinguished British Handel scholar Donald Burrows has spent many years sorting out the various versions that Handel collated for his performances, first in Dublin and then in London at both Covent Garden and the Foundling Hospital. Burrows's researches have shown, after the fact,

61

that some of the recordings that have been made by adventurous conductors who have experimented with various combinations among the various alternatives have unintentionally, serendipitously and fortuitously resulted in the recreation or near recreation of some of Handel's own opportunistic performing versions.

Some of Handel's alterations were intended to improve the work's pacing, but most were changes dictated by the strengths or weaknesses of singers available for particular performances. In at least three seasons, Handel was, for reasons now unclear, compelled to use two different casts, and thus two different performing versions. Still, Handel's motives notwithstanding, later settings almost always ended up being his preferred ones, and with only one or two exceptions have become a part of what we now consider the 'standard' score. For instance, the aria 'But who may abide the day of His coming' was originally scored for bass soloist. In 1750, 1751 and 1753, Handel was blessed with the services of the remarkable castrato alto Gaetano Guadagni (later to create the role of Orfeo in the Gluck opera *Orfeo ed Euridice*) for whom he wrote the now universally familiar revised version of 'But who may abide'. About thirty years after his death, this version, with its vibrant prestissimos, began to be assigned to a bass soloist – which it *never* was by Handel – a practice that persists to this day, even in some otherwise 'historically accurate' performances.

Handel, of course, wouldn't have given a damn about such later adaptations. A pragmatist and businessman, he knew that changes and compromises are often necessary for the show to go on. *Pace*, ye righteously indignant purists, Handel surely would have endorsed the changes, cuts and additions that have helped to ensure *Messiah*'s status as the longest-running hit in musical history; its universal popularity has not waned for nearly 250 years.

In the twentieth century, however, we have become accustomed to think in terms of 'final' or 'definitive' versions of compositions, musical and otherwise. By the late nineteenth century, a 'standard' version of *Messiah* – a combination of the various alternatives that tallies with no version that Handel himself presented – came to be accepted by performers and audiences alike. These choices, made for extra-musical as well as musical reasons over the nearly 150 years since Handel's death, have their roots in the Mozart–Hiller arrangement first published in 1803, and were codified once and for all – for the English-speaking world, at least – by Ebenezer Prout in his performing edition, published in 1902. For numbers that exist in more than one authentic form, Prout selected and printed only the version then most popular; since these are the versions that most of us know as 'definitive', a list of his choices is given below.

Handel: *Messiah*

Prout's *Messiah*

PART I
1 Sinfony
2 Comfort ye My people (tenor recitative)
3 Ev'ry valley (tenor aria)
4 And the glory of the Lord (chorus)
5 Thus saith the Lord (bass recitative)
6 But who may abide the day of His coming (alto aria)
7 And He shall purify (chorus)
8 Behold, a virgin shall conceive (alto recitative)
9 O thou that tellest good tidings to Zion (alto aria and chorus)
10 For, behold darkness shall cover the earth (bass recitative)
11 The people that walked in darkness (bass aria)
12 For unto us a Child is born (chorus)
13 Pifa (long version)
14 There were shepherds; And lo! the angel of the Lord (soprano recitative)
15 And the angel said unto them (soprano recitative)
16 And suddenly there was with the Angel (soprano recitative)
17 Glory to God (chorus)
18 Rejoice greatly (soprano aria) (4/4 version)
19 Then shall the eyes of the blind (alto recitative)
20 He shall feed His flock (alto, soprano aria)
21 His yoke is easy (chorus)

PART II
22 Behold the Lamb of God (chorus)
23 He was despised (alto aria)
24 Surely He hath borne our griefs (chorus)
25 And with His stripes (chorus)
26 All we like sheep (chorus)
27 All they that see Him (tenor recitative)
28 He trusted in God (chorus)
29 Thy rebuke hath broken His heart (tenor recitative)
30 Behold and see (tenor aria)
31 He was cut off out of the land of the living (tenor recitative)
32 But Thou did'st not leave His soul in Hell (tenor aria)
33 Lift up your heads (chorus)
34 Unto which of the Angels (tenor recitative)
35 Let all the Angels of God (chorus)
36 Thou art gone up on high (bass aria)
37 The Lord gave the word (chorus)
38 How beautiful are the feet (soprano aria)

63

39 Their sound is gone out (chorus)
40 Why do the nations (bass aria) (long version)
41 Let us break their bonds asunder (chorus)
42 He that dwelleth in heaven (tenor recitative)
43 Thou shalt break them (tenor aria)
44 Hallelujah! (chorus)

PART III
45 I know that my Redeemer liveth (soprano aria)
46 Since by man came death (chorus)
47 Behold, I tell you a mystery (bass recitative)
48 The trumpet shall sound (bass aria)
49 Then shall be brought to pass (alto recitative)
50 O death, where is thy sting? (alto, tenor duet) (short version)
51 But thanks be to God (chorus)
52 If God be for us (soprano aria)
53 Worthy is the Lamb (chorus)

DUBLIN VERSION

As is well known, Handel wrote *Messiah* in twenty-four days during August and September 1741, rested a week, wrote the oratorio *Samson* in one month, rested a few days, and then left for Dublin to present a series of subscription concerts. While he worked on *Samson*, his longtime friend and business associate John Christopher Smith, Sr, was busy deciphering the *Messiah* composing score and preparing the fair copy from which Handel would direct his performances for the rest of his life. This manuscript contains much invaluable information concerning who sang what in which production and – together with the evidence that can be gleaned from the composing score, surviving wordbooks, and contemporary manuscripts copied by Smith and his assistants – reveals a great deal about the various changes Handel made during the eighteen seasons prior to his death on 14 April 1759, eight days after he directed the work for the last time.

During the winter of 1741–2, Handel began to tamper. He rewrote the opening of 'Thus saith the Lord', shortening it by two bars and changing it from an arioso to an accompanied recitative. He also suppressed the original form of 'How beautiful are the feet', a *dal segno* aria that has as its central section a setting of the words now familiar from the chorus 'Their sound is gone out'. He substituted another number, an alto duet leading into a chorus, to a different text that also begins 'How beautiful are the feet'. The first performance of *Messiah* in the spring of 1742 did not include a setting of 'Their sound is gone out'.

Indeed, the *Messiah* Handel introduced in Dublin was a rather makeshift affair, and he never again presented the oratorio in that form. Having taken with him only three vocalists — two sopranos and an alto — from England, Handel had to rely on local talent for the rest of his soloists. Probably for reasons of dramatic pacing but perhaps because he was hampered by the weakness of his tenor and bass soloists, he ended up substituting recitatives for three arias — the original bass versions of 'But who may abide the day of his coming' and 'Thou art gone up on high' and the tenor aria 'Thou shalt break them'. He also re-assigned other solos to his own singers, taking care not to tax them more than necessary. The 'original' Dublin version, therefore, was, as Christopher Hogwood has observed, 'a small-scale performance, minus the oboes and just with strings and trumpets, being put on for the Lord Lieutenant of Ireland. And, obviously, Handel was worrying very much about this, the only non-dramatic oratorio he'd ever indulged in, and whether this meditative piece might just lack dramatic pacing.'

Notwithstanding the captions emblazoned across record covers, *Messiah* has *never* been recorded as Handel first gave it on 13 April 1742 — nor is it possible to do so, since the recitative substituted for 'Thou art gone up on high' has not survived. Jean-Claude Malgoire's CBS account (1) is the most recent to be billed as the Dublin version, yet, as even the most cursory scrutiny of the extant sources and relevant literature shows, the musicological preparation for this recording was embarrassingly slipshod. To catalogue the most egregious mistakes:

1 'Ev'ry valley' is given in the familiar post-1745 version with two measures excised from the opening and closing ritornellos.
2 'But who may abide' and 'Thou shalt break them' are not sung in the recitative forms; the correct aria forms of those numbers and of 'Thou art gone up on high' are used, however.
3 'Rejoice greatly' appears in a curious, completely un-Handelian hybrid of two early forms. Handel initially set the text as a strict *da capo* aria in 12/8 time. Early on, probably between the first Dublin and London performances, he shortened it appreciably by splitting the original opening section into two segments, separated by the original central section. Malgoire gives the opening section complete in the original form, then follows with the central section and the shortened reprise.
4 'Then shall the eyes', 'He shall feed His flock', and 'If God be for us' are all sung by soprano, as written, not by alto, as was actually the case in Dublin.
5 'How beautiful are the feet' appears in the *dal segno* version Handel discarded before the Dublin premiere. Ironically, this error inadvertently furnishes one of the album's strongest selling points: this first recording of the aria's original version fills a gap in the discography and makes the set invaluable for every true *Messiah* enthusiast.

6 Malgoire presents 'The trumpet shall sound' in the post-1745 *dal segno* form, rather than as the full *da capo* aria that Handel preferred in his first three productions, and he cuts the reprise of the opening ritornello of 'He was despised', which Handel never treated as anything but a full *da capo* aria.

7 The duet 'O death, where is thy sting?' appears in its revised 24-bar version rather than the original 41-bar form that Handel favoured until 1749 or 1750.

Using period instruments and a choir of men and boys, Malgoire follows Handel's instrumentation scrupulously, perhaps too scrupulously, for he omits the two French horns which the surviving bills for Handel's later performances at the Foundling Hospital suggest doubled the trumpets in the choruses at the end of Parts II and III. (Conversely, Malgoire's inclusion of oboes and bassoon may also be incorrect, if Hogwood's view of the Dublin performances is accurate.) With an instrumental ensemble somewhat smaller than Handel's, Malgoire stresses the dancelike qualities inherent in many of the movements. This approach works to the definite advantage of the jig-like 12/8 setting of 'Rejoice greatly', but it detracts seriously from a contemplative aria like 'I know that my Redeemer liveth'. At times – such as in the arioso 'All they that see Him' and the ensuing chorus 'He trusted in God' – Malgoire's striving for interpretative effects seems fussy, and his undue stress on strong beats makes the instrumental articulation a little too forceful and unnatural. Mirella Giardelli's harpsichord continuo is overly reticent, particularly in bravura arias like 'Why do the nations'. The sound of the instrumental ensemble, particularly the strings, is raw and scrappy. Patches of painfully poor intonation abound, and the playing, like the musicology, reeks of inadequate preparation.

The Worcester Cathedral Choir sings the choruses to a fare-thee-well, but the soloists do not join in, as Handel's did. Soprano Jennifer Smith is most impressive. Obviously schooled in authentic performance practice, she has a rich, well-focused voice with a molten-gold tone that invites comparison with Rosa Ponselle's. Treble Andrew J. King's singing of the Nativity recitatives and ariosos becomes downright uncomfortable. Charles Brett's is a fine, full and focused countertenor, but his strangely detached air, particularly in 'He was despised', is disconcerting. Predictably, tenor Martyn Hill's contribution confirms his thorough mastery of Handelian idiom; a pity, then, that his voice is suffused by so much anachronistic vibrato. A sensitive and effective bass, Ulrik Cold offers a lovely reading of 'Thou art gone up'.

For all its failings – including a trilingual booklet that provides no information about which performing edition is used or which soloist sings which numbers – this is nonetheless a valuable addition to the discography. Along with the gramophonic 'first' already noted, the rousing 'Hallelujah', one of the most thrilling renditions ever recorded, justifies the cost of the entire album.

Handel: *Messiah*

The coolly received first London performance is documented by Neville Marriner's first recording, accurately described as 'based on the first London performance of 23 March 1743' (2). The performing edition was prepared by Christopher Hogwood, who also plays organ continuo and who provided the excellent annotations that are just one of the many strong points of this superb recording.

Apart from restoring at least two of the arias replaced by recitatives in Dublin, Handel made three major changes in this version: in the duet and chorus version of 'How beautiful are the feet' he substituted a soprano for one of the altos. He added a tenor arioso setting of 'Their sound is gone out' – sung by a soprano at some of the first London performances. In the Nativity sequence he replaced the accompanied recitative 'And lo, the angel of the Lord' with the arioso 'But lo, the angel of the Lord', composed expressly for the singing actress Kitty Clive, who had gained fame as Polly in *The Beggar's Opera*. The presence of such a singer, the eighteenth-century equivalent of a Lotte Lenya or a Bernadette Peters, must have been specially annoying to those antagonistic to Handel's presentation of a sacred oratorio in the theatre.

Though commendably accurate, Hogwood's performing edition does contain two vestiges of the Dublin and pre-Dublin versions – the original arioso form of 'Thus saith the Lord' and the abbreviated form of the 'Blessing and honour' segment of 'Worthy is the Lamb'. A pencilled indication in the composing score, evidently in Handel's handwriting, directs the omission of bars 39 to 53 of the chorus; doubtless associated with the Dublin production, this abridgement, which Handel may never have used, lends a different balance to the final chorus that is not without its peculiar appeal. Technically not part of *Messiah* as first performed in London, these variants are nevertheless well worth having on record.

Marriner's first *Messiah* otherwise recreates the first London production right down to the restoration of the two bars in the opening and concluding ritornellos of 'Ev'ry valley'. Using modern instruments and a mixed chorus, this is, quite simply, one of the finest accounts of *Messiah* ever recorded. From the initial bars of the marvellously wrought 'Sinfony', the instrumental playing is both inspired and impeccable. Aside from the concluding 'Amen', a bit flaccid and lacking in momentum, the choruses are light-footed and brisk, but tempi in the slower choruses are never inappropriate. The soloists all give sensitive, stylish, and finely honed performances. Soprano Elly Ameling is especially noteworthy; her 'I know that my Redeemer liveth' is meltingly beautiful, and the extended, but not excessive cadenza that she interpolates into 'Rejoice greatly', correctly performed in the revised, short 12/8 version, is in and of itself cause for rejoicing.

The use of the abbreviated form of 'Worthy is the Lamb' and, curiously, the Mozartian anachronism of muting the strings in the 'Pifa' and in 'He shall feed His flock' are among the few things, other than a fleet and vibrant reading, that Marriner's second account (3) has in common with his first. This later recording is nowhere near as important, for from the outset it is of interest only to a specific and limited market. Recorded in co-operation with the Süd-deutscher Rundfunk, it is a complete, 'authentic' *Messiah* with the text translated into German. (And, at the risk of stating the obvious, Handel did not set, perform or intend to perform *Messiah* in any language other than English.) As is generally the case in German-language recordings, Handel's original note values at bars 37–39, 51–53, and similar passages in 'The trumpet shall sound' are retained, since the use of a translated text obviates any charge that the declamation is 'awkward'. Marriner opts for the 'standard' score with but one exception: as Karl Richter did in both of his recordings of *Messiah*, Marriner follows the revised soprano setting of 'How beautiful are the feet' with the arioso for high voice setting of 'Their sound is gone out' sung by the tenor. (This combination, one which Handel never used, may well be considered standard in Germany or, at least, in West Germany, for in the three East German recordings – the two conducted by Helmut Koch and the one led by Karl Forster – the Prout sequence for these numbers is followed.) 'But who may abide the day of His coming' is correctly assigned to the alto and the four 'Passion' solos are sung by the tenor.

As seems to be the practice in most of the authentic recordings, whether with modern or period instruments, the use of harpsichord and organ as continuo instruments is mutually exclusive; they are not used together in the choruses, with the organ reinforcing the vocal parts as seems to have been Handel's usual practice. Marriner also capitulates to the current faddish practice of using organ continuo in the 'Nativity' recitatives, something that Handel almost certainly never did. There are other bits of *Uraufführungspraxis* 'funny business': in the 'Pifa', presented in the familiar long version, the *da capo* reprise, for some unknown reason, is played by a concertino, and a similar unwarranted intrusion of string soloists, doubtless the result of a misreading of the significance of Handel's *senza ripieno* and *con ripieno* markings in his conducting score, is found in the opening semi-chorus segments of 'Lift up your heads'. (Associated with the 1749 season, the year of the double chorus oratorio *Solomon*, in which Handel had a much larger orchestra than usual, these directions indicate when the extra strings were to play.)

The soloists are unexceptional; only bass Robert Holl rises above the others; his voice is dark, rich, well-focused and unforced, his interpretation dignified, sincere and unpretentious. The chorus – some fifty strong – is larger than the orchestra, which appears to be only a hair larger than Handel's customary ones; his ratio of singers to instrumentalists, therefore, is inverted – a practice that is the rule, alas, rather than the exception. Yet it must be said that, musicological errors notwithstanding, in his second recording Marriner once more directs a forceful, dramatic interpretation that emphasises the theatrical side of *Messiah*'s pedigree; only the Tobin, Bonynge, and Beecham recordings can be said to be more overtly operatic in flavour.

1749–1759

1749 and 1750 were watershed seasons for *Messiah*, and the productions mounted in those years prompted Handel to make revisions that to a large extent have become 'standard'. 1749 witnessed the composition of the best-known form of 'Rejoice greatly', in 4/4 time, and the equally familiar choral form of 'Their sound is gone out', prefaced by a version of 'How beautiful are the feet' that is a slightly abridged form of the opening section of the soprano *dal segno* aria that Handel had deleted from the score before the Dublin premiere. In 1750, he wrote the 'Guadagni' versions of 'But who may abide the day of His coming', 'Thou art gone up on high', and 'How beautiful are the feet'. (This last alternative version, by the way, is not an exact transposition of the soprano air, as is commonly thought.) In 1749 and 1750, Handel was also blessed with the services of an especially talented treble. Who this gifted child was is not known; Handel refers to him in his conducting score simply as 'The Boy', but whoever he was, he figured prominently in 1749 and in both of the 1750 casts and was given much to do in 1751 as well.

As Donald Burrows's recent researches have shown conclusively, when Guadagni was in Ireland in 1752, Handel appears to have been compelled to use two different casts – and as a result, two different performing versions – for his annual series of *Messiah* performances. The version that Handel performed at the Theatre Royal in Covent Garden on 25 and 26 March 1752 calls for a 'modern' solo quartet of soprano, contralto, tenor and bass, and is the one fortuitously recreated in the first Robert Shaw recording (4), now more than two decades old but still one of the most satisfying. Of all the combinations of the various alternatives that Handel himself arranged, this production is the one that comes the closest to the standard Victorian sequence confirmed by Prout in his edition and thus, ironically, the version which most 'authentic' *Messiah*s come nearest to recreating. For this 1752 production Handel assigned the Guadagni versions of 'But who may abide' and 'Thou art gone up' to an alto and made use of the revised soprano form of 'How beautiful are the feet'. In addition to the most familiar version of the recitative 'Then shall the eyes' and ensuing aria 'He shall feed His flock' in which the alto sings the recitative and the first part of the aria, the soprano the rest (which Handel appears to have used a number of times between 1743 and 1753 and perhaps again in 1758), the short, eleven-bar form of the 'Pifa' (generally miscalled the 'Pastoral Symphony') and the short version of 'Why do the nations' (which, with its terse and dramatically intense recitative ending, Handel evidently preferred to the familiar long version) were chosen.

Especially in the choruses, Shaw's tempi are brisk and energetic, yet controlled. As one might expect, his chorus, only slightly larger than Handel's, acquits itself impeccably. All four vocal soloists are also first-rate; their embellishments and cadenzas, though conservative, are not too restrained. The orchestra, about the same size as the bands Handel used for his benefit performances, is of like calibre.

If one makes the correct allocation of the Passion solos between tenor and soprano, Alfred Mann's performing edition, first published by the Rutgers University Press in 1963, as part of its 'Documents of the Musical Past' series, also replicates the 1752 solo quartet version. Just such a correct assignment is made in the second recording of the Mann edition, recorded at the Eastman School of Music by the Eastman Chorale and Philharmonia under the direction of Donald Neuen (5). In this thrilling recording, which ranks among the very best ever recorded, there is no lack of the essential, intangible emotional clout that quickens the listener's pulse and makes the adrenaline flow. Neuen's interpretation is straightforward, devoid of mannerism, and almost perfectly paced. The singing from soloists and choir alike is fine, the orchestral playing first-rate.

With additional guidance from the noted Danish Handel scholar Jens Peter Larsen, Dr Mann, a professor of musicology at Eastman, acted as musical adviser to the project. Musicologists, whatever their stripes, tend to interpret evidence according to their instinctive and intuitive preconceived notions of how the music in question should sound. Both Mann and Larsen are basically conservative in their views of Handel's performance practice, a bent reflected in the Eastman performance. In keeping with Larsen's considered opinion that Handel's oratorios were not sung in the heavily ornamented *opera seria* style, vocal and instrumental embellishment is restrained, as is the realisation of the harpsichord continuo. The final chords in recitatives are delayed and the *Grave* in the 'Sinfony' is not double-dotted, since Larsen – and he is not alone in this regard, by any means – feels that the case for doing so is by no means proven. (Not only is the validity of over-dotting by no means certain but also a cogent case can be made for considering the 'Sinfony' to be an Italian *sonata da chiesa* rather than a French *ouverture*.) There is one extraordinary textual error above and beyond those customarily made: In 'Lift up your heads', the choir sings 'Who is *the*' rather than '*this* King of glory?'.

Mann's and Larsen's annotations are maddening in one particular: they provide no exact information about the make-up of either the orchestra or the chorus. From the lone session photo and from the recording itself, it seems that the vocal and instrumental complements conform closely to Handel's own.

The performance features an especially large group of soloists – the largest on records, in fact: three sopranos, two mezzo-sopranos, tenor, bass-baritone and bass. All have solid, 'modern' voices, with warm vibrato, and there is an equality among them rarely encountered in *Messiah* recordings. Marcia

70

Baldwin's burnished trumpet-like voice proves particularly effective in 'But who may abide' and 'O thou that tellest', Jan DeGaetani gives an affecting reading of 'He was despised', and Seth McCoy's singing of the tenor solos is rich and impassioned.

Evidently made up largely of Eastman students, the orchestra and chorus perform with a boundless enthusiasm and commitment that is apparent in every measure. Practically without exception, Neuen's tempos are well chosen, neither rushed nor sluggish, and carefully balanced, one to another. While it may not have either the cumulative excitement of Hogwood's or the quasi-operatic drama of Tobin's, Neuen's is, overall, one of the best-paced on records. Word's natural-sounding recording is rich, mellow, and well-focused, but not overtransparent.

The first recording of the Mann edition was made in 1977 by Thomas Dunn and the Handel and Haydn Society of Boston (6). There are five soloists, and the two sopranos share the four Passion solos and the recitative that precedes 'He trusted in God', a division of these numbers that Handel seems never to have tried. While Dunn uses modern instruments and a mixed choir, his is a particularly stylish *Messiah* — the only complete one in which the soloists sing the choruses, as they did for Handel. The instrumental complement — except for the missing horns — conforms closely to that documented by the Foundling Hospital ledgers for the 1754 and 1758 performances. Dunn also scrupulously follows the *solo* and *ripieno* indications that Handel entered into his conducting score for his performances in 1749. This is without question one of the better 'authentic' *Messiah*s.

In 1753, Guadagni returned to the cast, but Handel stuck to the 1752 four soloist sequence nonetheless. He compensated the Italian castrato for the loss of the alto version of 'How beautiful are the feet' that had been specially composed for him by assigning him the final aria, 'If God is for us'. Andrew Parrott has chosen this 1753 version for his recent period instrument recording (7), but he allots the solos among six singers — two sopranos, contralto, countertenor, tenor and bass — rather than four. The size of the choir and orchestra are close to, but not identical to the configuration that Handel is known to have employed at the Foundling Hospital in 1754. Significantly — and correctly — there are more instrumentalists (37) than choristers (21), as there appear always to have been in Handel's own performances.

The quality of the playing and the singing, from soloists, choristers and instrumentalists alike, is of a particularly high standard in Parrott's well-paced reading. The passionate and powerful voice of countertenor James Bowman, for example, has never sounded better, and the liberal decoration that he adds to 'But who may abide' is both tasteful and exquisitely sung. David Thomas is first-rate, as is Emma Kirkby, who fortuitously sings all the major soprano solos that were not allocated to her in Hogwood's set. The voice of tenor Joseph Cornwell, however, suffers from a mildly annoying tight bleat that detracts from an otherwise exemplary account of the tenor role. Throughout, the embellishment of the vocal lines in general is liberal, the cadenzas extended, but always in the best taste.

The harpsichord continuo is restrained but colourful; apart from its subtle appearance in 'For behold, darkness shall cover the earth' and 'The people that walked in darkness', in which it is the only continuo instrument, the organ apparently is used only in the choruses, in which it either realises the continuo or doubles choral lines. On an instrument made by John Harris of London about 1717, Crispian Steele-Perkins plays the obbligato in 'The trumpet shall sound' with technical security, profound emotion and particular beauty of tone; no better performance of this fiendishly difficult solo part exists on records. Two horns are employed, doubling the trumpets at the lower octave in the final choruses of Parts 2 and 3, as appears to have been the custom in Handel's performances, at least at the Foundling Hospital.

Overall, however, for all of its many strengths, the Parrott interpretation doesn't quite jell. Inexplicably, this intimate, straightforward interpretation as often as not lacks focus, power, charisma and incisiveness; it frequently simply fails to inspire the listener. The whole, alas, proves to be less than the sum of the parts.

The best-documented of all of Handel's productions of *Messiah* is the annual benefit performance of 15 May 1754. A complete statement of the number of participating vocalists and instrumentalists is preserved in the minutes of the Foundling Hospital's general committee, and the set of parts and the full score that Handel bequeathed to the hospital, copied from the performance parts used in the 1754 benefit, are still extant. The orchestra consisted fourteen violins, six violas, three cellos, two double basses, four oboes, four bassoons, two trumpets, two horns, and timpani, with harpsichord and organ continuo. The chorus, six boys and thirteen men, was augmented by the five soloists, who, the partbooks make clear, sang all the choruses, as concertists in this period customarily did. Second soprano Christina Passerini, who had been recommended to Handel by his old friend Georg Philipp Telemann, was allotted only three arias – but what three arias they were! In addition to 'If God be for us', she sang two of the 'Guadagni' numbers – 'Thou art gone up on high', transposed up a fourth, and 'But who may abide', raised a fifth. This latter transposition entailed extensive reworking of the violin parts, which otherwise would have lain awkwardly high. (Incredibly, until the recent appearance of Donald Burrows's *Urtext* score published by Edition Peters, this A minor revision for soprano was the one authentic alternative version for a number in *Messiah* that had not been published.) Otherwise, the 1754 *Messiah* was essentially identical to the one Handel presented in Covent Garden in 1752.

The 1754 'Foundling Hospital version', as it is commonly known, is recreated with extraordinary accuracy by Christopher Hogwood for his own recording (8), still far and away the finest authentic instrument account and one of the best *Messiah*s ever recorded. Hogwood deviates from Handel's practice in only one important particular: 'As soloists cannot be expected to sing choruses nowadays, the original balance is here restored by the use of a choir slightly larger than Handel's, though fundamentally the same in constitution.' Alas, boosting the number of trebles and male altos to compensate for the absence of the soprano and alto soloists does not result in quite the same choral timbre Handel expected. Why couldn't the requisite number of additional adult female vocalists have been engaged to preserve Handel's own balance? Still, in the face of Hogwood's magnificent achievement, such a cavil is perhaps ungracious.

(Apart from the Thomas Dunn recording, there is only one in which the soloists sing in the choruses, albeit for the wrong reasons. It is a particularly fascinating disc of excerpts from *Messiah* conducted by Wilhelm Ehmann recorded at a broadcast given in honour of the 40th anniversary of the Nederlands Christelijke Radio Vereiniging, Hilversum (9). The performance reflects Ehmann's obsession with the contrast between *favoritchor* and full chorus. In a way that is inapposite to Handel's own practice, choruses feature solo, *favoritchor*, and full chorus passages, as well as ornamentation of the vocal lines.)

There are those who do not share my enthusiasm for the Hogwood. Yet, after numerous rehearings over a long period of time, its immediate appeal and interpretative persuasiveness remain undimmed and have been enhanced by familiarity. Particularly thrilling are soprano Emma Kirkby's performance of the revised 'But who may abide the day of His coming', incomparably exciting and compelling, and the concluding choruses, with their shattering emotional clout and near-perfect dramatic pacing.

True, there are moments, like the rushed and rather perfunctory 'Grave' in the 'Sinfony', where that quicksilver spark of inspiration eluded the performers; some of the choruses could have been just a hair faster and more vibrant. Yet no listener should hold his breath waiting for a more exciting or more moving account on period instruments. Oiseau-Lyre's sound is bright, transparent and natural, and the annotations, by Hogwood and Anthony Hicks, are excellent.

Robert Shaw's second recording (10) of *Messiah* is described in the mediocre annotations as 'patterned' on the version performed on 15 May 1754, but that representation is less than accurate: four of the alternative versions Handel used in 1754 are not among those selected by Shaw, who, as it turns out, sticks quite closely to the 'standard' sequence, deviating from it in only two major respects. As he did in his 1966 recording, he opts for the short form of the 'Pifa' and the 'Guadagni' form of 'Thou art gone up', sung by the alto. He also gives the second of the two pairs of 'Passion' solos − 'He was cut off' and 'But Thou did'st not leave' to a soprano.

Shaw has clearly rethought his interpretation over the years. Gone are the almost startlingly brisk tempos. The choruses, particularly, are slower and weightier. Still, Shaw, who is arguably the greatest choral conductor in the United States, gives them clarity, verve, and atmosphere; momentum never flags, even in the slowest and most contemplative passages. 'Atlanta Symphony Chamber Chorus' is something of a misnomer; the group numbers sixty singers, more than Handel ever used – even in 1749, when he employed an unusually large chorus and orchestra. Shaw's Atlanta Symphony contingent – twenty-eight strings, four oboes, three bassoons, contrabassoon, two trumpets, timpani, organ and harpsichord – is, however, only slightly larger than Handel's customary band. While he strikes a fine balance between chorus and orchestra, Shaw, therefore, like the overwhelming majority of those who perform and record 'authentic' *Messiah*s, has turned the tables by using more singers than instrumentalists. Handel seems always to have had more instrumentalists than singers.

For the most part, the solos, like the choruses, proceed at leisurely but ardent tempi. Jon Humphrey's voice is especially appropriate to his numbers, emotionally warm but vocally pure and cool. Alfreda Hodgson negotiates the perilous *fioritura* of the 'Guadagni' version of 'But who may abide' with aplomb, although her trills do not emerge clearly and precisely. While anachronistic, her pronounced vibrato enhances the molten quality of her distinguished interpretations, especially in 'He was despised'. Sylvia McNair has a pure, well-focused voice. Her vibrato is less pronounced than that of Karen Erickson, whose work, marred by a touch of the goat's trill, sometimes borders on the querulous. Richard Stilwell sings with flair and power; the vibrato that suffuses his voice is inoffensive in this neo-baroque context.

The approach to vocal embellishment is inconsistent. Some cadential points in the solos are floridly decorated, others hardly at all. In the recitatives, elementary performance conventions regarding appoggiaturas are sometimes ignored, and the concluding chords are delayed (the now standard practice) rather than played as written (Handel's own practice according to Winton Dean's researches). As a whole the performance is well paced, one number leading into the next with nearly operatic intensity. Telarc's digital recording is exemplary, with rich room sound and just the right amount of reverberation – chapelish not churchy.

During the last five years of his life, Handel made no further alterations in the score. All he did was reassign various numbers – 'Rejoice greatly' was sung by a tenor one season – and revive alternative versions. For one series of performances in the late 1750s, he appears to have harked back to *Messiah*'s first performances in Dublin and in London by reviving the duet and chorus form of 'How beautiful are the feet'.

When all is said and done, however, relatively little is known for certain about the differences between *Messiah* as Handel gave it in the Theatre Royal,

Covent Garden, and *Messiah* as Handel gave it at the Foundling Hospital. As his use of different casts and thus different versions in the same season indicates, Handel was an extremely flexible performer. Among the issues that have so far gone unresolved is his choice of keyboard instruments at the Foundling Hospital. The gallery surrounding the organ was not large. Did Handel, therefore, take maximum advantage of the available space, forego the harpsichord, and use only organ for the realisation of the figured bass? We simply do not know.

The recording of *Messiah* made in concert in St John's Church, Smith Square, in London in December 1986, by The Sixteen, under the direction of their founder, Harry Christophers (11), provides an invaluable glimpse into precisely this particular aspect of Handel's performance practices at his Foundling Hospital benefit performances. It is the only period-instrument recording to use the organ as the only keyboard continuo. The glitter and jangle that the cembalo provides is gone, lending the oratorio what to our ears at least is a more reverent, less theatrical aura. Christophers's is, however, a vibrant and extroverted reading and it would give the Hogwood a good run for the money as the best 'antique instrument' *Messiah*, were it not for the more than occasionally scrawny and out-of-tune string playing, and a group of five soloists who, with but one significant exception, are little better than adequate.

While duplicating none of the known Handel orderings, Christophers's sequence of selected alternatives comes very close to Prout's; there are only three deviations: the short version of the 'Pifa', the revised, short 12/8 form of 'Rejoice greatly' and the Guadagni version of 'Thou art gone up'. There are five vocal soloists; the alto solos are divided between contralto and countertenor; countertenor David James is assigned the duet 'O death, where is thy sting' and the recitative that precedes it, in addition to the Guadagni forms of 'But who may abide' and 'Thou art gone up'. Of the five soloists, the only one who is truly outstanding is soprano Lynne Dawson, whose affinity for this repertoire and skill at interpreting it is emphasised by the varying insufficiencies of her fellow soloists in this recording.

For this recording, The Sixteen turn out to be a choir of nineteen singers, and they are accompanied by an ensemble of twenty, including the two trumpets, timpani, and organ. There are no French horns. Handel almost certainly never performed the oratorio with such limited forces, even in Dublin.

Like the Christophers recording, the inspiring and sensitive Trevor Pinnock period instrument account, with The English Concert & Choir (12), provides much insight into *Messiah* as Handel's audiences heard it in the 1750s. At first glance, Pinnock's selection from among the various alternatives seems to tally quite closely with the sequence that Handel arranged for the first of his 1750 casts; the only actual textual divergence is the choice of the long form of 'Why do the nations'. A closer examination of the vocal assignments – soprano rather than treble, countertenor rather than contralto – shows how subtle the changes were from season to season and from cast to cast. Handel appears to have carefully assessed the effect of male rather than female voices in his assignment of soprano and alto material, and vocal timbre may have been every bit as important to him as the singers' ability to negotiate the solos given to them.

Pinnock also divides the alto solos unevenly between a man and a woman. The first-rate countertenor Michael Chance is assigned the same numbers as David James in the Christophers recording: the alto part in 'O death, where is thy sting', the recitative that precedes it, and two of the three 'Guadagni' numbers. 'How beautiful are the feet' is beautifully sung by the redoubtable and ever-wonderful Arleen Augér, whose warm and clear voice is especially affecting in 'I know that my Redeemer liveth'. Anne Sofie von Otter gets the rest of the 'standard' alto solos plus the C minor version of 'If God be for us'. Her account of this last, rarely heard alternative is every bit as satisfying as Anna Reynolds's moving interpretation in the Marriner recording of the 1743 London score. Howard Crook is far and away the more satisfying of the two male soloists; he interprets the tenor solos with warmth and understanding and is one of that tiny handful of singers who know how to use vibrato as an embellishment. John Tomlinson's big, woolly voice suffuses the bass solos with the aura of Bayreuth and Wotan; strangely, he is most agile and straightforward in the demanding *fioriture* of 'Thus saith the Lord' and 'Why do the nations'.

The mixed choir of thirty-three voices is slightly larger than the instrumental ensemble: a basic ensemble of twenty-two strings and six winds augmented where appropriate by two trumpets, two horns and timpani. Pinnock leads from the harpsichord, and there is organ continuo in the choruses. A post-Handelian anachronism or two has crept in; recitative endings are sometimes delayed, rather than played as written, and Pinnock succumbs to the inauthentic and cutesy trend of using organ rather than harpsichord for the accompaniment of the 'Behold a Virgin shall conceive' and 'Nativity' recitatives.

It would be churlish to finish a discussion of *Messiah* recordings based on his own performances without mentioning the extraordinary disc of portions of Part I that documents a complete performance of the oratorio that was given at a four-day *Messiah* symposium held at the University of Michigan in December, 1980 (13). Performed by the University's period-instrument ensemble Ars Musica and the Early Music Ensemble Chorus under the direction of harpsichord-continuist Edward Parmentier, the record features four of the world's finest baroque specialists as soloists. All of them – Emma Kirkby (assigned the soprano form of 'Then shall the eyes' and 'He shall feed His flock'), René Jacobs (given the 'Guadagni' form of 'But who may abide'), Marius van Altena and Max van Egmond – are in superb form and sing with conviction, sensitivity and impeccable taste. The instrumental playing is of

76

an equally high standard. With almost nothing of the eccentric in Parmentier's interpretation, this is a period instrument performance of *Messiah* that can hold its own with the Hogwood, and one regrets that the University of Michigan was unable to underwrite the release of a recording of the complete performance.

The single disc of excerpts directed by Martin Neary is also a worthy recording. The Winchester Cathedral Choir − men and boys − appears to be about the size of Handel's, as does the accompanying period instrument ensemble. All five soloists are more than satisfactory, and the sensitive listener cannot help but be curious about Neary's approach to the complete oratorio. With the exception of the 'Pifa', all of the excerpts are performed in the standard versions (14).

WESTMINSTER ABBEY, 1784

As early as 1744, Handel authorised and even encouraged the presentation of *Messiah* by ensembles other than his own, and by the time of his death in 1759, it had been performed in Oxford, Bristol, Bath, Salisbury, Gloucester and in Worcester, where it was sung at the triennial Three Choirs Festival, establishing an enduring tradition. After Handel's death, John Christopher Smith, Jr, and then the blind organist and composer John Stanley continued the annual benefit performances through the year 1777.

In 1784, more than 500 vocalists and instrumentalists gathered in Westminster Abbey to commemorate the centenary of the composer's birth, giving rise to the tradition of gargantuan Handelian performances. In the performances of *Messiah*, there were eleven soloists! Two of them had sung for Handel in Foundling Hospital performances of the oratorio nearly forty years before, and one wonders what went through the mind of Samuel Champness, who had been Handel's principal bass in 1758, as he sang 'Why do the nations' with King George III among the more than 3,000 listeners. Apart from trombones doubling the vocal lines in 'Hallelujah' and the final choruses, there were no added instruments other than, apparently, French horns doubling the trumpets down an octave in those same choruses, and a double bassoon reinforcing the bass line.

An especially interesting distillation of the various alternatives was employed at the Westminster Abbey Commemoration performances and it is possible to reconstruct that sequence with almost complete accuracy, thanks to the lone surviving wordbook now in the collection of that worthy British Handelian, Gerald Coke. The original bass forms of both 'But who may abide' and 'Thou art gone up' and the all too rarely heard alto version of 'How beautiful are the feet' were selected and the Passion solos were divided between tenor and soprano soloists. The wordbook for the 1784 performances also reveals the first documented cut: the central section and the *da capo* reprise of

'The trumpet shall sound' were omitted, most likely because the fine art of baroque tromba playing was all but extinct by that time. Since none of the performing materials for the 1784 performances appears to have survived, it is no longer possible to determine for certain whether the long or the short versions of the 'Pifa', 'Why do the nations', and 'O death, where is thy sting' were used, but contemporary reviews make it quite clear that the familiar form of 'Rejoice greatly' was sung.

A sensitive recreation of the spirit, if not the letter, of the 1784 Westminster Abbey commemoration *Messiah* was recorded in concert at the 1984 Maryland Handel Festival (15). The vast reverberance of the National Cathedral, Washington, DC, is not unlike that of Westminster Abbey, and the performance, under the direction of Antal Dorati, crackles with charisma and excitement. The Smithsonian Concerto Grosso, some 100 strong, was the largest period instrument ensemble assembled since 1784, but, of course, is less than half the size of the orchestra in the Abbey in 1784; conversely, with 325 singers, the combined Cathedral Choral Society and University of Maryland Chorus are substantially larger than the choir at the Commemoration. A particularly fine solo quartet – soprano Edith Mathis, counter-tenor James Bowman, tenor Claes Ahnsjö, and bass Tom Krause – sang the solos divided among the eleven vocalists in 1784. The Westminster Abbey Commemoration version has been duplicated as exactly as possible in the Dorati recording. In addition to those alternative versions that the wordbook shows were sung in 1784, the short versions of the 'Pifa' and 'O death, where is thy sting?' were used. (The sole surviving copy of the libretto for the Westminster Abbey Commemoration performances is reproduced in facsimile in the booklet that accompanies the recording; the annotations were provided by the author of this chapter.)

MOZART AND HILLER

In 1789, a performance of *Messiah* that was to have a radical effect on the course of the oratorio's performance history was given in Vienna. Baron Gottfried Van Swieten, who later translated and edited the text for Haydn's *Creation*, had, as a diplomat in London during the late 1760s, become an ardent Handelian. Among other Handel scores, he took back to Austria a copy of the first edition of the full score of *Messiah*, published by Randall and Abell in 1767. Beginning with *Judas Maccabaeus* in 1779, he introduced works by Handel into the annual oratorio series given for the benefit of the Tonkunstler Society, a Viennese musical charity. In 1789, he presented *Messiah* and, for this first Viennese performance, commissioned Mozart to fill out the accompaniments, largely dispensing with keyboard continuo and replacing the tromba parts – practically unplayable for late eighteenth-century trumpeters.

Using the Randall and Abell score and a German translation of the text

78

by Daniel Ebeling, Van Swieten had a copyist prepare a score containing the vocal lines and Handel's string parts, together with the original dynamic and tempo markings. On to the staves left blank for his use, Mozart added his woodwind, brass and string parts; those of Handel's woodwind or brass parts that he chose to retain, he copied from the Randall and Abell score.

Since that score contains some, but not all, of the alternative versions either in its main body or in an appendix, Van Swieten had to decide which of the various forms to use. He doubtless chose the versions that he had come to know in London twenty years earlier; by and large he selected the versions favoured by Handel in the last years of his life and subsequently by the younger Smith and by Stanley.

Van Swieten reassigned some of the solos to voices other than those that Handel specified. He divided the six tenor numbers beginning with 'All they that see Him' between the two soprano soloists (there was no alto soloist *per se*; those solos he allotted to the second soprano), assigned the 4/4 form of 'Rejoice greatly' to the tenor, and gave the Guadagni version of 'But who may abide' to the bass. Ironically, the only one of these re-assignments with no precedent whatever in Handel's own practice – namely, the last – is the one that became 'standard' during the nineteenth century and the first half of the twentieth. And this seems as good a place as any to deal once and for all with the 'problem' of the various versions of 'But who may abide the day of His coming'. Handel originally set this number as an aria for bass in 3/8 time without the vibrant *prestissimo* sections that distinguish the bravura rewrite for Gaetano Guadagni. At Dublin and in other early performances, a recitative setting for bass was on occasion substituted and, in at least one season, Handel gave the original bass version, transposed up a step, to the tenor soloist. After Guadagni returned to the continent in 1753, Handel assigned the setting of 'But who may abide', that is now so familiar, to a female alto or, as we have seen, to a soprano. There is not a scintilla of evidence that he ever assigned this version to a bass.

Since Mozart's version of *Messiah* was to become the basis for most, if not all, further accompaniments added to the oratorio throughout the nineteenth century, Van Swieten must also take credit – or shoulder the blame – for initially shaping the 'standard' score that was finally codified by Prout. Neither Mozart nor Van Swieten, however, can be blamed for turning 'Why do the nations' into a *da capo* aria; they were merely following the indication in the first edition. As Walsh's heirs, Randall and Abell had reused the plates from his *Songs in Messiah* in order to hold down costs in assembling a full score. Since no choruses figured in that collection, a *da capo* was indicated at the end of the aria to provide a return to the tonic key; Handel had used the chorus 'Let us break their bonds asunder' as an exciting and dramatic substitute for a reprise of the aria's opening section. Walsh's *da capo* expedient was carried over into the full score in error.

Van Swieten and Mozart also made a few cuts. They omitted the chorus 'Let all the Angels of God' and the aria 'Thou art gone up on high'. Mozart replaced the aria 'If God be for us' with an accompanied recitative of his own composition. His abridged version of 'The trumpet shall sound' gives most of the demanding tromba part to a horn. Perhaps most surprisingly, Mozart wrote no additional accompaniments whatever for quite a few numbers. 'He trusted in God', for instance, is utterly free of added instrumentation.

Mozart's woodwind complement includes paired flutes (piccolo in the 'Pifa'), oboes, clarinets, bassoons and horns. In addition to two trumpets and timpani, his scoring calls for three trombones – in the 'Overtura' and the chorus 'Since by man came death'. The original performance materials, which have been preserved, show that the trombones also doubled the alto, tenor and bass lines in the *tutti* choruses, according to the standard Austrian practice at that time. In addition, these parts show not only that portions of some choruses were sung by the soloists, but also that the tutti choir – and this is confirmed by annotations on a surviving wordbook – consisted of but twelve singers!

Precisely because Mozart's additions were so exquisite in and of themselves and were written by a universally acknowledged master unabashedly working in the style of his own age, their validity and propriety have been debated. The negative view was perhaps best expressed by Moritz Hauptmann, who complained that Mozart's arrangement 'resembles elegant stucco work upon an old marble temple, which might easily be chipped off again by the weather'. Perhaps, but to extend the architectural analogy, I for one find Mozart's work as congruent with and as complementary to Handel's as Sir Christopher Wren's late seventeenth-century additions are to the original Tudor portions of the palace at Hampton Court.

The arrangement was published by Breitkopf und Härtel in 1803, with editorial assistance from Thomascantor Johann Adam Hiller, who had done much to promote *Messiah* in Germany. Influenced no doubt by reports of the 1784 Westminster Abbey commemoration, he had presented the oratorio, with additional accompaniments of his own, using enormous forces; at the first performance he directed, in Berlin in 1785, 302 vocalists and instrumentalists participated.

Editing Mozart's arrangement must have been a bittersweet task for Hiller, who surely would have preferred to have seen published his own performing edition, for which both the score and the performing parts now appear to be lost. Still, Hiller's alterations to Mozart's arrangement were nowhere near as extensive as Prout, Franz and others believed. (Mozart's autograph score and the original performing materials turned up only in the mid-1950s, and the arrangement was not published in *Urtext* form until 1961.) Apart from the substitution of a German text that is a combination of the Klopstock and Ebeling translations, Hiller's only crucial change was to substitute his own

80

arrangement – with bassoon obbligato! – of Handel's 'If God be for us' for the accompanied recitative that Mozart had written.

There have so far been four recordings of the Mozart *Messiah*. The first (16), recorded live in Salzburg in 1953 under the direction of Josef Messner, is based on Mozart–Hiller. Crippling cuts (can you imagine a *Messiah* without 'All we like sheep'?), lugubrious tempi, dry and wan singing and cramped sound make this out-of-print recording expendable for all but the archivist. The second recording based on Mozart–Hiller (17) is of a similarly limited appeal. Like the Messner, it dates from the early 1950s and is marred by crippling cuts and mediocre singing. The conductor, Walter Goehr, also favours slow tempi, but his come off as loving and caressing rather than stodgy, and he leads a rousing 'Hallelujah'. The score is sung in English, not German. For his second recording of *Messiah*, however, Goehr chose to use the original instrumentation; in all other respects, however, it parallels his earlier account (18).

By contrast, the third recording (19), glorious in almost every way, is essential to the library of anyone seriously interested in *Messiah* or Mozart. Conducted by Charles Mackerras (his second *Messiah*) and produced by Andreas Holschneider, who prepared the *Urtext* edition for the Neue Mozart Ausgabe, the recording accurately represents the original production in all important respects save two: Firstly, the chorus consists of fifty-two singers rather than twelve and the solo passages Mozart indicated in some choruses are sung by a *Favoritchor* rather than by the soloists. Secondly, the second soprano's part is divided between soprano Edith Mathis and alto Birgit Finnilä, who, with tenor Peter Schreier and bass Theo Adam, make up one of the finest group of soloists to grace any recording of *Messiah*. Overall, the performance is indescribably charismatic and atmospheric and, despite the use of modern instruments and other minor inauthenticities, succeeds admirably in conjuring up images of the Palffy Palace premiere in Vienna on 6 March 1789.

Early in 1988, Mackerras recorded the Mozart arrangement a second time, with the Huddersfield Choral Society, the Royal Philharmonic Orchestra and a group of the finest oratorio soloists in Britain today (20). Philip Langridge's account of the tenor solos is especially sensitive and his voice has nearly as much bloom as almost fifteen years earlier when he made so worthy and valuable a contribution to the Marriner recording of the 1743 London version of *Messiah*. Felicity Lott's soprano may be a bit tender at the top, but her interpretation is both elegant and mature. Felicity Palmer, who has become a mezzo since she recorded *Messiah* with Raymond Leppard in the mid 1970s, and Robert Lloyd both turn in more than satisfactory performances. As is to be expected from this greatest of the British provincial choruses, the Huddersfield Choral Society sings this music with gusto and empathy; the Royal Philharmonic provides support of equivalent quality.

Still, as exhilarating though it may be as a performance, Mackerras's second 'go' at the Mozart arrangement is, alas, a disappointment. This English-language performance with a large orchestra and chorus is neither fish nor fowl. Nineteenth-century forces and authentic performance practice – the scrupulous observance of the appoggiatura convention and the final chords of recitatives played as written, for instance – rub shoulders uncomfortably. This interpretation is further compromised both by cuts and by an uneasy *mélange* of Handel–Mozart and the original score. Besides making the standard cuts in Parts II and III, Mackerras omits 'Their sound is gone out'. 'The trumpet shall sound' is performed without the central section and the *da capo* reprise, rather than in Mozart's reworking. In addition, with the exception of the assignment of the Guadagni version of 'But who may abide' to the bass, the 'traditional' vocal assignments are preferred to Mozart and Van Swieten's occasional reallocations. Mackerras's decision not to follow either pure Handel or pure Mozart in its entirety is particularly regrettable because he passed up a perfect chance to fill an important gap in the *Messiah* discography by recording the Mozart–Hiller setting as it was known in Britain in the latter half of the nineteenth century thanks to the Novello full score, published in 1859 with the original English text.

NINETEENTH CENTURY

During the century after his interment in Poet's Corner in Westminster Abbey, Handel, revered like a demigod, had increasingly fallen victim to the notion that bigger is better. The most notorious and elephantine performances of his music, without question, were those given at the triennial Handel festivals held in the Crystal Palace. At the 1859 commemoration of the centenary of Handel's death, before an audience of some 20,000, Sir Michael Costa led 2,765 vocalists and 460 instrumentalists in *Messiah*; he added parts for a full Romantic orchestra that included contrabassoons and ophicleides. Emma Albani, Adelina Patti, Nellie Melba and Clara Butt were among the galaxy of opera stars who appeared as soloists in the Crystal Palace festivals, which continued until 1926. English Columbia issued discs containing five choruses recorded at one of the performances given at this last Crystal Palace Festival (21). Sir Henry Wood conducted a choir of 3,000 and an orchestra of 500. In the absence of more definite evidence, it has to be assumed that Sir Henry used Sir Michael's additional accompaniments which appear to have been used exclusively at the Crystal Palace.

Since this facet of *Messiah*'s history has not been adequately documented on records, it had been my hope that one of the major international record companies would have the guts to ignore the purists' howls of horror and engage a quartet of topflight opera stars and one of the giant choruses like the Mormon Tabernacle Choir to record the Costa arrangement of *Messiah* and recreate a full-blown Romantic Crystal Palace production, right down to the string *portamenti*, thereby not only performing an invaluable musicological service but also avoiding — as Andrew Davis, for instance, failed to do in his recording — a misguided attempt at a pseudo-authentic *Messiah* with anachronistically large forces. Alas, it seems that this cannot be, for the Costa parts, like the Hiller ones, appear to have been irrevocably lost. Costa bequeathed the performing parts and the conducting score to his arrangement to the Novello family, who added them to their company archives, and this unique set of *Messiah* materials was one of the casualties of the disastrous fire that struck the Novello library at Sevenoaks in Kent in the late 1950s.

In the 1870s and 1880s, the German organist and academic Robert Franz made quite a reputation by preparing editions of choral works by Bach and Handel with additional accompaniments for 'Modern orchestra'. His edition of *Messiah*, published in 1885, was used for many years by the Handel and Haydn Society of Boston, which had given the first complete American performance in 1818. (The alternatives selected for that premiere can be easily determined from the contents of the first American edition of the oratorio, printed under Handel and Haydn's auspices in 1816.) It formed the basis of the score used by the late Thompson Stone for the Society's 1955 Unicorn recording (22), now long out of print. Although Stone made numerous cuts and alterations and was cajoled — or more accurately shamed — into allowing a harpsichord into his orchestra, his recording gives a clear idea of Franz's approach, which 'though founded on Mozart[–Hiller], with the necessary completions', is both tasteful and inventive.

Messiah as it was performed in nineteenth-century Britain is documented in the first comprehensive recorded representation of the oratorio, a remarkable series of twenty-five single-sided G&T 78s made in 1906 (23). Although arranged for woodwinds and brass to accommodate the limitations of primitive recording methods, the Mozart score, including the assignment of the 'Guadagni' version of 'But who may abide' to the bass, was followed. Tempi are consistent with those considered the norm today. The soloists, however, provide surprises. Theirs are not large, vibrato-ridden operatic voices; the tone is light, pure, well focused and free of vibrato. Vestiges of the performance practice of earlier times can also be detected in the treatment of the cadential points; the soloists actually dare, albeit conservatively, to interpolate high notes and other embellishments. Tenor John Harrison's interpolations at the end of 'Thou shalt break them' bear a close enough resemblance to Paul Elliot's in the Hogwood recording to drive the point home: these soloists could have walked into Hogwood's recording sessions and, with a modicum of coaching in baroque embellishment, recorded *Messiah* in an impeccably stylish manner. *Plus ça change ...*

The soloists in the G&T *Messiah* also observed the so-called appoggiatura convention. This important bit of seventeenth- and eighteenth-century vocal style was, ironically, one of the casualties of the new-found interest in the 'pure' musical text that burgeoned in the 1920s and the 1930s. As Watkins Shaw has pointed out, soprano Elsie Suddaby, for instance, observes the convention in the Nativity recitatives leading into 'Glory to God' in Kennedy Scott's 1931 HMV single disc of excerpts (24), but, in Sir Thomas Beecham's 1947 recording of the complete score, she sings these recitatives as written. The inexorable progress of the eradication of the appoggiatura convention can be traced by listening to the many important individual recordings of solos from *Messiah* that were made between the bloody chunk of 'Ev'ry valley' on an 1898 seven-inch Berliner flat disc that represents the oratorio's gramophonic debut and Alfred Deller's hauntingly beautiful accounts of three *Messiah* solos (with the Prout added accompaniments, ironically) in the waning days of the 78 in the early 1950s. Without regard to whether or not the appoggiatura convention is observed, or whether the vocal production is 'modern' or 'old style', no account of the discographical history of *Messiah* would be complete without mention of the many superb recordings of *Messiah* solos made by such distinguished singers as Emma Juch, Louise Homer, Kirkby Lunn, Marian Anderson, Aksel Schiøtz, Kirsten Flagstad, Helen Traubel, Ria Ginster, Peter Dawson, Margarethe Matzenauer, Evan Williams, Walter Widdop, Heddle Nash, Keith Falkner, and Herbert Witherspoon.

TWENTIETH CENTURY

As *Messiah* entered the twentieth century bedecked in Classical and Victorian raiment, seeds of the return to Handel's original were being sown. In 1902, two important scholarly editions appeared. The first, prepared by Friedrich Chrysander after a careful, though not exhaustive collation of primary and early secondary sources, is an *Urtext* – the forerunner of such modern editions as the Schering-Soldan, the Coopersmith, the Priestman, the Watkins Shaw, the Tobin and – most recently – the Donald Burrows. The other, produced by Ebenezer Prout, Professor of Music at the University of Dublin, is an uneasy compromise between a pure, accurate text and the practical need for a performing edition that could gain wide acceptance in Edwardian England.

Besides codifying the standard Victorian form of *Messiah*, Prout confirmed the customary cuts by relegating to an appendix the numbers 'always omitted in performance' – the three separating the choruses 'Lift up your heads' and 'The Lord gave the word' and the four between 'The trumpet shall sound' (from which the central section and the *dal segno* reprise were excised) and the final chorus 'Worthy is the Lamb'. Prout did, however, correctly assign the Guadagni version of 'But who may abide' to the alto.

Although he considered his edition 'an honest effort to reproduce as nearly as possible both the letter and the spirit of Handel's greatest oratorio', Prout had to admit that, 'while Handel's text has been scrupulously respected, no attempt has been made to preserve his orchestral colouring'. Though he restored most of Handel's original tromba parts − but not his oboe parts except in three choruses in Part II − Prout based his accompaniments on Mozart's, striking out those he found 'un-Handelian' and retaining those he considered 'strictly pertinent to Handel's subject matter'. In essence, he removed almost all of the colour from Mozart's arrangement; his own accompaniments, careful and competent yet discreet and nondescript, frequently do little more than muddy the texture with unison doublings. The resultant opacity, of course, is exactly the opposite of the shimmering transparency of Handel's original. Chicken consommé is transformed into *crème de volaille*.

BEECHAM AND SARGENT

It's not surprising, therefore, that no recording uses Prout's accompaniments exactly as he wrote them. The one closest to 'pure' Prout is the first (25) of the three recordings made by Sir Thomas Beecham. Dating from 1927, it fills eighteen twelve-inch 78s and is the first true attempt at a 'complete' *Messiah*. In addition to the standard cuts, Beecham made further excisions: the 'Pifa' (which he had recorded previously on a single Columbia twelve-inch 78); the central section and *da capo* of 'He was despised'; 'The Lord gave the word'; 'Their sound is gone out', and − believe it or not − the concluding 'Amen', which means the recording ends in the dominant! (A 78 collector did not have to be left hanging, however; he needed only acquire Malcolm Sargent's single twelve-inch HMV 78 containing the 'Amen'.)

Beecham's outspoken aversion to the harpsichord notwithstanding, his first *Messiah* did much to hasten a return to the spirit of Handel's original. As alto soloist Muriel Brunskill recalled, 'His tempi for this work, which now are taken for granted, were revolutionary; he entirely revitalized it, the old slow progress was gone forever. *Messiah* was reborn.' Though myriad early recordings of excerpts, including fascinating renditions of 'And the glory of the Lord' and 'Hallelujah' recorded by '60 selected voices from the Leeds Festival Choir', under the direction of H. A. Fricker, FRCO, in 1907 (Gram. 04760), suggest that prevailing tempi may not have been all that lugubrious, Brunskill does not exaggerate the importance of this exciting and virile recording. Its recent reissue by Pearl on CD is particularly welcome for both musical, historical and artistic reasons.

For his second *Messiah* (26), recorded in 1947, Beecham used many of the Mozart and Prout accompaniments, frequently altered, and supplanted others entirely, substituting his own reorchestrations; these he also provided for numbers that neither Mozart nor Prout had rescored. Beecham's handiwork is less academic and much more colourful than Prout's; unlike the professor, who held Handel's brass and string parts sacrosanct, Beecham avoids opacity and, paradoxically, manages to preserve the glittering clarity of the original by changing Handel's instrumentation rather than merely doubling lines.

Beecham II is the first complete and uncut *Messiah* recording, originally released on twenty-one twelve-inch 78s and re-issued on four LPs. The engineer who made the LP transfer did not know the score, for in addition to perpetrating some god-awful side breaks, he carried over an unintentional gaffe from the 78 set: Nos. 34 and 35 were inserted between Nos. 52 and 53. Furthermore, as often happened in the 78 era, *da capo* reprises were not separately recorded; following the aria's central section, one simply turned the 78 back over to create the *da capo* repeat. (Ironically, this quirk makes Beecham II the first *Messiah* to feature an alternative version – the early, full *da capo* form of 'The trumpet shall sound'.) The LP transfer does not incorporate the *da capo* reprises.

These faults and some scrappy moments aside, Beecham II, though less frenetic than Beecham I, is every bit as inspired and thrilling, and this especially satisfying interpretation, which cries out for reissue, remains one of the tiny handful of truly stellar *Messiah* recordings, one of those that sets a standard against which all others must be judged. The quartet of soloists, Elsie Suddaby, Marjorie Thomas, Heddle Nash, Trevor Anthony, were all in superb voice, and Beecham adjusted the size of his choir to fit the character of the individual choruses.

In 1959, Beecham made his third *Messiah* recording (27), a stereo spectacular that has been the vortex of controversy ever since the moment of its release. Once more, this iconoclastic conductor opted for a reorchestration. Attributed to Sir Eugene Goossens, whom Beecham had commissioned for the task out of fury and compassion because his old friend and colleague had been pilloried because of his penchant for pornography, the arrangement, in fact, is largely Sir Thomas's own handiwork. According to Ward Botsford of Arabesque Records, who worked with Beecham for several years, Goossens's orchestration was delivered about four weeks before the recording sessions were due to begin. Beecham didn't like it and redid it himself.

Here, too, he bases his arrangements on those of Mozart and Prout, reorchestrating the latter's additions to give them the colour that their creator had so scrupulously avoided. Beecham calls for an enormous orchestra, including piccolos, cymbals, triangle, harps and a full battery of brass. The orchestration is *Klangfarben*-esque in its kaleidoscopic instrumental colours – especially in the solos – and once again Beecham succeeds in preserving the shimmering transparency of Handel's original by expanding the texture with upper octave doublings rather than clogging things up with sombre unison doublings. Met on its own terms without puristic prejudice, Beecham III proves a thrilling experience.

The format of the original issue is curious. Beecham made the standard cuts but relegated the deletions – except for the central sections of the two *da capo* arias, which were not recorded – to an appendix on the last side of the set.

One would think that, with three recordings of *Messiah* to his credit, Sir Thomas would hold the record. No fear. His great rival, 'Flash Harry' — Sir Malcolm Sargent — recorded the oratorio no fewer than four times between 1946 and 1964. All four epitomise *Messiah* as it was known and loved in the provinces during the decades between the two World Wars. The standard cuts are made, a large chorus is used, and the soloists declaim with imperial vigour, warmth and reverence. Of the four Sargent *Messiah*s (28, 29, 30, 31) the first is the best. It is especially noteworthy because of the participation of that British nightingale, Isobel Baillie, who has blessed posterity with the additional bonus of a supremely beautiful separate recording of the customarily omitted 'If God be for us'.

Three other *Messiah*s use Prout's accompaniments, but only selectively and with harpsichord added to various degrees. The first (32), recorded in Canada in the early 1950s under the baton of Sir Ernest MacMillan, has become something of a cult item among collectors. Why is beyond me. Apart from Lois Marshall's exquisite singing, it is somnolent and murky in the extreme. In addition to making the standard cuts, Macmillan omits 'And He shall purify'. This recording apparently marks Jon Vickers's disc debut, but I am sure that this great tenor, who is first-rate in Beecham III, is delighted that the MacMillan set is as scarce as the legendary hen's tooth.

A few years ago, the noted English choral conductor John Alldis, who has certainly prepared more choirs for *Messiah* recordings than any other chorus master, recorded the Prout *Messiah* (33) — a good but not great account in which some of the Dublin Academic's accompaniments are discreetly dropped. Alldis prepared the chorus for the single disc of excerpts conducted by Douglas Gamley (34), in which certain discreet additions from the Prout accompaniments augment the original instrumentation.

Also derived from the Prout edition is the brass band arrangement of the accompaniments used by Geoffrey Brand for his disc of 'favourites' from *Messiah*, featuring the Black Dyke Mills Band (35). One finds it difficult to argue with Mr Brand's contention in his notes for this unintentionally hilarious record, 'That [Handel] would have been intrigued (dare we say, fascinated?) with the sounds of soloists, chorus, and brass band, is conjecture, but not outside the realms of possibility.'

And, while we are on the subject of hilarity, if not abuse, the single disc of excerpts conducted by Randolph Jones (36) is a travesty, despite the use of the original orchestration. The selections are tossed on to the record in scrambled order, and many are severely cut. For example, thirty-eight bars are dropped from 'For unto us a child is born', and 'Why do the nations' ends with the last notes of the main section; the needle rises up from the turntable, a colleague remarked, before 'the kings of the earth rise up'. It seems, too, that Randolph Jones is a pseudonym, for the same bird's breakfast of brutalised excerpts appears on Spinorama, credited to the Stradivari Strings (37), and on Premiere with the Homburg Symphony conducted by Kurt von Baum (38).

The selections conducted by John Pritchard (39) are also served up in an unnecessarily scrambled order and, though the original orchestration is used, a few lingering vestiges of the Mozart arrangement are in evidence: muted strings in part of the 'pifa' and the delightful echo trills in the ritornellos of 'Ev'ry valley', albeit played on the harpsichord.

The Jones disc is a model of respect for the score compared to Andy Belling's simply gruesome 'pop' version of *Messiah* issued in the early 1970s under the title *The New Messiah* (40). This attempt at a new and improved product is a monument to bad taste. *The Electronic Messiah* (41), a record of synthesizer accompanied choruses sung by the Elmer Iseler Singers is better, if only because Handel's notes are not tampered with to any significant degree. The choir, up to its customary high standard, cannot be blamed for not being entirely 'in sync' with the obviously dubbed-in and quite colourless electronic accompaniments.

In the early 1950s, there was also a 'budget' recording of the 'complete' score available in the USA (42). With the standard cuts, this account featured four relatively unknown soloists and an unidentified chorus that was conducted by one John Cartwright, who also played the accompaniments in an organ reduction. Of greater significance to the history of *Messiah*, however, is a group of excerpts that appeared first on 78s and then on a 10″ LP on the Bibletone label (43). This odd recording documents, alas not particularly effectively, *Messiah* as it was then performed at Augustana College in Rockford, Illinois, where the oratorio has been performed regularly for more than 100 years. The selections, some of which have been abridged, are sung by soloists and a chorus of 300, with organ accompaniment.

But for all intents and purposes, in the decade after the end of the Second World War, Beecham, Sargent and diluted Prout held sway; however, that was soon to change.

'AUTHENTIC' VERSIONS

In March 1954, the first 'authentic' *Messiah* was released by Nixa in Great Britain and by Westminster in the United States — Hermann Scherchen's first recording, billed as the 'original Dublin version (1742)' (44). In fact, it contains the standard Victorian choices from among the various alternatives, except that for the first time on records the Guadagni version of 'But who may abide' appears in its original form for alto. Hermann Scherchen directs a tiny orchestra and chorus, using Handel's original instrumentation, but there is hardly any ornamentation of vocal or instrumental lines. Although it sounds dated today, even in the superbly cleaned up digital transfer to compact disc, this seminal interpretation, with its typically Scherchenian iconoclastic extremes of tempo, was a revelation in its time and should be heard by all interested in the recorded history of *Messiah*. After the release of Scherchen's 1954 recording, there was no turning back. *Messiah* as Handel wrote it had been recalled from exile.

Less than a year later, Decca/London issued Sir Adrian Boult's first recording (45), which reflects traditional British notions of how *Messiah* ought to go, although with the original instrumentation restored. His is a worthy interpretation on all counts, some sluggish tempi excepted.

Both Scherchen and Boult re-recorded *Messiah* in stereo. Scherchen's second account (46), a technical shambles replete with such inanities as a side break between the central section and the *dal segno* of 'The trumpet shall sound', is a carbon copy of his first as to edition, tempi and interpretation, but the performance simply does not jell. Léopold Simoneau provides the one bright spot in the recording; he handles the tenor part exquisitely.

While Boult's second effort (47) is also, for all practical purposes, a copy of his first, he benefits from improved sound and an even better solo quartet. Released in 1961, the performance is mildly compromised by an artificial balance of the otherwise natural and rich sonics, which affords the instruments an unrealistic clarity in the choruses. Aside from David Ward's tendency towards mannerism and pretension, the soloists sing especially well. Just one seizes the opportunity to ornament – Joan Sutherland, who embellishes her solos thoughtfully and elegantly, if in an anachronistic, early nineteenth-century *bel canto* style. Her notoriously murky diction intrudes only in 'Thy rebuke' and 'Behold and see', which she sings, as Handel's soprano soloists often did, in addition to her 'standard' solos. (How magnificent she would have been in one of the soprano versions of 'But who may abide'.) Boult's tempos tend to be slow, although not unreasonable except in some of the choruses. 'Hallelujah', unfortunately, is sluggish; 'The Lord gave the word' and the 'Amen' are both ponderous.

Eugene Ormandy's (48) and Leonard Bernstein's (49) two-disc versions make extensive – often seemingly mindless – cuts; both conductors use additional accompaniments derived more or less from Prout. Bernstein, moreover, shuffles numbers from Part II into Parts I and III, reorganising the oratorio into a Christmas and an Easter section. Neither Handel nor his librettist Charles Jennens would have been amused.

It may seem surprising to many, but, when he made a single disc of excerpts from *Messiah* for the Decca/London 'Phase 4' series in the late 1960s (50), Leopold Stokowski approached the oratorio with respect and understanding. The original instrumentation is used and the novel distillation of selections, including the four Passion solos and 'Since by man came death', is presented in the correct order. Because 'Let us break their bonds asunder' is not included, Stokowski elects to present 'Why do the Nations' as a *da capo* aria, *à la* Walsh's *Songs in Messiah* and Mozart.

Joan Sutherland has also recorded *Messiah* twice − the second time in a 1970 release conducted by her husband Richard Bonynge (51). With its plethora of ornaments and embellishments, elaborate continuo realisations, effusive cadenzas (including one for the trumpeter in 'The trumpet shall sound') and use of five soloists (a boy soprano sings in some of the Nativity recitatives), the interpretation is extroverted, exciting, and theatrically gaudy − Handel with a frosting of Bellini.

Basically, Bonynge follows the standard score, but he opts for the short form of the 'Pifa' and the Guadagni versions of 'But who may abide' and 'Thou art gone up', both sung by the alto Huguette Tourangeau. Once again, Sutherland sings 'Thy rebuke' and 'Behold and see'. There is, however, one bizarre cut. Some sixty-six measures are omitted from the *dal segno* reprise of 'The trumpet shall sound'. The soloists − apart from Tourangeau, whose tone is veiled and whose diction often sounds smothered in onions − sing magnificently. The *fioriture* and embellishment trip off their tongues with the greatest of ease, yet their primary goal always seems to be to convey the meaning of the texts. The same is true of conductor, chorus and orchestra.

1966−7, a pivotal season for *Messiah* on records, witnessed the release of two of the most important versions yet recorded, one by Sir Colin Davis (52) and the other by Sir Charles Mackerras (53). Davis uses the standard Victorian sequence but with the original instrumentation; while the vocal and instrumental embellishments now seem a little tame, the recording came as a revelation at a time when an 'authentic' *Messiah* was still a rarity. Featuring an especially fine solo quartet, it has stood the test of time and remains an excellent choice for those who want an authentic account of the standard score. The only fly in the ointment is Davis's decision to turn 'He was despised' into a *dal segno* aria by clipping off the reprise of the opening ritornello.

In his digital remake nearly two decades later (54), Davis has changed the essentials of his interpretation very little, but he has reworked myriad details to such a degree that his masterful view of Handel's 'Sacred Oratorio' is now veneered with a disconcerting fussiness. Once again he follows the standard Victorian sequence and turns 'He was despised' into a *dal segno* aria. A chorus of fifty-five to sixty is balanced against an orchestra of about thirty, a marked departure from the 1966 recording in which forty-one instrumentalists and forty choristers participated. In keeping with his statement that *Messiah* is a product of 'the world of the Italian opera', Davis strains for dramatic effects that have no basis in what we know to have been Handel's own practice. Apart from a one-bar *forte* outburst, 'Behold the Lamb of God' is sung *pianissimo*, and 'And with His stripes' is performed *a capella* throughout. Davis also applies the baroque principle of *soli* vs. *tutti* extensively in this recording, but once more in a manner that directly contravenes what we know to have been Handel's practice; the same is true of his finicky alternation, sometimes within the same number, of harpsichord and organ as continuo instruments. With

90

the exception of Stuart Burrows, who sings the tenor solos with a conviction, understanding, elegance and a pure rich tone that recalls both John Harrison and Heddle Nash, the soloists are not quite the equal of the excellent quartet in the 1966 recording.

Although Karl Richter opted for the tenor arioso form of 'Their sound is gone out', preceding it incorrectly with the soprano form of 'How beautiful are the feet' in both his fine but abridged German-language account (55) and his uncut but uneven English-language remake (56), Mackerras's first recording was the first to offer a substantial number of alternative versions. His recording, using an edition by Basil Lam that has not as yet been published, includes the shortened 12/8 form of 'Rejoice greatly', the Guadagni forms of 'But who may abide' and 'Thou art gone up', the alto duet and chorus version of 'How beautiful are the feet' (superbly sung by Janet Baker and Paul Esswood) and the tenor arioso setting of 'Their sound is gone out'. Subsequent theories of baroque performance practice have made this recording, too, sound a bit dated. The 'rules' are often over-applied − the use of over-dotting in both 'Hallelujah' and 'Worthy is the Lamb', for instance − yet this detracts not one whit from the enjoyment of what was, and is, a wonderful *Messiah*.

No recording did more than Mackerras's first to show that *Messiah* was not graven on stone and, ever since its release, recordings have fallen essentially into two categories: those that follow the familiar Victorian sequence in the main and those that do not.

The former category, whether released before or after the first Mackerras recording, includes Otto Klemperer's grandiose and moving interpretation using the original instrumentation (with 'Then shall the eyes' and 'He shall feed His flock' exquisitely sung, like the rest of the soprano part, by Elisabeth Schwarzkopf) (57); Raymond Leppard's solid, middle-of-the-road 'authentic' *Messiah* (58); David Willcocks's English 'collegiate' account, in which the soprano solos are sung by massed trebles, thus limiting its interest primarily to boy-choir buffs (59); Johannes Somary's bland if stylish performance (60); Frederick Jackson's less bland but less stylish reading (61); and Walter Susskind's undistinguished recording (62). Of limited interest is the recording by The Masterwork Chorus, conducted by its founder, the American classical radio personality David Randolph, who presents a severely abridged version of the oratorio, with organ accompaniment (63).

Karl Forster's German-language version (64), in which the Schering-Soldan edition − one of the earliest *Urtext* scores − is used, follows the standard Victorian sequence, but with 'Then shall the eyes' and 'He shall feed His flock' once again sung by the soprano. In his recordings (65, 66) − both of them complete and uncut − Helmut Koch follows Schering-Soldan, but he uses a different translation of the text. He deviates from the standard Victorian sequence only twice: the Guadagni version of 'Thou art gone up' is used,

TERI NOEL TOWE

rather than the original bass form, and 'The trumpet shall sound' is given as a full *da capo* aria. Like Forster, Koch leads an earnest, crisp performance.

Among the more recent recordings of the standard sequence is a Polish one (67), recorded in concert in Warsaw, apparently in the late 1970s or early 1980s (there is neither a date nor a copyright notice to be seen anywhere). Under the direction of Kazimierz Kord, the Warsaw National Philharmonic Orchestra and Choir and a fine cast of English soloists turn in a performance that is tasteful and quite idiomatic, especially for a country with no *Messiah* tradition; tempi tend to the leisurely by and large. Only the heavily accented English of the chorus reminds the listener that it is not a British or an American production. With the exception of the increasingly ubiquitous substitution of the Guadagni alto version of 'Thou art gone up' for the early bass version and the substitution of the short form of the 'Pifa', the Prout score is followed throughout.

A far less distinguished, in fact a positively noxious, account of what is essentially the standard score is Anders Öhrwall's *Messiah* (68), recorded live in February 1982, in the Adolf Frederik's Church in Stockholm, where he is choirmaster. A fine harpsichordist and a member of Holmiae Musicae, one of Scandinavia's foremost period instrument ensembles, he founded the Stockholm Bach Choir in 1964; he has turned it into one of the finest small choirs in Europe. Yet Öhrwall's is perhaps the fussiest interpretation of *Messiah* ever recorded – unpleasant in almost every particular, despite the obviously high quality of both the choral singing and the playing.

As he does for Malgoire, Martyn Hill sings with such a wonderful understanding of the idiom that one forgives his anachronistic vibrato. Paul Esswood turns in yet another fine account of the alto part, with particularly affecting embellishments in 'He was despised'. Soprano Yvonne Kenny's vibrato, though strong, is inoffensive, her voice clearly focused, her diction excellent. Baritone Magnus Linden, on the other hand, possesses one of the driest, ugliest voices it has ever been my misfortune to hear; for once, the absence of vibrato is not a virtue but a defect. He is especially unpleasant when straining for high notes – a fatal defect for a bass or baritone singing *Messiah*, since the bass parts tend to lie high.

Apart from his assignment of 'Thy rebuke' and 'Behold and see' to the soprano, Öhrwall deviates from the standard sequence but twice: he elects to use the Guadagni form of 'Thou art gone up' and the short version of 'Why do the nations'. Considering his obsessively fussy application of his misunderstanding of Handel's performance practices, it is, however, surprising to discover, towards the end of Part II, that Öhrwall starts to make cuts. Although magnificent from the technical standpoint – with especially realistic and distortion-free sound – Öhrwall's *Messiah* is an interpretative disaster, superfluous for all but the archivist.

Much the same verdict has to be reached, alas, about another *Messiah* recorded live in Stockholm in 1982 (69). Nikolaus Harnoncourt makes few digressions from the Prout choices, opting for the eleven-bar form of the 'Pifa' and the alto form of 'Thou art gone up' and assigning 'Thy rebuke' and 'Behold and see' to the soprano, thereby coming very close to Handel's 1752 solo quartet version, as the conductors of so many 'authentic' recordings unknowingly do when paying lip-service to the various alternative settings. The Concentus Musicus Wien, Harnoncourt's venerable period-instrument band, has too few oboes and bassoons for the number of violins and other strings, and this divergence from Handel's balances is keenly felt in the 'Sinfony' and in the choruses. Still, Harnoncourt gets plenty of mileage out of the oboes and bassoons that he does have. The surviving performing parts from Handel's time show that oboes and bassoons were used only in the 'Sinfony' and the choruses, not in the 'Pifa' or in any of the solos. In direct contravention of the composer's practice, Harnoncourt adds oboes to 'Ev'ry valley', the 'Pifa', 'He shall feed His flock', 'How beautiful are the feet' and 'Thou shalt break them'. Harnoncourt is yet another conductor who misconstrues the *soli* and *ripieno* indications that Handel entered into his conducting score for his 1749 performances. Instead of adding strings where Handel calls for ripienists, Harnoncourt cuts back where Handel asks for soloists, exactly the opposite of what the composer did in 1749, when he had contracted for a much larger orchestra than usual.

Although not without its lovely moments, Harnoncourt's *Messiah* is infected with an indisputable aura of contrivance, affectation and pretension; it lacks momentum, charm, charisma and enthusiasm, and is often almost offensively prissy and precious. The interpretative exaggerations notwithstanding, the Concentus Musicus Wien plays superbly in the main.

Harnoncourt's tempi are often unconvincing and unrelated to those that Handel indicated. Not only is the chorus 'And He shall purify', for example, disfigured by unnatural sways and swells that the distinguished Bach scholar Gerhard Herz complains 'sound like turning a water faucet on and off' but also it is taken at a slothful pace that can hardly be described as 'Allegro'. Such treatment is the rule, not the exception. The Stockholm Chamber Choir, a first-rate ensemble of mixed voices superbly prepared by Eric Ericsson, gives Harnoncourt exactly what he asks for, even if he is misguided.

None of Harnoncourt's four soloists adds much embellishment to the vocal lines. Of the quartet, the contralto Marjana Lipovšek acquits herself the most laudably. Like that of the tenor Werner Hollweg, her English is accented, which may disconcert those accustomed to British oratorio singers, but Handel would not have objected. Not only did he speak English with a pronounced accent, but also he regularly engaged continental singers as soloists for his oratorios, and *Messiah* was no exception. Lipovšek is especially fine in 'He was despised' and 'But who may abide'. Here is a rich, dark voice without much of the anachronistic vibrato that colours the otherwise lovely performance of Elizabeth Gale, who shows great sympathy for and understanding of the soprano solos. Despite his tendency to be stentorian and bombastic, Hollweg gives a fine account of the tenor solos. While not devoid of colour and richness by any means, Roderick Kennedy's voice has more than a soupçon of dryness about it; nonetheless, he sings the bass solos with flair and sensitivity, even if he does from time to time stab at pitches with the shameless aplomb of a Gilbert and Sullivan star negotiating the parlando of a patter song.

Like Harnoncourt, John Eliot Gardiner (70) uses the Tobin edition and, by assigning 'He was cut off' and 'But Thou did'st not leave' to the soprano and opting for the revised, shortened 12/8 form of 'Rejoice greatly' and the alto form of 'Thou art gone up', deviates minimally from the traditional selection of alternatives codified by Prout. While not misled by the 1749 *soli* and *ripieno* markings by and large, Gardiner does, inexplicably, assign the violin obbligato in 'If God be for us' to a solo violin. Although Elizabeth Wilcock plays the part with elegance, poignancy and sensitivity, Handel clearly directs that this obbligato be played by the first and second violins in unison.

Gardiner divides the solos among six singers: a soprano, a treble, a mezzo-soprano, a countertenor, a tenor and a bass. As is the case in the other complete *Messiah*s with a treble soloist – the Bonynge and the Malgoire – Saul Quirke has been given only the Nativity recitatives to sing. Handel gave the boys he engaged to sing as soloists in *Messiah* much more to do; in fact, in 1751, the unidentified boy soloist sang all the soprano solos! I doubt that Quirke, although better than Andrew J. King in the Malgoire recording, would have been equal to any of those demanding numbers, but one ought not forget that boys' voices broke at a much later age in Handel's day and were thus more mature and probably better trained than one can reasonably hope for today.

An especially sensitive interpreter, Margaret Marshall gives us a magnificent 'If God be for us' and a reading of 'I know that my Redeemer liveth' that, at once impassioned and awed, ranks among the best ever recorded. At its best her unusual voice has a solid, tawny quality about it that heightens the keenness of her interpretations; at its worst, as in 'But Thou did'st not leave', her voice is like curdled cream, besmirched by a tight, narrow vibrato with a pronounced bleating quality. The effective Catherine Robbin gives a sensitive, if conservatively embellished account of 'He was despised'. Charles Brett sings with much greater conviction for Gardiner than he did for Malgoire. (He sings entirely different segments, too.) His range is somewhat limited – tender at the top and not full at the bottom. He is the only alto that I can recall who takes advantage of Handel's own octave-upward alternative for the last three notes of the vocal line in bar 72 of 'But who may abide'. But Brett sings this air and the alto form of 'Thou art gone up' so marvellously and with such conviction that one regrets that Gardiner assigned him just those two numbers and did not give him the rarely sung Guadagni version of 'How beautiful are the feet', too.

Handel: *Messiah*

Although he sounds a touch pressed by the extraordinarily brisk tempo at which Gardiner takes 'Ev'ry valley', Anthony Rolfe Johnson is up to his customarily high standards. Robert Hale's voice is perfect for the authentic rendition of Handel's music. His rich, focused tone is practically vibrato-less and is strong at the top, as it must be to bring off the bass solos in *Messiah*. Hale's is a spectacular account of the familiar long version of 'Why do the nations', and his powerful and sincere reading of 'The trumpet shall sound' is the best on records, hands down, even if he does elect to use the altered declamation and note values for 'incorruptible', an editorial second-guessing of Handel's ability to set English words that is adopted in every English-language recording of *Messiah* other than Hogwood's, Weaver's and Parrott's. Although the changed declamation and note values date from an early stage in *Messiah*'s history and have become the accepted text, the appalling practice of 'correcting' Handel's deliberately awkward accentuation of the 'wrong' syllable has no basis whatever in his own practice and destroys his carefully planned symbolic play on the word 'incorruptible': even when the word's pronunciation is corrupted, it is still 'incorruptible'.

The 32-voice Monteverdi Choir has no trebles, but the alto section is made up entirely of countertenors. The group sings with lightness and grace and with a potent solidity when appropriate. The period instrument band, the English Baroque Soloists, also performs superbly. In addition to the leader Elizabeth Wilcock, the trumpeter Crispian Steele-Perkins must again be singled out for particular praise. His execution of the demanding tromba solo in 'The trumpet shall sound' rivals Michael Laird's in the Hogwood recording for sheer beauty of tone and interpretative sensitivity; he is every bit the equal partner of Robert Hale.

In the main, Gardiner favours brisk, occasionally practically breakneck tempi, particularly in the choruses. There are a couple of exceptions, however, and one of them creates a serious – for me, fatal – defect in the recording. Like all too many conductors before him – Boult, Scherchen, Westenburg, Colin Davis in his second recording – Gardiner chooses to take the concluding 'Amen' at, to put it euphemistically, an excessively reverent tempo. Such a slow pace causes all of the momentum built up in the preceding 'Worthy is the Lamb' and 'Blessing and honour' segments of this concluding 'French *ouverture*' chorus to dissipate. When one remembers that this choral fugue and the fugue in the 'Sinfony' are both *allegro moderatos* in common time, such an extreme variance in tempo between the two destroys Handel's subtle but carefully conceived 'Alpha and Omega' symbolic linkage between the opening and concluding movements and, therefore, can be justified only on purely subjective grounds.

For his recent recording (71), Sir Georg Solti opted for the original instrumentation, albeit with an orchestra of forty and a chorus of approximately 100 – forces not only larger than those Handel customarily employed

95

but also in inverse ratio of orchestra to chorus. Solti employed the Tobin edition and, with one exception – the Guadagni setting of 'Thou art gone up' – opted for the standard Prout sequence.

In almost every respect the Solti *Messiah* runs hot and cold. While the sound is rich and natural, most of the choruses give the curious impression that the orchestra and the choir are in different rooms; there is no sense of an enveloping auditory atmosphere. The keyboard continuo is rarely prominent enough, except in the recitatives, and is usually inaudible in the choruses.

The soloists are also uneven. Though sensitive and understanding, Keith Lewis is saddled with a tight, discomfiting vibrato, evocative of the 'goat's trill' so derided by baroque critics. Anne Gjevang's particularly wide vibrato, on the other hand, lends her solos an anachronistic *verismo* air. Despite strain on the high notes in 'The trumpet shall sound', Gwynne Howell sings with much the same sensitivity, dignity and rich, focused tone he displayed in Marriner's recording of the 1743 version. The great surprise, however, is Kiri Te Kanawa. Her voice overflows with a burnished gold warmth, her interpretation evinces both profound sincerity and discerning restraint and her diction, for once, is precise and crisp. Her account of the soprano solos recalls that of the legendary Isobel Baillie, and the knowledgeable listener cannot help but regret that she was not asked to sing some of the other numbers Handel occasionally assigned to his soprano soloists – the 'Passion' solos, 'But who may abide', and even 'Comfort ye, my people' and 'Ev'ry valley'.

The Chicago Symphony Orchestra and Chorus perform superbly, with commitment and assurance, but Solti, whose tempo choices are practically always right on the mark, seems strangely uninvolved and insecure, if not uncomfortable with the music, and he evokes little passion, charisma, or even enthusiasm. Despite an energetic and sinewy 'Sinfony' and a powerful, incisive and joyfully majestic 'Hallelujah', the interpretation seems not entirely Solti's 'own', particularly in the choruses. One can't help but wonder if the maestro abdicated the interpretative design of the choral movements to the redoubtable Margaret Hillis, the more than competent conductor who founded and prepared the Chicago Symphony Chorus. Cute dynamic effects and choral *legerdemain* display the ensemble's prodigious talent and superb training to the utmost but interfere with the direct expression of the music and the texts.

The Solti *Messiah* is proof positive that the ubiquitous obsession with authentic performance practice is being carried too far. It has become so voguish to be 'authentic' that the interpretative and aesthetic purposes served by *Uraufführungspraxis* are often lost in the shuffle. Performers and listeners alike ought not to lose sight of the reality that any piece of music can be performed validly in the style of any period subsequent to its own as well as in the style of the period in which it was written. Solti himself understands this principle, as his superb Mendelssohnian account of Bach's *St Matthew Passion* so clearly shows. Perhaps the incongruity between his still-born

Handel: *Messiah*

Messiah and his radiant *St Matthew* can be explained in terms of culture shock: a central European, Solti grew up with a Bach performance tradition that grew out of Mendelssohn's and that pervaded Central Europe during his youth. On the other hand, he apparently had no such relationship with *Messiah*. How much better his interpretation would have been and how much more valuable his recording would have been to *Messiah* buffs everywhere had he elected to record the Mozart–Hiller, the Franz, or the Prout edition, with any one of which he would have felt a greater natural affinity.

The most recent recording adhering to the traditional Victorian sequence is a Torontonian production (72). A scintillating and by-and-large satisfying account led by Andrew Davis, it is, like Mackerras's English-language recording of the Mozart arrangement, neither fish nor fowl textually, being a hodgepodge of authenticity and added accompaniments. Davis, alas, is yet another conductor who blew the chance to fill a yawning gap in the discography and give *Messiah* collectors a first-rate account of one of the very badly needed and as yet unrecorded post-Handelian arrangements: a complete Mozart–Hiller or Franz *Messiah* or, better yet, a pure and 'authentic' recording of the Prout edition, complete with piano continuo in the recitatives. Instead, we have what is essentially a large orchestra and chorus traversal of the original orchestration, with, to use Davis's own words, 'the full complement of brass and woodwinds in the choruses'. The soloists are all major artists: the frigidly brilliant Kathleen Battle; the mildly fuzzy Florence Quivar; the warm but bleaty John Aler; and the potent and exciting Samuel Ramey, who is particularly effective in the one aria Handel would not have assigned to him: the Guadagni version of 'But who may abide'.

In addition to Mackerras I and the numerous recordings discussed earlier, there are yet more in which alternative versions figure significantly. James Weaver's (73) is the second of the now-numerous *Messiah* recordings to feature period instruments. Once again, the size of the ensemble was determined on the basis of the Foundling Hospital ledgers; while horns are used, the soloists do not sing the choruses. Weaver opts for the short form of the 'Pifa', the Guadagni versions of 'But who may abide' and 'Thou art gone up', the alto duet and chorus form of 'How beautiful are the feet', the original 41-bar form of 'O death, where is thy sting?', and the alto transposition of 'If God be for us'.

Despite its many virtues, not the least of which is the exquisite singing of countertenor Jeffrey Gall in thrilling readings of 'But who may abide' and 'If God be for us', Weaver's *Messiah* leaves much to be desired. In addition to a pussyfooting 'Hallelujah', the harpsichord continuo realisations are often annoyingly four-square, and a certain tentativeness pervades the enterprise, contributing significantly to its lack of charisma.

There is nothing tentative, however, about John Tobin's recording (74). Editor of the Hallische Handel Ausgabe *Urtext* edition and the author of two books on *Messiah*, Tobin devoted thirty years of study to the work, researching the details of Handel's performances and putting his conclusions into practice. The result, the culmination of years of annual London performances, is a dramatic, operatically paced interpretation with an unsurpassed grandeur and emotional conviction that may come closer to the spirit of the elderly Handel's own performances than any other reading so far recorded.

Tobin's account does have its eccentricities, however; one can't help but feel that Tobin occasionally bends the results of his researches to fit pre-conceived notions − rooted in Victorian tradition − of how the work ought to go. A case in point is the *Grave* of the 'Sinfony'. Not overdotted, it builds gradually in volume from an almost inaudible *pianissimo*. Thrilling and convincing though it is, the effect is nonetheless a bizarre *mélange* of the Italian *sonata da chiesa* and Mendelssohn; it is doubtful that such an effect could have been achieved with period instruments. Tobin also disregards Quantz's dictum that vocal cadenzas should be singable in one breath and gives his excellent battery of soloists prepared cadenzas of excessive length. Yet for all its eccentricity and iconoclasm, the Tobin recording is unquestionably another of that handful of *Messiah*s against which the others must be compared.

In addition to the alto forms of 'But who may abide' and 'Thou art gone up' − both sung with style and aplomb by Paul Esswood, Tobin opts for the duet and chorus version of 'How beautiful are the feet', which he, alone, presents with two countertenors as Handel did in Dublin in 1742. He follows it with the tenor arioso form of 'Their sound is gone out'.

In his 1982 account (75), Richard Westenburg uses the edition prepared by the noted Handel scholar Watkins Shaw and opts for the revised 12/8 form of 'Rejoice greatly' and the soprano/alto variant of the duet and chorus version of 'How beautiful are the feet', which he follows with the choral form of 'Their sound is gone out', a combination that Handel seems never to have tried. Westenburg, however, retains two vestiges of the Mozart arrangement: the assignment of the Guadagni version of 'But who may abide' to the bass and the use of muted strings in both the 'Pifa' and 'He shall feed His flock'.

Without a doubt one of the world's finest choral conductors, Westenburg founded and directs Musica Sacra, which he has made into one of the world's truly great choruses. As an interpreter of *Messiah*, however, he falls short. While he has many good ideas which he brings off with great effect, he often seems to let his justifiable pride in his splendid chorus get in the way of the music. He can't, it seems, resist the temptation to show off his talented choristers like trained seals.

As a group, Westenburg's soloists are minimally satisfactory. John Cheek's is a full, powerful bass voice, and his 'The people that walked in darkness' is both sensitive and compelling; yet on the whole his stentorian bluster would be more appropriate to the role of the Grand Inquisitor in Verdi's *Don Carlos*. Nor is John Aler, who is in much better voice in the more recent Andrew Davis recording, particularly pleasant to listen to, notwithstanding his obvious affection and empathy, because his voice is afflicted with a pronounced, narrow vibrato. Katherine Ciesinski is the weakest of the group, lacking character in both voice and interpretation, and her vibrato − as pronounced as Aler's − is wide enough to drive a Mack truck through. Judith Blegen turns in the one truly outstanding performance, even though her voice is 'wrong' for the music: too much vibrato, and diction that rivals Tourangeau's in unintelligibility. Her interpretations of 'Rejoice greatly', 'I know that my Redeemer liveth', and 'If God be for us' − and the exquisite embellishments that she adds to all three − are sublimely sincere and hauntingly beautiful.

Westenburg's is the first digital *Messiah*, and it has a wonderful sonic aura. The atmosphere is intimate, not operatic, the sound is crisp and clear, and the instrumental parts − especially the continuo line − are distinct yet unobtrusive.

For his recording (76), made in concert in 1983, Ton Koopman uses a period instrument ensemble much smaller than any that Handel is known to have used: nine strings, two oboes, one bassoon, two trumpets, timpani, organ and harpsichord. Koopman's choir numbers but sixteen singers, half the number that Handel had at the Dublin premiere in 1742. An error in the vocal underlay in 'Hallelujah' makes it clear that Koopman is using the John Tobin edition. Several 'non-standard' alternatives are adopted: the 1743 arioso 'But lo'; the soprano version of 'Then shall the eyes' and 'He shall feed His flock'; the Guadagni form of 'Thou art gone up'; the *dal segno* form of 'How beautiful are the feet' that Handel rejected before the Dublin premiere; and the original long form of the duet 'O death, where is thy sting?'. The Passion solos are divided, two and two, between the tenor and the soprano. Incredibly, given his alleged concern for authenticity, Koopman, in the manner of Mozart and Van Swieten, assigns the familiar Guadagni version of 'But who may abide' to the bass, something that, as we have seen, Handel never did.

Of Koopman's four soloists, three turn in magnificent performances. Marjanne Kweksilber's voice has deteriorated alarmingly since her astonishing recording of Bach's *Jauchzet Gott in allen Landen*, BWV 51, with Gustav Leonhardt; alternately hooty and covered, it lacks focus. James Bowman is in superb voice, however, singing without strain and with clarity, vibrance, intensity and telling emotion. His interpretation of 'He was despised' (which Koopman, like Colin Davis, turns into a *dal segno* aria by omitting the reprise of the opening ritornello) is among the most compelling on record, and the ease with which he dispatches the florid lines of 'Thou art gone up' makes one all the sorrier that it is not he who is singing 'But who may abide'. Both Paul Elliott and Gregory Reinhart project a clear, well-focused tone and use practically no vibrato, but Elliott's interpretation is rather cool compared to his performance in the Hogwood recording (a reflection of Koopman's approach?), and Reinhart, though he has little difficulty with Handel's *fioritura*, does occasionally stab at the high notes. The vocal embellishment is unusually generous, but at times it sounds anachronistic, as in the cadential flourishes in 'If God be for us'.

The Sixteen, superbly prepared by Harry Christophers, sing with an appropriate baroque purity of tone, but Koopman indulges in those annoying, precious swells on strong beats that have marred more than one 'authentic' *Messiah* recording. The Amsterdam Baroque Orchestra plays with complete ease and security. Koopman, whose tempos are brisk yet gracious on the whole, leads from the harpsichord, and his especially enjoyable continuo realisations evince a daring and a sense of the horizontal all too frequently lacking elsewhere. But there has always been a tendency to over-interpret *Messiah*, and Koopman falls into the trap. In general, his interpretation, which has been captured in a bright, crisp, digital sound that is almost unnaturally transparent, is too 'loving' − overly reverent and lacking the fire, the ardour, the blood and thunder, the pathos that make for a truly compelling reading.

SUMMARY

Because of the changing versions, a core collection of *Messiah*s should include:

1 Marriner's recreation of the first London performance, which is an excellent representation of the oratorio as it sounded between 1742 and 1749;
2 Hogwood's inspired and nearly flawless exact re-creation of the 1754 Foundling Hospital benefit that gives the listener an accurate view of *Messiah* as it sounded during the last decade of Handel's life;
3 Dorati's exciting evocation of the gargantuan 1784 Westminster Abbey Commemoration performance which has the additional virtue of offering at least one alternative version not included in any of the other essential *Messiah*s;
4 Mackerras's first recording of the Mozart arrangement, which documents a wonderful meeting of two supreme musical minds and provides an exciting glimpse into the complex history of *Messiah* after Handel's death; and
5 Tobin's grandly operatic and eccentrically authentic account, the legacy of a maverick who devoted much of his life to the study of Handel's 'Sacred Oratorio' and the only recording to include the duet and chorus version of 'How beautiful are the feet' sung by two countertenors as it was at the Dublin premiere in 1742.

Messiah as it was heard in England in the latter half of the nineteenth century and first half of the twentieth is imperfectly documented on record, but those who can find the second of Beecham's recordings or the first of Sargent's will have an exhilarating idea of that performance tradition at its best. In their absence, however, the CD reissue of severely abridged 1927 Beecham set will prove a satisfying substitute. Still, recordings of the Mozart–Hiller, the Franz and the Prout editions in their pure forms are badly needed, as is a recording of the version of *Messiah* as it was premiered in the United States in Boston in 1818.

Also worthy of inclusion in the collection of a *Messiah* buff is the Neuen, a finely paced modern-instrument recording employing Alfred Mann's thoughtful edition, a fortuitous recreation of the oratorio as we now believe Handel performed it in 1752.

You insist that you have room on your shelves for but one *Messiah*? Let it be either the Hogwood or the Neuen.

Mozart: Requiem Mass

INGRID GRIMES

Mozart's last, sombre masterpiece, the Requiem in D minor K.626, has caught the public imagination as few other works, largely because of the mystery surrounding its origins.

The bare facts are now known: Count Walsegg von Stuppach, a passionate music-lover, commissioned the Requiem in the spring or summer of 1791, in memory of his young wife who had died earlier that year. Walsegg was a harmless eccentric whose practice it was to recopy works he had commissioned, in order to test his chapel-musicians' powers of deduction, and who seemed to derive much innocent amusement when flatteringly credited with their authorship. Hence his insistence on retaining the copyright of the Requiem so that it could not be published prior to his own first performance, thus spoiling his little joke. The contract between Mozart and the Count has recently been discovered, proving that their business together was above board and conducted with total propriety.

Nevertheless, the legends persist, and even today commentators are divided over the more colourful theory that Mozart had a premonition of his impending death, regarded Walsegg's 'grey-clad emissary' as a messenger from the other world, and became obsessed with the idea that he was composing the Requiem for his own funeral. Though a letter in which Mozart confides these fears to Da Ponte has long since been discredited as a forgery, it is significant that the account given by his widow Constanze to contemporary chroniclers seems to corroborate this view.

In the event, Mozart did not live to finish the Requiem. This placed Constanze in a delicate position, since a large amount of money had already changed hands, and more was outstanding subject to the Requiem's completion. Accordingly she first sought the help of Mozart's talented pupil Joseph Eybler, and only after he — and several others — had refused did she approach Franz Xaver Süssmayr. And yet it appears that in the final stages of his last illness Mozart had frequently discussed the completion of the Requiem with Süssmayr — though whether it is likely that, even *in extremis*, Mozart would

102

have entrusted such an important undertaking to a man for whose musicianship he was known to have scant respect must remain open to conjecture.

Nor can we be certain how much of what has come down to us is Mozart's
own work. Süssmayr claims to have composed the Sanctus, Benedictus, Agnus
Dei and all but the first eight bars of the 'Lacrimosa', but Constanze maintains
that the score was virtually complete, and that, in any case, Süssmayr worked
from Mozart's own sketches. The fact remains that no definitive version of
the score exists. Süssmayr's workmanlike completion, regarded by many as
unsatisfactory and unMozartian, has undergone two major revisions (Beyer,
Eulenburg 1971; and – more radically – Maunder, O.U.P. 1987), in addition
to minor emendations in performances by Walter, Beecham and Scherchen
inter alia, but the question of what Mozart might have written, had he lived,
remains tantalisingly unresolved.

Similarly, there seems to me to be no one 'definitive' interpretation of the
Requiem, which, beyond the narrow context of Mozart's late church-music
and its evocation of the idioms of an earlier age, might itself be regarded as
'unMozartian'. Does this 'one-off' quality perhaps absolve conductors of the
duty to make the Requiem sound 'like Mozart'? Most have sensed – and
responded to – the baroque 'otherness' of the work, by opting for a clean,
steely string-tone, paring down the instrumentation at the beginning of the
'Recordare', and introducing double dotting in the 'Rex tremendae'; but
beyond these stylistic details, whether the emphasis has been on drama or
lyricism, pathos or terror, sanctity or theatricality, spiritual doubt or Divine
assurance, or whether indeed the work is recreated in terms of cathedral,
church or concert-hall, has been a matter of individual choice.

There is no denying the fact that, generally speaking, performance standards
have improved immeasurably over the past fifty years. Is it that conductors
are more demanding, or that performers are more self-critical, or the public
more discriminating? And, beyond the niceties of pitch, rhythm and ensemble,
has scholarship played as crucial a part as it would have us think in shaping
– and sharpening – our awareness of what is (and is not) acceptable? Of
course, perceptions – and fashions – alter: moving up the evolutionary scale,
one notes the gradual demise of the contralto in favour of the mezzo, a steadier
top line to the choral texture, a predominance of faster tempi, but also fewer
dramatic fluctuations between extremes of speed in individual performances.
(It is arguable that some interpretations may have become blander in the
process.) One notes with interest the contemporary assessment of Richter's
version as 'too rhythmic', or Davis's as 'authentic' and 'small-scale', especially
in the light of more recent performances by Gardiner *et al.*, though no one
has yet suggested the appositeness of the 'one to a part' Rifkin approach.

All the critic can hope to do when faced with a work that lends itself to
a large (though finite) number of interpretations is to decide to what extent
each recording has been true to that particular conductor's vision of the work

and, in attempting to assess the integrity and validity of individual readings, to express preferences that are inevitably subjective. Of course, recordings are in some ways as artificial as photographs, preserving for posterity every detail of what are, essentially, transient experiences. Perhaps for this reason, we are less tolerant of recorded imperfections, knowing that they will be endlessly replicated. Even so, basic musical criteria must surely be satisfied, and I cannot help but feel that it would have been kinder to respect Bruno Walter's judgement in suppressing his 1937 recording, rather than dragging it forth, fifty years on, in all its shambling, ill-tuned inadequacy. There are undoubtedly inspirational moments: the 'Lacrimosa' is graceful, the tugging syncopations of the 'Hostias' have a rare Brahmsian intensity and Anton Dermota sings with affecting ardour. But the brass are abysmal, especially in the lumbering 'Quam olim Abrahae' fugue, the 'Confutatis' displays all the aural sophistication of a train pulling out of a station, and the beginning of the 'Tuba mirum' is certainly neither Alexander Kipnis's – nor the trombonist's – finest hour.

Bruno Kittel's account, dating from 1941, is as authoritative as one might expect from a conductor who already had one of the earliest recordings of Beethoven's *Missa Solemnis* under his belt. His choir and the Berlin Philharmonic respond with fervour to his energetic direction of the first (and last) three movements, but the solo singing is definitely not for the squeamish. A more sinister sign of the times: the words 'Jerusalem' and 'Abrahae' have been removed from the text.

Predictably, Victor De Sabata makes no concession whatsoever to period, be it that of Adolf Hitler or the Emperor Leopold II. To him, Mozart is indistinguishable from early Verdi, complete with sobbing tenor, throbbing accompaniments and a 'Lacrimosa' that sounds uncannily like the Chorus of the Hebrew Slaves from *Nabucco*. De Sabata takes a somewhat nonchalant view of the Requiem's more intimate moments and clearly cannot summon much enthusiasm for Mozart's more academic polyphony; nonetheless, he offers an uncompromisingly severe (and fast) 'Rex tremendae', and a 'Dies irae' in which all Hell is let loose. It may be theatre rather than real life-and-death drama, but it makes for riveting listening – which is more than can be said for Josef Messner's turgid account. It is not simply that every movement is taken unbelievably slowly – a comment one could equally well make about either of Karl Böhm's recordings – but that Messner fails to elicit any expressive nuances from his performers. Indeed, one begins to wonder whether they are capable of responding, since even at these speeds much of the score seems to be technically beyond them. His normally distinguished soloists enter fully into the lack of spirit of this performance: Josef Greindl adopts a hectoring, aggressive tone in the 'Tuba mirum', Rosette Anday slides up a good semitone to most of her entries and the opening chains of suspensions in the 'Recordare' are both poorly tuned and in imminent danger of bringing the movement to a complete standstill.

Little wonder then that the crude vitality and directness of Josef Krips's boy-singers come as something of a relief, though it must be admitted that undisciplined fervour has a strictly limited charm. The Vienna Hofmusik-kapelle Chorus seem to have no more than a rudimentary grasp of phrasing, they lack the intensity to sustain the 'Rex tremendae', 'Lacrimosa' and Agnus Dei at Krips's rather ponderous tempi, and the trebles tend to sing sharp. Furthermore, the vulnerability of the solo singing cannot be blamed entirely upon the two boy-soloists, and the orchestra is embarrassingly approximate in places.

Hermann Scherchen, on the other hand, secures some effective and well-articulated playing from the Vienna State Opera Orchestra in his 1954 recording, which still creates a powerful dramatic impact. He takes the outer movements very slowly, imbuing them with a deep solemnity, gives a searing account of the 'Dies irae', and a thrusting rhythmic impetus to the 'Rex tremendae'. The choral singing is generally expressive, though marred by the unfocused sound of the sopranos and altos below *mf*. The glory of this version, however, lies in its outstanding soloists: Magda László and Hilde Rössl-Majdan are beautifully matched, and the balance in the Benedictus is, for once, first-rate. I did wonder whether Richard Standen was just a little too gentlemanly and suave in the 'Tuba mirum' – I felt he might have been sounding the dinner-gong, rather than the Last Trump.

In comparison with Scherchen, Eugen Jochum's Requiem may at first seem a rather low-key, muted affair, yet somehow it carries with it a conviction that Scherchen's lacks. The greater sensitivity of Jochum's choir is noticeable at the end of the 'Confutatis', and in his gently lilting 'Lacrimosa', while the tenors in the 'ne absorbeat' fugue of the 'Domine Jesu' are wonderfully passionate. Kim Borg – the first bass to discover that 'Tuba mirum spargens sonum' can actually be sung in one breath – rolls his consonants with great aplomb, and the angel-bright innocence of Irmgard Seefried's 'Te decet hymnus' is touching and appropriate.

With Sir Thomas Beecham's recording, one simply reaches a higher plane of experience. Like Colin Davis, Beecham has an apparently unerring knack of hitting upon the 'right' speed for each movement: virtually all the choral sections in this performance are brisk, yet none is perfunctory. From the first vocal entries, one senses the subtle interplay and growth of lines, rather than the customary sea of voices. The 'Dies irae' is exhilarating, the monumental 'Rex tremendae' is complemented by a beautifully focused 'Salva me', and the rasping tenors and basses in the 'Confutatis' really lead one to the brink of the abyss. Beecham's 'Lacrimosa' and Agnus Dei are the fastest on record, but while the former is tender and consoling, the latter has an almost unbearable intensity. The solo quartet is particularly well blended, nowhere

105

more than in the delicate and understated 'Recordare'. Elsie Morison's clear, sweet soprano is delightful, and Alexander Young is suitably heroic in the 'Tuba mirum'. The orchestral playing is splendid; there is much shapely and sensitive phrasing and, despite its age, the recording captures an astonishing variety of instrumental colours – more, indeed, than most of us will remember, since Beecham makes fairly free with the scoring, adding extra wind parts to the solo movements, and substituting an enthusing and over-decorous solo cello in place of the much-maligned trombone obbligato in the 'Tuba mirum'. Nevertheless, this is a performance that holds its own among the finest.

Though Bruno Walter's second version is a vast improvement on his first, I still find it a trifle heavy-handed. Tempi are better-judged (and adhered to), the singing is spirited, with the Handelian angularity of the Kyrie fugue nicely caught, and a strikingly sibilant 'Dies irae'. As one might expect, the emotional weight of this performance is borne by the orchestra, and while the strings play with anguished eloquence in the Agnus Dei, during the fugal sections of the 'Domine Jesu' they tend to drown the singers. (Incidentally, the pitch drops suddenly in this movement, just before the solo entries.) The soloists are no more than respectable, and Seefried sounds distinctly reedier than under Jochum.

Böhm's earlier recording is thoughtful and dignified, with a weighty string-tone and unusually prominent use of organ. Tempi are predominantly slow; this allows much beauty of orchestral detail to emerge from the Agnus Dei, but robs the 'Confutatis' of its menace. In the 'Lacrimosa', the second quaver of every beat is anticipated and lengthened, imparting a curiously Viennese instability to the rhythm. The solo movements are urbane, and lack Beecham's special intimacy; but for me, the exquisite, boyish purity of Teresa Stich-Randall's *tonus peregrinus* is what will linger in the memory.

Instantly forgettable is Jascha Horenstein's overblown operetta of a Requiem. His choir sing rather worse than the average amateur choral society, their guttural entries and tinny, unblended tone accentuated by the forward choral balance. Horenstein's soloists (charitably described as 'operatic' by a contemporary reviewer) are a further liability; Wilma Lipp and Elisabeth Höngen are rarely in tune, Ludwig Weber starts each phrase as if clearing his throat, and even the redoubtable Murray Dickie quacks his way unpleasantly through the 'Domine Jesu'. The orchestra play well enough, though ironically the star of this particular show is the anonymous trombone soloist, whose musicianship leaves everyone else standing.

Rudolf Kempe's overtly devotional approach strikes me as far more convincing. His recording is characterised by committed choral singing and warm orchestral support, although there is some lack of instrumental definition in the 'Recordare'. Among the soloists, the magisterial Gottlob Frick is outstanding, though of the 'lower profile' Requiems of the 1950s, Böhm's probably has the edge.

106

Mozart: Requiem Mass

There is little left to the imagination in Scherchen's second recording. Theoretically it should be virtually indistinguishable from his first, since he uses the same choir and orchestra, and adopts similarly extreme tempi. In practice, his earlier version is streets ahead. To be fair, the 'Dies irae' and 'Rex tremendae' are as punchy and thrilling as ever, but the 'Hostias' and Agnus Dei are disconcertingly unlinear, the 'Confutatis' sounds laboured, the 'Lacrimosa' lurches, and the fugues all tend to plod. Furthermore, instead of his previous sublime quartet, we now have Sena Jurinac — who sings flat, Lucretia West's acidic top notes, the operatic tenor of Hans Loeffler, and Frederick Guthrie's gravelly bass.

With the arrival of stereo we move, so far as Herbert von Karajan's 1961 recording is concerned, into the wonderful world of deluxe sound. His is a soothing, sanitised way of death, with most of the fear and ugliness smoothed away. The Berlin Philharmonic accompany with bland elegance, and in the Agnus Dei, which might otherwise have been the emotional high-spot of this performance, the Wiener Singverein are late on the attack, short on consonants and slightly flat. Walter Berry and Anton Dermota are in fine voice, but the ungainly vocal scooping and swooping of Wilma Lipp leave much to be desired.

Reviewers gave Karl Richter's version the thumbs-down when it first appeared, but I feel it has a great deal to commend it. I like Richter's positive tempi, and find his unique blend of severity and fervour quite appealing. This is a purposeful reading, stronger perhaps on polyphony than pathos, but exemplary in the superb attack and articulation of the Munich Bach Choir. The sopranos are rock-steady on 'Salva me', at the end of the 'Rex tremendae'; the Munich Bach Orchestra are especially impressive in the pulsating 'Domine Jesu', and also manage to make rhythmic sense of the syncopations in the 'Hostias'. Some may find the soloists too forthright, but I thought they chimed acceptably with the lack of artifice of the whole performance.

It would be unfair to judge Erich Leinsdorf's recording in the light of others, since it forms part of a two-disc set of the Memorial Service for President Kennedy held in Boston's Catholic Cathedral. Most of the detail is lost in the welter of sound and the balance is inevitably poor. Even so, hearing the Requiem in its proper liturgical context is a profoundly moving experience.

In terms of forces, Ferdinand Grossmann's account may be nearer what Mozart had in mind, but I found it just too, too rococo. The outer movements lack weight and *gravitas*, and in the 'Dies irae' the Vienna Boys sound suspiciously like fugitives from the *Liebeslieder* Waltzes. They are no less coy and ingratiating in the 'Domine Jesu', and there are moments in the fugues where there seems to be only one to a part. Had the others simply given up? Roland Bader fares little better with his pedestrian choir, hearty soloists, and an orchestra whose intonation comes to grief within the Requiem's first two bars. Wolfgang Gönnenwein's reading, on the other hand, is the very epitome

107

of restraint. His languidly legato approach works well enough in the Requiem's more reflective movements, but generates little heat in the 'Dies irae', and hardly a tremor in the 'Confutatis'. Even the vocal contributions of Teresa Zylis-Gara and Peter Schreier are insufficient to elevate this workmanlike performance beyond the decorously passionless.

Under István Kertész's muscular, Romantic direction, the Vienna Philharmonic Orchestra play superbly. The Vienna State Opera Chorus sing no worse than many choirs on earlier recordings and rather better than they did under Jochum, but by 1968 standards they sound slightly frayed at the edges. Elly Ameling's 'Te decet hymnus' is one to cherish, but I found Ugo Benelli's fulsome 'Quaeren*sh* me' and 'redemi*sh*ti' too much to cope with.

I have no such reservations about Sir Colin Davis's marvellous, glowing account. He seems to grasp the relationship between individual detail and overall structure better than almost anyone else: each phrase is lovingly shaped, yet one section flows inevitably into the next. In the 'Rex tremendae', 'Confutatis' and 'Domine Jesu' (all of which Davis takes remarkably slowly), he heightens the music's emotional impact by his avoidance of gratuitous rhetoric. The singing of the John Alldis Choir is extraordinarily vivid and responsive, never more than in the hushed, other-wordly 'Quarum hodie memoriam facimus' of the 'Hostias'. For once, the solo quartet is ideally matched; the 'Recordare' and Benedictus capture that special intimacy of ensemble that distinguishes Davis's Mozart opera recordings. Musically, I found this Requiem one of the most satisfying, but those with a predilection for incense and brimstone may well prefer Rafael Frühbeck de Burgos's more full-blooded approach, where death looms larger than life. Here, the gestures are theatrical yet effective. The 'Rex tremendae' is grimly authoritative, the 'Confutatis' vengeful, the 'Dies irae' strikes terror in the heart. Edith Mathis, Grace Bumbry, George Shirley and Marius Rintzler are more Romantically assertive than Davis's team, and blend less well. The New Philharmonia Orchestra and Chorus are excellent, though where Davis opts for subtle shading, here the colours are boldly applied.

Pierre Colombo might have scraped by in the early 1950s but here he is hopelessly outclassed. Can this possibly be the same choir that served Scherchen more than adequately? Their loud, insensitive singing and messy work-endings are further exaggerated by the unacceptably close recording quality. Kieth Engen bashes his way through the 'Tuba mirum' like some bar-room baritone, Thomas Page sings persistently through his teeth ... need I go on?

Maarten Kooy's version, typical of the enterprise and fallibility of the first generation of Saga records, offers the earliest performance using original instruments. Indeed, the Netherlands Singers Orchestra play quite respectably, but Kooy's choir sounds frail and undernourished, and cannot cope with his hectic tempi, particularly in the 'Confutatis' and 'Lacrimosa' – which jerks along clumsily like a marionettes' waltz. Of the eight soloists, the boy treble is passable; the others are clearly untrained, and one of the tenors sings much of his part in falsetto. Authenticity is more than just a matter of small choirs and old instruments.

Daniel Barenboim's essentially flexible, Romantic approach produces one of the most dramatically potent interpretations on record. The 'Dies irae' is electrifying, the 'Lacrimosa' combines poignancy with power, the muscular 'Domine Jesu' eschews the dynamic contrasts of Davis and de Burgos but is no less gripping, the Sanctus is mighty and triumphant. Barenboim takes a more lyrical, expansive view of the solo movements, and here he is served well by his vibrant soloists. Janet Baker and Dietrich Fischer-Dieskau are un-equalled in their shaping of the opening duet of the 'Recordare', but later in the movement one can hear few of Sheila Armstrong's words. Once again the John Alldis Choir are magnificent, the English Chamber Orchestra play with great feeling and the recording is vivid and atmospheric.

In his second reading, Böhm takes the Requiem more slowly than anyone else. It is beautifully played and sung, but most of it is rather portentous. The 'Dies irae', for example, smacks of admonitory, rather than punitive, zeal; and the 'Confutatis' virtually grinds to a halt. Noble and impressive it all certainly is, but I am a little disappointed that Böhm – a committed Mozartian – should have turned his back so completely on the passion and drama of this score.

Gerhard Schmidt-Gaden is the first conductor to record Franz Beyer's edition of the Requiem. The most striking changes are, I think, extremely effective: Beyer shuts up the trombonist of the 'Tuba mirum' once the dead have been wakened; he removes the pre-emptive chord on the second crotchet of the 'Rex tremendae'; he adds acceptably Mozartian codas to the perfunctory 'Osanna' choruses; and prepares the otherwise absurdly abrupt modulation into E flat major at bar 32 of the Benedictus by adding a third-inversion dominant 7th A flat to the bass-line of the preceding bar. There are literally hundreds of more minor alterations of harmony and scoring; the overall impression is of textures that are leaner, more economical, less adorned. At the time of writing, Beyer's edition is slowly gaining ground in both 'tra-ditional' and 'authentic' camps, but has not won general acceptance.

The Collegium Aureum play stylishly under Schmidt-Gaden's brisk direction, but frankly, the chesty, forced tone of the Tölz trebles and altos does not appeal to me, even though it imparts a rawness and urgency to the 'Dies irae' which is not inappropriate. In the 'Rex tremendae' there is no tension between the long-held choral notes and the rhythmic instrumental underlay because – apparently – the boys cannot sustain a line. The treble and alto soloists in the 'Recordare' seem to have enough problems, without attempting to embellish their parts. I found it difficult to concentrate on textual minutiae in the face of such distractions.

109

There is a much greater sense of emotional involvement in Karajan's second recording than in his earlier account; here, the 'Lacrimosa' is hushed and devotional, the 'Domine Jesu' is urgent and sung in a conspiratorial whisper, the 'Dies irae' really blazes. The orchestral sound is better focused and the playing more committed, though the strings are still rather silky-smooth, and the solo trombonist tends to wallow. The soloists, too, are excellent, and José van Dam's rich, sonorous bass is one of the best on record. What a pity that after fourteen years the Vienna Singverein Chorus still sing flat!

In comparison with Karajan's warmly Romantic interpretation, Michel Corboz's reading seems monochromatic and subdued, the singing soft-grained, the accompaniment muted. At the beginning of the 'Introitus' Corboz ignores Mozart's markings and brings the choir in quietly, which typifies his 'quasi religioso' approach to the whole work. I liked the neurotic angularity of the 'Quam olim Abrahae' fugue, but such moments of heightened tension are few and far between.

There is nothing lacklustre about Hans Gillesberger's spirited account, which trips along with an unselfconscious freshness of tone. The legend assures us we are listening to three choirs and two (inauthentic) orchestras, but the textures throughout are delightfully transparent, and the balance could not be better. The soloists are unusually eloquent, particularly in the 'Recordare', where the underlying anxiety of 'tantus labor non sit passus' is caught with aching poignancy. But the jewel in the crown of this remarkable reading is surely the astonishingly accomplished treble soloist, whose impeccable intonation and sensitivity to line put several established prima donnas on other recordings to shame.

Sir Neville Marriner is less inclined to wear his heart on his sleeve; his sober, at times introspective view of the work is well suited to the greater austerity of Beyer's edition. Unlike many conductors, Marriner is prepared to let the music speak for itself, without recourse to exaggerated word-painting or excessive tempi. The opening of the 'Confutatis' can so often sound raucous and uncontrolled; here, it is both menacing and musical, and contrasts superbly with the quieter 'voca me fons pietatis'. The soloists are generally excellent, though I find Robert Tear too unrestrained at times for this essentially classical reading.

Those expecting a Verdian Requiem from Carlo Maria Giulini may be surprised by his mellow, lyrical account. From the first bars of the 'Introitus' there is a sense of linear growth, and in the Kyrie the contrasting characters of the two fugal subjects are emphasised to splendid expressive effect. Giulini's 'Dies irae' does not flash past, but it *does* have musical substance − which is more than can be said for the vulgar pyrotechnics of some performances. Time and again, Giulini avoids the obvious, large-scale gesture, opting for a more searching, three-dimensional approach to bring the Requiem's devotional and dramatic elements to the fore. Of the soloists, Helen Donath is less secure than under Davis, but all sing well, though only Robert Lloyd is outstanding.

Like Richter and Gillesberger, Helmuth Rilling offers a kind of 'half-way house' to authenticity, in terms of fast tempi, clarity of textures and size of forces. I cannot say that I would choose his version to the exclusion of at least half a dozen others, but I must admit to being bowled over by the extraordinary intensity of his Stuttgart choir. Their attack on the 'Rex tremendae' is shattering, and the lines are maintained with awesome power (take note, Tölz boys). The weakness of this performance lies in its poorly matched quartet, and, in particular, the edgy tone of Arleen Augér.

Listening to Janos Ferencsik's recording, one could well imagine oneself in the nave of a cathedral, probably near the back. This over-resonant acoustic suits his reverential reading but tends to blur the music's rhythmic contours, making everything sound slower than it actually is. Even so, it is possible to hear the lack of unanimity of his otherwise accomplished choir on such words as 'excel(chel)sis', and to note that his soloists are frequently below par — and pitch.

The washy acoustic rather takes the edge off Nikolaus Harnoncourt's original instruments and softens the focus of his choir, but the performance still has plenty of vitality. I liked the quiet start to the Kyrie fugue, and the *sotto voce* 'Quando tremor est futurus' from the tenors and basses in the 'Dies irae', but am less convinced by the way 'Rex' is spat out as if summoning one's dog from a neighbour's garden. Beyer's judicious prunings make the 'Offertorium' feasible at these speeds, though Harnoncourt seems to take issue with the 'Osanna' codas. The soloists are good, though why does Robert Holl need *three* breaths to get through 'Tuba mirum spargens sonum'?

Peter Schreier elicits a rare degree of commitment from singers and players alike, but for me, his interpretation somehow misses the emotional core of the work. The 'Hostias', for example, is slow, and full of stark contrasts, but seems to lack genuine fervour; the 'Lacrimosa' is reflective and gentle, yet the words 'Dona eis requiem' manage to sound oddly forthright; one is struck more by the sheer physicality of the 'Rex tremendae' than by any interpretative finesse. The solo numbers bowl along just a shade too briskly, and though Margaret Price sings exquisitely, I do not find this rather operatic quartet ideally balanced.

Christopher Hogwood's recording must be reviewed in splendid isolation, for he alone uses Richard Maunder's edition, which — unlike Beyer's face-lift — involves major surgery to the score. The results will not please everybody. I do not mourn the departure of the jarringly grandiose D major Sanctus (which Mozart would almost certainly not have sandwiched between movements in E flat and B flat), nor of the elegant, yet vapid Benedictus. Maunder's masterly reworking of the 'Lacrimosa' using a chorale-like texture derived from material from the 'Introitus' is wholly convincing, and the concluding 'Amen' fugue, based on a recently discovered Mozart sketch, is a stunning coup. The book in which Maunder justifies these and a host of less radical emendations is immensely persuasive, and reads exactly as a first-rate 'whodunnit' should; it is only on listening to the music that one becomes aware of the same arbitrariness for which Maunder unabashedly slates the opposition. There is more than a hint of molasses and treacle about some of his reorchestration, particularly at the beginning of the 'Tuba mirum' (which I have never found offensive anyway). The word-setting in the 'Cum sanctis' fugue is a definite improvement, but I fail to hear what advantage a German 6th has over a diminished 7th in bar 45 of the Agnus Dei. The law of precedent − which Maunder constantly invokes − is not always the elixir that turns Süssmayr into Mozart. Nevertheless, I cannot fault the impassioned and eloquent advocacy of Hogwood and his all-male choir. Unlike Schreier's, this is a reading that shirks none of the more uncomfortable issues. The urgency of the singing is constantly accentuated by the sensitive instrumental pointing and the balance is exemplary. This is one of the few recordings I would not wish to be without.

Barenboim's second account has all the expressive subtlety of the Mighty Wurlitzer. I do not really warm to his 'tidal wave' approach to the 'Introitus' and the 'Hostias', nor am I especially taken by the great roar that goes up on 'de ore leonis', and the mannered whispering of 'Qua re-sur-get' (and later, 'hu-ic er-go'). The solo singing teeters on the brink of melodrama but does little to disguise the banality of the Benedictus. Insofar as it offends fewer sensibilities, Robert Shaw's reading, with its attractively blended quartet, Beyer score, and lack of pretension, is marginally to be preferred.

Karajan's 1976 recording surprised many (including me) by its uncharacteristic depth of feeling and expressiveness. Unfortunately, this third time around it seems once again to be a case of the bland leading the bland. The largely wordless chorus is for the most part dominated by the orchestra and the Singverein ladies are *still* unrepentantly flat. The 'Tuba mirum' vies with the worst on record for the quality of its soloists, but that is no reason for the engineers to persuade us that the offending bass − Paata Burchuladze − has been shut in a distant broom-cupboard for the duration of the 'Recordare'. Only in the 'Confutatis' does this dreary performance spring momentarily to life; for the rest of the time it is too reliant on its velvety acoustic and its famous names.

John Eliot Gardiner's version is, in every sense, a revelation. He uses period instruments, heard to splendid and sonorous effect from the first bars of the 'Introitus', delicately phrasing the lithe, trio-sonata-like opening of the 'Recordare', and at the end of the 'Confutatis' − as in *Don Giovanni* − grimly pointing the way to Hell. In clarifying the textures and allowing lines to rise and fall naturally, without distortion, Gardiner frequently heightens our perceptions beyond the purely musical: the stark, disjunct quavers at the beginning of the 'Lacrimosa' seem to bring the human tragedy uniquely to the fore; the 'Domine Jesu' quivers with suppressed tension; the 'Rex tremendae' is majestic but not bombastic; the Benedictus has an ethereal lightness and grace; the Agnus Dei is insistent to the point of desperation. The choral and solo singing is excellent throughout, though Willard White's fruity bass does not blend perfectly with the other soloists. This Requiem may not appeal to the traditionalists, and is short on comfort, but musically, dramatically and emotionally, it is in a class of its own.

Sigiswald Kuijken presents a more eccentric view of authenticity. Unlike Gardiner's, his tempi vary widely; the Kyrie fugue bounces along with great vitality yet the 'Recordare' sounds laboured, and causes breathing problems for the soprano soloist. The clarity of this recording is very striking; nevertheless, I remain unconvinced by the 'Sugar-plum Fairy'-like opening to the 'Introitus', and the Dalek-style articulation in the 'Lacrimosa'. Such self-conscious mannerisms are merely distracting when introduced so sporadically and to no apparent expressive purpose. This is a performance that stands up musically, without needing to draw attention to its authentic designer-label.

After this bracing antidote to Romanticism, I have to say that I much enjoyed the impressive funereal solemnity of Riccardo Muti's epic reading. Its greater dramatic immediacy is apparent in the acrid 'Confutatis', and the ominous, muffled drums of the Agnus Dei. The choral singing is vivid, though in the 'Hostias' the women sound unattractively astringent. Patrizia Pace's cool, incisive soprano does not complement the more opulent tone of Waltraud Meier, but the soloists are pleasingly responsive to the text: I particularly liked the echo-effect of 'statuens in parte dextra' at the end of the 'Recordare'. The Berlin Philharmonic Orchestra provides an atmospheric, if at times under-characterised, accompaniment.

Recorded in the reverberant acoustic of St John's College Chapel, George Guest's interpretation, with its plangent altos and organ-dominated instrumental textures, leaves one in little doubt as to its Anglican pedigree. The treble line is excellent, though not as sustained as that of Gillesberger's Vienna boys, nor as earthy and direct as Schreier's Leipzig sopranos. This reading is not much concerned with drama or terror, though its devotional atmosphere and finely articulated playing and singing make it a strong contender.

In conclusion, what has surprised me most is that, of these forty-four recordings, no two are even superficially alike. The impossibility of selecting a clear, comprehensive 'winner' from among the dozen or so outstanding versions merely exemplifies the point that − as the ultimate subject − death transcends the scope of any single recorded interpretation. Hence I make no excuse in commending not one, but four: strikingly different though their readings are, Davis, Gillesberger, Hogwood and Gardiner seem to me to offer a wholly satisfying synthesis of superb musicianship, unparalleled emotional insight and a marked sensitivity to the Requiem's liturgical provenance.

113

Haydn: *The Creation*

PETER BRANSCOMBE

The Creation tends to bring out the very best in musicians, as innumerable performances by amateur and semi-professional bodies each year make clear — they rise to the challenge and indeed surpass themselves in the service of an inexhaustibly delightful work. Doubtless part of its continuing hold on the imagination of people in an age of materialism, selfishness and little faith lies in the firm trust in God that inspired Haydn throughout his life — variants of 'In nomine Domini' and 'Fine laus Deo' preface and conclude most of his autograph scores. 'I was never so pious as during the time when I was working on the *Schöpfung*', he told his biographer Griesinger, 'daily I fell on my knees and asked God that He grant me the strength to bring this work to a successful conclusion.' This simple faith is nowadays more to be envied than taken for granted; the appeal of the oratorio lies at least in part in that blend of confidence and humility that inspired the composer during his lengthy labours (1796–8), and then in the direction of the performance ('Now I was ice-cold all over, now a hot glow came over me, and more than once I feared I should have a stroke'). This confidence is something that we can briefly share, as performers or listeners, every time the work is given.

Haydn was sixty-five when he wrote *The Creation*, the most loved and most famous musician the world had yet known. The distant models for his oratorio were the great Handel choral and orchestral works whose inflatedly large-scale performances deeply impressed him during his first visit to London. And the story has it that the original of Haydn's libretto had been intended for Handel. Be that as it may, Haydn brought back from his second London visit an English text, perhaps given to him by (or from the library of) Thomas Linley, composer and manager of the Drury Lane Theatre (hence the name 'Lidley' erroneously given as author of the poem in German sources?). The text was skilfully adapted and translated by Baron Gottfried van Swieten, an influential Viennese patron of music, particularly of oratorio; his autograph of the poem (unlike Haydn's autograph score) fortunately survives. From it we know that his marginal notes provided Haydn with advice on how to set particular passages to music; Haydn usually complied. One example must suffice: 'The darkness could gradually disperse during the [opening] chorus, but so that enough of the darkness remains for the instantaneous transition to light to be felt very strongly. "And there was light" is to be said only once.'

Though van Swieten modestly belittled his own share in the achievement, we can see that he did more than merely provide a serviceable adaptation of the English poem; many of the marvellous descriptive and evocative touches in the music – the moonlight, the birdsong, the birth of the animals, the movement of the waters, dawn in Eden – owe much to the librettist, and even when Haydn went his own way, the marginalia affected his thinking. The structure too is van Swieten's: Parts I and II each celebrate three consecutive days of the Creation in a loose fusion of narrative recitative, lyrical solo and choral hymn, while in Part III, with reduction in the narrative element and replacement of solo singing by the 'pure harmony' of the duettings of the first couple in the Garden of Eden, a sufficient measure of synthesis and contrast is provided.

The ideal performance of *Die Schöpfung*, in church, concert hall or recording studio, will be equally responsive to every demand of the score – the orchestral scene-painting, the recitatives, dry and accompanied, the solos, duets and trios, the choral mutterings and the mighty outbursts of jubilation; sonically it must be able to convey truthfully the full dynamic range from both lightly and heavily scored *pp* to the weightiest *ff* outbursts of what were probably the largest musical forces ever yet required by a composer. If the conductor, in alliance with promoter or recording director, opts for the luxury of different singers for Adam and Eve in Part III, then they must be good enough to ensure there is no falling off in the performance of what is often (though unjustly) regarded as the weakest part of the oratorio. If just three singers are to be employed (and three were enough for Haydn), then soprano and bass must be skilful enough to suggest the archangelic quality of Gabriel and Raphael, and then the primal innocence and more earthy quality of the first pair in paradise.

Not surprisingly, rather few performances meet all these demands equally well. But it is a measure of the lure of the ideal performance, and of the inspiring nature of the challenge presented, that almost all the complete recordings convey most of the essential features. When we bear in mind that the very first recording was made in 1949 (and issued in 1953, the year of the first conquering of the highest of physical peaks), and that in the intervening forty years at least thirty commercial recordings of it have appeared, we should recollect that there are dangers in over-exposure, that we may run the risk of taking the work's availability for granted, and that in consequence a performance (let alone the playing through of records in the home) may lack that special sense of occasion that our ancestors had to wait patiently for. Nevertheless, of very few recordings of *The Creation* could one say that they lack conviction or distinctiveness. One surprising feature, given the fact that Haydn simultaneously set the German and English texts of the poem, is that only two of the recorded versions are sung in English.

No work, not even *Messiah* over half a century earlier, so swiftly captured the enthusiasm of the musical public, nationally and internationally; Haydn himself arranged the publication of the full score, and in Vienna alone there was a string of warmly received private and public performances – the former naturally using fairly modest forces, the latter employing positively vast bodies of players and singers (180 orchestral musicians and about 220 singers were employed in the Burgtheater on 19 March 1799, nearly a year after the first private performance in the Schwarzenberg Palace on 30 April 1798). The temptation to use forces of a comparable size in the recording studio can easily lead to congested sound and poor balance; interpreters seeking to model their account on one of Haydn's own performances have preferred to concentrate on the ones using more modest forces: Kuijken (1982) an orchestra of 45 (using period instruments) and a chorus of only 28; and Harnoncourt (1986), who in his accompanying essay specifies the Tonkünstler-Societät performances of December 1799 as his model, follows Haydn's example in basing his orchestra on a string body of 13/12/7/6/4. Such details must not distract attention away from the first priority, which Haydn himself would have insisted on: to give the work with the greatest possible attention to style and spirit.

The central place of *The Creation* in our musical heritage is perhaps exemplified by the echoes and pre-echoes it contains of works by other composers: Handel might be regarded as godfather to the whole work; specifically, the chorus 'Stimmt an die Saiten' ('Awake the harp') in Part I is the most Handelian in style. The glorious depiction of Eden that opens Part III, as well as several other moments in the oratorio, indicate Haydn's love of his late friend Mozart's *Die Zauberflöte*. And where would Weber have been in depicting the anguished plight of Max in *Der Freischütz* without the example of the minor key *Allegro moderato* section of Uriel's aria with chorus, 'Nun schwanden vor dem heiligen Strahle' ('Now vanish before the holy beams') in Part I? Such examples could be multiplied – but at the cost of implying that *Die Schöpfung* is important other than for its own unique qualities.

So spoiled have we been by superior recorded performances of *Die Schöpfung* over the last twenty years that it is hard to imagine how eagerly the first-ever version (made in 1949) was awaited – and how disappointing sonically it turned out to be when it at last came out in 1953. Clemens Krauss with the Vienna State Opera Chorus, VPO and good solo singers produced something special, even if it has to be listened to now with yet more generous ears. For the technical level is depressingly low: uneven balance, soloists right on top of the microphone, and shrill violin tone; *ff* choral and orchestral passages threaten or actually produce serious congestion. The performance

116

is stylistically inconsistent, with just a sprinkling of the required vocal graces and appoggiaturas, and piano accompaniment to the recitatives; the wonderful duet 'Holde Gattin' is omitted. Yet there are many pleasures. Trude Eipperle is a sound Gabriel, and in 'Auf starkem Fittige' more than that; Julius Patzak produces characteristically magical phrases, and gets better as the performance unfolds (the sunrise excitingly described, 'Mit Würd und Hoheit' clear in every detail); and Georg Hann, though he has problems in confining his ample voice and is uneven, impresses time and again. The label on the Super-Majestic pressings names Alois Pernerstorfer as singing the part of Adam. This would account for the unevenness just remarked on. Certainly, the voice of Adam changes for the later section of his music. Friedl Riegler is the Eve. As far as the acoustic allows one to judge, the choral and orchestral contributions are first-rate, and Krauss's direction is majestic yet sensitive, both firm and flexible.

Igor Markevitch directed his Berlin performance from the harpsichord. This is an interesting version if not an outstanding one. Tempi are for the most part well chosen and well sustained, there is no loss of impetus (except to accommodate the rather unwieldy bass of Kim Borg), and the mono recording is never less than adequate, even though there are signs of artificial manipulation of volume levels and the big numbers have rather a 'boxy' quality, with the orchestra receding. Both the St Hedwig's Cathedral Choir and the Berlin Philharmonic are in excellent form. Richard Holm sings boldly though with uneven quality. Easily the best of the soloists is Irmgard Seefried, who is prepared to take the occasional risk and sounds both radiant and tender, with exquisite control.

Mogens Wöldikc recorded *Die Schöpfung* for Vanguard in the Grosser Musikvereinssaal in the mid-1950s, using an orchestra and chorus (those of the Vienna State Opera) of about sixty each. With such a fine choral and orchestral fundament this should have been a grand, insightful performance, supported as it is by pleasing monaural sound quality and remarkably clean pressings. A distinguished group of soloists is in the event less consistent than one had hoped — Teresa Stich-Randall is shrill at times, cautious rather than soaring; Anton Dermota, however, is near his superb best, especially in his first aria. Frederick Guthrie, often under-rated, is a sonorous, stylish Raphael (with appoggiaturas in place — his colleagues should have followed his example), flexible and warmly responsive. Neither Anny Felbermayer's Eve nor Paul Schoeffler's Adam conveys the wonder of Eden, the latter disappointingly suggesting a day on the hustings rather than marital bliss. This lack of emotional commitment highlights the main deficiency of the set.

Jascha Horenstein's recording of 1960 was reissued on four stereo sides a decade later. Regrettably, it has little more than curiosity value. Mimi Coertse reminds us what a blessing she was on the Viennese scene in those years, and the ageing Patzak has incomparable moments; Dezsö Ernster is clumsy and

117

has a nasty wobble. The instrumental and choral achievements of Volksoper orchestra and Singverein are decent but not spectacular. Horenstein, marvellous in so much late Romantic music, hardly conveys the impression that he felt any special affinity with Haydn's score; certainly no sense of wonder, and little of joy, is communicated.

Karl Forster's version, made with distinguished soloists, the choir of St Hedwig's Cathedral and the Berlin Symphony Orchestra, is a mixed blessing. It begins with a dramatic but indecently fast Representation of Chaos; thereafter there is a nice spring to the tread of the choral numbers and good orchestral detail – the recording is congested in places, yet the woodwinds often come through freshly. The resonant acoustic is perhaps responsible for the choice of marginally slow tempi in several numbers. All the soloists (set rather close, and forward) do good things. Elisabeth Grümmer sings her arias with mature yet appealing tone and considerable fluency, Josef Traxel is a forthright if unsubtle (and ungrammatical) Uriel, and Gottlob Frick is warm, dark-toned but clumsy in Raphael's music.

Helmut Koch recorded *Die Schöpfung* for Deutsche Grammophon in 1964, using the chorus and orchestra of the Berlin State Radio. It is another good performance, with several pleasing features, yet hardly in the top class. Gerhard Unger, often thought of as a *Spieltenor*, proves a most musicianly if not especially eloquent Uriel, alert to all but appoggiaturas. By contrast the soprano, Ingeborg Wenglor, is thin and edgy in tone; she has the right ideas, but her technique is deficient. Theo Adam begins unsteadily, but he manages the arias well, with a ringing top F. As a whole this performance fails to take off – Koch controls the choruses with a firm hand, and rhythms are keen, but the recitatives are bare, even bleak. On this evidence he was probably lucky to have a second chance to record the work – which, as we shall see in due course, he took gratefully and to fine effect. Certainly he was not helped in the 1964 version by the over-resonant acoustic and the thin sound in richly-scored passages.

Walter Goehr's 1965 performance for the Concert Hall label is a thoughtful, sensitively shaped reading, with good sound quality (mono) that enables one to appreciate the gravely beautiful contribution of the Vienna Symphony Orchestra and fine, alert singing of the Vienna Academy Chorus. Agnes Giebel is a neat, shapely Gabriel, though guilty of intrusive h's, and taxed by the divisions. Richard Holm reminds us what a sensitive Max he was by his firm, stylish singing of the first tenor aria, with its foreshadowings of the infernal forces in *Der Freischütz*. Heinz Rehfuss, except when Goehr holds back the tempo in 'Nun scheint in vollem Glanze', is a well-focused and eloquent Raphael. There is the usual inconsistency with appoggiaturas, but for its period this is certainly a performance to reckon with, the grand choral numbers going particularly well.

Frederic Waldman's 1965 recording is one of the few to use the English-language text (well, American, with 'Gud' prominent). This is a nice performance, not strongly profiled yet sensitive and well paced, albeit with some over-emphatic phrasing, especially in the recitatives, and – a rare miscalculation – a rather lugubrious pulse for 'O happy pair'. The Musica Aeterna Chorus and Orchestra (the latter kept too much in the background) do very well, and all the soloists give pleasure: Judith Raskin blithe, at times inventive too; John McCollum a flexible, perceptive tenor; and Chester Watson happier with his faster-moving music than with the more statuesque numbers. The voices blend well in the ensembles. The sound quality is on the dull side, with congestion in the mighty climaxes.

Eugen Jochum is represented by two versions of *Die Schöpfung*, an 'official' one made for Philips in 1966, and a radio transmission from fourteen years earlier, which was not issued until 1980. Though the acoustic sounds cavernous, the recording is clean in all but the heaviest-scored passages. This is a less leisurely reading, and with less distinguished soloists, yet Jochum was never other than a fine Haydn conductor. The Representation of Chaos is slowly yet excitingly projected, but Gottlob Frick is set so far back that his opening phrases are murky. He rolls the recitative texts appreciatively round his tongue but is often unwieldy in the arias and ensembles. Agnes Giebel's lively artistry is obvious despite sour high notes in 'Mit Staunen'; she settles to give a poised account of the two later soprano arias. Waldemar Kmentt is variable – from the ringing delivery of his first phrases one hoped for more than one actually gets: the arias both reveal constriction of tone and a lack of evenness. What finally rules this set out of court is its deletion of ten pages from 'O glücklich Paar' (a cut which somehow damages Jochum's earlier live performance less gravely).

That excellent Haydn conductor Karl Münchinger recorded the oratorio for Decca in 1967. It immediately became the preferred version, and its supremacy was not seriously challenged for some years; it remains one of the most desirable of sets. Indeed, so vivid are memories of its first issue that it comes as quite a shock to realise that that event already lies more than twenty-one years in the past. Ray Minshull's Sophiensaal recording is good and true, if a touch rough in the boldest climaxes; careful attention to balance ensures that all the wonderful detail comes through without unnatural highlighting (something one can say of no previous recording of the work). The singing of the State Opera Chorus (in its Pitz years) is firm and joyous, and there is delightful playing from the Philharmoniker. This is a large-cast performance, with Erna Spoorenberg and Robin Fairhurst a somewhat earthbound first couple after the radiant, absolutely angelic singing of Elly Ameling (unfailingly pure and ethereal), Werner Krenn (sensitive, evocative, and in the arias fluent and ardent) and Tom Krause (alert, perceptive and entirely reliable). The conducting of Münchinger is, however, what gives this set its special quality: there is nothing inflexible here, or for that matter unusual – except the directness, the essential rightness, of his insights and his control. A warm, committed, continuously satisfying performance, equally inspired in the moments of calm contemplation, vivid narration, lyrical song, and choral and orchestral grandeur.

Leonard Bernstein's 1969 version with the Camerata Singers and New York Philharmonic has many pleasing features. The quite brisk approach, with no time wasted between numbers, and with a real sense of momentum, is supported by fine choral singing and alert orchestral playing; the woodwinds come over with particular clarity. If there is a criticism to be levelled against the pacing, it is that several of the numbers are taken marginally faster or slower than one could have wished. A harpsichord tinkles away rather ineffectively in the orchestral textures, and there are fussy touches in 'expressive' *ritardandi* and *accelerandi*. The solo singing is variable. Alexander Young sings stylishly and with ringing tone, but Judith Raskin, though quite fiery in attack in 'Mit Staunen' and firmly confident in 'Nun beut die Flur', is hampered by poor German and an apparent unawareness of what her words convey. John Reardon sings decently if with dry tone-quality. The stereo sound is generally bright, though middle frequencies suffer by comparison with rather shrill treble and prominent bass lines.

No performance has as many solo singers as Karajan's 1966–9 recording, the reason being the still deeply regretted death of Fritz Wunderlich before the sessions had been completed. What remained of the tenor music – mainly the recitatives – was nobly and very successfully sung by Werner Krenn. There is no sign in this stately, glowing performance of the length of time that elapsed between the start of the sessions and the final release of the records. There are reservations occasioned by the cuts – small but damaging in the first duet for Adam and Eve, and the devastating ten-page deletion in the second that other recordings have also inflicted. In other respects this is a performance to treasure. Karajan is at his most warm and committed, and his forces rise to the occasion. Gundula Janowitz sings with relaxed ardour and pure line (if without the trills), in agreeable contrast to Christa Ludwig's warmer, earthier tones (she is less happy in the runs). One or two moments of over-emphasis apart, Fischer-Dieskau is a superb Adam, and Walter Berry, despite a few rough high phrases, is a firm, flexible and musicianly Raphael. Most moving of all is Fritz Wunderlich, with his feeling for the drama of the score as well as an easy elegance of line. The Vienna Singverein and Berlin Philharmonic are in glorious form. All that is lacking is a touch more spontaneity – the story told in this work is of the Creation itself, not of polished re-creation.

Helmut Koch's second recording of the work, in 1974 (not issued in Great Britain), used the Symphony Orchestra and choirs of East German Radio. Though his solo singers are of variable quality he directs a perceptively conceived and finely executed reading, marked by judicious integration of tempi, a good ear for texture, and the ability to sustain momentum through to the end of a number whilst conveying an awareness of the contours of the work as a whole. Regina Werner, not otherwise known to me, displays a lovely, unforced line, good breath-control and neat ornaments, though she does have problems with intonation. The ever-dependable Peter Schreier soon recovers from a bumpy start to deliver the recitatives with authority and poise, and he sings the arias with appropriate dignity and exaltation. Theo Adam, cautious in his semiquaver runs, is otherwise sensitive and firm. This is definitely a performance to be reckoned with. It is also above average technically, with clear detail and an attractive sheen to the string tone – once serious pre-echo problems have ceased to haunt the Representation of Chaos.

David Willcocks's peformance of 1974 is an urgent, resonant English-language account of this miraculous score. With the fresh, open timbres of the King's College Choir and alert yet expressive playing from the Academy of St Martin-in-the-Fields it comes over with admirable directness, and there is exquisite detail too – the *divisi* lower strings (inspired second thought of the composer) at God's command 'Be fruitful all, and multiply!', and much tender yet incisive wind-playing. John Shirley-Quirk is equally good as Raphael and as Adam, with clean coloratura, though he might have preferred a somewhat livelier approach to the recitatives. Heather Harper cannot conceal moments of strain in high-lying passages, yet she and Robert Tear (in rather dry voice) both show fine stylistic insight if too few appoggiaturas. The solo voices blend well, and are expertly balanced with orchestra and chorus. The acoustic (King's College Chapel) is of course somewhat cavernous, and the LP surfaces are disappointingly rough.

The award to Günter Wand's recording of the French Grand Prix du Disque seems very surprising on both musical and technical grounds. To dispose of the latter first, the recording is rather raucous, with hiss prominent, and with shrill violin tone. From a stylistic viewpoint it is a very old-fashioned reading; even Schreier, in other recordings of *Die Schöpfung* a sensitive advocate for essential vocal gracing, is constrained to avoid appoggiaturas; once or twice the strain shows. He is below his best in the arias too, not helped by Wand's slow tempi. The soprano, Jeannette van Dijck, displays a neat, girlish voice that tends to sound harsh above the stave. Theo Adam is dependable but stilted, the recitatives in particular are stodgy. The Gürzenich Choir and Orchestra are good, the former reliable if a bit beefy, though the challenge of the final chorus is well met. Balance favours the solo trio in the concerted numbers, where a rather husky quality clouds definition; the timpani reverberate dully. Wand shows awareness of the dramatic elements in the score, but the slower tempi are inclined to drag. Disappointing.

Wolfgang Gönnenwein is surely underrated in Britain, yet his Vox set of *Die Schöpfung* is not likely to help him make the breakthrough in popular estimation. His reading, with the South German Madrigal Choir and the Orchestra of the Ludwigsburger Schlossfestspiele, is forthright and also dignified, with very good work from choir and orchestra. The delivery of the recitatives is sometimes mannered, yet numbers like the ones depicting the birds and beasts are finely characterised. Ornamentation is inconsistent but unusually adventurous. Helen Donath is in lovely voice, very neat if lacking an air of primal simplicity of the true Gabriel. Adalbert Kraus displays a round, free tenor voice and a nice sense of style. Kurt Widmer sings well but is inclined to exaggerate in the search for expressiveness; he is at his best in recitative. The recording is of mixed merit: the open, resonant acoustic can lead close to distortion; on the other hand balance is good and detail tells. A purchaser could well feel cheated who bought this three-disc set only to find the ten-page-long cut in 'Holde Gattin', which leaves side 6 with only just over thirteen minutes of music.

Antal Dorati's proudest monument is his pioneering achievement in recording all Haydn's symphonies and most of the Italian operas. He also made impressive recordings of the two late oratorios. His *Die Schöpfung* was made in The Kingsway Hall in December 1976, and it is very pleasing – though not, I think, quite in the short list of the four or five finest versions of all. There are a couple of curious textual matters: in the duet 'Von deiner Güt' (No. 30) the oboe enters half a bar after the normal place; and the recitative for Adam and Eve that follows it, a *secco* in the editions of the score known to me, is here endowed with string figuration for part of its course. Lucia Popp is an affecting, rather effortful Gabriel, Werner Hollweg a forceful Uriel in the more extrovert parts and less interesting in the more contemplative music. Kurt Moll too is happiest when he can sing out, or where he can bring due solemnity to Raphael's lower-lying phrases. This is one of the performances that import vocal reinforcements into the Garden of Eden. Helena Döse is a gusty, mature-sounding Eve, Benjamin Luxon a sympathetic, even-voiced and crisp Adam. There is lovely playing from the RPO, nicely detailed in the recorded ambience, and the singing of the Brighton Festival Chorus is unfailingly alert, balanced and idiomatic. Dorati directs the whole with dramatic insight, love and spirit, and he himself leads from the harpsichord. There is a refreshingly stylish approach to appoggiaturas, though an unusually wide dynamic range and some jerky accents do provide mild distractions, as does the occasional extreme of tempo (the *Andante* of No. 2 is taken uncomfortably fast).

Rafael Frühbeck de Burgos's 1978 recording with the Philharmonia Chorus and Orchestra is definitely one of the better versions, yet in the final analysis I find it just a little lacking in character and impact. It begins marginally too slowly for full clarity and awe to be maintained, though the nobility and restraint of José van Dam's Raphael (marred somewhat by untidy runs later) helps make the case for a very leisurely tempo. There is excellent choral singing, and the recording comfortably accommodates both loud and soft extremes. Donath is pure-voiced and agile, though a bit fluttery in 'Nun beut' (where the tempo is on the slow side). And Tear is musicianly and neat, if uningratiating in tone. Balance and blend within the solo trio is excellent, and rhythms are springy, the whole performance quietly perceptive.

Eugen Jochum's live performance of *Die Schöpfung* at Munich in 1952 (issued in 1980) sounds as though it took place in winter, to judge from the coughing. It is a constricted, bass-heavy transfer, and detail is often unclear in the true *pianissimi*, though the timpani bang away like a shed-door in a winter gale. In almost every other respect this is a very special performance, the direction strong and sympathetic, the vocal soloists ardent and inspired, and the Bavarian Radio Chorus and Orchestra rising to the occasion with sensitivity and precision (though they suffer from casual microphone placing). The Representation of Chaos is taken unusually slowly (as if Haydn had never countermanded his original *Largo assai*), but is well sustained. Irmgard Seefried sings Gabriel's music with radiant voice and long phrases (and a reluctance to take ornaments); her Eve, apart from dazzling runs in the solo passages in the final chorus, which are anyway more angelic than human, sounds not inappropriately more earthbound. What a splendid tenor Walther Ludwig was! He brings ringing tones and precise articulation to the recitatives and an engaging lyricism to the arias. Hans Hotter combines all the virtues one could desire: easy, dignified delivery, unaffected intellectual penetration, weight of utterance without a trace of ponderousness. There are the tiny flaws almost inseparable from a live recording, yet the splendours of a special occasion make one forget all else.

Though the sessions for Neville Marriner's recording took place in January 1980, before the general introduction of digital techniques, remastering of the analogue originals has produced sonic excellence to equal the musical glories of the performance. This taken all round is the finest of all the thirty versions I have listened to, my clear first choice to have washed up with me on to my desert island shore by the 'outrageous storms'. It stands the test of time superbly; the freshness of Haydn's vision, and the subtlety of his realisation of it, are conveyed with wonderful directness by Marriner and his forces; the rhythmic buoyancy and sure sense of shape and timing are outstanding. For almost every other version one's enthusiasm is tempered by reservations about one or another of the singers, or by technical shortcomings; here all is worthy of the 'new created world'. The solo trio is outstandingly fine, both individually and in consort: Edith Mathis serene yet vibrantly involved, Aldo Baldin tempering bold, youthful timbre with maturity of insight, Fischer-Dieskau in excellent voice and almost completely subduing the inflectional mannerisms that diminish his natural directness and dignity of utterance. The singing of the Academy's Chorus does great credit to Laszlo Heltay's training: it is signally full-toned, precise and alert to the implications of the text. The

Academy of St Martin-in-the-Fields has never given more pleasure than it does here, with playing of sparkling clarity, warmth and spirit. Marriner favours a very fast tempo for the *Più allegro* of 'Die Himmel erzählen', yet the result is wholly invigorating, with no hint of a scramble. The fugues have that clarity and cumulative force that is such a feature of a wholly rewarding performance. Since the recording is also all one could hope for − direct yet spacious, finely balanced and with a bloom that never inhibits clarity − the recommendation becomes irresistible. It's not just that Marriner and the Philips recording team do nothing wrong, they really do everything absolutely, memorably right.

Helmuth Rilling's recording, taken live at a concert in Tokyo on 20 April 1974, became available in Britain through Studio Import in 1982. The audience was slow to settle, so that the opening evocation hardly emanates from the primeval void, but thereafter one can have few complaints (the sudden cut-off at the end of Part I − to forestall applause? − is a pity). Rilling and his Gächinger Kantorei and Bach Collegium of Stuttgart are very experienced exponents of the German choral tradition; their involvement and their musical skills are patent. Arleen Augér conveys a proper sense of wonder in her music, equally happy at the two extremes of Gabriel's range, and equally assured as Eve in Part III. Niklaus Tüller's name is unfamiliar, but he easily outsings many a better-known Raphael, producing an easy flow of even tone, considerable flexibility, and due weight for the recitatives; only in 'Nun scheint in vollem Glanze' does he show signs of human fallibility. The tenor is Adalbert Kraus, confident and smooth in his delivery, just a shade over-ambitious in some of his added ornaments in the recitatives. Balance is fine, so that the important wind details make their proper impact; overall this is an enjoyable, impressive achievement.

Solti's *Creation*, using Chicago forces, has the distinction of being the first version in digital sound. Further distinctions are Sir Georg's fine, sweeping direction, and some particularly lovely singing from the Gabriel, Norma Burrowes. Her timbre is splendidly appropriate, almost androgynous, yet she is full of life as well as imaginative in her ornamentation. The other soloists are good in a more conventional way. Rüdiger Wohlers is careful in narration, eloquent in aria, and James Morris, if dry-toned and slightly dull in recitative, sings out finely in the lyrical numbers. Sylvia Greenberg and Siegmund Nimsgern are a worthy Adam and Eve, though Greenberg's diction is casual. The Chicago Symphony Orchestra Chorus is yet another very fine body to record the work, and the Orchestra too gives delight with its polished, eloquent playing. A harpsichord tinkles away to good effect almost throughout (distractingly in the wonderful wind-writing for the nightingale), and the whole performance has clearly been thought through carefully and lovingly. Just occasionally one may question a tempo (the *Allegro* of 'Holde Gattin' uncomfortably fast, for instance). And it was a miscalculation to go for such an artificial-sounding reduction in volume for the description of the moonlight

124

before 'Die Himmel erzählen'. This set is certainly in the 'special mention' class, but like so many others it does not command the listener's absolute approval.

Armin Jordan is hardly a name to conjure with outside France and Switzerland, yet his 1982 version is one of the very best we have had. Its first source of strength is Jordan's sure feeling for tempo (slow at times, but well sustained), texture and phrasing; he can rely on the excellent Lausanne Chamber Orchestra which won its Haydn spurs with the Dorati opera series, and the Pro Arte Chorus; and he has a strong team of solo singers. The recorded quality is not quite as steady as one could wish, but it is fully adequate, and balance is well judged. If the tempi are often on the fast side, that is all to the good − there is no unseemly haste, and certainly no sentimental lingering. Margaret Marshall is one of the few Gabriels who sound equally accomplished and at home in all three arias; her pure vocal line, neat ornaments and rapt delivery are alike splendid. Would that she, rather than the unlovely Horiana Branisteanu, had sung Eve too! Eric Tappy is not at his best throughout − there are quavery patches and bulges; he does manage the high-lying ornaments gracefully at the end of 'Mit Würd und Hoheit', however, and his bold singing is most refreshing. Kurt Rydl is a noble, slightly gruff Raphael, and Philippe Huttenlocher leaves nothing to be desired as the father of us all. This is a committed reading, stylistically admirable, with a proper sense of climax in the mighty choruses.

Gustav Kuhn's recording for German Harmonia Mundi chronicles a particular occasion, the 250th anniversary of Haydn's birth, celebrated by a performance in the Old University, Vienna, where on 27 March 1808 Haydn himself heard the work for the last time. At its best this is an outstanding performance, yet it is uneven − some miscalculations over tempi (at both extremes), and a less than ideally steady contribution from Roland Hermann as Adam (Walter Berry too shows signs of strain above the stave in Raphael's music, as well as some rather stolid phrasing). Augér is the pick of the soloists; indeed her Gabriel is among the very finest, with delicate ornaments, long breaths, radiant tone and keen insight (adequate as is Gabriele Sima as Eve, I longed for Augér here too). Schreier is his usual reliable self − one of the few Uriels with a true trill, and with distinction in his every utterance. Balance is a problem − the small string body of the Collegium Aureum is thin, even scrawny at times, and though the winds come through strongly, the perspectives are variable. Kuhn keeps the performance moving, with incisive fortepiano realisation in the recitatives; a marginally more spacious approach to the great choral numbers (the Arnold Schoenberg Choir in athletic yet also majestic form) would have reduced the danger of overloading. Apart from some coughs in the introduction to Part III the audience is pleasingly forgettable until the merited applause bursts in at the end. This is certainly a shortlisted version (though surface noise is an intermittent problem).

125

Karajan's live recording from the 1982 Salzburg Festival shows joy in the dynamic possibilities of the new techniques of digital recording – quality is very high, apart from some shifts in balance, and for the most part convincing, over a very wide sonic range. Tempi are deliberate, at times slow to the point of straining even the Vienna Singverein and Philharmoniker. The grandest numbers take on a glowing and rich quality, without any loss of excitement. Mathis begins some way below her best; the vocal honours go to Francisco Araiza, especially when he can sing out (the description of the first moonlight is almost crooned), and to José van Dam, who is dark-voiced, firm and noble of utterance. Momentum is lost towards the end of the marvellous water aria in Part I, yet Karajan sustains the pulse to convincing cumulative purpose through the last three connected numbers in Part II. An uneven achievement.

Given ever-rising production costs, and perhaps also as a reaction against the aseptic 'perfection' achievable in studio conditions with the splicing of takes, it is not surprising that in recent years several versions of Haydn's mighty oratorio have been recorded live at concerts. Sigiswald Kuijken made his version during the Festival of Flanders in October 1982, and very delightful it is. The performance began during the tail-end of a torrential storm, and its sound (and a few not unrelated tensions?) can be detected early on. Thereafter, despite some minor distractions from the audience, the digital recording (which used only four microphones) is of high quality. La Petite Bande and Philippe Herreweghe's Collegium Vocale of Ghent are splendidly alert, fresh-toned and precise, and there is abundant dignity in the more sombre passages. Neil Mackie easily holds his own in an unusually pure-voiced trio (which in Part I is set rather far back in the aural perspective), and the Raphael, Philippe Huttenlocher, is archangelic indeed. Krisztina Laki sings with a wistful beauty that is most affecting. 'Authentic' performances are often assumed to be fast and spiky, or full of expressive bulges. Not here: several of Kuijken's tempi are on the leisurely side, and certainly there is no lack of warmth and expressiveness about the singing or playing. Disciplined enthusiasm is a hallmark of this truly distinguished, indeed revelatory reading; it is one of the best of all.

A few days before Christmas 1957 Joseph Keilberth conducted *The Creation* with the Cologne Radio Symphony Orchestra and Chorus. Since there is no distraction of audience noise I assume that Melodram may have obtained an off-air tape of a studio performance. The sound is congested, though wind detail comes over well. Keilberth favours slowish tempi, but momentum is well sustained (loose strands, for instance in 'Die Himmel erzählen', are an intermittent disappointment). Annelies Kupper makes heavy weather of Gabriel's higher-lying music, with some ugly singing in 'Nun beut die Flur'. Josef Traxel displays his ringing tenor to advantage, though the sunrise is woodenly handled. Josef Greindl troubles me with his wide vibrato, and he is rough in the D-major section of 'Rollend in schäumenden Wellen', and hardly copes with the second half of 'Nun scheint'. As the first pair, Käthe Kraus and Walter Berry are on the whole distinctly good. Hardly an idiomatic account, all told, though there is a welcome rhythmic lilt to several of the numbers, and the choruses go well.

Nikolaus Harnoncourt's recording is one of those made at a live performance, this one at the Konzerthaus, Vienna, on 10 and 11 April 1986. It is – inevitably, with this conductor – a challenging, and in many ways a highly original, reading, based on careful study of the first printed edition and the engraver's copy. This gives us many fascinating and unfamiliar touches in phrasing, accentuation, and even instrumental line (the recitative bidding the beasts and fish to be fruitful here lacks the familiar *divisi* violas and cellos which were later added to the bare double-bass line that Haydn, following van Swieten's instruction, originally wrote). But this is emphatically not a performance just for the specialist. Harnoncourt, unlike Kuijken, is not using period instruments but the polished and assured Vienna Symphony Orchestra in a reading of vivid life and complete conviction. The recitatives go wonderfully well, paced and enunciated with natural regard for syllabification and meaning; a particular joy is Herbert Tachezi's imaginative and poised fortepiano realisation, in the fully-scored numbers as well as in the plain recitatives. There is abundant rhythmic life to the whole performance, and the contribution of Erwin Ortner's Arnold Schoenberg Choir is alert, perceptive and full-throated. The soloists give much pleasure both singly and in ensemble: Edita Gruberova offers exquisite ornamentation which is always properly subordinate to line and phrasing; Josef Protschka is a delightfully ardent and musicianly Uriel; and Robert Holl is a majestic and uncommonly supple Raphael as well as a warm and credible Adam. The recording is atmospheric and very clear, audience noise is minimal. A superbly rich and rewarding issue, lyrical and also dramatic.

Bernstein's second version was made at a concert in the Herkules-Saal, Munich, in June 1986. It seems to me to add up to rather less than the sum of its parts – which include exquisite detail from the Bavarian Radio Symphony Orchestra, bold yet owing to the recorded perspective somewhat cloudy singing from the Radio Chorus in Part III (reversing the balance favoured earlier), and intermittently fine contributions from five soloists who hardly live up to their reputations. That Kurt Moll is permitted on two occasions to take an unmarked octave drop is perhaps symptomatic of the seemingly insouciant approach that informs the whole. There is little of Haydn's wit and spirituality in Bernstein's phrasing, or in his choice of tempi, which are now faster, now slower than expected, and the dynamic range also exceeds the golden mean. Generalised expressivity relieved by idiosyncratic touches would be too harsh a judgement, yet I do feel a lack of that wonder and self-forgetting commitment with which musicians (and audiences) approached *Die Schöpfung* in the days when a performance, let alone a recording, was a special event. The Munich audience is silent and attentive, and the recorded quality, apart from shifts in balance, is spacious and sympathetic.

Rafael Kubelik's recording, like Bernstein's made in the Herkules-Saal with Bavarian Radio forces, was taken a full two years earlier, though not issued in Britain until nearly four years after the sessions had taken place. It too is rather disappointing, Kubelik revealing no obvious empathy with the score. Individual beauties stand out; overall it is a curiously lifeless account, with little feeling for the pattern and flow of the music, some uncomfortably slow tempi (and one or two hurried ones), and rather little solo singing of true distinction. Margaret Marshall is again above criticism — her radiant and unfailingly neat singing as Gabriel is among the few joys of Parts I and II. Vinson Cole either sings out lustily, or else (in the introduction to the scene in Eden) he croons softly (and with poor command of the German). Gwynne Howell is lugubrious and unwieldy. Bernd Weikl as Adam is not much happier, but Lucia Popp, without being at her most precise, is a lovely Eve. Fine orchestral detail from the woodwind players in particular is a plus, and the Bavarian Radio Chorus sings out boldly, if without subtlety or inspiration. It is of a piece with this lacklustre account that appoggiaturas are in short supply, and that the harpsichord realisation is fussy. The recording, if over-resonant, is clear and comfortable both in balance and dynamic range.

The most recent account is a recording made in March 1988 at Minnesota and using almost entirely American forces. The Saint Paul Chamber Orchestra and Minnesota Chorale are conducted by Joel Revzen. The performance is well sung, well played, well recorded. But it has rather little in the way of special quality. One or two of the features that do stand out are distinctly odd — the Representation of Chaos is almost the slowest known to me (Jochum's 1952 reading has an even broader *Largo* here, but it is more meaningfully sustained), whereas the Introduction to Part III, also marked *Largo*, is almost indecently fast in the new recording. Neither Neil Rosenhein (Uriel) nor John Cheek (Raphael and Adam) is more than adequate, the tenor being raw-toned, and in his higher-lying phrases under strain, the bass inclined to spread, particularly in slow-moving passages. Orchestra and chorus are alert and reliable, though the chorus does not come through well, and the German pronunciation is unidiomatic (with feeble final consonants). The recitatives, with fortepiano as keyboard continuo instrument, are neatly done. The first real touch of distinction comes with no. 4, 'Mit Staunen sieht das Wunderwerk'. It may smack of jingoism for a Briton to say so, but Lynne Dawson's radiant, sensitive and deeply moving account of Gabriel's music lifts the performance on to a different, truly angelic plane.

Disappointing as it is to conclude this chronological survey of complete performances with some rather unimaginative versions, we can turn in conclusion to magical (and some less magical) older versions of single arias

recorded by some of the great vocal artists of the 78rpm era. It is probably simplest to take in chronological order the versions that were available to me of the five solo arias, in the order in which they occur in the
oratorio.

'Rolling in foaming billows' was recorded by Robert Radford *c*.1927
(D 1213) in a style that strikes the modern listener as uncomfortably old-
fashioned: rather gruff delivery, constricted low notes (in spite of which
he sings the unauthentic octave drop at the close), and with a sharp drop
in tempo for the D-major section. Peter Dawson (C 2099; RLS 1077053)
three years later is altogether much more successful. He produces a smooth
bel canto line, has a sure technique, and though he too takes the major-
key section slower than one could wish, he does so with a confidence
and a sense of ease that are endearing (both singers make a sizable cut).

'With verdure clad' is the more popular of the two solo soprano arias
with both German and English singers; it has been very fortunate on disc.
Florence Austral was first in the field with a performance that, though
disfigured by cuts, is attractively if rather primly sung (D 775; 1923).
Elsie Suddaby (D 1287; 1927) by contrast is fresh, alert and greatly to
be admired, despite the fact that she was positioned too close to the microphone. Another lovely performance (in German) is that by Ria Ginster
(Homochord H-8758; LV 190; 1929); she sings with purity, precision
and effortless ease. Dora Labbette (DX 334; *c*.1934) is lively, but the good
impression created by her clean and rounded tone is to some extent dis-
sipated by her mannered rubato; like most of the singers, she makes a
large cut towards the end of the aria. Isobel Baillie, with the Hallé Orchestra
under Leslie Heward, sings the aria uncut (DX 1052; RLS 7703; 1941);
she does so with a staid purity that is in its own terms very affecting –
a slightly faster tempo would have given the interpretation more feeling.
Irmgard Seefried recorded both the arias in November 1946 with Krips
and the Vienna Philharmonic (LX 1011; EX 29 1056–3). 'Nun beut' (with
its recitative) is done with charm, not without some flutter, and at a rather
slow speed that detracts somewhat from the impact. An interesting curiosity
from the CD era is Catherine Bott's performance (Meridian ECD 84080;
1985) of the aria in a recital devoted to Haydn's late years and his British
connection. She sings it in the piano reduction published by Clementi
in 1801. With Melvyn Tan's sensitive accompaniment on a fortepiano
copied from an Andreas Stein instrument she sings expressively, though
not without mannered touches in her phrasing.

I was disappointed by the performance of 'Auf starkem Fittige' recorded
by the admired Norwegian soprano Eidé Norena (DB 5054). She was
in her middle fifties when she recorded it in 1938, and though there are
elegant phrases and some well-executed trills, her intonation is wayward
and the quality often shrill; further, there are hefty and clumsy cuts. In

129

delightful contrast is Isobel Baillie's 1946 version of 'On mighty pens', alertly accompanied by George Weldon and the Philharmonia Orchestra (DX 1392; RLS 7703): unfailingly musical and assured, even if the vocal quality once or twice resembles a little too much the 'tender dove' of which she sings. Irmgard Seefried was at her youthful and radiant best when she recorded the aria with Krips in the same year; the reissue of LX 1245 in the LP set EX 29 1056−3 was a long-awaited treat for two generations of admirers of this very special artist.

Not having been able to hear the performances by Nelson Eddy and Norman Cordon of 'Now heaven in fullest glory', I can comment only on Norman Walker's recording of the aria with its two preceding recitatives, *secco* and *accompagnato*, made in 1947 (DX 1407; HLM 7009). The singing is resonant and forthright, if less than memorable.

'In native worth' − or rather, 'Mit Würd und Hoheit angetan' − seems by a long way to have been the first number from *Die Schöpfung* to find its way on to disc. Felix Senius recorded it in 1908 or 1909 (Anker 04979; SYO 11) with a surprisingly eloquent orchestral accompaniment; the disappointment is that Senius's noble delivery cannot avoid sounding ponderous; he sternly checks the conductor's understandable desire to speed things up a little. Tudor Davies recorded this number around 1923 (D 839) with bluff, manly singing of impressive directness and no great subtlety; and Julius Patzak gave a characteristically distinguished reading in the early 1940s, with sympathetic and expressive accompaniment under Fritz Busch − a fine, ringing performance, with every syllable as usual crystal-clear (Rococo 5348). Other fine performances were recorded at around the same period. Aksel Schiøtz, with accompaniment under Mogens Wöldike (DB 5271), is neat, even-toned but just a bit dull. Webster Booth prefaces 'In native worth' by its recitative (in a rather clumsy orchestral arrangement); the aria has clarity of line and of diction, but the ornaments are rather limp and tentative (C 3571). Richard Tauber also sings the number in English (well, what he imagined to be English). There are lovely phrases, but also a rather jerky, mannered delivery, and no trill. Nevertheless this is a distinctive performance (R 20543).

As the patient reader will have noticed, there are many wonderful individual achievements among the thirty-odd complete performances; what a glorious cast (with worthy understudies) one could assemble for the performance to end all performances! However, there is hardly a set that lacks some distinction; and eight or ten can be confidently recommended. The conductors who seem to me to have something very special to offer are − in chronological order of recording-dates − Eugen Jochum (1952, issued 1980), Karl Münchinger, Neville Marriner, Sigiswald Kuijken and Nikolaus Harnoncourt. David Willcocks's version will admirably suit anyone who is particularly keen to have a recording in the English language

130

Haydn: *The Creation*

To choose between the very best is an invidious, even impossible task. Kuijken, if one is looking for a 'period' performance (but this holds its own with the finest of the more traditional readings); Harnoncourt, if one wants an historicising approach but modern instruments. If I had to give up all but one of my recordings of *Die Schöpfung*, I am fairly sure I would keep the Marriner.

Haydn: *The Seasons*

DAVID CAIRNS

In the great concluding achievement of his career Haydn looks back and celebrates his love of nature and his deep sense of man's harmony with the natural world. As Robbins Landon remarks, *The Seasons* is a valedictory work; Haydn is 'describing things – the first glow of dawn on the horizon, the hazy heat of midsummer, the ripe fields of autumn – which will soon retreat beyond his grasp'. Yet they are evoked with all his former energy and zest. Though Haydn complained that the task of setting Baron van Swieten's text exhausted him, there is little sign of it in the music. Age left its mark not on the freshness and vigour of his creativity but only on the character of the work, which culminates in the wonderful bass meditation on the brevity of human life, followed by the jubilant final chorus expressing the composer's sure faith in the eternal life to come.

It may be that Haydn would have liked van Swieten to have given him more opportunities for this sort of thing, as he had done in *The Creation* (on which the two men had collaborated a few years earlier), and less of what Haydn himself disparaged as 'Frenchified trash' – the musical imitation of frogs and other fauna and flora which he said was forced on him. Haydn also said that *The Seasons* was inferior to *The Creation* because it was about peasants whereas *The Creation* was about angels. But *The Creation* too has its roaring lion, its 'flexible' tiger and its crawling worm. In any case such momentary imitative effects are no more incompatible with deep feeling and a serious exploration of the subject than are the nightingale and quail and cuckoo in Beethoven's *Pastoral* Symphony. Nor do angels necessarily inspire better or more richly enjoyable music than peasants.

These particular peasants may be shadowy as individuals – only old Simon 'whistling o'er the furrowed land' and shooting with his eager pointer has any solid identity – but all three have some of the loveliest music Haydn ever wrote, and all play their part in his grand scheme. To quote Robert Anderson, 'the bewitching Jane, up with the sun and shrewd enough to send any young lord packing; Lucas, her sterling swain willing to back his choice against

132

the gay and painted city girl; industrious father Simon, watchful for the thunderstorm, the scenting spaniel, his daughter's honour, or the opening of heaven's gates − the Baron's three characters gave Haydn every chance to roam once more the countryside he loved and to produce at 69 a joyous masterpiece for the enchantment of a sorry world'.

The Seasons is a classic in German-speaking countries, but in Britain it has always lagged behind *The Creation* in popularity. Its greater length is against it: at nearly two and a half hours it makes a very long concert. (Cuts are common even in Austria and Germany, and several supposedly complete recordings unfortunately reflect the practice.) Nevertheless a British performance is the outstanding one among the twelve versions reviewed in this chapter. Of the conductors, it is Colin Davis who gets closest to the heart of the work and has the most thorough understanding of its character and style and its widely varied content.

Davis's sense of tempo is almost infallible. Time and again he sets a pace that can only be described as totally natural, combining strong momentum with the space needed for the evocative nature-painting to make its effect. To take one example, no other version so fully realises Haydn's picture of intense noon-day heat in the beautiful E major cavatina for solo tenor in 'Summer' (No. 13). The multitudinous detail of the score, brought out by scrupulous attention to dynamic contrast, is delightfully vivid. There is an infectiously uninhibited relish in Haydn's portrayal of the noises of the countryside − the sudden ponderous bellow of contra-bassoon, trombones and lower strings as the cattle return to their sheds (18), the crack of the gun's report (24), in which Davis's balancing of the instruments emphasises the flash of the explosion (flutes and oboes) as well as the bang (bassoons, drums, strings).

At the same time the human emotions − fear of the storm, joy in the abundance of the harvest, conviviality by the fireside, the excitement of the chase, the happiness of a fine summer evening − are communicated with a warmth of sympathy and a humour that are authentically Haydnish. Performed like this, there's not a dull bar. Orchestral and choral work, by BBC forces, is first-rate. The four horns in the great hunting chorus (26), led by the late Alan Civil, are as splendid as the best that Vienna or Berlin can produce, and the contrast in dynamics when the four divide into two pairs gives a depth of perspective and sense of distance that none of the other versions can match. There is a good trio of soloists. Heather Harper is perhaps a little mature for the saucy Jane but full of character and vocally accomplished; Ryland Davies makes a lively and pleasing Lucas (despite occasional flatness at the top of the stave); and John Shirley-Quirk is the best of all the Simons under review, the most vital, the most alive to the varied demands of musical characterisation and dramatic situation: listen only to the tense, atmospheric *pianissimo* of his opening phrase in the shooting aria, 'Behold along the dewy grass' (24). The performance is sung in English, which makes

133

sense in the English-speaking market, given that van Swieten's text was translated from the English of James Thomson, but which has obviously cramped its selling-power. Though this is the best *Seasons* on disc, Philips (at the time of writing) have not yet reissued it on CD.

In comparison with it, Nikolaus Harnoncourt's version — the most recent and one of the better ones — sounds a trifle cerebral, academic, and this in spite of being the product of a live performance (or rather, two combined) and not of the studio. It is full of telling detail, like the admirably prominent dotted figures on the trumpet which are an important part of Haydn's orchestral texture but which are often obscured. The bright sound of the Vienna Symphony trumpet is a continual joy. Altogether, the score's rich variety of orchestral, and choral, colour is well served. We are never left in any doubt about a decisive entry of clarinet, horn, trombone or timpani, as happens, frustratingly, in some of the other recordings.

As a pioneer of 'authentic' performance Harnoncourt has always worn his authenticity with a difference; purism has not been allowed to interfere with personal, often idiosyncratic artistic choice. The trouble is, the choice can be very idiosyncratic. Some of his tempi in *The Seasons* are slower not only than current historical orthodoxy would approve but than what musical common sense suggests. The *allegretto* bass aria with horn obbligato (10) at the beginning of 'Summer', for instance, is much more like *andante*, and the singer, Robert Holl, finds it highly awkward to sing. The discreet tinklings of the continuo fortepiano in the arias are extremely irritating; this is one period detail I could happily do without. It ruins the lovely descending chromatic passage for strings in the soprano aria in 'Summer' (15). The aria is very nicely sung by Angela Maria Blasi, the best of Harnoncourt's soloists.

The performance also boasts a chorus, the Arnold Schönberg Choir, that is well above the average. Some of the big choral numbers are done with considerable power (though the peasants get drunk surprisingly genteelly in the great final movement of 'Autumn'). The Spinning Chorus, 'with its effortless pivoting from D minor to A minor, C major, E minor and back to D minor, and its whirring orchestral accompaniment' (Rosemary Hughes), is particularly well done, at a perfect tempo, and so vividly that you can see the turning wheels. In sum, the performance has many virtues without quite persuading me that Harnoncourt has the instinctive musicality to match the fertility of his ideas.

Nonetheless it is easily the best of the Viennese versions. In Karl Böhm's set, the work's status as a national monument is the cue for a routine jog through the notes. The opening bass aria of 'Spring' (4) — heavily accented, po-faced — sets the tone. There is no sense of celebration, no response to the unique character of the work, no joy. The potentially fine male soloists, Peter Schreier and Martti Talvela, are encouraged to bawl unfeelingly. Gundula Janowitz alone, in lovely voice, sings well. The sopranos of the Vienna

134

Singverein are a very poor lot, their high notes intolerably woolly. And the Vienna Symphony is not recognisable as the orchestra that plays so alertly and crisply for Harnoncourt twenty years later. Half-way through 'Autumn' Böhm seems to mellow under the influence of Haydn's genius and allows some charm and humanity to creep into his performance. The last few numbers of the work have much more character, as one would have expected of a conductor so steeped in Viennese music of the period; but they come too late to save it.

The third recording from Vienna, conducted by Clemens Krauss, is a much looser, less regimented but also in places more human affair. It dates from 1942 and suffers from a primitive recording. The quality of sound is generally coarse, there is some pitch-wavering, and the woodwind and the solo soprano (Trude Eipperle) tend to distort. Krauss makes a big cut in the opening chorus of 'Summer' and another in the final number of 'Autumn', the choral passage where Haydn shows the newly harvested grape going to the heads of the revellers (Eulenburg miniature score pp. 447–57). He also sets some very slow tempi, which – to take one example – reduces the Prayer ('Spring', 6) to a wearisome trudge. Both the performance and the recording improve during the final part, 'Winter'. The strength of this version is the singing of the solo tenor, Julius Patzak – as so often, a model of clear, expressive diction combined with firm melodic line. Georg Hann starts at a relentless, hard-voiced *forte*, like many of the basses under review (how can they fail to respond to the sheer good humour of Haydn's whistling ploughman – as Friedrich Schorr responds on his famous 78rpm record, DB 1564, now on Pearl CD 9318), but in the second half of the work he relaxes and sings with more variety and character.

There are four recordings from Germany, spanning a period of about twenty years. The two more recent, conducted by Herbert von Karajan and Wolfgang Gönnenwein, both date from the 1970s. Gönnenwein's, with the Bavarian Opera Orchestra and the South German Madrigal Choir, is a likable, musicianly but slightly kapellmeisterly performance. Nothing is inadequate; nothing makes you sit up. Speeds are generally sensible, and the music's rustic roots are not forgotten (there is a nice touch of village fiddlers about the violins' semiquavers in the 6/8 section of the drinking chorus, and the customary 40-bar cut is particularly regrettable). The quality of the version is raised by its soloists: Edith Mathis fresh and radiant, Nicolai Gedda as stylish as usual, and Franz Crass the best of the basses apart from Shirley-Quirk.

In comparison with Gönnenwein's account, Karajan's performance gives a very sumptuous impression of the work. The Berlin Opera Chorus is weak (its sopranos only less woolly than the Vienna Singverein's), but the Berlin Philharmonic Orchestra is predictably superb. The playing of both strings and woodwind in the opening chorus of 'Spring' (2), and equally in the duet for Hanne and Lucas (22), is marvellously delicate. Equally beautiful are the

135

strings in Simon's meditation at the end of 'Winter' (38). The blaze of sound which Karajan summons for the rising sun (11), after a perfectly gauged crescendo, surpasses in power and physical excitement all the other versions. Throughout, there is the closest attention to contrasts of dynamics and texture. What I miss in this richly upholstered account is the simplicity of Haydn's evocation of country life. There are no peasants in sight, not even the somewhat idealised peasants that Haydn portrays. Some of the movements, too, drag uncomfortably. Karajan is no Furtwängler, and the very slow speeds he occasionally chooses – for instance, in the introduction to 'Summer' (9) or the soprano's B flat aria (15) – are not successfully sustained. His soloists – Walter Berry, Werner Hollweg, Janowitz (in less good voice than on the earlier Böhm set) – are inferior to Gönnenwein's. But it remains in many ways an impressive performance.

The two earlier versions from Germany both date from the 1950s. Ferenc Fricsay's, with the RIAS Symphony Orchestra and Chamber Choir (augmented by St Hedwig's Cathedral Choir), suffers like Krauss's, though not quite so badly, from poor recording. Here the main problems are that the level fluctuates, dropping drastically just before a big number (once, with ludicrous effect, in the middle of the final chorus), and the orchestra sometimes recedes so far that brass and drums become inaudible and you would swear they weren't playing.

Some of Fricsay's tempi in the devotional numbers are unconvincingly slow: their slowness, you feel, is due to simple lack of vitality, not to religious feeling. He is very free, indulging in generous rallentandi and mannered pauses, and sometimes changing the speed during a movement (though that may be due to careless tape editing). On the other hand, in the recitatives, which are apt to be treated with misplaced reverence, Fricsay has a welcome tendency to get on with it. His chorus, without being remarkable, is better than some; his soloists – Elfride Trötschel, Walther Ludwig, Josef Greindl – are average.

Fricsay makes the traditional cut in the drinking chorus and shortens the chorus in praise of hard work (20) by about sixty bars. Walter Goehr's version from Hamburg NDR Orchestra and Chorus (1950s) is more heavily cut, to accommodate it on two LPs instead of the usual three. The opening Trio and Chorus of 'Autumn' (20) and the soprano's beautiful cavatina in 'Winter' (30) are removed altogether, and sizable chunks disappear from Nos 6, 11, 22, 26 and 28. This is a pity, as the performance, though a little matter-of-fact and lacking in poetic atmosphere, and not especially remarkable for its soloists, has strong musical virtues, emphasised by a recording which, though shallow, is immediate and unusally detailed. Goehr has a keen ear for orchestral colour and shows a care for clarification of texture and the parity of woodwind and strings that anticipates the period-instrument movement. This is the only version in which you can hear at all clearly the offbeat oboes in the recitative which describes the rounding up of the hares (25). Tempi are mostly well

136

judged; the *adagios* never fail to flow; the opening section of the wine chorus is taken for once *allegro molto*, as marked, and made to sound right at that speed.

A little of Goehr's pep would have enabled Vittorio Gui to get much more of the work onto his two-disc set: the recording, made in Italy during the war, manages to include only about half of the score's thirty-nine numbers. On the other hand the performance would have lost the dreamlike gait and lazy lyricism which give it its curious attractiveness. The gentle playing of the Italian Radio Orchestra of Turin, the pleasantly sleepy chorus from the same source and the liquidity of the Italian language, especially in the mouth of the charming, intensely feminine Gabriella Gatti, bathe the music in an unaccustomed light. It may not by Haydn, but it is an antidote to the more unfeeling interpretations from north of the Alps.

Beecham made his recording of *The Seasons* when he was nearly eighty, an age at which it is difficult to summon the physical energy and stamina needed to animate large choral and orchestral forces and keep them together. It too has its sleepy moments when the ensemble grows slack. The Beecham Choral Society — as a former member, I am sorry to have to say it — is inclined to be sluggish in attack, and sometimes falls behind the beat. The recording also has its cuts: one in the recapitulation of the opening orchestral 'Passage from Winter to Spring' — no one else makes this one — and one in the Lucas/Jane duet (like Davis, Beecham gives the work in English). Sir Thomas rescores the *secco* recitative for strings and touches up the orchestration here and there, adding chimes to the horns' representation of the evening bell in the concluding number of 'Summer' (Fricsay, for that matter, adds percussion in the passage where Haydn depicts the croaking frogs). In short, this is not vintage Beecham. But it has characteristically lovely and rousing things in it. The soprano aria 'O how pleasing to the senses' (15) is beautifully done, and sung charmingly by Elsie Morison, the best of the three soloists. The Royal Philharmonic's horns are splendid in the hunting chorus, and in the spinning scene Beecham's rhythm sets the wheels whirring irresistibly, though the chorus drags.

Neville Marriner, the third British conductor to record *The Seasons*, could do with a bit of Beecham's affectionate warmth. Up to a point his version is admirable. After so many laboured German and Austrian performances Marriner's approach is refreshingly direct. He understands, for instance, that the ending of the spinning chorus is far more effective when played without *ritardando*. With smaller than usual, and excellent, orchestra and chorus — Academy of St Martin-in-the-Fields — everything can be heard (the drums, muffled in many recordings, are nice and loud). Each tempo, when it begins, seems right. But Marriner doesn't do much with it. In the Prayer (6), for example, the music keeps stopping and starting. And there is less atmosphere, less poetic awareness in his performance than in the best of his rivals'.

137

The work, the first half of it at least, doesn't seem to mean so much to him as it does to Davis or to Dorati. The soloists too are a little disappointing: Mathis less radiant and secure than in the earlier Gönnenwein recording, Fischer-Dieskau showing his age badly in 'Spring' and 'Summer' (though he recovers form in 'Autumn'), and Siegfried Jerusalem merely competent.

As the work proceeds, however, Marriner warms to it. 'Autumn' and 'Winter' have a more rounded, genuinely animated feel to them; the tempi, instead of being merely superficially correct, come to life. All the same it is Antal Dorati's performance that seems to me to come nearest to challenging Colin Davis's. Dorati recorded *The Seasons* in the late 1970s, after he had recorded the complete symphonies, and the affection and sense of identification learned during his years of absorption in Haydn's world and style are palpable in nearly every number. (He also restores, presumably under the guidance of Robbins Landon, two passages which Haydn cut from the introductions to 'Autumn' and 'Winter'.)

This is not to say that Dorati never miscalculates. The bass aria with horn obbligato (10) moves a little cumbersomely (and Hans Sotin is generally a rather laboured, unsubtle soloist). The tenor's cavatina in 'Summer' (13), though quite nicely sung by Werner Krenn, is a little slow, the *allegro* conclusion of the Hanne/Lucas duet a little breathless. Occasionally, in all the loving care and refinement Dorati lavishes on the enchanting score, I find myself wishing for less restraint and more earthiness. But he captures better than anyone except Davis the innocence of Haydn's vision. Beecham's old orchestra, the RPO, plays beautifully for him – the oboe obbligato in the B flat soprano aria is memorably done, an exquisite foil for Ileana Cotrubas's finely shaped, if less than ideally bright and focused, singing – and the Brighton Festival Chorus is among the best of the choirs. Dorati and his performers are particularly successful in the scenes of communal endeavour and celebration – the hunt (constructed out of traditional horn calls), the flax-spinning, the wine harvest – where Haydn creates popular music of Gargantuan energy such as must have satisfied even his exacting spirit.

Beethoven: *Missa Solemnis*

JOHN STEANE

The *Missa Solemnis* is exceptional among great choral works in its dependency upon a great performance. Byrd's four-part Mass can be sung by anxious amateurs and still move its hearers. Mozart's Requiem is given every year by countless school choirs and choral societies and still manages to impress. Bach's Mass in B minor would sound like great music even if sung by a few sopranos and a bass gathered round the piano on an old-fashioned 'musical evening' at home. But the *Missa Solemnis* is different. It makes almost superhuman demands of its performers, and the best that they can give will not amount to much unless an outstanding conductor is there to control the massive forces, give them a vision and inspire them. Of the orchestra it demands unrelaxing attention to details of rhythm, accentuation and balance. The five soloists (four singers, one violinist) have immense opportunities, including (for the violinist) the equivalent of a concerto's slow movement, but the responsibilities are correspondingly awesome. For the soprano soloist in particular, Beethoven's demands upon high notes and breath-control are almost extortionate. The greatest challenge of all confronts the chorus. No choir can attempt the *Missa Solemnis* without a strong tenor line: that sets a formidable condition for a start. By the end of the evening all voices are likely to feel sung out. 'One more page and I'd have died' they say to each other when it is all over. Again the soprano part is cruellest. Beethoven thinks nothing of sending them up to the B flat, there to stay singing 'Et vitam venturi' till they begin to wonder whether the life to come may not be more imminent than previously supposed. News that this is to be the work chosen for the local Philharmonic's winter concert can be enough to make loyal sopranos who also have family duties decide that now is the time to book for the long-deferred holiday in Australia.

Ultimately, once the forces are assembled, success depends on the conductor; and even a conductor whose mastery of the score is as unquestionable as his experience in handling such occasions will not fully succeed unless there is some rare communication of the spirit. In a way that it shares with hardly

139

any other music, or at least to a degree and with an intensity which surpasses any other music I can think of, it has to speak with the voice of the composer. Its form may be lyrical, fugal or whatever, but behind every page Beethoven's own voice presses for utterance and understanding. When, in the course of a highly efficient, perfectly sincere performance, one never seems to catch that voice, then the work can seem like so much sound and fury signifying much less than it portends. That can be depressing. Yet it is perhaps the necessary obverse of the exhilaration which a great performance can bring. In this respect it resembles *Fidelio*, which can be the greatest of all operas, but only once or twice in a lifetime.

The record companies, not surprisingly, have tended to think twice before committing themselves to a new version. An exception was made in the case of Herbert von Karajan, who would want to remake it at frequent intervals. He recorded it four times. Other conductors have recorded it more than once, most notably Toscanini, but on the whole it has been a matter of once for all. It is also not surprising to find that a number of versions require not much more than honourable mention while some scarcely merit that.

Among these is a crude if enthusiastic performance under Heinz Wallberg made with the Vienna Symphony Orchestra and Chorus. At least the choir is well forward in the balance, indeed rather too much so; many modern recordings have it too far recessed. Unfortunately the prominence finds them wanting in several respects: leads are sometimes smudged, the style is often rough and over-emphatic, the tone too heterogeneous. In the tenor line, for instance, individual voices obtrude, and the sopranos wobble tremulously on high. The soloists include Teresa Stich-Randall, whose hooty, fruity soprano is not effective here till the Agnus Dei. Murray Dickie is the patently inadequate tenor, making a feeble, flat effect in the 'Et incarnatus est' and simply *being* flat in the 'Et homo factus est'. Frederick Guthrie brings an infirm tone to the solo at the start of the Agnus Dei, which leaves Nedda Casei, the contralto, as the sole satisfactory member of the quartet. Such saving grace as the performance has is the sense it conveys of wholeheartedness in the chorus: they hit out for all they're worth. Not even that can be said for the shallow, badly balanced recording under Werner Kloor. The Pfalz Philharmonic Orchestra lacks weight, the Landau Oratorio Choir lacks tenors, and the soloists distinguish themselves chiefly by securing a place right in front of the microphone and singing loudly throughout. The style is prosaic, with a relentless thumping of the fugues and a minimum of shaping or shading.

In quite a different category is the performance conducted by Günter Wand, yet this also joins the company of rejects, partly because of the hard, gritty quality of recorded sound, and partly because the soprano soloist is not up to her fearsome responsibilities. This is not through any gross dereliction of duty but simply a matter of the voice, which is neither steady nor resourceful enough. The Cologne Chorus is another that includes tremulous sopranos in

140

its ranks, particularly thin and shaky in quiet high leads such as the 'Gratias agimus tibi' and first 'Et vitam venturi'. The tenors, on the other hand, are unusually strong and firm, so that the attacks on the 'Quoniam' and 'Et resurrexit' sections flash a victory signal and everyone takes notice. A well-paced performance with sensible speeds, it also pays attention to detail, sometimes throwing light on points in the score which several more exciting and eminent conductors leave unilluminated: an example is the way in which, in the second 'Et vitam venturi', the 'Amen's in crotchets and at the interval of a sixth are tossed from one voice-part to another. In the blissful 'Dona nobis pacem' too, the parts are admirably clear, while the orchestra (the Gürzenich Symphony) almost visibly purrs in the introduction. Yet shortly after that, at the *presto*, instead of intensifying, the performance lapses into workaday adequacy and the great work ends without the drive and feeling for dramatic tension that must be kept going if the last pages are not to seem like the prolongation of a movement that has run its course.

Antal Dorati has things to say about that *presto*. The recording of a live performance given in association with IPPNW (International Physicians for the Prevention of Nuclear War) includes some extracts from a rehearsal, with Dorati giving memorable instructions at this point. 'Play as brutally as you can', he says. The passage is 'böse', 'angry', full of 'disorder' which he then defines as 'inner disorder'. In performance the *presto* is very firmly held together and disorder never threatens; yet the instructions were surely right, and they often come to mind when a conductor treats it all too genially, almost as though it were a high-spirited scherzo. Careering through one key after another, stabbing at the second and fourth beats of the bar, it runs wild like the very spirit of anarchy, to be pulled up short only by a dictatorial military restoration of order which provokes the agonising cry of 'Dona pacem'. This is the kind of vision a conductor has to impart. One certainly feels that Dorati had it, and there is also a real sense of devotion to the task by both orchestra and choir. The European Symphony Orchestra was probably better able to give what the conductor wanted of them than was the University of Maryland Chorus, which, despite obvious dedication, lacks body and incisiveness in the men's voices. The soloists are also a somewhat uneven team, but led by a soprano with a most beautiful voice, Tina Kiberg, who rises with lovely tone and complete security to her high phrases in the Benedictus. It's a pity the recording is not sharper in focus, for in many ways the performance transcends the limitations of its forces.

In performances with original instruments, limited forces are deliberate and numerical rather than qualitative. Wolfgang Gönnenwein conducts the Collegium Aureum and South German Madrigal Choir of Stuttgart in a stylish performance issued in 1977, and ten years later the Hanover Band with the Oslo Cathedral Choir under Terje Kvam recorded the work in the Hall of Birmingham University on Nimbus. Both versions, particularly the latter, gain in clarity. Gönnenwein takes special care over the opening of the Gloria, which with a full modern orchestra and the resonant acoustics of a big hall often registers as a noisy free-for-all. Texture is a prime consideration, with fine woodwind playing at the start of the 'Gratias' section, and when the brass enter (as in the 'Consubstantialem Patri' fugato) they stand out with brighter colouring. Such performances can also risk quicker speeds – not always wisely, though, for if the 'In gloria Dei' fugue is taken simply *allegro* (the '*ma non troppo*' ignored) there is a great danger that the quavers of the still faster sections ahead will sound somewhat frantic, as they do here. The Hanover Band, constituted so as to be 'as near to Beethoven's forces as possible', take well-judged, moderate speeds in the Gloria, the Credo opening less spaciously than usual, and the end of the Agnus Dei broadening so as to prepare us for the ending of the whole work. Soloists in both of these recordings do their job well enough to muffle complaints about such matters as the imperfect focus of Sylvia Geszty's soprano in the Gönnenwein recording and the lack of body in Andrew Murgatroyd's tenor with Kvam. Gönnenwein's solo violinist in the Benedictus is placed so far forward that it is rather a relief when he stops playing; Roy Goodman is excellent in the Nimbus recording. Neither of these performances possesses the incandescent quality of the best, but Kvam and the Hanover Band have their moment of inspiration and brilliant achievement: this is in the syncopations and dancing rhythms of the second 'Et vitam venturi' fugue and the extraordinary intricacies of accent in the 'Amen's which follow.

Coming now into the middle ground, where admirable performances tend to be overlooked because they have no single distinguishing feature, we can find much to enjoy in Kurt Masur's recording issued in 1973, Colin Davis's of 1977 and Robert Shaw's of 1987. Masur has the excellent Leipzig Radio Chorus, which gives of its best and takes the challenge in its stride. In fact there may be too little sense of challenge in the performance, a rather matter-of-fact style of affirmation, gaining intensity only towards the end in the Agnus Dei. Anna Tomowa-Sintow (or simply Tomowa, as she was here near the beginning of her career) produces some bright-edged tone, with Peter Schreier ever reliable on the tenor line. Davis's care is to lift the *Missa* free from the weight that accumulates round the 'solemnis'. Without reducing status or depth, he sets the tone by avoiding all portentousness in the opening of the Kyrie. The Gloria begins in splendour but with nothing frenetic in the rush to praise. In this performance we realise how much of tenderness and lyricism there is, and it is characteristic that when the trumpets break into the Agnus Dei they seem to strike not the dreadful note of war so much as an awe-filled intimation of the Apocalypse. In comparison with, for instance, Solti's there is less drama, and yet the more beneficent sweetness that, with Davis, follows the dark intrusion brings its own reward. His soloists form a well-integrated quartet, recorded in sensible balance with choir and orchestra, the total effect placing the listener in a seat further back in the hall than the front-row

142

position of others such as Solti and Ormandy. The London Symphony Orchestra would have benefited from a more forward recording of the wood-wind, and the choir from a refinement of tone among the men's voices.

The excellence of the Atlanta Chorus constitutes a principal attraction in Robert Shaw's recording. It is perhaps at some point toward the middle of the Gloria that a feeling begins to grow within the listener that this is something better than the competent but commonplace performance which the opening seemed to suggest; certainly that conviction grows from the start of the Credo. The dancing 'halleluia' figure after the 'Et resurrexit', then the steadily increasing fervour of the 'Et vitam venturi' from its quietly hopeful initial statement, are all finely caught. In the Sanctus at 'Pleni sunt coeli' Shaw is faithful to the direction *Allegro pesante*, the point of the *pesante* becoming clear when the ensuing *presto* takes off with such a light-footed spring. The best of the soloists are the pure-toned soprano, Sylvia McNair, and the steady Tom Krause. Recording is well-balanced if slightly wanting in edge and brightness.

That is also true of the performance under Helmut Rilling: the recorded sound is comfortable but hardly exciting, clear but not bright. Working with the Gächinger Orchestra and the Stuttgart Bach-Collegium, Rilling instantly establishes confidence in the devotion of spirit which his musicians will bring to the work. He has a particularly fine choir, well furnished with tenors, who give a sturdy lead to the 'Quoniam' section of the Gloria and 'Et resurrexit' in the Credo. His soloists, too, are well balanced, with Andreas Schmidt equally at home in the high tessitura of the Benedictus and the deeper bass of the Agnus Dei. Competence is never in doubt; it's the *nature* of the devotion that has its limitations, rarely taking the form of any specific insight and tending to withdraw an active producer's hand from the drama of the Mass.

In both of these respects it contrasts with an English performance under Jeffrey Tate released in the same month of 1990. Brighter recording, smaller forces, sharper direction, all ensure a more alert response from the listener. In the 'Christe eleison' section of the Kyrie, Tate gives detailed attention to phrases which Rilling more or less allows to run their own course and speak for themselves: following the contours of each voice-part, making more of developments in orchestration, he reveals much more fully the life of the move-ment. As the Gloria approaches its exultant conclusion in the 'Amen' section Tate leads rejoicingly into the festival, and in the Agnus Dei as war and peace vie for supremacy the tension is headline-news: Rilling's milder, more generalised manner (though not lacking in inner strength) makes it more possible for the listener to disengage, or view as from a distance. In textual matters, too, Tate has the edge (soloists for the Osannas, focusing more clearly than Rilling's full choir, appoggiaturas for the soloists in the Agnus and so forth). Where the results are more questionable is in the character of the solo quartet and in the balance of the overall recorded sound. Carol Vaness is sometimes too much of a Verdian soprano here, and her vibrancy does not match well with the 'straighter' tone of Waltraud Meier; and the ample, rich bass of Hans Tschammer assorts ill with the drawing-room tones of Hans Peter Blochwitz. In the total balance, Tate's soloists are well forward, with the choir recessed, and while this perhaps makes for a more interesting perspective it also causes one to be more aware of listening to a recording. With Rilling one does at least feel part of an audience hearing through their own ears and not through what is fed to them through some other source.

Rilling, Shaw and Davis all present recordings to live with. Some of the more starry versions merit less claim on our attention. Eugene Ormandy has the Philadelphia Orchestra keenly defined and well forward, the soloists in a glaring spotlight, and the choir subject to some unnatural-sounding manipulation by the engineers. The Singing City Chorus numbers some edgy sopranos among its members, the soprano soloist herself, Martina Arroyo, having an unsuitably fast operatic vibrato. Cesare Siepi's rich bass is welcome in the Agnus Dei, and the others, Maureen Forrester and Richard Lewis, do well throughout. The performance has been carefully prepared and is often exciting without ever quite going to the heart. Giulini with the New Philharmonia Choir and London Philharmonic Orchestra presents a complete contrast. Everything here is in a mellow light, the recorded sound dully reverent, the chorus somewhat withdrawn, the speeds slow. Heather Harper and Janet Baker are excellent, Robert Tear is not flattered by the close recording (better with Davis in Philips) and Hans Sotin's big voice sounds uncharacteristically dry. Much is warmly felt, with sometimes a touch of the greatness that one hoped to find more pervasive. There is also something lax about it emotionally and technically, and this is shown up by comparison with Solti and the Chicago Symphony Orchestra and Chorus. The opening of the Kyrie, for instance, finds Giulini loose in attack and detail, the movement almost sluggish: Solti is not just brighter in sound and firmer in cohesion but has far more of the composer's own energy. His 'glorificamus te' is exact and excitingly dramatic, Giulini's heavy in an outworn oratorio style. The fault in the Solti is in the excessive prominence given to the soloists, including the violinist in the Benedictus. Choral and orchestral work is splendid, and the conductor's taut, decisive style helps to produce one of the most dramatic and compelling performances of the Agnus Dei, with its frightening interruptions of drum and trumpet.

When these recordings first appeared they were inevitably compared with Klemperer's of 1965. Almost as invariably, comparison favoured Klemperer, whose version has a scarcely contested place among the classics of the gramophone. This is in spite of an uneven team of soloists. Waldemar Kmentt, the tenor, is hardly in a league with Söderström and Talvela, who is surely not the right bass to sing the high-lying Benedictus. Söderström herself proves to be a less happy choice than seemed likely, for her vibrancy, as caught in

144

recording, like Arroyo's, is not appropriate. The contralto, Marga Höffgen, has wider vibrations in the voice, almost a beat, and the two do not go well together. All of this is widely held to be no more than an incidental weakness in an inspired performance, a stammer in the divine speech. My own principal objection is to part of the speech itself, which is heavy and dogmatic as soon as it begins to talk in fugue. 'In gloria Dei Patris' is marked *Allegro ma non troppo* (but still *allegro*) and *ben marcato* (but not *pesante*). Klemperer weights it laboriously, as he does the Credo fugues. At other points too when the performance should dance for joy, as in the 'Et ascendit' section (*allegro molto*), if it dances at all it is as though in clogs. Nor, after digital remastering for the latest CD, does the recorded sound satisfy – except in one vital respect, and that is in the vivid, forward placing of the choir. The Philharmonia Chorus sings magnificently, and with this closer contact their music communicates in a much more human way. There is also of course humanity in Klemperer's conducting; mastery too. This is felt in the very opening, the unanimity, the fine shading; and humanity runs deep in the Preludium and 'Dona nobis pacem'. One other small but exceptional point is that Klemperer follows the direction for 'Pleni sunt coeli' to be sung by soloists, and though it might be impractical in the concert hall it works well under recording conditions.

'Nothing ... shakes my conviction that Klemperer comes nearest to the heart of the matter, to the truth, the grandeur and spiritual intensity of Beethoven's vision.' Alec Robertson wrote this towards the end of a review (*Gramophone*, October 1971) of the version which probably comes nearest to satisfying a taste which finds such fulfilment in Klemperer's. It is by the Concertgebouw Choir and Orchestra under Eugen Jochum. The difficulty is that 'the heart of the matter ... truth ... spiritual intensity' can hardly be demonstrated as matters of fact, though to my mind Jochum has them. They desert him a little in the 'Dona nobis pacem', but that observation is another that can scarcely be put on a factual basis beyond mention of a slow speed for the initial *allegretto vivace*, which in turn moderates the *allegro assai* and *presto* thus reducing pace and tension. Otherwise Jochum is much more than merely sensible, and he is certainly that. In the Kyrie, for example, he controls very finely the rise and fall of the 'Christe elelson' section, and the 'lift' given to it by the pizzicatos. Then in the lingering final pages the suspensions have the same tender quality we find in the most sensitive and imaginative of the other conductors who have recorded the *Missa*, but instead of sounding just a little like Mahler (or even Elgar) they are Beethoven through and through. Some of Alec Robertson's detailed criticisms, such as inaudibility of the timpani just before the martial passage in the Agnus Dei, are obviated by more modern reproduction, but his point holds about the muffled tenors in the 'Et incarnatus est', a fault shared by many other versions. Jochum's soloists do well both individually and as a quartet, and choral and orchestral work is admirable.

We come now to conductors who have recorded twice, and to Karajan, who has made a habit of it. I should add that there are also two versions by Klemperer though essentially only one survives. A recording in mono squeezed onto a single LP dating from 1952 has poor soloists, an unpleasant sound quality and what was probably inevitable distortion. Karl Böhm's first recording was a great deal better than that, but it too had evident limitations and it comes as no surprise that he should have wanted to remake it. In his second, the recorded sound is certainly improved and better spaced, but the performance itself has less obvious superiority. The Vienna Philharmonic does not improve on the Berlin Philharmonic, and the State Opera Chorus with its wavery sopranos proves no good substitute for St Hedwig's Cathedral. Among the soloists, Christa Ludwig in place of Marianna Radev, and Martti Talvela for Josef Greindl represent progress. Anton Dermota and Wieslaw Ochman do about equally well with the tenor part. While Maria Stader was an able soprano in the first version, Margaret Price in the second is magnificent. She provides the single excellence in this recording, for Böhm does not take us up the mountain with him even if he has been there himself. Good judgement and careful control mark the limits here, and little that is special – excepting perhaps a lovely touch in the Benedictus – remains in the memory as a lasting distinction.

With Karajan there is always something special. Or rather, he is continually supplying evidence of some new specific insight, or trying out different balances and combinations in an apparent pursuit of the definitive. With four recordings of the *Missa* made over a period of nearly forty years, one might look to follow a kind of musical pilgrimage, a steadily maturing musical wisdom and spiritual ripeness. No such clear picture has formed in my mind, however, and I'm not even sure that the last recording is a great improvement on the first. That was made in 1958, with the Philharmonia Orchestra and the Vienna Singverein, the choir he used throughout. Elisabeth Schwarzkopf, sometimes ideal, is clearly taxed by her part; Ludwig and Nicolai Gedda are both excellent (Ludwig being one of the few soloists to take the long 'Miserere' in the Agnus Dei without a breath, at a slow tempo too); and the bass, Nicola Zaccaria of La Scala, provides a welcome Italian richness of timbre. Always one is aware of a purposeful hand and an observant eye. In the Kyrie, *sostenuto* has been noted as the prevailing term and there is an effect of careful, deliberate steps; then on the last pages a dreamy dying-away, the slow, half-sad ending of a summer's day. Speeds are sometimes extreme: the 'Quoniam' section of the Gloria, for instance, is very slow, taking its cue from the *maestoso* direction at the expense of the *allegro*. In all his versions he makes a special point of the flute in 'Qui propter nos homines', a vivid perception of its role (though at least as well realised by Jochum). It's a pictorial imagination that Karajan has, the 'Osanna' of the Benedictus swaying like a censer in slow-motion, the orchestra imparting a rustle of spring to the start of the 'Dona nobis pacem'.

146

What holds it back is a lack of excitement, a feeling that one must always be in control, and finally something very like exhaustion settling upon the company. A strange mixture then, for there is also no doubt that this is a recording of genuine distinction.

Over the two mid-period recordings (1966 and 1974) the soprano of Gundula Janowitz shines clear and fresh as early-morning sunlight. The first has probably the finest quartet of soloists in all these recordings. In addition to the gift of the sumptuous voice, Ludwig (again Karajan's elected mezzo) provides an imaginative treatment of the hushed Agnus Dei in recitative marked *timidamente*. Fritz Wunderlich has the ideal firm lyricism for the 'Gratias' and very nearly the ideal breadth and authority for 'Homo factus est'. The bass part always presents a problem: it really needs two soloists, a baritone for the Benedictus and a deep bass for the Agnus. Walter Berry, more baritone than bass, earns gratitude for his consistently fine tone and firm placing. Predictably excellent is the playing (in both recordings) of the Berlin Philharmonic; so too the mixed quality of the Vienna choir, its sopranos tremulous and feeble in quiet leads, especially in the 1966 version. That and the rather fuzzy recording of the choir may have been one of the reasons why Karajan wanted to remake. He seems not to have greatly changed his interpretation, though certain specific points are clarified. His handling of the 'Christe eleison' now has special effectiveness, giving prominence to the pizzicatos, bringing up the brass more strongly to fortify the crescendo, and caring imaginatively for the rise and fall of the solo voices. This was the recording which introduced the young Agnes Baltsa to most listeners, and she makes a notable impression. But this version too has its drawbacks as a recording, the rushing start of the Gloria being unpleasantly blurred and the whole thing creating an uneasy awareness of hands on the dials of complicated machines. In both performances there is also the element of self-consciousness that tends to be inseparable from a choice of extreme speeds, with disillusionment setting in when the Credo opens at a plodding pace rather than with the confident stride of faith.

The fourth and final version, appearing in 1985, has its own troubles. Lella Cuberli, of whom much was expected, lacks the tonal energy and resilience for the hurly-burly (however effective in the more ethereal passages) and her intonation causes a twinge or two. Again the modern vice of recessing the choir frustrates Beethoven's will to human contact; all too often the choir provides an accompaniment to the orchestra. Yet there is an extra depth here after all, felt most in the stillness which comes upon the last pages of the Kyrie and in the profound meditation of the Preludium.

With the grave gods and the philosophers Karajan was on speaking terms, but not, I think, with Dionysus, whose familiar in music is Leonard Bernstein. Possession means one thing to Bernstein, another to Karajan: to Karajan it was a thing to keep, while to Bernstein it is a happening. Beethoven of course is in control sure enough, but there are moments when the *Missa* seems possessed in the dionysiac sense. Something stopped Karajan from going along with this; for Bernstein, to be taken up in the flood of divine madness and at the same time to be the medium, the one through whom all the others can enter into it, may well supply the greatest satisfaction that conducting can offer. That, at any rate, is the impression he makes and I personally am often wary of it: but in this work it is an essential if the full greatness is to be unleashed. With Bernstein's two recordings a new element comes into play, and it is what all of the recordings up to now have lacked. Perhaps in a grim sort of way it was there with Klemperer (certainly the choir catches the 'possession') and perhaps it found another but less pliant medium in the compulsive energy of Solti. But Bernstein bears the thyrsus here, as Toscanini did before him.

This does not mean that all is well. In the first recording the Westminster Choir has more than its fair share of tremulous sopranos, and in the second the Hilversum Radio Chorus, a thoughtfully trained body of singers, has less than its rightful share of the microphones. In both the soloists are too close. Though the speeds usually gain ready acceptance, the 'Qui tollis' of version two seems a good deal slower than *larghetto*, the Credo in both hasn't much of the *allegro* about it, and the 'Pleni sunt coeli' while very decidedly *allegro* is not also *pesante*. There are several allargandos, not marked in the score but I would say well judged. The first quartet of soloists is excellent, with Kim Borg giving one of the best of all performances of the bass part. The second has Edda Moser occasionally edgy but strong in feeling (a dramatic cry for peace in the Agnus Dei), while René Kollo supplies too many unwanted aspirates but has the requisite incisiveness. Kurt Moll is another excellent bass. The great strength of both performances is that, sparingly but tellingly, they achieve ecstasy. The places are the right ones, usually the end of a movement but also in the Preludium. The dramatic conflict in the 'Dona nobis pacem' is at its most intense, and the tireless dancing of the second 'Et vitam venturi' at its most inspired.

All the same, responding strongly to the Bernstein performances and admiring so much in many others, I still know what it is that I am really wanting to hear. The three recordings under Toscanini known to me differ considerably from one another yet speak with essentially the same voice, and when listening I cannot doubt that it is Beethoven's.

This is in spite of all sorts of attendant horrors. None of the three versions will do as recorded sound. The most modern of them and the only one issued commercially has that dry acoustic Toscanini loved and which certainly plays a part in conducting what is usually referred to as the electricity of the performance. But it does not make comfortable listening. The others are from the Carnegie Hall in 1940 and 1935 respectively, the earlier of them having presumably been pirated from a broadcast in which much sounds odd and

148

a certain amount would be virtually unidentifiable without the score. In the 1940 performance a sudden squeak disturbs the sublimities of the Preludium, and in 1935 somebody takes advantage of the *pianissimo* 'Et incarnatus est' to whistle cheerily into the microphone. Yet even that strange relic is a treasured possession. Elisabeth Rethberg is the peerless soprano soloist, and Marion Telva (otherwise remembered on records by her duet from *Norma* with Rosa Ponselle) is a fine mezzo (though incorrigible in turning her 'é' vowels into diphthongs). Martinelli is the tenor, always special and memorable, scrupulously moderating his tense, trenchant tone in the quieter quartet work, and just occasionally rather painfully flat (though with the variations of pitch in the recording it is not always easy to tell). And there is Ezio Pinza, whose sonority and dignity of style no defects of recording range manage to disguise: his solo in the Agnus Dei is probably the most beautiful piece of solo singing in all of these recordings. The performance can hardly be judged as a whole, and though I feel it to be inspired the view might be difficult to establish critically. What is observable and interesting as a matter of fact is the slowness of many of the speeds. The Kyrie is amazingly slow, and it is notable that in a section such as the 'Quoniam', marked *allegro maestoso*, Toscanini uncharacteristically (one would have thought) takes his lead from the *maestoso*.

This slowness is in marked contrast to the last of the three. Here, slower passages such as the 'Qui tollis' are restless, and some of the fast sections are set whizzing furiously. The finale of the Credo (the second 'Et vitam venturi') now in all its complexity sounds almost primitive, tribal. At some points, with all its faults, this recording can be the most exciting of all; at others it can be tender, calm, deep. Even so, one may well feel that something halfway between the forward pressure of this and the stately measure of the 1935 version might prove ideal, and that is borne out in the marvellous performance of 1940 issued on records by the Toscanini Society.

This is the one in which all elements seem to be in equilibrium. The soloists look exciting on paper and if anything exceed expectation in the event. Zinka Milanov favours a broad *portamento* but it has a certain grandeur, and her tone is ravishing. Bruna Castagna brings the vividness of the operatic stage to her pleading in the Agnus Dei. Jussi Björling and Alexander Kipnis sing like gods. Choir and orchestra are keyed-up, responsive and precise. Uncannily, everything has the stamp of a Toscanini performance. The recorded sound is quite astonishingly clear even if not entirely well balanced. The total effect, it should be said, is not adequately represented by references to 'electricity', though the term is apt enough to denote one of the ingredients. There is nothing inhuman, or mechanistic, but on the contrary the widest range of emotions and the most deeply felt. 'From the heart, may it go to the heart': Beethoven's famous inscription is a simple enough proposition on the face of it. The trouble is that between the hearts there intervene choirs and orchestras, celebrated soloists and conductors, and where recordings are concerned their producers and technicians. Usually the cardiac transmission, from the pioneering effort of Bruno Kittel on 78s in the 1930s onwards, has been subject to interference of some kind, but on 28 December 1940, bypassing some modern channels of communication, the line was quite remarkably clear and direct.

Mendelssohn: *Elijah*

ALAN BLYTH

Elijah has been somewhat out of favour now for a number of years. The seemingly mild treatment of the biblical story has counted against it in an age which prefers something bolder than Mendelssohn's benign idiom. But, though the work may be overlong and some of its choruses excessively anodyne, it has a certain conviction and character all its own. Our problem may be that we are hearing a work written in 1844 through ears that have encountered all the Victoriana Mendelssohn engendered, but the kind of music he was composing was, at the time of its writing, comparatively new in idiom: Bach and Handel heard, as it were, through the light of mid-nineteenth-century harmony. However that may be, Elijah himself, in sure hands, emerges as a real, strong character, at once vehement, despairing and humane, and the rest of the solo writing is on the highest level of Mendelssohn's achievement. Besides, when the work is sung in the language (German) for which the notes were composed and with really purposeful and clean choral singing, as happens on the Sawallisch set, recorded in Leipzig with its genuine Mendelssohn tradition, his most favoured oratorio emerges as a picture newly cleaned, alive and immediate, not least because Sawallisch follows Mendelssohn in assigning the passages for concerted solo voices to these and not, as happens in most other recordings, to a boys' choir or to a reduced chorus.

The libretto is largely the work of the composer's theologian friend, Paul Schubring, who had helped him with *St Paul*. It tells of the Prophet's leadership, tribulations and triumph through quotations from a dozen books of the Old Testament, with additional citations from the Psalms and St Matthew. As Mendelssohn set Schubring's libretto, he felt wonder in his own creation, jumping round the room with joy. 'If,' he wrote to Jenny Lind, 'it is only half as good as I fancy it to be ...!' William Bartholomew made the English translation for the Birmingham premiere (26 August 1846). He had the hard task, accomplished with some if not complete success, of turning Martin Luther's German words into prose which, while trying to observe Mendelssohn's musical accents, should convey some feeling and flavour of the English Bible. Mendelssohn substantially revised the score after the premiere. The first performance of the work as we now have it took place in London on 16 April 1847. The 'action' of *Elijah* falls into eleven sections. The first, beginning with the opening recitative and overture, and extending until the end of No. 5, deals with the curse of drought and famine, and the prayers of the people of Israel. Nos. 6 and 7 (except for the concluding recitative) describe Elijah's journey into the wilderness, Nos. 8 and 9 his sojourn in Zarephath and his raising of the Widow's son, Nos. 10–18 the trial by fire between God and Baal, Nos. 19 and 20 the repentance of the Israelites and God's gift of rain. Part II begins with God's words of comfort to his prophet. Nos. 23–9 deal with Elijah's rebuking of Ahab for worshipping Baal, Jezebel's incitement of the people against him and Elijah's flight into the wilderness, where the angels keep watch over him. Nos. 30–2 deal with Elijah's journey to Mount Horeb, Nos. 33–7 his vision of God and his joyful return to his people, Nos. 38–9 his further prophecies and his ascent into heaven. The final three numbers predict the coming of Christ.

The absence of a continuous plot such as we find in most of Handel's oratorios is a drawback, but the individual episodes — the fruitless invocation of Baal (where Mendelssohn's writing is at is sharpest), the scene of the saving of the Widow of Zarephath's son, the setting of the rain miracle as a dialogue between a treble and Elijah, and Jezebel's brief but effective interjection — are all handled succinctly and effectively. The second part has its *longueurs*, but even in the most adulatory choruses, a close study of Mendelssohn's procedures evinces unexpected turns of harmony and counterpoint.

The pioneering set on 78rpm discs was recorded, very faithfully, in 1930 in Central Hall (in 1934 a potted version was issued). Stanford Robinson was the conductor of an anonymous orchestra and the BBC National Chorus (possibly a professional chorus). The work is appreciably cut but what is performed is sung with both accuracy, sincerity and gusto. The choir, unlike that on later British versions, isn't too large; in consequence it sings with precision and vivid attack. The ten-inch format leads to some rather hectic speeds, but also a deal of excitement. Blessedly, 'Cast thy burden' and 'Lift thine eyes' are sung by soloists (from the choir?). The principals are recorded with more truth and presence than on many modern versions. Harold Williams was already a noble, compassionate and authoritative Elijah, but was to improve on this early performance in 1947 (see p. 153). Isobel Baillie is in fresher voice and almost as vital as in 1947. Clara Serena is the rather uncommitted contralto but at least she doesn't hoot. Parry Jones is among the most affecting and firm-voiced of all the tenors in the sets. He phrases 'If with all your hearts' with the utmost sensitivity to tone, dynamics and word. His account of 'Then shall the righteous' was chosen by EMI to represent him on a 'Famous British Tenors' LP (HQM 1228), and rightly so; it is a forthright piece of singing even if the voice isn't one of the most ingratiating.

Mendelssohn: *Elijah*

The 1947 Columbia set conducted by Sargent is one of my favourites. In many respects it presents the British oratorio tradition at its best, near the end of the period when *Elijah* was performed frequently up and down the land by a myriad of choral societies. Here the Huddersfield choir is in stronger, less rusty form than in the 1957 remake, possibly because Sargent himself seems to be responding more readily and immediately to the work's dramatic possibilities. Unfortunately, except in the case of No. 15 where the solo quartet appear, those concerted items written for soloists are taken by the chorus, upsetting the work's balance a little. Nos. 36, 40 and 41 are cut.

The main advantage of this set is Harold Williams's superb Elijah, here more mature and more eloquent than seventeen years earlier. His long experience of the role is evident throughout. 'Lord God of Abraham' is the very epitome of sincere affirmation. His histrionic attack in 'O thou, who makest Thine angels spirits!' has the authentic ring of Old Testament fire, as does 'Is not his Word', where the tone is at once sturdy and supple. In his appeal to God in 19, the sense of urgency is nowhere better conveyed, nor, in 30, does anyone else quite so convincingly convey Elijah's suffering soul. 'It is enough' is nicely shaped with due care given to dynamic shading. In 'I go on my way' peace at last comes to Elijah and Williams's tone nicely counterpoints the old-fashioned, woody sound of the Liverpool Philharmonic's oboe player. Then I like the way Williams colours certain words, such as 'Jezebel's table' and 'I journey hence to the *wilderness*' where this Elijah seems to carry all the burden of his people in his wandering. Above all there is the easy security of the voice throughout its register and its perfect marriage to the text. Altogether this is a great piece of singing.

Isobel Baillie is among the most telling of the soprano soloists. Her performance also benefits from long experience in the work. She is deeply concerned as the Widow, ethereal and appropriately boy-like as the youth and aware of the awesome nature of 'Thy face must be veiled'. In 'Hear ye, Israel', she and Sargent show the advantage of their long association in a tellingly paced account of this famous solo with true conviction filling 'Be not afraid'. Gladys Ripley, like her colleagues, is so articulate that you don't need the text before you. She is a fiery Jezebel, and sings both her solos with firm tone and unaffected phrasing. James Johnston, not a frequent soloist in oratorio and better known in opera, is the sound but not particularly communicative tenor.

The 1954 Decca set is conducted by Josef Krips, a musician too little celebrated today. His direction here is typical of his no-nonsense, direct approach, which masks the score's few weaknesses and emphasises its attributes. He also varies textures nicely through his refined control of dynamics. He is helped here by some excellent playing from the LPO of the day and even better singing from the London Philharmonic Chorus, a welcome souvenir of that sterling choral-trainer Frederick Jackson. Though the Baal invocations are a little tame, the softer-grained choruses, such as 'He, watching over Israel', are pleasingly done. But it is a pity that Krips follows bad tradition by assigning all the solo quartet music to the chorus.

Bruce Boyce is a clear, articulate, fairly dramatic Elijah with a real presence. 'Is not his word' is suitably fiery but by no means the most steady or accurate on these sets. 'It is enough' isn't as inward as it should be and the *Allegro* section is laboured. On the other hand, 'Night falleth round me' has the right sense of repose. George Maran has a mellifluous tenor and sings with an eager response to the text, though his rhythmic sense isn't ideally stable. Jacqueline Delman's good intentions are sometimes marred by a faulty technique: hers is not a very personal voice. Norma Proctor is steady and quietly moving in 'Woe, unto them', smooth but not especially remarkable in 'O rest in the Lord'. As a whole, this is a worthwhile, middle-of-the-road performance that I enjoyed hearing again.

Sargent's 1957 set shows once more his affinity with the work. The overture announces a performance of urgent conviction that is carried through consistently by the Huddersfield Chorus, though not quite so convincingly as in 1947. Sargent controls the Baal invocations with a sense of their dramatic context, but the choral singing is as a whole too woolly and imprecise to benefit Mendelssohn's clarity of musical thought. Sargent once more refuses the composer's requests for soloists in certain concerted numbers and cuts the same numbers as before. John Cameron gives a very 'central' performance of the name part, always alive to the needs of the drama. He brings conviction to 'Now behold thy son liveth', attacks 'Is not his word' boldly and finds a sense of worry for 'I journey hence to the wilderness'.

Elsie Morison is perhaps the most technically assured, vital and sensitive soprano in any set (a pity she was not asked to sing the boy on the mountain top). She is urgent as the mother, quite wonderful in 'Hear ye, Israel', the reprise sung *pp* as intended, and determinedly forthright at 'Be not afraid' with the 'not' purposively accented. Only Felicity Lott today sings this sort of music so convincingly. Marjorie Thomas, always a pleasing artist, tends to sentimentalise her solos, largely because of Sargent's slow tempi. That for 'O rest in the Lord' may be traditional but it's not what the composer asks for. Richard Lewis, in fresh voice, phrases 'If with all your hearts' ideally, but 'Then shall the righteous' really calls for a more heroic sound than Lewis's soft-grained tone provides. It is sad Heddle Nash never recorded in this oratorio.

Eugene Ormandy's 1968 set on RCA, never issued in Britain, is dominated by Tom Krause's big-scale, fiery performance as Elijah: his steady, bronzed bass-baritone is just the voice for the part, his command of English (one or two strange 'rs' apart) is idiomatic, his technique well-nigh faultless. He starts without quite the required commitment, but soon finds his best form. I like the generosity of 'Lord God of Abraham', the heroic attack in 'Is not his word', the controlled *mezza voce* in 'It is enough' and the soft legato in

154

'For the mountains shall depart'. He projects a real sense of an anguished prophet, one with the requisite temperament and soul. Jane Marsh, the soprano, is quite inadequate. Shirley Verrett may not have the voice or style one is used to in the contralto music, but experience in spirituals gives her 'Woe, unto them' a special sense of heart-searching eloquence while 'O rest in the Lord' is consoling, unaffected, 'thy heart's desire' carrying real conviction. Richard Lewis's long experience in the tenor solos is still evident – the phrasing always natural and shapely – but the voice itself is heard to better advantage in the second Sargent set.

Ormandy's approach is often heavy-handed and anonymous. He seems to be merely beating his way through the score rather than offering an interpretation. The Philadelphia do, of course, play with technical acuity, but they and the American-accented choir want conviction and without that *Elijah* falters. We have soloists in 15 ('Cast thy burden') but a reduced or boys' choir in the other ensembles the composer assigned specifically to soloists.

The high reputation enjoyed by the 1968 EMI set conducted by Rafael Frühbeck de Burgos has always puzzled me. The musical direction is not particularly dramatic or vivid. The New Philharmonia Chorus seems to have lost some of the zip as compared with its earlier incarnation, and its singing, somewhat distantly recorded, is often woolly with Mendelssohn's counterpoint failing to tell, though the choir and Frühbeck do generate considerable excitement in the last of the Baal choruses and their 'Be not afraid' certainly catches the right note of solid affirmation. Unfortunately Frühbeck assigns all the soloists' concerted numbers to the main chorus or to the Wandsworth School Boys' Choir, which admittedly sings with ethereal beauty in 28.

Fischer-Dieskau, for all his intelligence and fairly idiomatic English, is inclined to bully his music, with annoying emphases on certain words: just a little less would often mean so much more. 'Is not his Word' is the most obvious example of his over-energetic singing, which sometimes comes near ranting ('The Lord hath exalted thee' recitative). But there are moments when he can produce insights beyond lesser singers – as in Elijah's consoling words to the Widow: 'Now behold thy son liveth', which are movingly inflected, or the touch of biting irony he gives to the statement addressed to Baal's adherents, 'peradventure he sleepeth'. Then, where reflection is of the essence at the start of 'It is enough', the baritone comes into his own, but the middle section is somewhat tame – cf. Harold Williams or Tom Krause at this point – the fault may lie with Frühbeck's staid conducting.

Nicolai Gedda's voice may be one of the most attractive ever to have recorded the tenor solos, but his operatically extrovert singing is distressingly foreign, in both senses, to the work's idiom. Like his Elijah he is inclined to attack words too vigorously at the expense of line and inner feeling. He is at his best in the 'Man of God' recitative and arioso, where his voice takes on a nicely caring timbre. The young Gwyneth Jones certainly possessed a most

155

lovely voice, but even in 1968 it was inclined to become too vibrant for the good of this kind of music. By the side of Baillie or Morison her diction is poor, but she makes an urgent Widow. The set is treasurable for just one performance – that of Janet Baker. Her account of the alto's important recitatives has just the classical restraint and sense of inwardness that her colleagues miss, and her reading of both her solos is at once refulgent in tone and masterful in phrasing: it surpasses that of all her rivals. Her special gift of projecting conviction is always in evidence: 'O rest in the Lord', which even the composer thought over-sweet, here receives its definitive interpretation, comforting yet never effusive. The properly bitter tone that Baker brings to Jezebel's recitative inspires the chorus to replies of equal nastiness, especially in 'Woe to him'.

The most recent version in English, issued by Chandos at the start of 1990, is a disappointment, all the sadder given the long time since a satisfactory performance in the vernacular has appeared. Richard Hickox, who has proved himself something of a Sargent *de nos jours* (and that is intended as a compliment), attempts to inspire his LSO forces to give a dramatic reading, but the soggy singing of the chorus (sopranos excepted) and the lacklustre playing of the orchestra vitiate his best efforts. The oddly out-of-focus recording hardly helps, nor does Hickox's decision to follow bad tradition in assigning the solo ensembles to a reduced choir: once again this procedure fails to provide the contrasts Mendelssohn so obviously intended.

Willard White sings strongly and flexibly, but his Elijah is a dull, conventional fellow with insufficient fire in the belly. White never suggests, by phrasing or verbal insight, that he has lived with the role in the manner of his most notable predecessors. The same stricture applies to the other soloists, all that is but the admirable Linda Finnie, whose manner is at once grave and reassuring and who has, unusually among her generation, the true contralto to fulfil her excellent intentions. Rosalind Plowright gives the Widow's pleas the proper sense of desperation as one would expect from an artist experienced in the opera house, but the high tessitura of 'Hear ye, Israel' taxes her unduly: hers is an uncomfortable account of this glorious solo even though the feeling for how it should go is obviously there. Arthur Davies also sings with a deal of intensity but it is of the generalised kind not suggesting the care and intelligence in moulding English shown by the likes of Evan Williams, Widdop, Nash and Lewis in this music. There is an admirable treble, Jeremy Budd, for the Youth's eager recitatives.

The first of the versions recorded in Germany immediately shows the marked contrasts with those made in English-speaking countries. The chorus is smaller, more flexible, more incisive, and the German language sounds more apt for Mendelssohn's writing. Although the Stuttgart choir may not be a first-class body, it still gives Mendelssohn's writing a more open texture and brighter sound than most British choirs manage. A hearing of 'Thanks be to God!'

or rather 'Dank sei Herr Gott' proves the point. The chorus is vicious as Baal adherents and in 'Woe to him', when Jezebel arouses her people to attack Elijah. The orchestral playing, somewhat distantly recorded, is above average, with a favourable balance to the wind. Roland Bader's conducting is direct and dramatic, particularly so in the chorus, 'Der Herr ging vorüber', which here really sounds as stark as Mendelssohn intended for the description of the mighty wind rending the mountains. Its slightly raw sound makes the chorus describing Elijah 'breaking forth like a fire' (38) really forceful. No. 7 is given to the chorus, Nos. 15 and 28 to the soloists, and a quartet of female soloists rightly answer the chorus in No. 35.

Eduard Wollitz, the best-known of the soloists, is a real bass rather than the baritone or bass-baritone heard on all the other sets. The added weight, and the richness of his tone, give his utterance authority; a real presence is felt. Although he is not a very subtle or moving interpreter – 'Es ist genug!' evinces nothing of the Prophet's inner anguish – and he is inclined to approach notes from below, he has the technique to make 'Is not his Word' properly convincing. Hans-Ulrich Mielsch, an artist unknown to me, sings much of the tenor part as musically and sweetly as anyone else: his tone is silvery, his line exemplary. Only 'Dann werden die Gerechten' finds him overparted. Margarethe Bence is the wobbly and rough mezzo – she is best-suited by Jezebel's scheming. Ursula Buckel makes her mark as the Widow, pleading eloquently, after which her somewhat strained account of 'Hear ye, Israel' comes as a disappointment. She returns to favour for her Grümmer-like account of the Angel's recitative.

The next set in German is also Stuttgart-based, recorded at a live performance in 1981. The choir, large and rather muddily recorded, begins a little tentatively – there is not enough of the barbarian in the calls on Baal – but soon gains respect, under Helmuth Rilling's alert direction. The singing is often most persuasively contoured as in that lovely piece, 'Siehe der Hüter Israels' and the chorale-like 'Wer bis an das Ende beharrt'. Then 'Der Herr ging vorüber' evinces real awe before the Almighty, and 'Heilig, heilig, heilig ist Gott der Herr' carries, for once, total conviction. Nos. 7 and 28 are given to the chorus, 15 to the solo quartet, who unfortunately sing it weakly.

Siegmund Nimsgern's Elijah is operatic and extroverted. At times his reading is too coarse, at others too lacrymose ('Es ist genug'). It is also roughly sung. 'Herr Gott Abrahams' exhibits just about all these drawbacks. On the other hand nobody else quite conveys Elijah's outburst of temper so furiously at 'Greift die Propheten Baal' or seems in such fearsome desperation at 'O Herrlich arbeitete vergeblich'. Sentimentality – and some questionable intonation – returns for 'Ja es sollen wohl Berge weichen'.

Gabriele Schreckenbach is a lugubrious contralto with little variation in tonal colour. Robert Tear sounds in uncomfortable voice and is, for him, surprisingly unresponsive to his grateful solos, but his recitative is sharply characterised, especially 'Du Mann Gottes' and 'Siehe, er schläft', good examples, incidentally, of Mendelssohn's instinctive response to his text. Arleen Augér, at the height of her powers when this set was made, is a reasonably distressed Widow. Her 'Höre, Israel' is among the best, sung confidently in a bright, keen-edged style. As a whole, this set commands increasing respect as it progresses.

But, like all the other sets considered in this chapter, it has to yield place to the 1968 version, recorded in Leipzig, conducted by Wolfgang Sawallisch. Leipzig has always been closely associated with Mendelssohn. Here his musical descendants perform his favourite oratorio with admirable heart, musicianship and energy. Theo Adam announces an Elijah of vigour and authority in his opening recitative. The orchestra plays the overture with an immediacy and rhythmic *élan* unequalled elsewhere, full of anticipatory energy. Then the Leipzig Radio Choir delivers the first chorus with an incisive diction, accuracy, and exact attack – all consonants sounded precisely in unison – not encountered on other sets, and the actual timbre of each section is keen and clear – listen in the recitative near the end of the number to the two words 'heischen Brod' (ask for bread), spontaneously uttered and full of the desperation intended. In No. 4, we meet Peter Schreier's inward, fluent Obadiah: he, above all others, gives us real *pianissimo* singing. In No. 5 the choir's unanimity of attack and control of dynamics is rewarding to Mendelssohn's Bachian counterpoint. In No. 7, at last we hear a double quartet of soloists and so the diaphanous sound the composer obviously wanted here. No. 8 finds Elly Ameling an anxious, urgent Widow. In No. 10 the clash of temperament between Elijah and Ahab is pointedly made by Adam and Schreier.

The Baal outbursts are masterfully handled by conductor and choir. The *grave e maestoso* is followed in 11, the *presto* 13 is full of nervous fury, the Baalites having been urged on in their fruitless labours by Adam's highly articulate Prophet. No. 15 is sung by a solo quartet different from the principals, giving us yet another texture. Adam's ideal acccuracy over notes and runs in 'Ist nicht der Herrn Wort' is notable, and he brings great sincerity to the plea to God for rain, answered by an ethereal boy soprano. An exhilarating account of 'Dank sei dir Gott', with its clashing harmonies emphasised, brings the first part to a superb close.

And so it goes on – due attention and care given to Mendelssohn's intentions constantly proving how right it is to trust the composer. Elly Ameling's poised 'Höre Israel' is true of line and note, though she isn't quite Morison's or Baillie's equal in the final section. The choir give a marvellous lift to the succeeding chorus. Annelies Burmeister, a noted Fricka of the day, makes a suitably vital and unpleasant Jezebel, forcefully answered by the choir – the verbal attack is again stunning. We are rather conscious of Adam's vibrato in 'Es ist genug', but are consoled by the natural legato and the ideal weighting of words. Schreier finds the rapt tone and diction for the juniper-tree recitative which leads into a flowing, serene account by soloists of the Terzett (No. 28) and by the choir of the most delicate of all Mendelssohn's choruses, 'Siehe der Hüter Israels', with singing of ethereal lightness. Adam makes Elijah's desperation in 30 very real. Sawallisch and Burmeister take away all the sentimentality of 'Sei stille dem Herrn', propelling it even faster than Mendelssohn's metronome mark of crotchet = 72. Those used to the British custom of taking it at about half the pace may be disconcerted. The choir sing the chorale 'Wer bis an das Ende beharrt' persuasively, No. 34 with a marvellous attention to rhythmic attack and verbal acuity, expressing all the wonder of the text and a magical *pianissimo* at the enunciation of the 'still small voice'. For No. 36 we have, gratefully, a quartet of female soloists to suggest the Seraphim, set against the mass of the chorus producing just the effects intended by the composer. Adam's cantabile and that of the oboe make 'Ja es sollen wohl Berge weichen' the moment of contemplative beauty it should be. Schreier, in a finely shaped account of 39, and the chorus then bring this glorious set to an appropriately affirmative end.

The version made in 1984 under the direction of Michel Corboz is characterless and uninspired. His chorus wants both energy and sensitivity and it is inadequately recorded. Benjamin Luxon, a noted Elijah, here sings with too much vibrato and his line is hampered by Corboz's lugubrious approach. Nonetheless he does evince something of the requisite anger and compassion. Edith Wiens is pale in the soprano music, Carolyn Watkinson uncommitted in the alto's. Keith Lewis is the most pleasing of the soloists, singing mellifluously and with a fine legato, but not much individuality. Indeed that is the characteristic missing from this too polite reading, which only serves to confirm derogatory comments on the piece.

The only version issued unofficially stems from a Cologne broadcast of 1962. I wondered how it had been squeezed on to two LPs until I realised that Christoph von Dohnányi, in other respects an admirable conductor of this work, sanctions many excisions, too numerous to recount here. His reading is reasonably dramatic, with tempi that invigorate even the most soft-centred of the choruses. Unfortunately his choir is not better than average, wanting the bite and exactness of their Leipzig counterparts on the Sawallisch set. The soloists have the best-endowed voices on any set – indeed three of them were distinguished Wagnerians. George London is a black-browed, authoritative Elijah, but not a particularly sensitive or compassionate one. 'Ist nicht des Herrn Wort' suits him best of the Prophet's solos. Ira Malaniuk is a wobbly alto. The young Ingrid Bjoner is an anxious Widow, but sounds unhappy in 'Höre Israel'. Waldemar Kmentt is the most attractive of the quartet, naturally expressive, brass-toned, sensitive in his word-painting.

The 1964 highlights from EMI conducted by Sargent are well worth a hearing. The Royal Choral Society sings with a beauty of tone that comes close to rivalling their Leipzig confrères of similar vintage. The young John Shirley-Quirk makes a splendid Elijah. His attack in 'Is not his word' is incisive and 'It is enough' has eloquent accents. In recitative he is the peer of Harold Williams; indeed the desperation before 'O Lord I have labour'd in vain!' has not been bettered elsewhere, with the final 'O that I might now die' quite heart-rending. What a pity his interpretation hasn't been recorded complete. Richard Lewis is even finer than in the 1957 Sargent set. 'If with all your hearts' is phrased with refinement of tone and precision of phrasing. Marjorie Thomas is also in better voice than eight years earlier, singing 'O rest in the Lord' with inward feeling. Elizabeth Harwood, only twenty-six when these extracts were recorded, provides silvery tone and an ideal legato for 'Hear ye, Israel' and bright attack for the *allegro maestoso* section of affirmation.

Throughout the era of 78rpm records, the best-known solos were being recorded, all of them fitting neatly on to one side. Robert Radford, the once greatly popular English bass, recorded all the Prophet's solos in 1907 on Black G&T, later transferred to double-sided discs on HMV. 'Is not his word' (E 76) is suitably fiery. Both 'It is enough' and 'Lord God of Abraham' (D 267) show his large, sonorous bass and his eloquent feeling to fine effect. The enunciation and use of *portamento* is 'old-fashioned' but none the worse for that. 'For the mountains shall depart' (E 76) is delivered with a refined legato, but the phrasing is wooden and the pitch uncertain.

These solos formed part of an early attempt to record the work as a unity, demonstrating just how popular the oratorio was in the first decade of this century. Of the twenty-eight single-sided 78s, I have been able to hear, apart from the Radford items, only a few, but they are significant because they throw a little light on performance practice at the time. For instance both 'Cast thy burden' and 'Lift thine eyes' are sung by soloists, not the choir, and tempi seem to be quicker than became the custom later in the century in Britain. We also hear some notable singers of the day. Where Radford isn't employed Peter Dawson sings Elijah in resonant and eloquent tones, especially when sending the lad up on high. The boy's music is sung in the pure and exquisite tones of Carrie Tubb. The two tenor solos are taken by Edward Lloyd (3–2801 and 3–2802), still singing with fine-grained tone and untramelled authority in his sixties, though there are inevitably moments of strain.

David Bispham, a famous Elijah, is disappointingly extrovert in 'It is enough' (Columbia 154), recorded in 1908. Horace Stevens, perhaps the most famous Elijah of the 1920s, recorded all four solos in 1923. The voice is a resonant bass-baritone, of exactly the right weight and consistency for the part. He sings off the words without ever exaggerating them and obviously identifies with Elijah's authority and situation. 'Is not his word' is keen and incisive. In 'It is enough' the middle section is taken very freely and the reprise broadly with a nice variety of tonal colour, also a feature in 'For the mountains shall depart'. On his electrical remake of the first two solos (Decca K 531), recorded

160

in 1930, the liberties taken are even greater, the voice marginally less fresh, but 'It is enough' here is undoubtedly one of the great performances of the aria with some peculiarly moving phrases and the fire in the belly the central section calls for. Malcolm McEachern recorded 'Lord God of Abraham' (Vocalion 02979; Sunday Opera SYO 1), where the 'rs' are over-emphasised and the style alternates the strenuous with the lacrymose.

Roy Henderson, a baritone of the next generation who became a noted Elijah, recorded 'Lord God of Abraham' and 'It is enough' shortly after the war (Decca K 1557). The tone may be a trifle tired but the manner is exemplary, especially in the second piece, where Henderson conveys as well as anyone else the prophet's weary desperation. With a more incisive voice and diction just as keen, Dennis Noble sings a fiery 'Is not his word', coupling it on C 3850 with 'It is enough', a performance etched into my memory, as I learnt the music from it: it still seems to me a piece of articulate singing and interpretation, aided by the baritone's operatic experience. The way he phrases 'And I, even I, only am left' and the repeat of 'It is enough', the tone subtly controlled and coloured, is quite special; so is the hollow tone at the very close. Michael Mudie and the Philharmonia help make this 1949 disc worthy of rescue from obscurity.

Noble is surpassed on separate 78s in 'It is enough' ('Es ist genug') perhaps only by Friedrich Schorr's extremely rare version (D 2017) in German and that only because Schorr's is the better and more appropriate voice for the part. His concentrated, intense, almost terrifying singing encompasses every aspect of the solo, bringing the despondent prophet before our eyes. The reprise, taken in a plangent half-voice, is wonderful and a vivid contrast with the *Heldenbariton* heard in the middle section – and then on the other side in 'Ist nicht des Herrn Wort'. Schorr takes this at a fairly moderate tempo which enables him to declare his anger all the more heroically. With a bit of recitative from earlier in the scene included and Albert Coates's vivid conducting, the performance is irresistible. I wish these solos had been included in 'The Record of Singing', vol. 3, rather than the more easily accessible 'Herr Gott Abrahams' (DB 1564), surpassingly beautiful and sympathetic as that is, the German text so finely intoned. Schorr's Elijah must have been as definitive as his Hans Sachs. I have heard three earlier German interpreters in 'Es ist genug'. Franz Steiner and Alexander Heinemann (042329), both concert artists in the early years of the century, are ordinary, but their distinguished contemporary Joseph Schwarz (042563) is another matter. His long-breathed phrasing, immaculate diction and above all steady and noble tone make him Schorr's peer in this solo: this is undoubtedly a subtle and moving piece of singing, notable in the reprise of the first words for an exquisite *mezza voce* and a catch in the voice. Seek it out if you can.

'Hear ye, Israel' is sung with clear, fresh tone and utter conviction by the American Lucy Marsh on a Victor acoustic (55178-B), a 1916 version preferable to that by Perceval Allen (Columbia 672), with the 'Liebestod' on the reverse! Obviously Wagnerian duties had affected the steadiness of her tone. I have not located the version by Eleanor Jones-Hudson from the early 'set', a pity as her other contributions to it are notable. The aria can seldom have been sung by such a strong and certain voice as that of Florence Austral in her 1926 version (D 1032). Though the words do not seem to convey much to her, the security of the singing makes this performance worth seeking out. The concluding section is foreshortened. (As a parenthesis, I should mention a version of 'For he shall give the Angels' on D 1144, with Austral leading a distinguished double quartet of soloists that includes Edna Thornton, the young Gladys Ripley and Howard Fry, under Albert Coates.) Isobel Baillie's contemporaneous version (Columbia 5487; Pearl GEMM 217), a rarity on 78rpm as it was superseded when she recorded the first 'complete' set, is a lovely disc: the voice is in its most fresh and pure state and the style is exemplary. Later Baillie was to sing the solo with a shade more involvement but she never surpassed this performance in terms of singing. I have not found Helen Traubel's American Columbia, but that may be as strongly delivered as any. Master Ernest Lough's 1928 version (B 2627; Pearl GEMM 211) is something else. For a boy just turned sixteen, the singing is amazingly confident in tone and attack. I am not surprised to read that Lough considers this his best disc.

Some of the earliest accounts of the tenor solos certainly recall the Victorian way with the work. Take the American Evan Williams (1867–1918), whose career was mostly in England. His 1907 account of 'If with all your hearts' (DB 454; Cantilena 6206), taken in very stately fashion, is a lovely piece of singing – a secure legato, long-limned phrases, unforced, clear diction (perhaps with too refined vowels for our day), and a delicate control of dynamics and rubato. His 1916 'Then shall the righteous' (DA 393) is also appreciable in the same vein. This is the old English oratorio style personified and a tenor counterpart to Radford. Walter Hyde's style (D 108; Rubini GV 5) in 'If with all your hearts' is not quite so aristocratic. The voice is more heroic in timbre, the line less smooth. Yet the manner is forthright, also responsive to the text and quite unaffected. He, too, is free with the music and occasionally allows a note to bulge uncomfortably. Hyde includes the recitative. Dan Beddoe, who had a success in the work as late in his career as 1925 at the age of sixty-three, recorded both solos about then (Brunswick 3482; Rubini GV 517), showing character and a still-lovely voice. His earlier performances are more smoothly vocalised, less affecting. 'Then shall the righteous shine forth' of 1911, finely phrased but a shade bleaty, appeared in vol. 1 of 'The Record of Singing' – later 'A Record of Singers' (Victor 64196; RLS 724, RLS 7705).

Combining the best of most of these singers is Walter Widdop (E 566; HQM 1164), whose versions date from 1930. He has a better voice than many of his predecessors, his style is as pure as that of Williams, his commitment as deep as Hyde's, and his plaintive timbre is here ideal. The only drawback is odd pronunciation of 'knew' as 'ni-oo' in 'If with all your hearts'. In that piece, Arthur Jordan is not such a finished singer, but his slightly untutored account (Columbia 807), accompanied only by a piano and cello (!), is more personal than that by Webster Booth (C 3095; HLM 7109), though Booth is obviously the smoother, more musical singer whose version has much to commend it. John Fullard, in the Booth vein (Regal Zonophone MR 3237), recorded around 1939, sings with an ingenuous freshness that I find likable. In 'Then shall the righteous', Tudor Davies (D 1312) gives one of the most fervent performances of all: it is very slow and free, but this gives the piece an extemporaneous feeling that is wholly welcome.

Clara Butt's 'O rest in the Lord' has wonderfully clear and meaningful enunciation but a rather too jaunty manner. I much prefer Margarete Matzenauer's flowing legato and her quite lovely quality of voice in her early electric (1925) version (Victor 6555), also that of the Welsh mezzo Leila Megane (D 1567), which has an estimable flow of tone and sincere, unaffected feeling. Kathleen Ferrier (Decca K 1556; numerous reissues) sings both alto solos with her customary all-enveloping warmth and conviction.

I suppose a performance of *Elijah* fit for the prophet in heaven would have Isobel Baillie, Janet Baker, Walter Widdop and Friedrich Schorr as its soloists, with the Leipzig Radio Choir and Gewandhaus under Sawallisch.

Rossini: *Stabat mater*
Petite messe solennelle

RICHARD OSBORNE

Even more than Verdi, Rossini has suffered from the prejudice which would have us believe that the sacred music of an Italian opera composer will be compromised both by its worldliness and by its lack of real scholarship. Down the years, his not entirely well-founded reputation as an unschooled, cynical, *bon viveur* has made it difficult for the listening public and a good many performers to treat his sacred music with the consideration and care it invites. On record, the result has been depressing cycles of performances that enact and re-circulate assumptions about Rossini's competence and sincerity that bear little relation to the letter or the spirit of the two fine sacred works he wrote in the years following his retirement from theatre composition.

When the Abbé Gallet de St-Roch put the usual ritual questions about belief to the dying Rossini in November 1868, Rossini is said to have replied: 'Would I have been able to write the *Stabat mater* and the *Messe* if I had not had faith?' Outwardly, he was not a religious man; his faith was neither formal nor institutionalised. Privately, he might well have nodded agreement at the words of his famous contemporary, the poet Tennyson, in his *In Memoriam*:

> There lives more faith in honest doubt,
> Believe me, than in half the creeds.

The spectre of doubt, expressed as a kind of serene anxiety, is certainly there in parts of the *Petite messe solennelle*, written in 1863–4, not least in the work's quizzical conclusion. Equally, Rossini was a man in whom the primary affections and loyalties, both sacred and familial, were strong; and it is these primary forms of belief that have often inspired some of the most personally affecting religious art. The *Stabat mater*, begun in 1832, clearly owes much to Rossini's own sombre contemplation of his mother's illness and death five years previously.

This is not to deny an element of extroversion or uninhibited sensuality in some of Rossini's choral work. When he was free of the burden of melancholia that afflicted him, on and off, for the last forty years of his life,

164

Rossini was as capable as the next Italian of confirming the justness of Théophile Gautier's assertion that Italian sacred music is naturally 'heureux, souriant, presque gai, toujours en fête'. This spirit permeates the delightful *Messa di Gloria* which sent the Neapolitans into paroxysms of delight when they first heard it in March 1820. The work was revived and recorded in the early 1970s in a new edition by Philip Gossett and the conductor, Herbert Handt, whose direction of the 1973 Philips recording is a delight from start to finish (Philips 6500 612, reissued on their Sequenza label on 6527 223). For once in a recording of sacred music by Rossini, the singers – Rinaldi, Gunson, Benelli, Mitchinson, Bastin and the BBC Singers – barely put a foot wrong.

With the *Stabat mater*, recorded surprisingly infrequently over the years, things have been rather different. Until Hickox's touchingly fluent and idiomatic performance appeared in early 1990 it was possible to think that no entirely satisfactory recording existed, though versions conducted by Giulini, Muti, and Fricsay had much to commend them. Perhaps the work's fragmented origin has been a hindrance to interpreters, making it difficult for them to find within the piece real stylistic consistency. Not that the work's history has been at all accurately related or understood. As late as 1966, one of *Gramophone*'s senior critics was noting the superiority of the four concluding numbers – added in 1841, readers were erroneously informed, and self-evidently more mature. Of the four concluding numbers, only the final 'Amen' was, in fact, an 1841 addition.

The *Stabat mater* first came into being as a private commission, proposed and begun in Madrid in the winter of 1831–2. The idea had come from the priest and state counsellor, Fernández Varela, a friend of Rossini's patron and travelling companion in Spain, the Parisian banker, Alexandre Aguado. Rossini had been reluctant to accept the commission, not least because of the fame and popularity of Pergolesi's *Stabat mater* written during the last weeks of the young composer's life in 1736. But Aguado was not to be gainsaid and Rossini completed six of the proposed twelve movements (Nos. 1 and 5–9 of the final ten-movement work) before an attack of lumbago, actual or strategic, overtook him, obliging him to delegate the remaining movements to the Bolognese composer, Tadolini. The Rossini–Tadolini *Stabat mater* was first heard in Madrid on Good Friday, 1833. Rossini was rewarded with a diamond-encrusted gold box but stipulated that the work should be neither sold nor published. After Varela's death in 1837 the manuscript was sold. When Rossini learnt that it had passed into the hands of the Parisian music publisher, Aulagnier, he was appalled, not least because of the work's dual authorship. Despite indifferent health, Rossini set about recovering the work and completing it by providing his own settings of the 'Cuius animam', 'Quis est homo', 'Pro peccatis', and concluding 'Amen'. The all-Rossini *Stabat mater* was triumphantly received in Paris and Bologna (where Rossini supervised and Donizetti conducted) in 1842, with audiences evidently as much moved by the sombre beauty of the long 1832 opening movement as they were gratified by the simpler, more melodic, more obviously soloistic 1841 additions.

Of these, the tenor's 'Cuius animam' has always been very popular. It has also, alas, become an exemplum of the kind of sacred music the Rossini of popular imagination is expected to write. However unoperatic the piece is in both form and orchestration – you will scour Rossini's thirty-nine operas in vain for an equivalent piece – it sounds 'operatic' to the public at large. Working in context, a conductor and a singer mindful of the words, not to mention Rossini's moderate tempo marking, will bring to the piece a certain reflective quality and a quiet intensity with, perhaps, a hint of major-key pathos. Too often, though, it has been a jolly or a cue for peacock display, though this is not a stricture one can extend to the aria as a 78rpm sweetmeat where a singer like Caruso (December 1913; RCA GD 60495) or Björling (DB 3665; CDH7 61052–2) was capable of producing a most agreeable effect quite independent of the work's larger purpose. By accident or design, neither Giulini nor Muti was able to engage a star tenor for his complete recording. Both conductors are concerned to give the aria a certain air of melancholy. If Giulini's is the better performance here it is because his tenor, Dalmacio Gonzalez, is technically more secure than Muti's Robert Gambill and better served by Giulini, who reserves his greatest expressive tempo fluctuations for the orchestral preamble. Both tenors are outclassed, though, by Fricsay's Ernst Haefliger and Hickox's Arthur Davies, who realise the music with spirit and an expressive grace that is entirely without affectation.

More conventional, but stylish, and singing well within himself despite being hustled by the conductor, is Chris Merritt on Scimone's Erato set, though the notorious high D flat at the end of the piece – an act of musical supererogation if ever there was one – sounds strained. The case for ignoring the D flat, as Gigli does on his 1932 HMV recording (DB 1831; HQM 1075), is a strong one, since Rossini would never have expected it to be taken with the full voice, particularly if the result sounded forced or strangulated. Pavarotti handles the D flat superbly. Indeed, he sings the whole aria, on the complete Kertész set, with a shining ease of emission that would be exemplary were the whole thing not so bereft of real involvement.

Lack of involvement is the Kertész set's besetting sin. In movement after movement, it is difficult to believe that Kertész has so much as glanced at the words his soloists are trying to articulate. According to successive issues of the Penguin *Stereo Record Guide*, this underplaying of the work's alleged 'open-hearted vulgarity' was no bad thing; but this is a clear misjudgement when brisk tempi persistently undermine the work's reflective mood. However generalised some of Rossini's word-settings may appear to be, moment by moment, the text's musical 'atmosphere' (Rossini's own term) should never be sacrificed. That said, Decca assembled a strong team of soloists for Kertész and the singing of Arthur Oldham's LSO Chorus is first-rate; so, for all its shortcomings, the set is never as drab as Karl Forster's 1960 HMV account where Pilar Lorengar is less well schooled than on the Kertész and where the tenor bleats, the bass is routine, and the mezzo is clearly out of her depth and class.

At the other extreme from Kertész's superficiality and Forster's dowdiness is the 1965 CBS recording conducted by Schippers with all the ferocity and jaunty extroversion that Rossini would have loathed. The 'Inflammatus', the work's 'Dies irae', survives, and to some extent thrives on, such an approach, and it is well sung by Martina Arroyo. It is also possible to hear in Beverly Wolff's account of the 'Fac ut portem' a certain sense of justifiable anger; and there is no doubting the brilliance of the choral singing in the concluding 'Amen'. The distanced calm of the singing in the unaccompanied 'Quando corpus morietur', a number Wagner much admired, shows that Schippers is capable of relaxation and reflection. But much of the performance is an abomination, though at the time it was widely recommended by critics working on the premise that the work is real fun when given the jazz-opera treatment. Stylistically, Sternberg's Viennese recording is preferable. True, the generally excellent soloists are not native Italians, but this is no real disadvantage given the Latin text and Rossini's musical eclecticism. Ilona Steingruber, Anton Dermota and Paul Schoeffler all articulate the music and the text firmly and with affection. But there are drawbacks: a choir that is not especially proficient, an edgy recording, and cuts. Culling bars from the orchestral preamble and postlude in 'Cuius animam' is one thing, reducing the 'Inflammatus' to a single verse is another.

In this song of maternal suffering, female voices are of obvious importance and it is typical of the frustrations surrounding recordings of the *Stabat mater* that some of the most accomplished and sympathetic Rossinians have never been invited to record the work complete. Perhaps the more guileless and plaintive of all recorded performances of the 'Fac ut portem' is the one by Teresa Berganza on a recital disc with Gibson and the LSO (Decca SXL 2132), though a pre-war recording by Maria Olczewska has great human warmth and an astonishing freshness across the whole of the aria's wide vocal range. Its confinement to white-label pressings suggests that someone somewhere was being hypercritical about the recording or pitch, both of which are generally clean and secure. Similarly, no one has given a stronger and at the same time stylistically 'finer' performance of the 'Inflammatus' than Montserrat Caballé on her famous *Rossini Rarities* record (RCA SB 6771), a version that outpoints the famous record Florence Austral made in 1928 with Barbirolli and the Covent Garden orchestra (HMV D 1506; COLH 147).

Not all mezzo-sopranos are at ease with the wide-ranging lines of the 'Fac ut portem'. Fricsay's Marianna Radev develops a beat in the voice in the higher register and Muti's Agnes Baltsa reduces the low B to a nearly inaudible hum. Yvonne Minton is technically secure but Kertész is the perfunctory

167

accompanist. Lucia Valentini Terrani, with Giulini, gives a very slow performance, but a searching one, as does the young Cecilia Bartoli on a 1989 recital record (Decca 425 430–2 DH). In the 'Inflammatus' Giulini has the honeyed tones and rather worldly manner of Katia Ricciarelli; but Giulini is at his most black-browed and Ricciarelli is nothing if not self-possessed. Cecilia Gasdia is hurried and harried by her conductor, Scimone; and Catherine Malfitano, on the Muti set, sounds scared out of her wits, a sad contrast with Hickox's Helen Field, who attacks the piece with real brilliance and flair. In the soprano and mezzo-soprano duet, 'Quis est homo', one of the 1841 additions, voices that need to shine out elsewhere in the work need to be well matched here. Gasdia and Zimmermann on Scimone's Erato set are rather starkly opposed in timbre. Stader and Radev, with Fricsay, are well matched (though less commanding, perhaps, in some solo numbers). Ricciarelli and Valentini Terrani are not only well matched, they are also accompanied with real discrimination and understanding by Giulini.

Giulini also manages to make cogent use of Ruggiero Raimondi's presence, encouraging the bass to produce cleanly focused, trombone-like sonorities that help enhance Giulini's essentially hieratic view of the work. Hickox, Muti, and Fricsay also have success with their basses, Roderick Earle, Gwynne Howell, and the not entirely stylish but sympathetic and malleable Kim Borg. No modern bass provides the trill Rossini asks for; and here it must be admitted that Pol Plançon's standard-setting 1904 recording of the 'Pro peccatis' (Victor G&T 52070; Rubini GV39) has never really been surpassed. Certainly not by Peter Dawson (HMV C 2099, RLS 1077053) whose stirringly sung account is rendered absurd by the English words: 'Through the darkness thou wilt lead me / In my trouble thou wilt heed me'.

The quality of the choral work has never been a problem with recordings of the *Stabat mater*. Giulini's Philharmonia Chorus is very fine. The Muti and Scimone choruses are skilful and have been atmospherically recorded in the *a cappella* numbers as though in some Renaissance cloister or sacred space. Fricsay makes imaginative use of the RIAS chamber choir. Occasionally, in the 'Quando corpus morietur', conductors have elected to give the music to the soloists, though this is fraught with problems. If the music is not to lose its sense of timeless, impersonal beauty, the voices must be perfectly matched, and the intonation flawless. But this is not the case with either the Sternberg or the Muti recording, where we are all too aware of stylistic discrepancies and clashing egos. Giulini with the Philharmonia Chorus or Hickox with the LSO are much to be preferred here.

In the end, it is possible to admire the readings of both Giulini and Fricsay, Giulini shaping the music sternly, stoically, Fricsay warmer, more compassionate, stressing more the mood of maternal grieving. But the most successful all-round performance is Hickox's: a performance of touching directness and simplicity, skilfully and affectingly sung, and conducted with expertise and unaffected good sense. It is difficult to imagine the *Stabat mater*, elusive work that it is, coming together more naturally than this. Eschewing all vulgarity and pretence, the performance touches the affections in a way that is profoundly at one with the spirit of the real Rossini: that is, an urbane and sensitive human being, a good deal removed from the cynical prankster of popular legend.

As has already been suggested, Hickox's soloists are all very fine and it is significant that in the quartet 'Sancta mater' all the elements come together, everything clear, no one compromising or up-staging anyone else. Under Hickox's direction preludes and postludes are expressively nursed, but his tempi in the main body of movements tend to be fluent and forward-moving, not out of a sense of general indifference, Kertész's failing, but out of a desire to realise something of the music's own natural breathing, burgeoning life. Only in the *a cappella* 'Quando corpus morietur' (sung by the chorus, not the soloists) does Hickox lead a relatively expansive reading, but such is the eloquence and beauty of the singing of the LSO Chorus the spaciousness is entirely justified. The recording, made in St Jude's church in north-west London, has an acoustic that is ecclesiastical rather than drily secular. Once or twice in the *tutti* of the opening movement the chorus loses out against the orchestra and the acoustic reverberation, but in general the recording is very fine. The *a cappella* movements are superbly atmospheric, the soloists are well recorded, and the final chorus reveals clarity in the recording as well as real buoyancy and finesse in the choral singing. It makes a fine end to one of the best – perhaps the best – recording of the *Stabat mater* the gramophone has yet given us.

The *Petite messe solennelle* is the unexpected late masterwork which Rossini wrote in Paris in 1863 at the age of seventy-one in the wake of his return to occasional composition and relative good health after two decades of political and personal unrest and louring depression. At a time when choral music was becoming ever grander and more bloated, the *Messe* is a singular achievement, wryly scored for twelve voices, two pianos and harmonium, glancing back to the music of Palestrina and forward to the sacred music of Fauré and Poulenc. It is a work touched with moments of airy joyfulness that suggest a spirit purged and liberated after deep gloom. But it is also a work that engages doubt and anxiety. With all his characteristic fastidiousness and reserve, Rossini does not bare his soul at any point; but his contemplation of the text of the Latin Mass inspires music – parts of the Kyrie, the Crucifixus or the Agnus Dei – that can haunt the imagination of the attentive listener for days afterwards.

And yet, as with the *Stabat mater*, critics and some performers have been misled into thinking that Rossini's approach to the Mass was flippant. In almost every booklet accompanying the recording of the *Messe* we read the preface Rossini wrote for this 'last mortal sin of my old age':

Dear God, here it is finished, this poor little mass. Is this sacred music which I have written or music of the Devil? [Est-ce bien de la musique sacrée que je viens de faire ou bien de la sacrée musique?] I was born for *opera buffa*, as you well know. A little science, a little heart, that's all. Be blessed, then, and admit me to Paradise. G. Rossini. Passy 1863.

In its quipping, punning way, it is a very witty preface, but it is also a defensive one, as though Rossini is reluctant to appear in public except as the public expects to see him. There are those who have even suggested that the title is a joke, observing that the *Messe* is neither small nor solemn. In fact, for all its novelty, the title gives a perfectly factual account of the piece: *solennelle* in the strict sense of this being a sung Mass, a *missa solemnis* as opposed to a *missa lecta*, and small in scale if not in length.

Since scale is a factor with this work, it is probably worth doing a little preliminary ground-clearing by removing from contention the two recordings which use Rossini's orchestration of the piece. Rossini undertook the orchestration in 1867 as a purely defensive ploy. If he did not do it, he reasoned, someone else would. In the years immediately following Rossini's death it was the orchestrated version that was most often heard throughout the world after Rossini's widow sold the rights of that version to the teacher and impresario, Maurice Strakosch. But though the orchestration is agreeable enough, it has little of the piquancy or originality of the *Messe* as Rossini first conceived it. The orchestration may appeal to those who find the original a trifle astringent, like the boy in the *Punch* cartoon who thought the claret much improved by the addition of a little sugar, but for much of the time it gives the work a curiously conventional, even maudlin feel. The earliest LP recording of the piece, directed by Alberico Vitalini on Nixa, uses the orchestration, albeit in a highly abridged form, and has the distinction of being one of the worst performances of a piece of music ever professionally committed to a gramophone record. The text is not only heavily cut, it is also so freely adapted that it is at times impossible to follow what is going on, and the singing of Rome's Società del Quartetto has all the finesse of a convocation of costermongers and fishwives. The 1972 Oryx recording of the orchestration, conducted by Werner Albert, is textually more reliable, but the conducting turns the *Messe* into a coarse, occasionally sentimental, brand of musical comedy. The choral work is heavy-handed, the soloists undistinguished. The tenor's voice is oddly caught by the microphone, Grace de la Cruz is unsteady at the extremes of her register, and the bass, Grimm, is well named.

Caruso also used the orchestral versions – curiously when, for once, the piano is the specified accompanying instrument – in his recordings of the 'Domine Deus' and the 'Crucifixus', the latter appropriated and transposed for tenor voice. These records (Matrix C 24473−2 and B 24474−1; RCA GD 60495) are of considerable interest since they are from Caruso's final recording session on 16 September 1920. That said, the results are not especially pleasing. By Caruso's standards, the tone is veiled, opaque even, and the rhythms and phrasing seem uneasy. Of far greater historical interest are the first extant recordings of music from the *Messe* made in Rome in 1902 and 1904 by Alessandro Moreschi, director of the Choir of the Sistine Chapel and the so-called 'last of the castrati'. As a boy, Rossini had himself only narrowly escaped the knife; and as a young man he had both heard and written for the castrato voice. He recalled for Edmond Michotte in 1858:

I have never forgotten them. The purity, the miraculous flexibility of those voices and, above all, their profoundly penetrating accent.

Moreschi was forty-one and evidently nervous of recording when Fred Gaisberg made the initial recording of the Crucifixus in April 1902. In their collection 'The Last Castrato' (Opal CD 9823), Pearl include this for completeness's sake; but it is the April 1904 re-recording, made in Rome by Gaisberg's American colleague, W. Sinkler Darby, that gives the fairer impression of Moreschi's art, with the voice's gleaming, trumpeting top and curiously otherwordly, almost disembodied quality. Moreschi's concentration also gives the performance a dogged, tenacious quality that is quite strange.

Under the auspices of the period instrument movement, two recent complete recordings have used pianos of Rossini's time. In his live 1986 Amsterdam recording, Jos van Immerseel uses two mellow-sounding Erard instruments dating from 1850 and 1852, as well as a French harmonium built in 1845 by the instrument's inventor, François Debain. The soloists on this Accent set are variable and there are some odd balances from the live recording; but it is an account of the work that is easier to recommend than the 1987 recording by the English group, Combattimento. This also uses pianos of the period, two Robert Wornum instruments dating from the 1840s, as well as the correct forces: twelve singers with the soloists drawn from within the group. Unfortunately, there is an unannounced cut in the 'Prélude réligieux', and some of the vocal lines have been randomly decorated. The brief sleeve-note claims that, in the nineteenth century, singers used methods that have died out everywhere but in jazz and pop music. This is a very naïve remark. Rossini, particularly the older Rossini, was known to dislike unauthorised ornamentation of his music and he would have been horrified to hear his text modified midway through the rising sequence of minor thirds at the heart of the Crucifixus. Again, it has to be stressed that the *Messe* is a courtly, classical work, considerably removed from the operatic style of its day, and no more susceptible to this kind of musical tampering than Fauré's Requiem or Poulenc's *Litanies à la Vierge Noire*. These stylistic solecisms spoil what is in many respects a musically sensitive account of the work by Combattimento.

Cutting or adapting the 'Prélude réligieux', and the bass's lengthy solo, the 'Quoniam', is not uncommon, and perhaps understandable. If the septuagenarian Rossini has a fault it is, oddly enough, a certain long-windedness.

But these modifications, and the substitution of organ for harmonium, are nonetheless to be regretted. They are all present on a live Bulgarian recording, made with the addition of plenty of off-stage audience noise, in Sofia in June 1987. Mihail Milkov conducts a sincere, if rather pedestrian and chorally mannered, performance with a choir that seems to quadruple Rossini's suggested twelve voices. The organist makes free with the 'Prélude réligieux' and the set's pianists are not always very good at spiriting away the occasionally rum-ti-tum elements in Rossini's piano writing.

Nowadays, it is odd to hear a large choir and an organ in recordings of the work, plus some cuts. The first complete recording of the original version of the Messe was made for HMV in 1955 under the direction of Renato Fasano. There is an organ and a mass of small cuts, mainly in preludes and postludes. But for its time, a time when there were no Rossini Urtexts and when his music was often freely adapted, it is a surprisingly well-judged affair. The excellent Oralia Domínguez is given the communion hymn, 'O Salutaris', as well as the Agnus Dei which follows it, but her singing merits this novel reallocation. Of the other soloists, only the tenor, Giuseppe Berdini, sounds over the hill.

If we assume the Messe is performed more or less uncut, with harmonium rather than organ, and with no textual meddling of the kind we have on the Combattimento recording, the decisive factors will be the scale and musical accuracy of the performance and the performers' sense of style. The Messe is not a concert-hall piece, nor was it designed to be performed in large churches or cathedrals. The Catholic Church forbade women's voices in church music, so Rossini was happy to write it for semi-private performance in rooms appropriate to a Mass with piano accompaniment. The first performance was in the private chapel in Paris of the Countess Louise Pillet-Will, an almost courtly, pre-Romantic setting. And, indeed, the work was partly inspired by the exquisite singing style of the young Marchisio sisters who were for Rossini a reminder of the gentler world that existed before 1830. Hand-picked singers, performing in a private place before a small, discriminating audience: this is the context the Messe invokes.

It is no use, therefore, casting and recording it as though it were the Verdi Requiem. Indeed, it might be as well to avoid to an extent choirs and singers trained in the Italian manner that Rossini had long abandoned or never fully engaged. The 1979 Ars Nova recording, later issued by Decca, is heavily Italianate with Mirella Freni, Valentini Terrani, Pavarotti and Raimondi. To take just one example, Raimondi's groaning, hung-over, heavy-lidded singing is an abomination, and even Freni is prone to overstatement and distracting underlinings and prolongations. Gandolfi's direction, some lugubriousness apart, is clear enough, but the playing and choral singing are often lumpy and loud, and the recording is inappropriately close and big-bodied. By contrast, a 1960s recording on the Ricordi label has a powerful line-up of singers — Renata Scotto, experienced in Rossini's French salon music, Fiorenza

Cossotto, Alfredo Kraus, a little cool in the 'Domine Deus' but stylish as ever, and Ivo Vinco. Of the various Milanese choirs who have recorded this work, the Coro Polifonico, directed by Giulio Bertola, is the best by some distance. In the end, only the recorded quality, moderate by the standards of the time, and the set's rarity tell against it.

Looking hopefully to the French can be a disappointing experience. The Erato company has twice recorded the *Messe*, once in 1969 and again in 1987. Of these, the earlier is decidedly superior. Directed by Edwin Loehrer, it is a performance that takes full account of the work's intimate scale. The pianist, Luciano Sgrizzi, who appears on both Erato sets, favours a rapid, staccato manner that leaves some figurations rather naively exposed; but Loehrer's lyrical and affectionate direction, and the reflective style of the singing, is never directly at odds with the pianists' style. The performance may seem too reflective at times, with a sacramental calm that verges on the coy. But this is preferable to the brittleness and haste of the 1987 Erato set directed by Michel Corboz. Despite the presence of Cecilia Gasdia, and some skilful singing from the Lausanne choir, the direction veers between the provincial and the prosaic. The performance is the quickest on record. Indeed, Erato emblazons the figure 72'10" on the CD cover. But it is astonishing to hear the lovely unaccompanied 'Christe eleison' dispatched in a mere sixty seconds or the 'Cum sancto spiritu' rendered comic and conspiratorial at a tempo that almost matches Scimone's. Scimone's Philips performance would itself be a possible front-runner were it not for his hell-for-leather locomotion in this most gracious and gamesome ecclesiastical peroration since the time of Haydn. In general, Scimone's direction is rather restless and the performance has a slightly inflated air about it, though it is blessed with a good choir and first-rate soloists. Still, there is a nicer sense of scale, as well as a greater degree of stylishness, about the performance of the London Chamber Choir, trained rather in the Oxbridge choral style, by Laszlo Heltay for the 1977 Argo recording. Here there are two excellent female soloists, Margaret Marshall and Alfreda Hodgson, and this is the only set which offers us the 'Prélude réligieux' played on the harmonium, an option the score allows. It is astonishing, though, that Robert Tear was permitted, or permitted himself, to sing the 'Domine Deus' in so hefty and stentorian a manner. It is a black mark against a good set.

Happily, it is possible to end this survey of years of mismanagement of Rossini's choral music on record with two recordings of the *Messe* which it is worth seeking out: the recording made for HMV in 1984 by the Choir of King's College, Cambridge directed by Stephen Cleobury, with the Labèque Sisters and four − admittedly − not especially well-integrated international soloists; and, finest of all, a live performance recorded in June 1972 in the Baumburg Monastery chapel, Chiemgau by Ariola-Eurodisc in association with Bavarian Radio and South German Television, with the Munich Vokal-solisten, four incomparable soloists in Karl Lövaas, Brigitte Fassbaender,

Peter Schreier and Dietrich Fischer-Dieskau, with Wolfgang Sawallisch as conductor and principal pianist.

It must be said that Rossini would have been decidedly nervous about the *Messe* being sung by boys' voices. 'Sour and out of tune' was his verdict on all Italian choristers of his day. Yet if any choir could be guaranteed to make Rossini change his mind it would be the King's choir. Their singing is wonderfully pure and buoyant, and the Labèque Sisters, whom Rossini would have adored to have at his *soirées*, play throughout with great verve and sensitivity. The soloists do not quite match the choir, or their rivals on Eurodisc. Gedda is past his prime, Lucia Popp is less rivetingly intense in the 'Crucifixus' than Lövaas, Kavrakos is no match in mobility and intelligence for Fischer-Dieskau, and even Fassbaender sounds better, live and younger. Sawallisch's playing and conducting on Eurodisc are beautifully scaled but very compelling, the phrasing intense, the ear for bizarre and disturbing colours acute. There is a sense here of keen, living involvement with the music, of fresh discovery linked with real understanding, that brings out the music's contrasted elements – faith and doubt, innocence and experience – in a remarkable way. Performed like this, the *Petite messe solennelle* is one of the most original, and affecting, of all the great Mass settings of the last 150 years.

Berlioz: *Grande Messe des Morts*
Te Deum
L'Enfance du Christ

DAVID CAIRNS

For a professed agnostic, if not an atheist, Berlioz shows a remarkable interest in sacred music. A significant proportion of his output is concerned with religion — and this in a period when sacred music was in decline in France. Three of his major works — those dealt with in this chapter — are religious works; and in each case the original impulse came from within, from the composer himself, not from a commission. Even in his secular works one is struck by the frequent recurrence of religious imagery. This is more than just a reflection of the Romantic vogue for religion as a picturesque detail of landscape: it is a preoccupation.

Yet the paradox is easily explained. 'For seven years', wrote Berlioz of his boyhood, religion was 'the joy of my life'. The very loss of that joy left a deep imprint on his consciousness, and his music reflected it. It is not the music of a believer; but it conveys an intense regret at the inability to be one, and a profound awareness of the need, the desperate need, to believe, to worship. The Requiem, or *Grande Messe des Morts*, evokes the possibility of a universe without God; the God of the *Te Deum* is more terrible than compassionate; *L'Enfance du Christ* looks back nostalgically to a time when the healing myths of Christianity were received unquestioningly and nourished all.

Berlioz's own lack of belief is, as it were, used to suggest the eternal hopes and fears of the human race, faced with the enigma of death; his intuitive understanding of the religious instinct, his unsatisfied yearning for faith, enable him to respond to those immemorial feelings and express them in his art. His imagination believes, though his intellect does not. The result, with all its unorthodox elements, is true religious music. As Wilfrid Mellers has said, it has what Wordsworth calls 'the visionary gleam'.

The restraint and chamber-music delicacy of texture of *L'Enfance du Christ* surprised critics and public alike when the work was first performed, in Paris, in 1854; it didn't conform at all to the accepted idea of Berlioz. In fact, as he said, it marked no radical change of style, merely a change of subject. The huge forces employed in some (by no means all) of the movements of the

175

Requiem and the *Te Deum*, and the important spatial element in their composition, are in the direct tradition of the grand musical rites which had been such a prominent part of public life in the Revolutionary and early Napoleonic eras, not many years before, and which embodied the grand concept of the people of France united in a communal act of prayer and worship. The tradition was transmitted to Berlioz by his teacher Jean-François Le Sueur. Le Sueur's Symphonic Ode of 1801, written to commemorate the anniversary of the Revolution, used four separate orchestras, one at each of the corners of the Invalides – the same church where, thirty-six years later, the *Grande Messe des Morts* had its first performance.

What Berlioz does, in his renewal of that tradition, is to universalise it. Its local, patriotic origins are transcended; the Revolutionary community becomes the community of men and women in all ages – the voice of humankind calling from one generation to another down the centuries, coloured by the note of the tragic which is Berlioz's natural language. This visionary quality is the thing that above all one looks for in a performance of the *Grande Messe des Morts*.

The Requiem and *Te Deum*, being composed in the monumental style which Berlioz (following Le Sueur) chose for his ceremonial music, and which features deliberately slow harmonic movement and simple, boldly juxtaposed contrasts of colour, mass and dynamics, give far less latitude for 'interpretation' than his symphonic works and cantatas (or than *L'Enfance du Christ*). Nevertheless there is scope for conductors to go wrong, and some of them take full advantage of it, usually by ignoring the composer's tempo indications. Berlioz's metronome marks, like Verdi's, demand serious consideration; they mean something. So, when the 'Judex crederis' in the *Te Deum* is taken at a speed half as fast again as is indicated (dotted crotchet = about 104 instead of 69), as it is on Daniel Barenboim's recording, or when the crotchet = 96 of the Requiem's Dies irae becomes, in the hands of Theodore Hollenbach, a crawling 58 (only for the score's subsequent 'slightly faster' to be the signal for an acceleration to more than double the speed), the result is not surprisingly a nonsense.

Where smaller variations are concerned, acoustics may be an influential factor. A performance recorded live in a very resonant acoustic – as Gary Bertini's Requiem was, in Altenberg Cathedral – will tend naturally to be on the slow side, and may not suffer all that much because of it. As I say, it is the feeling behind that counts most.

The feeling behind Jean Fournet's recording of the Requiem – the earliest of all, made in France towards the end of the Second World War and issued on eleven 78s – goes quite deep. Fournet sets convincing tempi (though the Dies irae loses its initial momentum and becomes sluggish) and gets idiomatic playing and singing from the Emile Passani Orchestra and Choir. 'Mors stupebit', to take one example, is powerfully atmospheric. Georges Jouatte is a heroic, even-toned soloist in the Sanctus. Unfortunately all this good work is partly undermined by a recording which, though quite impressive by the standards of its day and sometimes remarkably sensitive to orchestral detail, fails to meet the larger demands of the work. Thus the brass unisons and surging timpani rolls which intensify the sense of terror in the reprise of the Lacrimosa are barely audible. The recording was made in a resonant building but the microphones were placed so close to the choir that you can hear individual voices, in particular one uncomfortably reedy tenor.

Hollenbach's Requiem of 1956 with the Choir and Orchestra of Rochester Oratorio Society — the earliest LP version — fluctuates between drastically slow tempi, like the one just mentioned, or like the Offertorium, which begins at about 52 crotchets to the minute (as against Berlioz's 84), and others that are hysterically fast, like most of the 'Rex tremendae'. The chorus sings with fervour, but the conductor's response remains on the surface of things. There is drama here, but of a rather crude sort. However, there are a few good points. The dialogue of flutes and trombones in the 'Hostias' and the Agnus Dei is given plenty of space (several conductors hurry over it) and the articulation of the funeral drum rhythm at the end has the right weight. Ray de Voll gives quite a good account of the tenor solo in the Sanctus.

The version conducted by Fritz Mahler with the Hartford Symphony and Hartford Symphony Chorale — one of three recordings made in 1957 — is also on the crude side, lacking the elegance of style and purity of tone that are essential to Berlioz even in his most apocalyptic outbursts: ill-focused choral interjections in the Offertorium, an absurdly loud solo flute in the Sanctus, and tempi that, though not often spectacularly wrong, never feel quite right. The recording is not too bad, but the trombones in the 'Hostias' and the Agnus Dei sound more like tubas, and the first two bars of the Sanctus are missing. David Lloyd's singing suffers from excessive tremolo, but he manages the first, awkward high B flat better than many of his rivals.

The other two versions dating from 1957, those of Dmitri Mitropoulos and Hermann Scherchen, especially the former, are much more like the real thing. Indeed Mitropoulos's, with the Cologne Radio Orchestra, is one of the best on disc, or would be if it weren't for the primitive recording, apparently taken from a live broadcast. The balance is lopsided, with prominent choir and woodwind, and strings very backward — the limping Mephistophelean bass at 'mors stupebit' is almost inaudible, so is the offbeat pizzicato bass which should quicken the tension half-way through the Dies irae, and the violins, whose role is so often to lighten the darkness with a gleam of hope, are sadly indistinct. The sound of the massed brass is also less than imposing. Nor does the tone of the combined Hamburg and Cologne Radio Chorus justify the prominence given to the voices, being often thick and wobbly, the sopranos especially. It is redeemed, however, by an uncommon sensitivity to the meaning of the words and the poetry of the music. The whole performance has the visionary quality I spoke of.

This is not solely due to the fact that Mitropoulos observes nearly all the tempo markings (and, in the Dies irae / Tuba mirum, the proportions between the different tempi); but the two things are undoubtedly connected. He is also unusually careful about dynamics and articulation. The different rhythms of the brass choirs in the 'Tuba mirum' are exceptionally clearly distinguished, making you realise that rhythm plays almost as important a part as sonority in the total effect. Beyond all this, Mitropoulos constantly penetrates the surface of the music and lays bare – though never with an alien emotionalism – the expressive intensity beneath. The performance is suffused with a sense of awe, humility, grandeur, mystery, whether in the sopranos' heartfelt threefold 'salva me' – softer at each repetition – or in the atmosphere of universal lamentation evoked in the 'Lacrimosa'. The young Nicolai Gedda gives a splendidly exalted yet unforced account of the Sanctus.

Scherchen's version, with the Paris Opéra Orchestra and the Chorus of Radio France, isn't quite in the same class. Like much that Scherchen did, it is marred by sudden eccentricities, and the recording – made in a large church, from the sound of it – is one of the worst. The engineers don't attempt to cope with the massed drums of the 'Tuba mirum', and the balance among the four supposedly equal brass groups is non-existent (group 1 much closer than the other three). But, as also is common with this conductor, there are flashes of genius, and a seriousness of approach which shows up his more dependable but more worldly rivals. If nearly all the tempi are well under what is marked, Scherchen uses this slowness to build up an epic sense of suffering which rises above the technical limitations of the performance (including weak, though enthusiastic, sopranos and tenors). The ascending chromatic scales in the Dies irae are electrifying. And for once the hushed choral reaction to the Day of Judgement – 'judicanti responsura' – is sung at a true *sotto voce*. The Sanctus, in which Jean Giraudeau sensibly sings all the high B flats with head voice, is invested with an extraordinary tenderness.

The solo tenor on the earlier (1959) of Charles Munch's two recordings, Léopold Simoneau, gives a marvellously rapt, effortless account of the Sanctus; the whole performance of this movement has an ethereal, serenely contemplative quality that lifts it far above most other versions. Munch's interpretation is among the better ones. The Boston Symphony plays superbly, and the New England Conservatory Chorus sings with character and feeling. There are few disappointments: a too slow Dies irae (*c*.80, as against Berlioz's 96), a perfunctory exchange between the flutes and trombones (like several of the conductors, Munch for some reason accelerates in these bars instead of giving them space). The recording, which has a wide dynamic range, wears its thirty years pretty well, though the drums in the 'Tuba mirum' are rather weak.

178

Munch's second version (1966), made in Germany, in some respects improves on the first. Speeds are nearer to those indicated. The Dies irae moves quicker and flows better. So does the opening 'Requiem' and 'Kyrie'. The Deutsche Grammophon recording gives the drums much greater prominence, and generally picks up more detail, than the RCA. Nonetheless I find the earlier performance preferable because more atmospheric. Peter Schreier's Sanctus, though good, is not to be compared with Simoneau's. The Bavarian Radio Orchestra plays well, but the Boston Symphony does more than that. The chorus − Bavarian Radio − is efficient (though the men's intonation in the Agnus Dei is shaky), but sings with less character than the New England Conservatory Chorus. And Munch seems to me to go less deep than before.

The performance conducted by Eugene Ormandy (1966) has quite a lot to commend it: well-judged tempi, the Philadelphia Orchestra in full command of the score, and choral singing by the Temple Choirs which, if sometimes overstretched in the upper soprano and tenor registers, is well prepared and expressive. The recording has both clarity and weight. Towards the end, however, recording and performance both deteriorate slightly. In the 'Hostias' the chorus, recorded too close, with individual voices sticking out, sings mechanically, without feeling. The Sanctus, taken rather fast and sung in an inappropriately operatic style by Cesare Valletti, has a feverish quality, all stillness banished, and in the reprise the soft strokes of the bass drum are more like a thud.

The next version to be recorded, Colin Davis's with the London Symphony Orchestra (1969), had the advantage not only of the conductor's proven insight into Berlioz's music but also of the ambience of Westminster Cathedral, a building whose resonance, because of the large areas of unfaced brick, is less extreme than that of others of comparable size. Unfortunately this advantage was partly neutralised by the too close miking of the chorus, which also exposed the weakness of the London Symphony Chorus's tenors, especially in the 'Lacrimosa', but also in the 'Requiem' and 'Kyrie'. (The *Grande Messe des Morts* really demands, if not a professional chorus, at least a substantial professional element.) What is magnificent in the Philips recording is the glowing, spacious sound of the orchestra − the bloom of the violins, the crunch of the double basses' *sforzati*, the fathomless booming of the tubas, the woodwinds' wailing unisons, the trombone pedal notes resounding as the composer imagined them. Davis's interpretation has the grandeur and searching intensity one would expect. Even when the tempo is, ideally, too slow, as in the Dies irae and the Offertorium, it carries conviction. The high B flats in the Sanctus stretch Ronald Dowd to the limit, if not beyond, but his singing has a certain heroic dignity.

In comparison with Davis's, the performance conducted by Louis Frémaux with the City of Birmingham Symphony Orchestra and CBSO Chorus (1975) is earthbound and unimaginative. The 'Rex tremendae' sounds merely jolly, the rhythmic drive of the 'Lacrimosa' strictly mechanical. Frémaux sometimes sets a correct tempo but then does nothing with it. Only in the Sanctus, where dramatic emotion is not required, is he really successful, achieving, with Robert Tear, the timeless, motionless quality that can elude other conductors. Lack of dramatic involvement can't be held against Leonard Bernstein's version, made in Paris in 1975 with the French National Orchestra and Chorus and the Orchestre Philharmonique. Bernstein is freer with the time than any of the other conductors, exaggerating the tempo changes in the 'Tuba mirum' ('très peu' becomes 'beaucoup'), and making a big *ritenuto* for 'mors stupebit', though none is marked. He takes the 'Quid sum miser' very slowly, milking it of its 'sentiment d'humilité et de crainte'. Such things are the obverse of the interpretation's conspicuous virtues, a minor consequence of Bernstein's wholehearted response to the emotions embodied in music and text. The opening 'Requiem' evokes a profound desolation, the 'Lacrimosa' an awesome sense of struggling, panic-stricken humanity, the Sanctus a lovely floating serenity, with both the choir and the fine soloist, Stuart Burrows, quite distant, not of this world. The men of the chorus are not among the most sensitive or exact on record, and there are one or two mistakes in the orchestra as well as some ragged ensemble. Was this version recorded live? It certainly has the feel and vitality of an actual performance.

The next two versions, André Previn's with the London Philharmonic Orchestra and Chorus and Lorin Maazel's with the Cleveland (both 1979), are technically speaking among the very best. Previn has a first-rate chorus, well trained (by John Alldis) and, I suspect, leavened by professionals. The LPO plays splendidly, and the recording could hardly be bettered. But I find it emotionally too cool, communicating little sense of dramatic urgency – efficiently generalled but never deeply felt.

Maazel, too, settles for sensation rather than feeling. His chorus matches the power of the Cleveland Orchestra to which it belongs, and the effect of the whole body of performers in full cry at the tempo prescribed is – in passages like the climax of the 'Lacrimosa' – undeniably grand. But such things as the excessive opulence of string tone in the Offertorium and the surface excitement of the exaggerated *accelerando* in the 'Rex tremendae' are indicative. Kenneth Riegel, once past the first high B flat–A natural, is a fine soloist. Maazel, like Ormandy, restores the dozen bars cut from the 'Quaerens me' in the revised edition of 1853, and also adds a passage cut from the Offertorium, without, however, persuading me that Berlioz was wrong to remove them.

Barenboim's version (1980) begins so well, with a 'Requiem' and 'Kyrie' of tragic sweep, that its subsequent falling off comes as a sad disappointment. A note of wilfulness obtrudes, which I do not remember from the noble performance I heard him conduct with the same forces – Orchestre de Paris and its splendid choir – in Washington a few years earlier. The austere dignity of the interpretation is disturbed by sudden unmotivated changes of tempo. Yet with a little more restraint, you feel, it might have been very good. Plácido Domingo, recorded too close, declaims the Sanctus with ringing burnished tone but seemingly little idea of what it is about.

Gary Bertini's recording with the Cologne Radio Symphony Orchestra (1987) was made at a live performance in Altenberg Cathedral, and the evidently very reverberant acoustic imposes 'cathedral tempi' throughout. The 'Lacrimosa' is the slowest on record, and most of the others are well below the metronome. The recording is heavily biased in favour of the chorus, with the all-important violins very backward in the 'Requiem' and 'Kyrie' and the brass and drums making a muted effect in the 'Tuba mirum' and the 'Lacrimosa' (where, too, the great cymbal stroke is feeble and the tam-tams not to be heard at all). All the same I like this version. The combined choirs of Cologne and North and South German Radios are magnificent. Bertini generally manages to sustain his very slow speeds, and achieves an atmosphere of momentousness and mystery despite the lack of physical impact in the big numbers. In the Agnus Dei he gives the flutes and trombones plenty of space; and the final bars of the work have an impressive air of calm resignation.

The most recent version, Eliahu Inbal's (1988), also comes from Germany and uses part of the same excellent chorus, and the same soloist Keith Lewis (less at home with the B flats than on the Bertini recording). Otherwise, being a product of the studio, it is very different. The Denon engineers have gone to town with the big numbers − the reprise of the 'Tuba mirum' is the most tremendous on record, and the sustained horn writing in the reprise of the 'Hosanna', which barely registers in most recordings, is glowingly present. Speeds, too, are much faster − sometimes significantly faster than indicated, and occasionally Inbal is lured into merely superficial excitement. But the performance has an infectious enthusiasm and dramatic fire.

Though Robert Shaw's recording with the Atlanta Symphony Orchestra and Chorus was made a few years before Inbal's, in 1985, I have left it till last because in some respects it is the best. Perhaps it lacks the imaginative flair that illuminates the performances of Mitropoulos, Scherchen Davis, Munch and Bernstein. The sobriety of Shaw's reading does too little with the strings' rising chromatic scales in the Dies irae, which, breaking in on the timeless desolation of the choral chant, should make our hair stand on end. On the other hand the Lacrimosa, taken at exactly the speed indicated, acquires more vividly than any other version the character of the medieval Dance of Death that Berlioz intended.

What Shaw demonstrates in this performance is just how much can be achieved by devoted attention to the score. In matters of tempo, dynamics, phrasing, articulation, balance, this is of all performances on disc the most faithful to what the composer wrote. Chorus and orchestra have been scrupulously prepared and rehearsed (the flutes' and trombones' poor intonation in the Agnus Dei is virtually the only flaw) and imbued with the conductor's clear-sighted, deeply felt conception of the work. The result is very satisfying. The recording is sonorous and exceptionally clear and, in the Sanctus, by placing both the fine tenor soloist (John Aler) and the female chorus unusually far from the microphone, magically enhances the stillness of the music.

As against seventeen recordings of the Requiem, the *Te Deum* has had only four. The least satisfactory version is Barenboim's (1977), and this despite first-rate choral singing (by Arthur Oldham's Choir of the Orchestre de Paris), plenty of telling detail from the Orchestre de Paris, and a recording, made in a resonant building, that is notable both for clarity and for warmth of sonority. Barenboim, at his most capricious, sets unidiomatically fast speeds – nearly half as fast again in the opening movement, forcing him into a violent gear-change at 'omnis terra'. Even faster is the tempo of the 'Judex crederis'; at this pace the grandeur of the music is left far behind. Jean Dupouy is a dull tenor soloist, singing the 'Te ergo quaesumus' in a laboured style, with little line to speak of.

On the brisk side, with some ragged ensemble and a recording of no great éclat, Beecham's version with the Royal Philharmonic Orchestra and the London Philharmonic Choir (1953) nonetheless served a very useful purpose. For fifteen years it had the field to itself, and it still commands respect. Alexander Young gives a strong, slightly theatrical account of the 'Te ergo' (he also sings, most expressively, the chorus tenors' part in the 'Christe Rex Gloriae'). But by that time Sir Thomas was in his mid-seventies, an age when the controlling and animating of large choral and orchestral forces becomes physically too demanding. The version made by Colin Davis in 1968 with the London Symphony Chorus and Orchestra and the Wandsworth Boys' Choir offered a more suitably majestic and at the same time more vital interpretation. It too has its faults, among them a soloist, Franco Tagliavini, who has audible problems with the more chromatic passages, some perilously threadbare tone from the divided tenors and basses of the chorus, and a recording (made in Watford Town Hall) which misses a lot of important string detail, especially in the 'Tibi omnes'. But the general effect is impressive.

The version has a challenger in the one conducted by Claudio Abbado and recorded live in St Alban's Abbey with the European Community Youth Orchestra, LSO Chorus, London Philharmonic Choir, Wooburn Singers and assorted boys' choirs. Abbado's interpretation is in its way as masterly as Davis's (only the 'Christe' has slightly less rhythmic élan), and it has a better soloist, Francisco Araiza, as well as being both more clearly and more sumptuously recorded: the trombone pedal notes at the return of the 'Judex crederis' theme, after the middle section, make a truly awe-inspiring sound. The disadvantage of a live recording is that things can go wrong which it

182

may not be possible to put right later. In the 'Dignare' the organist, Martin Haselböck, plays a wrong note near the beginning and at the end of the movement hurries the chords badly. (Both Nicolas Kynaston, on the Davis disc, and Denis Vaughan, for Beecham, are much to be preferred.) But these are minor blemishes on a performance of great power and brilliance.

To perform *L'Enfance du Christ* adequately is more difficult. Broad effects, enthusiasm, sincerity of feeling are not enough. The work is a mosaic of different tempi, moods, poetic evocations, atmospheres. It demands delicacy of touch, refinement of tone and sensitivity to the music's subtle and constantly changing colours. Everything is in the score; but the score is an exacting taskmaster. Of the nine recordings that I have heard (a tenth, conducted by Pierre Dervaux, I have not managed to find), two must regrettably be ruled out entirely. They happen to be the two earliest: André Cluytens's (1951) and Thomas Scherman's (1953). Scherman's, despite soloists of the quality of Donald Gramm, Martial Singher and the great Simoneau, is a paltry affair. The conductor hardly seems in control of what is happening. The angels bellow their way through the final section of Part 1, the Alleluias at the end of Part 2 ('The Flight into Egypt') go at nearly twice the speed of the rest of the movement, the chorus hold the last chord of the 'Shepherds' Farewell' too long, the tuning of the final chord of the work is excruciating, the tempi, apart from being ill judged, are unsteady, and there are several cuts. The Little Orchestra and Choral Art Societies no doubt do their best, but it is not sufficient.

Cluytens's 1951 recording (the first of two conducted by him) won the Grand Prix du Disque of the Académie Charles Cros, but it is a coarse performance, its generally routine character and lack of care for balance, tone and dynamics accentuated by the very close recording. Jean Giraudeau gives a pleasant account of the tenor solo in Part 2, and Cluytens finds an excellent tempo for all three movements of 'The Flight into Egypt'. But the good qualities of his interpretation are nearly all to be found in more refined form in the recording he made fifteen years later, with the Paris Conservatoire Orchestra (hardly recognisable as the same band which played the earlier version) and the Choeurs René Duclos (distinctly superior to the Choeurs Raymond Saint-Paul). This time Cluytens has Nicolai Gedda as his Narrator, in excellent form and producing some lovely soft singing at the end of Part 2. Ernest Blanc is an authoritative Herod, if a little stentorian, and Roger Soyer a fine Joseph. With Victoria de los Angeles and Xavier Depraz they make up a strong team. Cluytens takes both the march and Herod's aria rather fast and the chorus of Ishmaelite children and servants rather ploddingly, but again he judges 'The Flight into Egypt' just right – only conductors brought up in the French tradition seem to understand that the 'Shepherds' Farewell' is a carol, not a hymn; the final verse, too, is sung at a real and rare *ppp*. This time the off-stage angels behave in a reasonably angelic fashion. The opening of Part 3

('The Arrival at Saïs') is also well done, and the trio for flutes and harp is among the better versions.

The other recording from France, by Jean Martinon with the Orchestre National and choirs from the French National Radio, suffers, by comparison, from less good choral and orchestral work and a rather churchy, lachrymose Ishmaelite Father (Juan Soumagnas). Jane Berbié, too, is too fruity for Mary and Claude Calès a no more than competent Joseph. Alain Vanzo's mellifluous voice does not have a great deal to say. The best soloist is Roger Soyer, a poised, elegant Herod with a wide expressive range. Martinon's jaunty tempo for the march takes away all the uneasiness, but he gives welcome attention to its dynamic shading and shows the same care for detail in Herod's aria. Though the string playing and the choral singing is not of very high quality, Martinon coaxes some expressive moments from his forces. In his hands the performance feels better than it sounds.

In the case of Charles Munch's version (1957) the orchestra, being the Boston Symphony, has no need of transformation: it plays beautifully. But the New England Conservatory Chorus, oppressed by the French text, gives a very stilted account of itself and, in spite of all the conductor's efforts, cannot conceal the poor quality of its tone (far worse than the same choir's singing on the Munch recording of the Requiem made two years later). Of the soloists, Gérard Souzay (Joseph) is the best. The others – Cesare Valletti, Florence Kopleff and Giorgio Tozzi – are adequate but not very interesting. Despite these drawbacks, Munch does some fine things, especially when he comes closest to the tempo indicated.

The Gallic flair shown in varying degrees by Munch, Martinon and Cluytens is conspicuously absent from the version conducted by Philip Ledger with the English Chamber Orchestra and John Alldis Choir (1985). This is a punctilious and worthy but kapellmeisterly performance. Even when Ledger chooses the right tempo, metronomically speaking, it is apt to seem stiff. Choral and orchestral work is sound but rarely distinguished and the soloists are more painstaking than inspired. Anthony Rolfe Johnson has sung the Narrator's part more memorably than this. Fiona Kimm is better in the dramatic music of Part 3 than in the lyrical music of Part 1. Richard Van Allan and Benjamin Luxon do quite well in the two bass roles but William Shimell is an unconvincing Joseph.

Of the two versions conducted by Colin Davis (1960 and 1976) I find the first, with the Goldsbrough Orchestra and the St Anthony Singers, more atmospheric than the second (LSO and John Alldis Choir). It is generally slower, and sometimes quite a bit below the tempo indicated, but for all that it is more alive, and to my mind more moving (thus demonstrating that the metronome isn't everything). True, it has the benefit of Peter Pears's marvellous Narrator – Eric Tappy, though not at all bad, is not to be compared with him. From his opening 'Dans la crèche en ce temps Jésus venait

184

de naître' Pears establishes a mood at once elevated and direct, hieratic and momentous yet fundamentally simple. The ensuing march is excellent; on Davis's later version it is still good, but its colours and dynamic contrasts seem here more freshly felt. Joseph Rouleau makes a more affecting Herod than Jules Bastin; and the singing of Janet Baker and Thomas Allen on the later recording, good as it is, doesn't eclipse Elsie Morison and John Cameron. With a touch of the extra pace of the second Davis version the first would be a clear choice. As it is, some of its tempi are a little too slow.

The most recent recording, by John Eliot Gardiner with the Lyons Opera Orchestra and the Monteverdi Choir (1987), comes near to being the answer to one's prayers. José van Dam is a powerful Herod, Anne Sofie von Otter and Gilles Cachemaille a touching pair of parents, and Jules Bastin a genial Ishmaelite Father. The Monteverdi Choir, though too loud in the final chorus, predictably sings its rivals out of court − lovely offstage angels, their haunting sound enhanced by the first-rate recording (made in the church of Sainte Madeleine in Pérouges). Gardiner's performance surpasses all the others, even Davis's, in its sensitivity to orchestral colour, whose vital role in the drama is realised as never before in my experience, so that the score glows like the illuminated missal to which Berlioz likened it. Dynamics too are meticulously gauged, with fine-drawn diminuendos (achieving, for example, a profound sense of desolation in Herod's aria) and true pianissimos. The duet in the streets of Saïs is intensely dramatic, the overture to Part 2 perfectly paced.

But tempo is, finally, where this version just fails to be exemplary. The tenor solo in Part 2, at dotted crotchet = c.63, compared to the composer's 52, is simply too fast − the lilting, slightly melancholy tranquillity of Berlioz's gently rocking 6/8 is lost at this pace. (Nor does Anthony Rolfe Johnson's Narrator approach Pears's in eloquence or vocal power.) And the 'Shepherds' Farewell', at exactly half the speed indicated, turns a noël − the simple seed from which the whole work sprang − into a pronouncement from the pulpit. For tempo in Berlioz's music, the score really is the surest guide.

Verdi: Requiem Mass

ALAN BLYTH

Toscanini's interpretation of the Verdi *Requiem* was once described, by Alec Robertson, as the Old Testament reading, Giulini's (his first) as the New Testament, an apt and illustrative distinction that sums up, if too simplistically, the impression left by these two classic performances of the work. 'Dramatic' as compared with 'devotional' might be another description of their differences. Yet, for all this contrast in approach, there is a greater similarity between the two Italians than there is between their performances and those by many other conductors who have challenged their ascendancy. Indeed with three notable and unexpected exceptions, it is the Italians who come closest to understanding the spirit of the work and to conveying it in a truthful and unexaggerated manner. I use those two epithets advisedly, for it is on fidelity to Verdi's text, particularly to his dynamic and tempi markings, that the success of so many of the most cogent interpretations rests, whether those interpretations be dramatic or devotional.

To show just how much licence some conductors have taken, compare the time taken in two sets from the start of the work to the entry of the tenor soloist. Sir John Barbirolli, one of the most dilatory of all interpreters, begins at crotchet = 50 (instead of Verdi's 80) and allows himself 6 minutes 13 seconds over the passage. Toscanini, conforming to the composer's tempo in his 1951 version, goes through the same music in 4 minutes 33 seconds, an amazing difference, when you consider the section is only of seventy-seven bars length. Nobody expects, or wants, a conductor to obey Verdi to the letter, but there should be an attempt to match his intentions if the music is to retain its proper character. Too many conductors ignore that fact.

Timing was of the essence, in another sense, in Toscanini's reading, as Spike Hughes pointed out in his detailed study of the 1951 performance.[1] Not something easily analysed, it permitted him to include *ritardandi* and *accelerandi*, even unmarked ones, while maintaining a basic pulse; and those

1 *The Toscanini Legacy* (Dover Books, 1969).

186

subtle variations feel natural and unforced.'In all three of Toscanini's extant performances, one also notes his attention to pertinent orchestral detail, and an incandescence of manner and spirit that imbues them with a single-minded, unfettered view of the Requiem.

Toscanini I derives from a 1938 Queen's Hall performance, part of a London Music Festival. All who remember hearing or taking part in it agree that it was a very special occasion, and that sense of being present at the experience of a lifetime can be felt through the somewhat dim recording. I do not think it is fanciful to hear just how much the famed Queen's Hall acoustics contributed to the aura of the evening. Toscanini's speeds are close to those in the score, and time and again one remarks on the beauty of the detail and the way it is played by the BBC SO. In the Kyrie the staccato semiquavers (bar 96) are *leggierissimo* in delivery as required. The bassoon and cello precision near the movement's close (129ff) are as precise as you will hear them. In the Dies irae, taken at absolutely the right tempo, the amount of detail to be heard, in particular the piccolos (32ff), is common to all three Toscanini readings; as is the tremendous incandescence − the word must be used again − of the interpretation, though here the superb singing of the BBC Choral Society remains unrivalled. Later in this movement one observes Toscanini's secure pacing of the 'Salva me' ensemble, his sympathetic attention to the needs of the soloists, the timpani at bars 504 and 506 in the 'Oro supplex', here slower than in 1951, but at the same pace as 1940; in the Offertorio, the ethereal wind over the cantabile passage for soprano, in the Sanctus the diaphanous orchestra sound, again unique to Toscanini, and once more the vivid quality of the chorus, in the Lux Aeterna, the way Toscanini (bar 20) insists on articulation of the triplets by the soloists. In the finale, apart from the terror of the hell-fire implicit in the conductor's approach, there is yet again so much detail clarified that it is usually left to fend for itself.

The 1938 soloists are an impressive team. Kerstin Thorborg's 'Nils' in the 'Liber scriptus' have a shivering, frightened effect all their own. Throughout she sings in grave, steady if hardly Italianate tones which, in the 'Recordare' and Agnus Dei, finely set off Zinka Milanov's clear, fresh soprano. 'Huic ergo', with its rise *pp* to a high A, is predictably radiant, ethereal, while the 'Sed' dropping from E to E flat *pianissimo*, always a supreme test of the soprano's mettle, is here done as well as anywhere and the final solo phrase of the movement is legato and *dolcissimo* as marked. Against that has to be set a placid Libera me (1940 far superior in that respect), some sliding in 'et timeo' (41ff) and a break (also present unfortunately in 1940) before the change of key in the *andante* section, which at the right pace (crotchet = 80) is finely phrased. It might be as well to state here just how important it is that this section should be taken *andante*, not *adagio*, in order that it should be a reflective moment in the otherwise dramatic finale, not something separated from it. Helge Roswaenge sings stoutly, but is too Germanic in delivery. The 'Ingemisco' (same speed as 1940, slower than 1949) is sensitively phrased and ends with a ringing B flat, but it is a trifle lachrymose in expression. The important 'Hostias', which Toscanini, again rightly, takes strictly, is adequate, no more. The wholly non-Italian team is completed by the reliable, uninteresting Greek-born Nicola Moscona.

He is transformed by the time we reach Toscanini II, taken from a performance at Carnegie Hall on 23 November 1940. Authority, and a neo-Pinza timbre, are now evident. The 'Oro supplex' is properly sombre and imploring and the support at the bottom of the ensembles is exemplary. Milanov has also grown in stature as an artist in every respect, steadier and more ethereal where needed, finely urgent in the Libera me, providing a soaring high C at the movement's climax. Her voice is clearly contrasted with Bruna Castagna's in the Agnus Dei, where both catch the chantlike, monastic quality of the writing. Elsewhere Castagna is rather dull, breathing too often for the good of her legato, failing to dig deep into her phrases or to grasp their full import. But, apart from hearing yet again Toscanini's masterly interpretation, the reason for listening to this performance is to catch Jussi Björling, at his very best, in a classic account of the tenor part. The 'Qui Mariam' is nowhere so plaintive or *dolce*, or the 'Hostias' so poised and inward (no trill, however) and throughout his perfect pitching in the unaccompanied passages for the four soloists is a source of strength. The American choir sounds small in size, confident in execution, but not comparable to the BBC chorus. Björling apart, this is the most dispensable of the Toscanini sets.

For a detailed description of Toscanini III the reader is referred to Hughes. 'A great spiritual and emotional experience' is his general description of this 'near-ideal performance'. Toscanini has undoubtedly grown more severe with the years, but at the same time no less spontaneous and loving in his attitude towards a work that so obviously moved him deeply. The recording is the most tolerable of the three, and greatly improved in its CD form. One notices the even tauter control of form, the terrifying intensity now of the Dies irae, the still more overwhelming 'Tuba mirum', the turmoil so vividly depicted at 'Confutatis', the expressive cellos introducing the Offertorio, the *leggiero* strings at 'Pleni sunt coeli' in the Sanctus, the lightness of the *Falstaff*-like orchestral support to the Lux aeterna, the clipped tension of the resumed Libera me fugue (312).

A notable indication of the conductor's late, more impatient style is the quicker tempo adopted for both the 'Ingemisco' and the 'Oro supplex': Hughes states that the former is thus given lyrical warmth without sentimentality, but I would suggest that the 1940 'Ingemisco' with Björling at Verdi's crotchet = 72 is in fact even more restrained and lyrical than the 1951 with its suggestion of hurry. On the whole, Toscanini here boasted his best integrated quartet of soloists. Herva Nelli does not scale Milanov's heights but she does not commit her colleague's occasional solecism: her tone, in her most important recorded performance, is fresh and full, her singing unfussy, to the point, the very antithesis of, say, Schwarzkopf in this music. Fedora Barbieri, bumpy to start with, gains in steadiness and feeling as the work progresses and laments with the best mezzos in any set at the start of the 'Lacrymosa'. Giuseppe di Stefano, not in his best voice, is nonetheless fervent and appealing in timbre and expression. Completing this happily Italianate quartet is the solid, malleable bass of Cesare Siepi, inspired by Toscanini to be more positive in expression than was his custom. The disciplined choir gives its all in the Toscanini cause to help create one of the gramophone's true classics.

His disciple, Guido Cantelli, had he lived, might have presented us with another. As it is, we have to be content with his flawed 1954 'live' performance. Without quite the master's authority, Cantelli achieves much of the same impact, but some of the detail, so inevitable in Toscanini's accounts, here becomes exaggerated. Where the older conductor gives us *animando* just where Verdi asks for it, Cantelli anticipates it. The American-sounding choir is not as infused as Toscanini's with the meaning of the text. In brief, the performance was probably not as well rehearsed as Toscanini's, but the beseeching cellos in the 'Recordare' (437ff) indicate Toscanini's influence. The soloists are unidiomatic in utterance, unsatisfactory in voice. Herva Nelli, now less confident than under her mentor, goes completely awry near the start of the Libera me, turning the passage between bars 24 and 40 into some kind of atonal parody of Verdi. She only just regains her confidence for the *andante* section. Claramae Turner, unsettled and edgy, at least suggests good intentions until she loses her voice towards the end of the Lux aeterna. Eugene Conley's monochrome, hard tenor is not equal to the task in hand. Moscona, rusty to start with, begins to show his experience in this work from his contribution to the 'Hostias', showing Conley how to phrase its solemn, sweet melody. As a memento of Cantelli's often compelling direction, this is interesting, but not for much else.

Cantelli is, as it were, only a parenthesis to Toscanini, whose close contemporary and fellow-Italian Tullio Serafin comes closest in his two remarkably similar versions to matching Toscanini's faithfulness to Verdi. Let me take Serafin's second version first. For those who think he may have laid a more yielding, indulgent hand on the work I would recommend a hearing of the Dies irae or Libera me in this version. Both are released with tremendous energy and with the same conviction that marks out Toscanini from his inferiors, and the opening movement, with tempi properly managed, unfolds naturally, inevitably. Detail is clear if not given the same point as by Toscanini. The chorus is heard as typically Italian — the Rome singers are obviously of mature years, vibrating uncomfortably and sounding, for better and worse, Italian. When the soloists enter, they immediately announce themselves as a most interesting and individual group. That they confirm in their succeeding solos and ensembles. The Lebanese Shakeh Vartenissian, who has a real Verdian soprano, is matter-of-fact in expression, too phlegmatic one might surmise not knowing any of her other work, but the steadiness is welcome; so is the soaring over the orchestra in the 'Salva me'. The young Fiorenza Cossotto immediately suggests the right manner and voice in the 'Liber scriptus', conveying awe before the seat of judgement, and deeply expressive at the start of the 'Recordare' without the hardness that later afflicted her tone. Eugenio Fernandi, a tenor rightly appreciated by Walter Legge, is plangent and beseeching (as he should be) in the 'Ingemisco' – 'qui mariam' taken in one phrase and ended with a *morendo*. Nor is an extra breath needed in the final (and very difficult phrase), which here rises immaculately to the high B flat. Just before that, Serafin and tenor reserve the *animando* until bar 488 as Verdi enjoins. Boris Christoff, who has earlier shown his authority in keen consonants and impressive delivery, is a little over-emphatic in the 'Oro supplex' with Serafin yielding too much to him in the matter of tempo (too slow). Christoff cleverly changes vocal colour for his 'Lacrymosa' entry, which is now warmer, more pliant. The three lower soloists make the most of the Lux aeterna. There is much else to admire in this well-recorded, perceptive and unhackneyed performance.

Serafin I, recorded in Rome with similar forces twenty years earlier (no change of chorus-master in all that time, I note), is the set by which I learnt the work. Returning to it after a long absence, I found it no less admirable than in the past. Just like the later version, it flows along with a natural inevitability, and conveys a tradition passed on without growing stale. As in 1959, Serafin's tempi are right, and in the 'Oro supplex', with Pinza as the unsurpassed bass soloist, the speed is here up to Verdi's metronome mark. The choral singing is fresher in sound. As *The Record Guide*[2] commented, 'Serafin achieves a high degree of precision without any loss of intensity or fire.' That book also described Pinza's account of the bass part, quite rightly, as 'flawless'. Listen to the second verse of the 'Oro supplex' if you want to hear the epitome of Verdian style. Listen also to his contribution to the start of the Lux aeterna: he is like a high priest answering the supplications of mezzo and tenor. Earlier, the 'Mors stupebit' suggests horror without exaggeration. Ebe Stignani is almost as exemplary in her richly etched account of the mezzo music: how grateful to the voice it sounds, how easy to deliver, when sung so satisfyingly as here, the tone grand yet heart-easing. Gigli is Gigli in his third period, soulful, impassioned, inimitable, indeed definitely not to be imitated, all the nudges to the line forgiven in pleasure at the sweet, warm voicing of emotions. Maria Caniglia deviates from pitch in the earlier part of the work, but matches up to most of the challenges of the finale in her own, somewhat melodramatic way. The blend with Stignani is fine, but here as in other ensembles Verdi's dynamics are too often ignored; that is forgotten in enjoying the sheer opulence of all four singers.

2 Collins, London, 1955.

Verdi: Requiem Mass

For those who find Toscanini's blinding vision and dramatic impulse almost too terrifying to contemplate or Serafin a little too predictable, Giulini's is the eloquent approach personified — at least in his earlier recording. This is a Requiem for a human and lovable person, not the final rites for the whole world as encompassed by Toscanini. Ever since its first appearance in the catalogues in 1964, it has been accepted as more or less the *fons et origo* where the Requiem is concerned, in stereo at least, and on reappraising it for this study I found little reason to quarrel with the verdict of the years — or indeed with much of what Alec Robertson said in his original review. He wrote that 'There is no lack of vitality [in Giulini's reading] but always he is remembering that the *Requiem* mourns the man, Alessandro Manzoni, whom Verdi worshipped "as the purest and holiest of our glories". This gives a special depth and pathos and warmth to his interpretation.'

Contrary to what is often said about Giulini's conducting here, it is not by any means slow, rather yielding within basically correct speeds, and the marvellous responses he obtains from chorus and orchestra are the result, surely, of long preparation, long familiarity each with the other. As with Toscanini, nothing is left to chance, yet spontaneity can be felt in every bar. From the start we are aware of the detailed care over dynamics taken by the Wilhelm Pitz-rehearsed Philharmonia Chorus. To quote AR again, 'Many choruses can sing Dies irae: but how many can sing the unaccompanied "Te decet hymnus", ranging from *f*, through *diminuendo* to *ppp*, the men observing the staccato marks at "votum in Je(rusalem)", *crescendo* to *f*, *p* to *f*, with *diminuendo* to the exquisitely modulated close (24 bars) with the perfection here shown.' On the larger canvas of the Sanctus, the singing is no less acute, no less pleasurable to the ear, nor has the unaccompanied support to the soprano in the Libera me ever been sung with such hushed beauty as here. The orchestral performance is as imaginative, matching the subtlety and appropriateness of Verdi's writing. The offstage perspective of the trumpets in the 'Tuba mirum' is perfectly adumbrated, as is the pining wind in 'Quid sum miser'.

The soloists are as well balanced a team as in any set, and highly accomplished, at times inspired as individuals. Schwarzkopf is the most controversial among them. No other soprano has lavished so much intelligence on her phrasing or (perhaps) caught so precisely the passages of meditative loveliness — the poised high G flat in the 'Salva me', 'huic ergo' in the 'Lacrymosa', that difficult 'sed' in the Offertorio, practically all of the *andante* of the Libera me: in all of these the technical control is beyond praise. Yet, when that is said, it has to be admitted that hers is not the ideal voice for Verdi, and here, more than in her earlier set (see below), the strain of the *spinto* sections of the work is self-evident. Her voice blends with and sets off Christa Ludwig's to perfection in the 'Recordare' — 'quaerens me' is inexpressibly beautiful and in the Agnus Dei the lower voice is a pure shadow of the high one. On her own,

191

Ludwig is rewardingly opulent whether she is using her dark lower register to depict terror or her free upper one to proclaim hours of judgement, and her contribution to the Lux aeterna, in particular her long-breathed phrasing at the start is impeccable. Nicolai Gedda is not in her class. For all his musicality, exemplified in fidelity to the score in so many respects, his is a dullish account of the solos, the 'Hostias', where his trill is neat, apart. Nicolai Ghiaurov also lacks individuality, but one is thankful for his strong voice and often stirring accents: only inner feeling seems wanting. In the many unaccompanied passages, however, both men surpass almost all their rivals in sensitivity, by which I mean dynamic control (producer Walter Legge's influence?), and careful modulation of their voices to those of the women. The recording, at least in its CD format, provides a fine balance among soloists, chorus and orchestra, all caught in a warm acoustic. For that and the time spent in perfecting the performance, we must thank Legge.

Unfortunately Giulini's 1989 remake hasn't many of the virtues of its predecessor. The choral singing of the Ernst Senff Choir is, if possible, even more disciplined than that of the Philharmonia Chorus, and, of course, the Berlin Philharmonic responds willingly to Giulini's call for legato playing tinged with the ethereal. But in the quarter of a century since the conductor's former reading, he has so refined his ideas about the work as seriously to debilitate its dramatic force. The Dies irae remains awe-inspiring but elsewhere speeds have become noticeably slower in every movement, conveying a fatal sense of lassitude. One still admires Giulini's wonderful control of details of expression and dynamics, but much of the earlier urgency has given way to flaccid rhythm. We are left only with the sense of the spiritual, which is only half the story.

With one notable exception the solo singing is anonymous in character. That exception is Sharon Sweet, who possesses just the Verdian sound that Schwarzkopf failed to muster. Somewhat overawed in the earlier part of the work, she sings a superb Libera me, vivid in tone and word, and delicately phrased in the reprise of the Kyrie music. Florence Quivar is always adequate, but seldom much more. She, like the tenor Vinson Cole, wants the individuality of utterance to fill her music with life and feeling. Simon Estes is simply wooden and dull. I cannot think why Giulini accepted three singers with so little imagination among them.

Continuing with Italians, we come to the two sets conducted by the problematic Riccardo Muti. Without a doubt, the first enjoys a sound quality unimagined in the Toscanini era. We hear a conductor who has, in many respects, followed in the Toscanini tradition in tempi (two major ones excepted), care for detail, and indeed incandescence. What may be found missing is the spiritual element, admittedly difficult to define and, almost as hard to explain, a comparative failure to encompass that imperceptible mastery of timing already referred to. In brief, there is occasionally a slightly contrived and self-regarding character about the interpretation. It is most to the fore in the two sections where Muti strays furthest away from Toscanini – and Verdi – namely the Dies irae chorus, raced through and hard-driven at each appearance, and the brisk Sanctus, which only a professional choir such as Muti employed could manage at this pace. The advantage of having these professionals is to be heard in the manner by which the singers respond to his demanding beat with flair and virtuosity, itself caught by the engineers in a truthful, full-blooded acoustic (Kingsway Hall). Every fast semiquaver is in its place and can be heard as such. Yet there is no want of feeling when that is the overriding need. The appeals of the 'Salva me' are as pliant and beseeching as the sound of the Last Trump is arresting. The Philharmonia players, though marginally less precise than their predecessors in the same band in the early sixties, provide the singing tone (strings) so essential in Verdi.

Muti's solo quartet is a felicitous ensemble, obeying most but not all of Verdi's myriad instructions. Renata Scotto, as is the case in her later career, sounds strained at the top of her voice under pressure. A few other notes discolour, but from her ethereal entry in the Offertorio right through her marvellously vibrant use of the text in the Libera me, with an imaginatively phrased account of the *andante* section, she is direct in expression, spontaneous in reaction to the text. Agnes Baltsa's mellifluous, even mezzo lacks weight for the 'Liber scriptus' and could be said to avoid temperament, but she uses it with consistent intelligence and feeling. Veriano Luchetti's plaintively urgent 'Ingemisco' and prayerful, finely accented 'Hostias' are the work of a dedicated artist. Yevgeny Nesterenko is the firm, unaffected bass, secure in his musicianship though not tonally quite idiomatic. The start of the Offertorio shows the team at its best. The piece is up to tempo from the start, the cellos phrase eloquently, the three lower soloists demonstrate their blend, then Scotto floats in tenderly on 'sed', makes her *crescendo* and draws back to a *pianissimo* for the semitone drop. All in all, a version that is consistently thought-provoking, never dull (as are so many of its near contemporaries) and always alive – perhaps it can be characterised as a young man's long-distance look at death.

Muti's second recording is very different by virtue of the fact that it was made live at La Scala with La Scala forces. The performance is altogether grander in scale but no less carefully crafted. In place of the more incisive Ambrosians the Scala chorus offers bold, black-browed singing at 'Rex tremendae' and the awed *senza misura* incantation at the start of the Libera me. The chorus copes well with Muti's hard-driven Dies irae and his nifty speed for the Sanctus (not quite so fast as previously). There are refined details in the instrumental playing, but not more so than in 1978. Recording live means that no adjustment can be made to the slightly hesitant start to the work, not helped by Cheryl Studer, the soprano replacing Margaret Price at a very late moment. There is some cloud on her tone at 'huic ergo', but she soon recovers her best form. The final phrase of the Offertorio is ideally managed. The whole of the Libera me is delivered with impassioned urgency and splendid control. Even the slow speed of the *andante* section, reflecting that of the Kyrie, is easily encompassed by Studer with the voice carried over from 'domine' to 'et lux'. Her slightly resinous tone blends well with that of Dolora Zajic in the 'Recordare' and the Agnus Dei. The dark grain of Zajic's sappy voice in the lower register contrasts with a degree of brilliance at the top. Hers is among the best accounts of the mezzo part. Pavarotti is in as good a voice as for Solti (see below) and sings with more subtlety and is solicitous of his colleagues in the ensembles. Ramey sings with consistently firm tone and consideration of phrase, even trumping Pavarotti's ace in the 'Hostias'. In spite of the range of the recording it wants immediacy, a serious drawback in this piece, and one vitiating the set's many virtues.

Claudio Abbado, also with La Scala forces, gives a curiously blank interpretation. There are few of Muti's idiosyncrasies, few of his perceptions. Abbado conducts the work as though overawed by it. He is not helped by the recording, which emphasises the extreme ends of the dynamic range and varies in its acoustic properties. The choral singing is assuredly authentic in its operatic approach – the men sound, not inappropriately, like the priests in *Aida* at 'Rex tremendae' – but often one is conscious of doubtful intonation, imprecise ensemble and ill-adjusted vibratos. Tempi often accord with the metronome, or thereabouts (a slow 'Oro supplex' being an exception), but they tend to plod because of Abbado's slack pulse – the 'Lacrymosa' is a case in point. The total effect is anonymous and enervating.

The work of the soloists, an ill-assorted quartet, does little to redeem this version. Katia Ricciarelli is the most satisfying of the four. Cloudy and poorly focused notes are forgiven for the generally easy and fresh character of her singing. 'Huic ergo' is ethereally done and the difficult phrase, a few moments later in this section, from bar 651, rising to a high B flat, one of the most rewarding but difficult to bring off in the entire work, here receives its due; so does the final phrase of the Offertorio, starting 'fac eas'. The *andante* of the Libera me has true inwardness but is spoilt by an unsteady B flat at its close: as ever with this singer the most laudable intentions are often vitiated by incomplete technique. Ricciarelli's verbal definition also leaves something to be desired. Shirley Verrett's husky timbre is a poor match for Ricciarelli's voice in the Agnus Dei, but on her own, as at the start of the Lux aeterna, she offers a customary commitment and largeness of heart, aware of the text's import. Domingo is in staid, uncommunicative form, as if completing just another recording assignment: he is heard to greater advantage under Mehta (see below). Ghiaurov, in his third recording of this part, is less convincing than of old and now reaches for high notes previously attacked without fear.

The last (the early 78rpm version apart) and least admirable of 'official' versions conducted by an Italian is surprisingly, given his reputation in the work in his own country and in Britain just after the war, that conducted by

Victor De Sabata. The supplement to *The Record Guide* described his speeds as 'positively grotesque', a verdict I wholeheartedly endorse. All are far below Verdi's metronome marks with disastrous results on the work's structure. The opening is almost as ponderous as Barbirolli's, 'Oro supplex' static, the Agnus Dei soporific. The chorus is operatic in the worst sense with over-tremulous women, superannuated men. Some consolation is to be found in the work of the soloists. Oralia Domínguez, the mezzo (who created Madame Sosostris in Tippett's *A Midsummer Marriage*), is the most telling of the four. The great weight of the seat of judgement is felt in the 'Liber scriptus', and her voice blends ideally with Schwarzkopf's in the 'Recordare' and the Agnus Dei as if a penitent and her *alter ego* were being heard. Schwarzkopf, in youthfully fresh voice, sings 'huic ergo' with perfect poise, but takes a huge breath just before the B flat a few minutes later, a point she had corrected by 1964 with Giulini. Throughout she uses all her artistry and pure, technically assured singing to make us forget that hers is not a Verdian soprano, at least until her exaggerated chest register in the Libera me. Giuseppe di Stefano is too overt with his emotional responses and refuses to sing *pianissimo* until 'Hostias', where he spoils the calm of his intoning by carelessness over note values. Siepi sings with less inspiration and variety than for Toscanini. This set is perhaps best sampled in the 'Lacrymosa'. Schwarzkopf and Domínguez begin by pouring out the lamenting phrases with feeling and the whole section is built to an overwhelming climax by De Sabata.

De Sabata's 'off-the-air' performance, given on 27 January 1951, the fiftieth anniversary of Verdi's death, is a much more inspired performance than the studio effort of three years later. Speeds are again on the slow side, but this is a warmer, more vibrant interpretation. A total view of the work can be felt, also a keen ear for relevant detail. Nell Rankin is a secure but uninteresting mezzo, Nicola Rossi-Lemeni an idiomatic but wobbly bass. In contrast Giacinto Prandelli's liquid, sensitive tenor (of a kind apparently extinct today in Italy) is among the best, and here is the only representation of Renata Tebaldi's fervent, soaring soprano in music that ideally suited her, a poised 'huic ergo', finely floated 'sed signifer', electrifying, as is De Sabata, in the Libera me, its *andante* section up to speed and quite beautifully and spontaneously sung. All in all, this version takes a very high place in the discography of this work.

A number of non-Italians have recorded the *Requiem*, none with complete success. Three of the best are among the most recent. That directed by Zubin Mehta is an unexaggerated, devout reading that nicely relates tempi one to another. It is true that he starts slowly (5 minutes 33 seconds to the tenor's entry), but there he is more or less at one with most recent interpreters. Elsewhere he is reasonably faithful to Verdi. His choir and orchestra are precise and involved. The choir, larger than Muti's or Abbado's (among recent competitors), is more spiritual than the Ambrosians, more accurate than the La Scala Chorus. The New York Philharmonic provides strong strings and some affecting wind solos.

The soloists make a well-blended team – two Spanish stars, two American stalwarts. Montserrat Caballé surpasses even her lovely singing for Barbirolli (see below) some twelve years earlier, floating the A flat at 'huic ergo' ideally and carrying up to the B flat a little earlier, a difficult moment, with consummate ease. Similarly, the phrase marked *cantabile dolce* in the third movement at bar 69 is as ethereal as one could wish, also the *andante* of the Libera me. Only descents to a weak chest register and a few moments of self-indulgence give cause for complaint. Bianca Berini, whom I once much admired in this work at the Festival Hall, is a generous-voiced, impassioned mezzo, not often bettered elsewhere – try her at 'et lux perpetua' in the sixth movement. She matches Caballé's timbre in the Agnus Dei.

Domingo, in the best of his recorded Requiems, equals Björling in plangent sound and pure phrasing in the 'Ingemisco'. He is inclined to overlook *piano* marks, except in the 'Hostias', which he delivers in a rapt *mezza voce*. Paul Plishka is sound vocally and involved emotionally without calling on histrionics; the 'Oro supplex', taken at Verdi's tempo, proves just as supplicatory that way.

The Polish recording conducted by Kazimierz Kord is a good middle-of-the-road reading. Tempi may be on the slow side, but they are sensibly integrated, relating one to the other, and they allow the resplendent contributions of the Warsaw forces to make their effect in a spacious but not too reverberant acoustic. This performance may be a trifle staid but it commits no solecisms. Nor are his soloists to be overlooked. Teresa Zylis-Gara, alive to her part's meaning, passes most of my tests of vocalisation and phrasing, while never being very individual in accent. Her mezzo partner, Krystyna Szostek-Radkowa, has a fruity tone but is no mean artist. Wieslaw Ochman is mellifluous rather than positive in the tenor music. Leonard Mróz boasts one of the most telling basses in any set, beseeching in his solos, a solid bottom line in the ensembles.

Robert Shaw's 1987 set is probably the most successful set to date in terms of sound and it is also a more even-handed, central performance than any of its recent rivals. Toscanini, Shaw's mentor, may have been the model – and an excellent one. No other modern version has choral singing to equal this one in dedication and precision. Indeed the unanimity of approach in this reading is one of its strong points. All know what they are doing individually and collectively. The Atlanta Orchestra responds confidently and naturally to its conductor. Speeds are just throughout, near to Verdi's markings and seldom strayed from.

You may hear certain solos sung with more personality elsewhere, but in few other sets is there such a well-coordinated team. The voices blend truly because all four singers have firm tone and avoid ego trips. Only the un-accompanied passages, marked *piano*, are disappointing: they are sung *mezzo forte*. Susan Dunn, here at the outset of her career, floats finely at 'huic ergo' in the 'Lacrymosa' and the soprano's first entry in the Offertorio. Her voice has the bite to soar over the whole ensemble, and she overcomes all the danger points in a moving account of the Kyrie reprise in the finale. Diane Curry is less interesting but consistently firm and incisive in her delivery. Jerry Hadley's timbre is hardly Italianate, but he finds the right style and feeling for the 'Ingemisco', the final phrase taken in one breath, and the 'Hostias'. Plishka's bass is sympathetic, pliant, not quite weighty enough. Although the single parts of this set are excellent, it is the sum of them that is so admirable.

The second of Solti's performances catches the sense of a real occasion, having been recorded after live performances in Chicago. A vivid recording allows us to hear more orchestral detail than on almost any other set, indeed sometimes it seems unrealistically highlighted. Much of the fire and sensitivity in the conducting suggests a close study of Toscanini's recordings, and there is more sense of an occasion than in Solti's lifeless Decca set. The well-trained choir has an American flavour to it, an innate eagerness and quick response, a fresh, though not particularly Italianate sound. Sometimes, as happens in the Sanctus, the voices are almost overwhelmed by the large orchestra. Tempi are well maintained; consolation tempers the drama of the earlier reading, even if there is still no shape to the piece as a whole.

Janet Baker is, in every sense, an exceptional mezzo soloist. Hers is not a voice intended by nature for this music, but her singular intelligence gives new, or at least renewed, meaning to the text. The 'Liber scriptus' indicates the occasional strain put upon her resources, but we are soon made aware of her distinction of phrase, her involvement in her work, even when this leads to the occasional overemphasis as at the start of the 'Lacrymosa'. The dark sorrow of 'Judex ergo' earlier and the radiance of the Lux aeterna, shining through darkness, are just two instances of a wonderfully individual approach. It is crowned by the real benediction of 'quia pius es'. She pairs well with Leontyne Price in the Agnus Dei. Price herself offers a lovely piece of singing in the *andante* of the Libera me to make up for an uneven performance earlier in the work, where glorious phrases alternate with many disturbed by unequal tone or uneven phrasing. There is too much here that was better done at the start of the great Verdian soprano's career for Reiner some seventeen years earlier (see below). José van Dam is steady, even noble at times, a tower of strength in ensemble but finally a little too phlegmatic for this work. Luchetti is much as for Muti, special thanks being due for his simple, restrained 'Hostias'. All in all a puzzling version, off-centre in some ways as an interpretation but never uninteresting.

And 'uninteresting' is, I fear, just the epithet for Solti's 1967 set. Its rhythmic stodginess, bland orchestra (the Vienna Philharmonic having a poor session) and overblown sound are relieved only by a diaphanous Lux aeterna in which the Vienna violins recover their laurels; tempo and dynamics are finely controlled by Solti, and the unaccompanied passages go particularly well. Elsewhere, the Vienna State Opera Chorus is wobbly without being Italianate and not well disciplined. Joan Sutherland is yet another singer out of her element in this work, groping at a 'role' she does not seem to understand and worrying the music to the extent of destroying line: her final contribution to the Offertorio is obvious evidence of this point. Her opening of the Libera me, melodramatically intoned, has become a classic of mistaken interpretation. Yet the sound remains as lovely as ever, most obviously in the *andante* of the finale. Marilyn Horne is the formidable mezzo, but her firm impressive singing is seldom lit by interior feeling. The young Pavarotti excels at 'qui Mariam' in the 'Ingemisco', but is hampered in this solo by four-square support; the 'Hostias' is too heart-on-sleeve – but the sheer beauty of the tenor's tone is hard to resist. Martti Talvela sings sonorously, with feeling, but lacks graceful legato. In many ways, Sutherland excepted, this is a safe, 'gramophonic' performance, but not one to take anyone to the inspired heights on which Verdi's genius is working.

Eugene Ormandy's set comes into a similar category. His is a typically big-scale American performance, a massive, extroverted reading of the work. Ormandy is in some respects more faithful to Verdi's intentions than, say, Giulini; Ormandy does not anticipate *rallentandi* as did the Italian in his roughly contemporaneous version, but obeying the letter of the score in this case does not mean catching its spirit. He is also attentive to detail as at 'quantus tremor' in the Dies irae, but the playing of the Philadelphia is respectful rather than persuasive. None of the soloists offers a specific insight into his or her part. Lucine Amara has the power to dominate ensembles, but her voice, often fluttery and uncertain, cannot mould the quieter sections with any degree of security. Maureen Forrester's closed vowels and gusty, unsubtle approach leaves a 'plummy' impression on all the important alto solos. A *pianissimo* seems to mean nothing to Richard Tucker, who sings most of his part *mezzo-forte* and betrays not a sign of sensitivity even in the 'Hostias'. George London's voice does not carry the weight needed for the bass's contribution, but his 'Mors stupebit', full of foreboding, is among the best.

The version conducted by Erich Leinsdorf has much more to offer, including a Boston chorus and orchestra technically accomplished and imaginatively inclined. Tempi are well adjusted, and those averse to Giulini's free way with the score ought to respond to Leinsdorf's stricter approach which, like Solti's, owes something to Toscanini (they both worked with him before the war at Salzburg). The music flows, there is a give-and-take by everyone, preparation has been careful. Ezio Flagello is a reliable rather than inspired bass. Carlo Bergonzi is musical and suitably reverential, obedient to Verdi's dynamics, taking the final phrase of the 'Ingemisco' in a single breath, and giving us a refined, unaffected 'Hostias'. Offering a full tone throughout a wide range, the mezzo Lili Chookasian is firm in attack, never dull in her inflections. All three make much of the Lux aeterna. There they are spared the company of Birgit Nilsson; her pitch is too frequently suspect, she slides uncomfortably between notes, and in general does her reputation much harm, in spite of her thrilling top, most in evidence in the finale.

Bernstein, Barbirolli and Karajan are the next three 'international' conductors to have given us their variously flawed readings. Bernstein's 1970 set, recorded in the Albert Hall after a performance there, is nothing if not involving, but throughout one has the sense that everything is being manipulated for emotional effect. The start is exaggeratedly hushed and slow, even turgid, in the Dies irae vigour and drama are lessened by ear-splitting timpani, the double-dotting and *sotto voce* at 'Quantus tremor' are overdone, the *andante* in the Libera me is a dragging *adagio*. Against that, and the unwanted *accelerandi* and *rallentandi*, has to be set very many points left unobserved by other conductors, such as the *frizzante* horns in the 'Tuba mirum', the real *cupo* in Josephine Veasey's voicing of the end of the 'Liber scriptus' and the *dolce pp* Domingo manages at 'inter oves'. The Sanctus, at the correct speed, is marvellously alert and, at 'Pleni sunt coeli', light. The fugue in the Libera me has bite and real precision. In both these movements the LSO and the Arthur Oldham-trained LSO Chorus are commendable. The results of having a dark-toned soprano and a light mezzo are not always felicitous, but Veasey is at all points deeply eloquent, not least at the start of the 'Lacrymosa', which is really mournful. Martina Arroyo, by contrast, is no more than correct, and her vibrato becomes intrusive after a time; nor can she float the relevant passages. Domingo sings 'inter oves' prayerfully as already noted and an inward 'Hostias'. He is stylistically admirable, if not individually communicative. Ruggero Raimondi, with a tone like a light, dry Burgundy, shows sensitivity when he can avoid sliding up to notes, but is not a perceptive interpreter.

Barbirolli's must be the most perverse version ever recorded. I have already noted the ludicrously slack start, but that is only the beginning of an interpretation that plods its way wearily through even the most dramatic passages. Indeed Barbirolli conducts the piece as though he was in charge of his own Requiem. As if to match the reading, the sound is curiously muffled and soft at the edges, obscuring what seem to be good performances by New Philharmonia forces. What merit resides in this interpretation comes from the solo quartet. Together they make a refined, well-balanced team: the unaccompanied 'Jesu pie' has not been surpassed elsewhere for sensitivity and good vocal manners. Montserrat Caballé and Fiorenza Cossotto catch the hieratical character of the Agnus Dei: the effect is 'as if one voice had acquired a halo of overtones' (John Warrack in *Gramophone*). Caballé answers a prayer in her accomplishing of 'huic ergo' and in the Offertorio, her held E natural at 'sed' moves down to the E flat with imperceptible grace while the following phrase, 'signifer sanctus Michael', is filled with the 'holy light'. Then in the Libera me, one senses not the customary melodrama but the terror of a youthfully trembling soul. The control of the *andante* section is exemplary, with the most lovely singing reserved for 'et lux perpetua': the section might have been written with Caballé in mind. Cossotto, though not as pleasing as with Serafin, still responds with much warmth and passion to the mezzo's grateful music, her attack as secure as ever. Vickers, as ever working intelligently on his music, sentimentalises much of it by sliding up to notes or almost crooning; the 'Hostias' is the worst example of this. Ruggero Raimondi is generally not as impressive as he is for Bernstein, but never less than involved: one just wishes that his technique was more secure.

The first of Karajan's two 'official' readings is also most notable for its soloists. Christa Ludwig repeats her rich, personal account of the mezzo solos; Mirella Freni is a straightforward, wholly committed soprano; Carlo Cossutta, despite some fur on his tone and a slight excess of vibrato, is a purposeful tenor; Ghiaurov gives perhaps the best of his four performances, secure and impassioned. What rules this set out of consideration is the inconsistency of the recorded quality and Karajan's slack conducting, often at slow tempi (the Sanctus is the worst example). Accents are too often smoothed away, legato overdone, 'quantus tremor' almost inaudible.

Karajan's second 'official' set, made in 1985, shows his reading still smooth and/or ponderous, but it gains from a more natural recording and the measured tread and poise of the conducting cannot be gainsaid. There is some ethereal playing from the Vienna Philharmonic, especially in the 'Ingemisco' and 'Lux aeterna', and altogether the orchestral sound has more presence than in 1972. Karajan's insistence on really *sotto voce* and *piano* singing from chorus and soloists when that is called for is a bonus, and you sense Karajan personally moulding the expressive treatment of the Lacrymosa *concertato*. If you view the work as a solemn rite, this version may be for you. That impression is enhanced by the backward placing of the soloists, who are less individual supplicants than part of a general pleading. Anna Tomowa-Sintow phrases with consistent accuracy and aristocracy, but her expression and timbre are not Italianate. She rises with distinction to every aspect of the Libera me. Baltsa is more impressive than for Muti I, finding more weight here for the 'Liber scriptus' and combining well with Tomowa-Sintow in the 'Recordare' and the Agnus Dei. Carreras moulds the 'Ingemisco', at Karajan's slow speed, with few signs of effort, but the voice sounds in indifferent shape. José van Dam intones the 'Mors stupebit' sepulchrally but is a shade phlegmatic in the 'Oro supplex', yet another movement taken way below Verdi's metronome mark.

Karajan's earliest performance, taken off-the-air from a 1949 Salzburg Festival performance, is itself a much more vivid affair, the Sanctus here taken at its proper tempo, and the Vienna forces energetic and enthusiastic. Even then, Karajan was supportive of his singers, and allows Helge Roswaenge, now

200

effortful as compared with his pre-war form but still an important singer, too much leeway to make a meal of his 'Ingemisco'. Margarete Klose's glorious mezzo is still in good trim, though whether it was ever a suitable vehicle for this kind of music is another matter (the Germanic 'Kvee' is much in evidence). The youthful Christoff is already imposing his own terms on the music, somewhat to its detriment. Much the most appealing of the soloists is Hilde Zadek, whose soft-grained yet strong soprano (she once sang Aida at Covent Garden) is used expressively throughout, culminating in a totally unaffected, natural, unmannered account of the *andante* section of the Libera me, taken up to tempo. *(See also Postscript)*

Two other faulty readings need not detain us long. Fritz Reiner's is debilitated by drawn-out tempi and too many *rallentandi*, indifferent chorus and orchestra, but to some extent redeemed by its soloists, a notable team, headed by Leontyne Price, here at the peak of her career, not only in wonderful voice but intensely personal in her utterance. Rosalind Elias is scarcely less admirable, offering an even mezzo intelligently used: only the last ounce of passion and inwardness is missing. Björling, in his last recording of any work, cannot match his performance in the unofficial 1938 Toscanini set, but by any other standards sings with impeccable style and great feeling. Giorgio Tozzi, lacking a true Verdian bass, compensates for that with the sincerity of his approach.

If it is possible, Alain Lombard is even more lethargic than Reiner, and there is no redemption here from the soloists, of whom only Paul Plishka's bass is in any way up to his duties. Joyce Barker has the right voice, but is dull in phrasing. Mignon Dunn is tentative and uneven, Ermanno Mauro pseudo-Italian in the very worst way. Carlos Paita's version is more orthodox but betrays many signs of hasty preparation. The choral singing and orchestral playing are often slack and poorly co-ordinated. The impression this conductor makes is of being overheated to the point of intemperance. As one would expect, Heather Harper gives a well-considered account of the soprano role. Josephine Veasey is much as for Bernstein but in less equal voice. The ladies react intelligently to each other in their duets. Carlo Bini is a run-of-the-mill tenor, Hans Sotin an impassive bass.

Now we begin to travel back in the LP era, meeting first on the way the set conducted by Igor Markevitch, recorded in Russia with superb Bolshoi forces. Here, indeed, is a thrilling, immediate view of the work that, as John Warrack has pointed out, should show 'how an element of drama plays a crucial part in so sincerely felt a work' or what Luigi Barzini refers to as the 'element of spectacle' in Italian consciousness. It can be heard in the élan of the brass in the 'Tuba mirum', the direct passion of the 'Salva me' ensemble. After a slow start, tempi tend to be on the fast side, the Dies irae particularly so. The whining tenor apart, the soloists are all of interest. Galina Vishnevskaya sometimes phrases awkwardly or sings sharp, but everything she does is inspiriting, alive with meaning and, in the finale, spine-tingling. Nina Isakova, the mezzo, is still better. The way she cuts off her 'Nils' almost in terror, starts 'Lacrymosa' *piangente* as asked, or blends with her soprano in the Agnus Dei adds to the impression she at once makes of a strong and serious singer. Ivan Petrov starts a little roughly but comes into his own with a sympathetic, eloquent 'Oro supplex', and follows Vladimir Ivanovsky's bland 'Hostias' with a more inward account of the gratifying music. The helter-skelter of the Dies irae apart, this is a set to be reckoned with.

So is the one conducted by Paul van Kempen, whose records were much admired in the fifties. Speeds, dynamics, and detail are all given due respect. The Santa Cecilia Academy Chorus is excellent, as is its orchestra. Oscar Czerwenka makes an uncouth bass soloist, Petre Munteanu a reedy, ineffective tenor. But the ladies are admirable. Maria von Ilosvay, taking time off from duties on Valhalla, proves herself throughout an appreciable Verdian. Everything, from her double-dotting in the 'Liber scriptus' to her glorious launching of the Lux aeterna, bespeaks an innate musician and a heartfelt one. Gré Brouwenstijn, though not Italian, was acknowledged as an eminent Verdian and confirms that repute here, even if we might ideally ask for warmer tone, a more immaculate attack. The slightly uncomfortable tonal quality mars an otherwise fine Libera me, in which one feels the world trembling about this supplicant.

More widely distributed in its time was the Ferenc Fricsay set, now on CD. Indeed the authors of the *The Record Guide*, in one of their few questionable judgements, dared to prefer it to Toscanini III. However, one can agree that it is 'scrupulous in its adherence to Verdi's demands' and that Fricsay's tempi are 'thoroughly convincing', also with the praise for the St Hedwig's Cathedral Choir. The marvelling at the sound, superb for its day, no longer applies. The four non-Italian soloists continue the good work with their rapt singing of unaccompanied passages and generally, as a team, eschew untoward histrionics or excessive rubato. Maria Stader, a Mozartian soprano, might seem light for this music, but she achieves much through perfect intonation, clean movement from note to note, and thoroughgoing musicality, although her Libera me lacks dramatic thrust. Marianna Radev is a sympathetically expressive mezzo, Helmut Krebs a mellifluous but restrained tenor, Kim Borg a firm bass. The Italian language is subjected to Germanic perversion.

Fricsay's 'live' 1960 recording, first issued in Germany in 1978 and in Britain as late as 1989 (on CD), is another matter and certainly bids fair to compete with Toscanini. Here Fricsay, mortally ill, conducted a performance that seems to deal in immortal matters with immense urgency. The reading is much freer than the earlier one, also more spontaneous, the same forces, now even more attuned to Fricsay's ways, responding with unanimity and dedication to Fricsay's obviously beseeching hands. Everything here seems immediate and convincing, carefully conceived yet wholly without contrivance. There could be no better monument to an undoubtedly great conductor than this riveting set.

Stader repeats her fastidious performance from 1954 but is slightly less firm in voice. Oralia Domínguez is the superb mezzo, strong and secure in voice, sensitive in accent, bold in attack as for De Sabata I. Both tenor and bass are Hungarian by birth but Italian in training. Gabor Carelli, a Gigli pupil, copying the master to good and bad effect, is always interesting, particularly so in a well-varied 'Ingemisco'. Ivan Sardi produces a sustained, keen bass throughout, and is admirable both in ensemble and solo. The mono sound is more than acceptable. Indeed this latecomer proves one of the most telling performances ever committed to disc.

The 1938 Stuttgart Radio performance is notable for Joseph Keilberth's lyrical, unafraid conducting and for some rich, old-fashioned singing from the Munich-based mezzo Luise Willer. Roswaenge is his accustomed self, emotive and full-blooded, Margarete Teschemacher too Germanic in expression. Georg Hann is the rough bass.

We are left with odds and ends, among them an ancient Nixa set conducted by one J. H. Ossewaarde, using an organ instead of an orchestra and third-rate soloists, the Concert Hall version conducted by Gianfranco Rivoli of no more than provincial standard if we except brief moments of distinction from Gloria Davy (soprano) and Heinz Rehfuss (bass-baritone – a prayerful, tenderly phrased start to the 'Salva me' for instance); the Remington performance conducted by Gustav Koslik with Austrian forces than boasts one or two notable phrases from Ilona Steingruber (soprano), one or two imposing ones from the veteran but *passée* Rosette Anday; and the uninteresting unidiomatic Patané set. I have not heard the listed sets conducted by Ricci, Walter Goehr, Balzer or, in more recent times, by Marinov and Buchei.

Of complete versions, that leaves me with the earliest recording of all, the 1929 La Scala set (recently transferred to CD by Pearl), which held the platform alone for eleven years until the first Serafin version was sent from Rome to rival it. Carlo Sabajno, who was then HMV's Italian chief, conducts a fiery, intense performance, well caught in the CD transfers. His tempi are much as Serafin's were to be, except when he was to hurry to cope with the length of 78rpm sides. The chorus and orchestra are distinctly superior to their successors who were to record the work twenty-five years later with De Sabata. The chorus, in particular, sing with brio in the Dies irae and lightness in the Sanctus.

Two of the soloists are at the very highest level of achievement. Irene Minghini-Cattaneo, a much underrated artist, sings throughout with full tone, complete steadiness and opulent phrasing, while not forgetting to consider the meaning of what she is interpreting. She may not be a subtle artist, but in every other respect she is to be admired. Pinza is even better than for Serafin, seemingly more involved in the sense of the text and providing a secure resonant lowest line to all the ensembles. Maria Fanelli, the soprano, is a no more than average Italian soprano, an honest worker but uninspired, and she sings with a too consistent loudness. Franco Lo Giudice has a fiery, strong tenor, but tends to use it too tearfully, particularly in his 'Ingemisco'. There is a small cut in the Lux aeterna.

The 78rpm discography of individual items is not extensive. The most frequently recorded extract is the tenor's 'Ingemisco', starting with Francesco Marconi, then already retired from active service, in 1904 (052057; RLS 7705). We hear the remnants of a fine, free voice and a respectable style, but the primitive recording and the failure to modulate at 'qui mariam' make this version little more than a curiosity. Giovanni Zenatello (Edison 82214; Club 99.49) sings strongly, but the phrasing is rough and ready. Caruso's famous 1914 record (DB 138; GD 60495) is invested with his customary full and golden, third-period sound, but the tempo is treated in rather a cavalier fashion. Evan Williams's 1910 disc (DB 458) is secure enough, but unvaried in tone and expression and curiously pronounced. Moving into the electric era, we find Alfred Piccaver in his most opulent voice and more involved than usual in a version well worth seeking out (Poly. 95354; Discophilia P2): the ease of delivery indicates that Piccaver had one of the most glorious tenor voices of the century. But even he is surpassed by Björling, whose 1938 version (DB 3665; 1C 147–00947/8) trumps that on Toscanini II. This performance has everything: ideal tone, right tempo, no hurrying, prayerful interpretation but no lachrymose intrusions. So does the recently re-discovered live performance from a 1939 concert issued on a Bluebell CD (ABCD 006). The 1954 account on the same CD shows a marked decline.

Two late 78s, by John McHugh (DX 1469) and Luigi Infantino (LX 1080), are both strongly sung but without any special qualities. In the LP era the performances by Franco Corelli (ASD 599), weepy and coarse, Mario Del Monaco (SXL 6234), simply coarse, and Kenneth McKellar (SKL 6118), over-parted, are best forgotten. Versions by Louis van Tulder, Rudolf Schock and Robert Ilosfalvy are no more than souvenirs.

Records of the 'Confutatis' begin with Oreste Luppi in 1906 – except that he doesn't start until the 'Oro supplex': the voice is strong, but the phrasing awkward and wooden. Vittorio Arimondi's 1907 version (Columbia Tricolour 30100) has confidence and character. José Mardones (Victor 6420; LV 268), recorded in the early twenties, colours his magnificent tone most sympathetically but articulates the text in lazy fashion. Not so Heinrich Rehkemper in 1924 (Poly. 66005; LV 107), who gives proper weight to the words with his lighter but not inconsiderable voice. Pinza, in a disc (AGSB 103; GEMM CD 9306) made at almost the same time as his first set, is as resplendent as ever in this music. Has it ever been better done? Tone, attack, feeling are all in perfect accord. Pinza's earliest, 1924 version (DB 956; HLM 1435561) is a little lighter in tone, but still magnificent. Mark Reshetin (Melodiya 33SM 02091/2), in his slow, woolly version, sounds tame beside Pinza. Thomas Denijs

204

(Dutch HMV FD6), more baritone than bass, sings with fervour, but insufficient weight.

I end this survey with two fine discs of the *andante* section of the Libera me. That by Margherita Perras from the 1930s (C 2794; LV 73) is pure and poised. That by Elise Elizza, Viennese in spite of her name, made in 1903 (43445; CO 318), comes nearer to the ideal than any soprano on the complete sets. The voice sounds full yet it is perfectly placed and pure. At the same time the music seems deeply felt and it is phrased with great plasticity rising to a poised, floated B flat − a disc recalling a golden age indeed.

My heavenly 'cast' for the Requiem would be Tebaldi or Milanov, Minghini-Cattaneo, Björling and Pinza with the BBC forces of 1938 under Toscanini.

***

Postscript: In the spring of 1990, DG issued a Laserdisc version conducted by Karajan (071 142−1) that has apparently never appeared in another format. It is by far the most vital and heartfelt of his interpretations. Recorded at La Scala in 1967, it benefits enormously from the participation of that theatre's superb chorus and orchestra of the day. The solo quartet proves as formidable as any that has recorded the work. Leontyne Price is grand and expressive. The young Cossotto sings confidently and with long breath. The even younger Pavarotti is the lyrically refined and beseeching tenor, Nicolai Ghiaurov the sonorous bass, heard more advantageously here than on his other versions. Karajan urges everyone to give of his or her astonishing best. The film, directed by Henri-Georges Clouzot, positively enhances the performance by virtue of its searching but seldom obtrusive camera-work, the sound image is electrifying, all proof of this medium's advantages over video tape.

Brahms: *A German Requiem*

JOHN STEANE

Such works as his *German Requiem* endear themselves to us as being musically great fun; but to take them quite seriously is to make them oppressively dull.

G. B. Shaw: *The Music of the Future*

Shaw first reported on Brahms's *Requiem* in an article called 'Gas and Gaiters' which appeared in *The Star* in May 1890. 'A solid piece of music manufacture ... it could only have come from the establishment of a first-class undertaker.' The tedium of sitting through it had been intolerable, and for years the memory haunted him: 'There are some sacrifices which should not be demanded twice of any man; and one of them is listening to Brahms's *Requiem*.' The experience, he said, 'is patiently borne only by the corpse'.

This, I had always thought, was Shaw being Shavian. In fact there were plenty who shared his boredom if not his happy way of expressing it. *The Musical Times*, writing on the first London performance in 1873, detected 'a feeling of weariness in the audience', and the *Monthly Musical Record*, which was of opinion that 'Herr Brahms is a very unequal composer', felt that the work would 'have certainly gained in effect by judicial curtailment'. What has surprised me is to find the sentiment echoed at this very day by friends and colleagues who, as they say, 'cannot stand it'. The precise grounds for criticism or disaffection have not been made clear but, having listened to the work in nearly thirty recordings, I can certainly see one possible cause. Conductors should have the sentence from Shaw's *Music of the Future* stamped at the top of each page of their score, as it is at the head of this chapter. So many of them take this music, which was meant for comfort, and play large sections of it at the tempo of a dirge. If the detractors formed their opinion on the basis of many of these recordings, it would be no wonder if 'judicial curtailment' were among the milder of their wishes. Shaw, whose mode of operation was, as he explained, to think with the utmost seriousness of what he meant to say and then to say it with the utmost levity, provides an adroit corrective to over-earnestness. The serious content of the *Requiem* can hardly be missed

206

in any competent performance; what is more rarely caught is the exaltation, the energy, the liveliness: in short, the fun.

That kind of fun, as denoted by abstractions such as energy, is probably not what Shaw had in mind: he was thinking of a musician's enjoyment of a work that is 'learnedly contrapuntal, not to say fugacious'. For most of us, spiritual fun in music is often at the mercy of tempo; and while it is not at all true to say 'the quicker the merrier' or 'the slower the sadder', finding the right tempo is like tuning into a radio wavelength where there is a small point that is absolutely central and a relatively large area that is possible but not right. A composer's metronome marking ought to be the equivalent of waveband-information, for it indicates the precise point he had in mind. Unfortunately for simplicity's sake, metronome markings are widely held to be too restrictive of the interpreter's freedom, and in this instance it appears that the markings were given in the first vocal scores but later omitted, and not included in the full score at all. The implication, presumably, is that they are not to be taken as definitive, though they must surely remain at least an authoritative suggestion. The scores are also in some disarray in the matter of verbal instructions over tempo. In the full score some are in German, some Italian; vocal scores generally sort out this anomaly by having everything in Italian, but create a new discrepancy by not agreeing about the terms. This perhaps goes some way to account for the wide range of tempo found in the recordings; it also weakens somewhat the position of a critic who would like to be able to refer to 'what the score says' and judge the deviationists accordingly.

Even so, I wonder whether it is generally realised how wide the deviation is. The chart printed below takes the first two of the seven movements and shows the speeds chosen by a representative selection of conductors. The first movement, *Selig sind, die da Leid tragen* ('Blessed are they that mourn'), sets the mood. The second, *Denn alles Fleisch, es ist wie Gras* ('Behold, all flesh is as the grass'), has four sections, with different metronome markings; omitting the third, as a short link-passage, I give the other three separately, to show how careful or otherwise conductors are in following the relative values of the markings. For readers unfamiliar with the metronome it should be explained in brief that the lower the figure, the longer the note and therefore the slower the tempo.

I 'Selig sind'		II (i) 'Denn alles Fleisch'		(ii) 'So seid nun geduldig'		(iv) 'Die Erlöseten'	
SCORE	80	Mengelberg	66	Walter	120	Barenboim	132
Walter	80	SCORE	60	Klemperer	116	Walter	
Klemperer	72	Walter		Maazel }	108	Sinopoli }	120
Kempe }	63	Kempe }	60	Kempe }		Mengelberg }	
Levine }		Maazel }		Levine		Levine	
Maazel	60	Karajan }	58	Barenboim }	100	Previn }	114
Sinopoli	58	Ansermet }		Previn }		Tennstedt }	

207

continued

I 'Selig sind'		II (i) 'Denn alles Fleisch'		(ii) 'So seid nun geduldig'		(iv) 'Die Erlöseten'	
Karajan	}	Previn	55	Tennstedt	97	Ansermet	113
Mengelberg	} 54	Klemperer	}	Karajan	96	Klemperer	112
Previn	}	Sinopoli	} 54	Sinopoli	92	Solti	110
Ansermet	53	Tennstedt	}	Solti	91	SCORE	108
Solti	52	Solti	51	Ansermet	88	Kempe	}
Tennstedt	49	Barenboim	50	Furtwängler	} 84	Maazel	} 108
Barenboim	46	Furtwängler	48	Mengelberg	}	Furtwängler	}
Furtwängler	44	Levine	47	SCORE	80	Karajan	100

A number of caveats should be added. One is that some are difficult to be certain about because the beat changes: in the first movement, for instance, Maazel sometimes increases his basic tempo and Sinopoli, more markedly, decreases his. Then at the end of the second movement most conductors pull back to a much slower tempo, the final pages being marked *tranquillo*, though no *rallentando* is specified at any point in the score. The first column, showing all except Bruno Walter to be slower than the score marking, is also a fair general guide to the last movement of the *Requiem*, and this, clearly, can be very influential in giving both an initial and final impression of slow-pulsed gravity, hence tedium. Add to this that the soprano solo (No. 5) is taken by most at a slower speed than marked, as are the first, slow, sections of numbers 3 and 6. Against that we have to note that few conductors are content with the fairly moderate markings for the faster sections in 2, 3 and 6, and so, in most instances, contrasts are heightened.

That, of course, may be a polite way of saying they are exaggerated. In the first movement, exaggeration is certainly not confined to the matter of tempo. At the start several of these recordings are next thing to inaudible. The score is marked *piano*, with a *pianissimo* for the horns only. The choir is to enter softly, but *piano* not *pianissimo*. In most recordings it is as though Brahms had written the *pppppp* that Verdi felt was advisable if he wanted his baritone to sing at something below a *mezzo forte* in *Otello*. Previn, Solti, Maazel, Tennstedt, Sawallisch (more particularly in his recording on Orfeo), Sinopoli, Barenboim and Kempe are among those who seem to have instructed the choir to sing as softly as they possibly can. Karajan, who made four recordings, can join the list in all save the first. Particularly depressing is the opening as recorded in Berlin under Fritz Lehmann, his tempo among the slowest of all, the style laborious, the choral entry a sanctimonious murmur. The choirs themselves show their quality early on in these opening pages. The Vienna choirs singing for Karajan improve with each recording, but are certainly pretty bad to begin with. Joyce Grenfell used to have a sketch about Ivy Trembly of the Choral Society: the Viennese soprano-line seems to be composed entirely of Ivy Tremblies. The Vienna Opera Chamber Choir singing for Giulini and Haitink has a new generation brought up in the old school.

Brahms: *A German Requiem*

Worse are the Stuttgart ladies under Marcel Couraud; better but still edgy on occasions are those of Chicago in the Levine and Solti recordings. Best are the Philharmonia under Klemperer: the blend of voices, the tone-quality, their cleanness and responsiveness are all outstanding. Others are fine too; the Danish Radio Choir under Corboz and Ansermet's Suisse Romande give much pleasure. So do the Ambrosian Singers under Previn, except that here is another of the tiresome features of modern recording, that in works such as this the choir tends to be discriminated against in balance with the orchestra. Sometimes it is as though they are away in a world of their own: 'et ô ces voix ... chantant dans la coupole'.

The second movement opens with the Funeral March in triple time. Here, especially with the crescendo leading to the choir's second entry, *forte*, the qualities of the orchestras come to the fore. Here the standard is much more consistent, and indeed no version can be said to be let down by the orchestral playing as opposed to the recording (where, for instance, the 1976 performance under Wolfgang Gönnenwein suffers from a hard, rather shallow recorded sound). That crescendo does, however, sort out the conductors. With some, its dramatic effectiveness goes for little. It depends largely on what they do with the brass. Those who make much of the horns pushing up in octaves and then chromatically include Previn, Barenboim (full of menace), Sinopoli (keeping a reserve till the last bars), Furtwängler (Wagnerian), Klemperer (seeing that they tell from first entry), Levine and (particularly in later recordings) Karajan. Those who either play it down or let it combine rather than lead in the general crescendo include Tennstedt, (surprisingly) Maazel and Solti, Ansermet, Haitink, Giulini, Walter and Kempe. In the *più animato* section ('So sei nun geduldig') several make a rather charming pictorial effect of the harp and woodwind quavers suggesting the kindly rain: Sinopoli, Sawallisch and Giulini are particularly good here.

With the modulation to B flat major at 'Aber des Herrn Wort bleibet in Ewigkeit' ('But the word of the Lord endureth for ever') the gloom is banished, and again some conductors take fuller advantage than others of the dramatic suddenness. A strong, incisive choral attack is wanted, and it comes most effectively in Furtwängler (despite some distortion in the recorded sound), Mengelberg, Klemperer, Barenboim (the Edinburgh Festival Choir articulating 'Ahbair' for all they're worth) and Solti. Syncopation in the strings helps the feeling of excitement and is well brought out by Levine. Then the bass entry ('Die Erlöseten des Herrn') introduces the *Allegro non troppo*, and I see in the full score in front of me, in big red letters, the word SMILE. Not many of them do, but it is good to hear Mengelberg's Amsterdam singers suddenly spring up with a vivid sense of gladness. Most performances do well with the staccatos of 'wird weg' ('shall flee') and the energy of the off-beat choral entries. Differences then arise in the final pages, from the marking 'tranquillo' and the *pianissimo* timpani quavers, which can have a slightly ominous sound

209

even though the words tell of 'joy everlasting'. Karajan versions 3 and 4 have them well to the fore so that we are very conscious of them throughout, where Mengelberg catches a subdued excitement that is rather more effective. Barenboim and Sinopoli, both given to exaggeration, reduce speed drastically at the *tranquillo*. Otherwise it is interesting to see where a conductor decides to begin his *rallentando*. Furtwängler starts early. Sawallisch starts with the violins' upward scale; Barenboim also, but characteristically more extreme. Previn holds back till the last notes of the rising scale and leaves most of it to the descending scale in the last bars of all: less sentimental.

On the matter of tempo readers can draw their own conclusions from the metronome table, and of course the same questions of choice and then of the relationship between speeds in the different sections recur in the third movement and the sixth. Briefly, the third ('Nun Herr, was soll ich mich trösten?') goes into the fugal finale ('Der Gerechten Seelen') with, in the vocal score, a very slightly faster metronome marking. Kempe is the only conductor I have found to take the speeds exactly as suggested. Levine almost does, but his beat seems to be steady throughout the movement, just slightly slower than marked. Several take the first section more slowly, and most (Previn a notable exception) take the second section a good deal faster. Extremists are Sinopoli and Mengelberg: instead of a difference of two figures on the metronome scale, Sinopoli makes it 28 and Mengelberg 34. It may be that the effect justifies the presumption – but a presumption it is, for the full score gives no suggestion of a change of speed at all.

This is the movement that introduces the baritone soloist. He has the words from Psalm 39 which tell of man's mortality, his days but a handbreadth, his passing like that of a shadow. It will not do to be too robust. Hermann Prey in both his recordings sounds so healthy that it is hard to believe he is giving his mind to these grave matters. Andreas Schmidt, Samuel Ramey and Håkan Hagegård seem fairly indifferent to the general fate. With Thomas Allen one is always grateful for the steadiness and fine tone, but there is not really a lot of imagination here either. A sense of involvement is communicated by Robert Holl and Siegfried Lorenz (but how they could do with Allen's steadiness of production), Max Kloos (not too happy with the high notes) and Sherrill Milnes. The bass-baritones like Hans Hotter and José van Dam seem to cope without difficulty, and bring an extra depth which does not come amiss. Some of the less well-known singers such as István Gáti and Kurt Widmer penetrate nearer than most to the spiritual truth, infusing their tone, as does Jorma Hynninen, with a weariness of soul. But essentially there is one singer of these solos and that is Fischer-Dieskau. The inner acceptance ('haben muss ... davon muss'), the quiet acknowledgement ('mein Leben ist wie nichts'), a sighing quality in the 'Ach, wie gar nichts', a wistful insubstantiality in 'wie ein Schemen', a suggestion of fatherly sternness in the phrase about what is likely to happen to your money when you're not there to see: there are slight differences among the three performances, but each of them has this singer's uncanny way of getting through to what is *particular* in everything he sings, and making it matter.

This third movement is like a synopsis of the whole work. It has room for the grimness of death, but then, in a wonderful passage of nine bars ('Ich hoffe auf dich') it turns towards consolation. In recordings, 'Ich hoffe' is often made to start so quietly that the bass lead is more a matter of conjecture than anything else. Some (such as Barenboim) place it in a stained-glass window, slowing down excessively in order to do so. A fine performance of it is that under Klemperer, who is also convincing in the fugue, with the pedal note (symbolizing, probably, the ever-sustaining hand of God) which Shaw could never forget or forgive.

When that long-held bottom D is released and the resolution into a firm and final major chord has been achieved, there occurs − perhaps in the literal sense − one of the most heavenly moments in the *Requiem*. We are borne upwards in key by the short step of a semitone but then come to another plane of existence. *Wie lieblich sind deine Wohnungen* ('How lovely are thy dwellings') is the shortest of the movements, the most popular and the happiest. As a separate anthem, it often appears in church service lists, and there have been several recordings by church choirs, the earliest (I believe) being made by the famous Temple Church Choir with organ accompaniment by Thalben-Ball (B 3453). In context the piece can be like a dance of the blessed spirits. The first notes, high and remote from the earthly solidity of what has gone before, introduce a flowing, lyrical movement in triple time, the accompaniment lightened by arpeggios, as in a song accompaniment, and sometimes by pizzicatos. On the whole, this is the part of the *Requiem* on which conductors most agree, both with one another and with the score markings. Giulini is among those who see the Lord's house as a laidback sort of place where the living is easy and eternity passes slowly. The melody is caressed and details such as the playful horn triplet about halfway through are given time to gain notice. Previn is one whose rhythmic sense lifts the movement lightly and easily, though the choir's place in the courts of the Lord is too distant for my liking. Solti captures the lilt and sweetness as well as making good use of the occasional *sforzandi* for flavouring. Leinsdorf's New England Chorus impress as a well-trained body of singers, and again Klemperer's Philharmonia Chorus (or Wilhelm Pitz's one should perhaps say) is on top form, while the Vienna sopranos tend to be at their trembliest.

The soprano solo *Ihr habt nun Traurigkeit* is another movement sometimes sung outside its setting in the *Requiem*. It also appears occasionally as a church anthem when the choir has a sufficiently able treble soloist: several have made recordings, though as a listener one is usually too much aware of its technical perils to find the comfort which the music seeks to provide. Barbara Schlick, in the Bremen Cathedral recording, has something of the treble quality. Some

211

sopranos from the old days of 78s have sung it too, among them Emmy Bettendorf (E 11138), with the ideal gentleness and warmth though with crescendos that, as recorded, bulge and lurch a little too pressingly, Florence Austral (DB 1540) with glorious tone sounding out over the Covent Garden Chorus under Barbirolli, and Hildegard Erdmann (C 3107), clear-voiced and absolutely sure of her intonation. All of these take the solo at the suggested speed, and, again looking at the full score, I see that that same firm hand has written in red pencil a reminder to 'Keep it moving!'. Elisabeth Schumann does that (though not excessively) in a performance, in English, appearing on an out-of-the-way label (Perennial 1001) and probably taken from a broadcast of the complete work under Bernard Herrmann. Occasionally the *portamento* is too broad but her singing of 'You shall again behold me' characteristically opens windows and lets in sunshine.

Many lovely performances are to be found among the complete sets. Elisabeth Schwarzkopf is pre-eminent, the voice at its radiant best in her early recording with Karajan, a deeper humanity felt in the Klemperer. Somewhat similar are her successors with Karajan, Anna Tomowa-Sintow, silver and slimlined, more deliberately ethereal in manner; Gundula Janowitz phrasing still more broadly but with that light patina of metal that had settled by this time on her voice; Barbara Hendricks with more admixture of a quick vibrato than the others but also very sensitively moulding the phrases. Most of the voices are light in weight and texture: Maria Stader just a little too much of the Mozartian soubrette in colour, Helen Donath a little too bright and edgy, Edith Mathis rather similar, Lucia Popp introducing more variety but inclined to squeeze her tone, Ileana Cotrubas not entirely secure and placed too far forward of the choir, Barbara Bonney too much a Sophie voice (as in *Der Rosenkavalier*) where this needs a certain maternal warmth. In some ways the best of the lighter sopranos in it is Kathleen Battle, who has a smiling gentleness and whose voice as recorded here sounds surprisingly full-bodied in the louder passages. Further towards the centre of the lyric soprano spectrum than this last group is Irmgard Seefried, inclined to get ahead of Bruno Walter's by no means slow beat. Kiri Te Kanawa, on the contrary, is utterly secure, her voice surpassingly beautiful, her style tenderness itself. Montserrat Caballé makes a wonderfully ethereal thing of it, supporting the phrases on an apparently inexhaustible supply of breath. Jessye Norman has the second of Caballé's qualities here but not the first, for she is too vibrantly substantial. Margaret Price, with both Sawallisch and Previn, brings the fullest, roundest voice, responsive also in its colouring. She does something to remind us of the missing record from the old days: surely someone should have taken pains to ensure that Tiana Lemnitz bequeathed what might have been the ideal version. As it is, probably the nearest thing in tone, and possibly closer to present-day taste in style, is Elisabeth Grümmer for Kempe: a direct, finely controlled performance, touching in its sincerity.

212

Brahms: *A German Requiem*

This soprano solo is another of the movements in which one sometimes concludes that there must be some kind of slow-race competition among performers. Sawallisch, with both his sopranos, takes it at the score's suggested speed; Couraud too, partly at the behest of his strangely importunate soloist. But the general tendency seems to be to take as long as the soprano's breath will last out. If there is indeed a spirit abroad of 'anything-you-can-do' the matter should be regarded as having been closed years ago by Furtwängler. His soloist, Kerstin Lindberg Torlind, shows that if necessary she could go slower still. One thinks of Tennyson's 'such a tide as moving seems asleep', and perhaps that is the intention.

Performances of the remaining two movements follow a similar pattern. In *Denn wir haben hier keine bleibende Statt* ('Here we have no continuing state') the three sections tempt a number of predictable conductors into extremes. Sinopoli starts at a slower tempo than most of his contemporaries (except Barenboim) and at the sight of the dramatic *vivace* he outstrips them, then being unique in maintaining this speed for the fugue. Furtwängler is slow as expected in the first section but then surprisingly brisk in the fugue. The normally moderate Kempe is among the fastest in the *vivace*, and Karajan, whose first recording was fairly close to the metronome markings, takes the opening sections a good deal more slowly in his fourth. What matters is to catch mystery, excitement and then something not so easy to define in the fugue, though 'fun' is not too far off. An alertness to rhythm, rather than mere speed, helps to ensure it: Kegel, with the excellent Leipzig choir, catches it well. And then there is that remarkable passage that Tovey calls the Jacob's Ladder, where the brass, then woodwind and violins seem to stride from pole to pole. Maazel makes much of it, bringing out the effect more consciously than most. Previn is good at setting the fugue a-dancing. Klemperer is great at making it sound like Beethoven.

As for the last movement, *Selig sind die Toten*, it is very beautiful indeed, but sometimes, in the Musician's Glossary, for 'beautiful' can be read 'boring'. If taken very slowly it can be a near-fatal soporific. Karajan in his later versions, Furtwängler and Tennstedt are among those who risk numbingly prolonged beauty. Among those I have tested the only conductor who comes anywhere near the score-marking is Klemperer, and he gains accordingly. His is, I think, the finest of the recordings, all told, not only as a recording of the score but in the resources of choir, orchestra and soloists employed.

Yet this is not the dominant memory that remains in the wake of all this listening. Perhaps because it is the oldest (though there is certainly more to it than that), the most fascinating of these recordings has been the Mengelberg. A public performance, with some cuts in the sixth and seventh movements, primitive as recorded sound, extreme and wilful in many of its speeds and dynamics, pulling the time about from bar to bar, closer in style to Sinopoli than to its own near-contemporaries Walter and Furtwängler, it represents many of the qualities that have been singled out for criticism in this chapter. Yet it has left an impression, as none of the others has quite done, of a live encounter with the score, almost a tussle, albeit a loving one. Such recordings belong of course to the dusty archives, and are just the sort of thing that makes the archives the liveliest part of the library to visit.

Fauré: Requiem

MICHAEL OLIVER

The published text of Fauré's Requiem is a strange and contradictory document. On paper the work looks as though it is scored for a standard orchestra, but closer inspection reveals how very curiously used the instruments are. There is not a single bar for full orchestra. The violins are undivided into the customary firsts and seconds, they play in only four of the seven movements and often do no more than double one of the viola lines (Fauré suggested that the viola parts could be enriched by urging some of the better violinists to switch to violas during the violin-less movements). Flutes and clarinets (always doubling strings or organ) are heard only in the Pie Jesu, the second clarinet for less than four bars; timpani and trombones (doubling the horns in all but eight bars) appear only in the Libera me. The woodwind, in particular, are not so much restrainedly as invisibly used. The question of how this anomalous score should be performed can hardly be discussed without considering how it came into existence.

Fauré began writing the Requiem in 1887 and its first version was ready in time for the funeral of a certain M. le Soufaché at the church of the Madeleine in Paris, where Fauré was choirmaster, on 16 January 1888. He worked unusually fast, possibly under the impact of the illness and death of his mother: the manuscript of the Agnus Dei is dated 6 January 1888, less than a week after Hélène Fauré died, that of the Sanctus three days later. Fauré seems to have been reluctant, however, to associate the work with the grief of his bereavement (his father, too, had died eighteen months earlier). Pressed later to explain its origins he replied simply that 'my Requiem was written for no reason; I wrote it, dare I say, for pleasure'. When deaths in the parish occasioned subsequent hearings, he would invite his society friends along, asking them only to avoid sitting in a group together 'as though it were a *performance*! You should give the impression of being there by chance'. It is a tender and heartfelt work, but not grief-stricken or to be approached on one's knees. 'They say that my Requiem does not express the terror of death; someone has called it a "cradle-song of death"', Fauré wrote, 'but that is how I see death: as a happy deliverance, as an aspiring towards the joy that lies beyond, rather than as a sorrowful passing. Gounod's music has been criticised for inclining too much towards human tenderness, but his nature predisposed him to feel like that: in him religious emotion took that form. Must we not accept the artist's own nature? As to my Requiem, perhaps I too have sought instinctively to escape from convention, after all the time I have spent playing the organ for funerals! I know all that off by heart; I wanted to do something different.'

At this stage the Requiem consisted of only five movements (Introît et Kyrie, Sanctus, Pie Jesu, Agnus Dei and In Paradisum), scored for soprano solo, chorus and a strikingly individual and subtly used instrumental ensemble: solo violin (in the Sanctus only, playing an octave above the violin line in the published score), divided violas (including a solo viola in the In Paradisum), divided cellos, double basses, harp, timpani (only in the opening movement) and organ. Although not yet 'complete' (an erased but still legible note in Fauré's hand on the first page of the Agnus Dei says that 'the orchestration is unfinished'; but did he regard the instrumentation of the other movements as complete?), the character, colour and scale of the work are already clear. It is not a liturgical Mass for the Dead (much of the text proper to that Office is omitted; the In Paradisum comes from the Burial Service) but a humane and consolatory funeral cantata, even an anthology of funeral motets. The accompaniment is closer to an expanded continuo group than an orchestra: the low strings add grain and warmth to the omnipresent organ, but for much of the time do little more than double its melodic lines; the harp and the two solo strings (played by the same performer, presumably, who for the rest of the work joined the concerted violas?) provide touches of subdued or silvery radiance.

Although not a liturgical work the Requiem is decidedly an ecclesiastical one: it was conceived for the choir of the Madeleine, with boys' voices taking the upper lines and a treble soloist in the Pie Jesu. It was at that stage obviously a chamber work, also: a big choir would rarely have been available at parish funerals (Fauré as a rule could draw on no more than four tenors and four basses, plus a boys' choir of at the most thirty); and besides, the solo violin and viola would have made little effect against a large vocal and instrumental force. The singers and players would have been hidden from the congregation, since it seems that Fauré used for his performances the detached Choir Organ of the Madeleine, not the Great, and grouped his choir and orchestra around it; a small instrument of ten stops only, its console was placed behind the towering high altar.

It was perhaps for rather grander occasions, richer obsequies, and for concert performances that Fauré decided to add two movements. The Libera me, originally for baritone solo and organ, dates from as early as 1877; its choral section was added much later and the completed movement was first performed as a separate piece (i.e. not as part of the Requiem) in 1892. The Offertoire was also composed in stages; the baritone solo 'Hostias' dates from 1887–89, the choral 'O Domine Jesu Christe' probably from some time in the late 1890s (the first performance of the expanded Requiem, in 1894, included only the 'Hostias').

Only four of the seven movements survive in manuscript, but it is evident from them that the orchestration also passed through several stages. It is difficult to date these, since Fauré wrote all his emendations into the original 1888 score, with additional instruments added at the top and bottom of the page, though parts for two horns and two trumpets were added very early, since an account of a performance in May 1888 mentions them. These modifications affected the character of the work (by introducing an additional solo voice and, in the Libera me, an overt reference – hitherto conspicuously lacking – to the Day of Judgement), but they did not alter its fundamental colour, save at those rare moments where brass instruments added drama. Woodwind instruments were still absent, as were violins in the plural.

In this light the final and most familiar version of the Requiem (until very recently the only available score; it was first performed in 1900 and published in 1901) looks less like a completion than a subsequent and puzzling arrangement. No manuscript of this version exists, and the many differences between it and the incomplete surviving autograph exclude any possibility that the latter was used as a basis for the 1901 score. It seems likely that it was prepared because Fauré's publisher Hamelle thought that the Requiem would sell better as a concert work if it were more conventionally orchestrated. Whether Fauré did the work himself or (as was frequently his practice in matters of instrumentation) farmed it out to a trusted colleague is unlikely to be proved. Would a skilled orchestrator (like Fauré's pupil Roger-Ducasse, his most likely emergency helper at this stage; it was he who prepared the vocal score) have perpetrated such pointlessly inconspicuous doublings? Could any conscientious assistant have passed the resulting printed text, which is riddled with misprints (they were corrected in a revised version by Roger Fiske and Paul Inwood, published by Eulenburg in 1978)? To add to the confusion there are many inconsistencies among the 1901 score, the orchestral parts and the vocal score; not surprisingly Roger-Ducasse's vocal score is the most accurate.

It seems at least likely that Fauré either capitulated unwillingly to Hamelle's demands and gave a few verbal or scribbled instructions to someone in the publisher's office, or that he made the amplifications himself, attempting to ensure that they affected the previous score as little as possible. All of his comments about the Requiem ring truer as descriptions of the 1888 and 1894 versions than of the published text of 1901. Most important of all, perhaps, he was still describing the Requiem, after the publication of the 1901 score, as 'based on a quartet of divided violas and cellos ... the brass and woodwind have very little to do, since the organ fills in the harmony throughout' (so he was expecting it to be *audible* throughout, evidently). And it is known that he approvingly attended performances of the Requiem at which some form of reduced scoring must surely have been used, such as that in the Brussels home of Mlle Boch in March 1906, which he described as 'intimate and perfect in execution and sonority'.

Although it is unquestionable that Fauré acquiesced in the publication of the 1901 score, in the light of its anomalies and questionable authenticity it has long seemed desirable that the 1894 score should be reconstructed, and in recent years two attempts have been made. That of John Rutter (recorded by him – see below – and published by Hinshaw Music/Oxford University Press) uses the fragmentary autograph as primary source, removing accretions to the remaining three movements to accord with the work's presumed scoring at its 'completion' in 1894. Much more recently Jean-Michel Nectoux has discovered a set of orchestral parts in the archives of the Madeleine. He was able to establish that they were copied by a M. Manier, a bass in Fauré's choir, and that they were corrected and annotated by Fauré himself, who also wrote out the parts for horns and trumpets. A provisional score based on this material has been prepared by Nectoux and Roger Delage; it too has been recorded (by Philippe Herreweghe – see below) and a published score is promised shortly by Durand.

Both Rutter's and Nectoux's scores leave some questions unanswered, but it is beyond question that Nectoux's represents a version of the Requiem that has Fauré's authority and was used at performances, possibly numerous ones, conducted by him. Several of the most conspicuous differences between Nectoux's version and Rutter's have a particularly direct authority, since they occur in the horn parts and are thus in Fauré's own hand. The horn writing is much more conspicuous in the Offertoire (there is a virtual horn obbligato to the baritone's 'Fac eas, Domine') and in the Sanctus, and the yearning modulation at letter C in the In Paradisum is given an inspiriting radiance by the addition of horn tone. No less important, the formidable brass entry at the reference to the 'day of wrath' in the Libera me has a quite different, more insistent rhythm. In this same movement the timpani are used to more dramatic effect, and there are numerous smaller differences. Unless some source postdating the Madeleine manuscript parts but predating the 1901 score can be found (preferably an authoritative manuscript of the latter, though that seems improbable at this stage), Nectoux's edition must be regarded as the most authentic account of Fauré's original conception of the work, Rutter's as a creditable but imperfect attempt to approach that conception, the 1901 score as a document to be used only with great care and in the light of all that preceded it. It cannot be cast aside entirely, however (it is hard to imagine, for example, that anything so radical as those altered horn parts in the Libera me could have been printed and performed without Fauré's sanction), and Nectoux is probably right to suggest that the 1901 score 'can still be recommended for performances in large concert halls'.

218

Fauré: Requiem

Recordings made when only the 1901 score was available cannot be blamed for taking it at face value (though its 'pre-history' has long been common knowledge, readily available to inquiring performers), but Fauré's descriptions of the work as a 'cradle-song of death ... aspiring towards the joy that lies beyond' and as 'a little Requiem of a GENTLE nature, like my own' are crucial to an understanding of the spirit in which that score should be read. So is his estimate of its duration, after much experience of performing the work in the reverberant acoustic of the Madeleine (which would have made swift tempi difficult) as '30 minutes, 35 at the outside'; a literal interpretation of the metronome marks (albeit they do not appear in the manuscript) gives a similar timing. It is not impossible to perform the 1901 score in accordance with Fauré's own view of its nature, but remarkably few recorded performances seem to do so. The misleading appearance of that score has all too often led to readings which treat it as a solemn Mass for the Dead in full orchestral vestments, and with a manner pitched somewhere between Mozart's Requiem and Verdi's. In such performances the relatively unimportant (indeed entirely dispensable) violins often outnumber and outweigh the centrally crucial violas and cellos and the organ is often obscured for much of the time.

One of the work's most persuasive early advocates was Fauré's pupil Nadia Boulanger, and we are fortunate to possess a recording by her which could in some ways serve as a model. It is let down by a claustrophobic studio acoustic and a narrow dynamic range − a true *pp* is seldom heard − and the bass Doda Conrad's voice is worn and unsteady (he is also placed very close to the microphone), but the urgency of the performance will come as a shock to any listener who thinks of the work as sweetly pious. The string group (not too large) has sinew and expressive intensity to it, the climaxes in the Agnus Dei and Libera me are strong, and the orchestral detail throughout is beautifully clear. Gisèle Peyron is quite a touching soprano soloist, but she sounds uncomfortable at the slowish speed of the Pie Jesu. The radiance of the Sanctus is diminished somewhat by the recording's close focus on the chorus. But the scale is right, the tempi are pretty well right (the playing time only a fraction over 35 minutes) and Boulanger has persuaded her (anonymous) chorus to sing out with attack as well as purity.

Among other early recordings, that by the Société Bach, conducted by Gustave Bret, has particular interest since Fauré is known to have admired Bret and his choir. This, too, is an urgently expressive account (save in the mystic, hieratic and extremely slow Sanctus), with real anxiety to the 'day of wrath' reference in the Libera me and a feeling of suspense to the 'Requiem aeternam'. The recording is recessed and indistinct − it is difficult to be sure how large Bret's orchestra is − but a firmly articulated bass line is perceptible. So is the full-voiced fervour of the choral singing; the soloists (Malnory-Marseillac and Louis Morturier, both devoutly restrained) are excellent. Ernest

Bourmauck's reading is not dissimilar in general approach, though he takes the Sanctus distinctly faster, with no loss of reverence. He is rather fonder, though, than Bret or Boulanger of gilding Fauré's lilies with 'expressive' slackenings of tempo, and the brightly edgy recorded sound makes the close-microphoned soprano (Suzanne Dupont), the very light-voiced baritone (Maurice Didier), the reedy choir and even the orchestra sound nasal.

Ugly and unatmospheric sound has marred numerous more recent French recordings and very few conductors have been as successful as Boulanger or Bret at inducing French choral singers to abandon the weightless crooning which seems to be their besetting sin. An interesting reading by D.-E. Inghelbrecht echoes Boulanger in its clarity of detail, and the light-voiced cantabile of the baritone soloist (Bernard Demigny) is agreeable, but the acidulated string sound is not so much reedy as papery, the chorus often sound harsh, and Inghelbrecht's praiseworthy expressive intensity leads him at times into hurried tempi: the Pie Jesu too fast for his thin-voiced soprano, Françoise Ogéas, the Libera me seeming restless at about 50 per cent above the marked tempo. Nor does the congested sound of René Leibowitz's recording give much pleasure. His chorus is mediocre, his tempi fidgety and only his baritone soloist (Demigny again, sounding more like a tenor here) gives a real sense of Fauréan style. An American performance of roughly the same vintage carried much more conviction, with vigorous and forthright choral singing (by the Roger Wagner Chorale under its eponymous conductor), a gravely restrained and indeed rather French-sounding baritone, Theodor Uppman (though his unsteadiness gets close to a bleat at times) and for the most part sensible tempi. Wagner's expressive urgency is a trifle overdone at times and neither the rather full-sounding orchestra nor the choir seem eager to notice dynamic markings below *forte*, but at a time when only inadequate French recordings of the Requiem were otherwise available this was a welcome demonstration that it contains more than boneless lyricism.

The earlier of André Cluytens's two recordings has little to recommend it except the pretty voice of Marthe Angelici in an insensitively accompanied Pie Jesu. The baritone, Louis Noguéra, sings loudly and dispassionately, the chorus is dulcetly lethargic and Cluytens shows a tendency both to ponderousness and to over-inflection of the orchestral parts. His better-recorded later version has the great advantage of Victoria de los Angeles, touchingly childlike, in the Pie Jesu. Dietrich Fischer-Dieskau, too, makes intelligent and very beautiful sounds in his two solos, though at times his expressiveness is a bit too operatic and refined. The chorus is no worse than in Cluytens's earlier recording (cooing sopranos, soft-textured tenors) and there are fewer of them, but the conductor's own fondness for sleepy blandness has intensified: a suave and impactless Agnus Dei that gets slower bar by bar, a lumbering Dies irae.

For the first of his three recordings Jean Fournet used the same choir as in Cluytens's second version; they are still rather weightless, the sopranos still fragile and insubstantial, but at least they make more of their strongly French-inflected Latin than they did for Cluytens. The soloists are pretty well ideal: Camille Maurane (a ranking Pelléas in his day) light-voiced and attractively reserved, Pierrette Alarie chastely pure in a rapt Pie Jesu. However, the bland choral singing makes Fournet's on the whole well-chosen tempi sound slower than they are, and the recording is both dull and muffled. Fournet did not record the work with a French choir again; the recording which presents his sober but alert view of the work with fewest impediments was made with Dutch singers and orchestra. The choir is fairly large, competent but rather impassive; their backward placing, however, at least allows for clearly audible instrumental detail and for the orchestra to dominate at climaxes. Elly Ameling is a decent soprano soloist, if a rather tremulous one, but Bernard Kruysen's fast, goat-like vibrato is an unhappy sound. The baritone in Fournet's remaining account, Kurt Widmer, is no better: he is both wobbly and plummy and is placed very far from the microphone, seemingly outside the hall. So is the more acceptable soprano soloist, Edith Mathis, but Fournet's tempo for the Pie Jesu has now slowed to a snail's pace. The weird recording of this (live) performance also places the chorus (Swiss, this time) in the remote distance.

Ernest Ansermet's reading of the Requiem is another that is let down by an inadequate chorus: the grandly titled Union Chorale de la Tour de Peilz sound raw and poorly trained. Ansermet's stodgy tempi, however, (even the rather fast Agnus Dei plods because of his heavy beat) suggest that he had little sympathy with the piece. His baritone soloist Gérard Souzay sings beautifully, unhampered by Ansermet's arthritic tempo in the Offertoire, but Suzanne Danco's fast, tight vibrato robs the Pie Jesu of tranquillity. Among more recent recordings from Francophone sources Michel Plasson's is uncommonly dark and brooding, the orchestra at times opaque and with the slowish tempi that seem inevitable when a fair-sized orchestra is used. Light is provided, however, by his admirable Basque chorus, the Orfeón Donostiarra, whose clearly enunciated but curiously pronounced Latin, whitish and almost boyish sopranos and firm tenors and basses provide a welcome contrast to most of the recordings considered so far. Barbara Hendricks makes lovely if rather studied sounds in the Pie Jesu; José van Dam, a bass-baritone and a rather curious choice for the other solo part, in fact fines down his tone effectively and sings with sensitive musicianship. But the apparent implications of the 1901 score hang frowningly over this performance, too.

Sylvain Cambreling frees himself from those implications rather more successfully in a live recording with mostly Belgian forces. The chorus (that of the National Opera of Belgium) is accomplished and of reasonable size, though robbed of impact by very backward placing in the recording perspective. The soloists, on the other hand, are placed forward and at the extreme edges of the stereo picture: Britt-Marie Aruhn is tremulously unrestful and

221

colours her Latin with markedly Teutonic vowels; John Shirley-Quirk yaps loudly and vehemently (partly the fault of the recording), but the sober urgency of Cambreling's direction is impressive. The same can scarcely be said of Michel Corboz despite his use of a pure-voiced (if short-breathed) treble in the Pie Jesu and the admirable Philippe Huttenlocher (who, however, is placed absurdly far away) in the baritone solos. Corboz's is one of the slowest and most weakly articulated performances that I have heard, and with a lumbering and lugubrious overall sound that is intensely dispiriting. Nor is Bernard Thomas much better. The pure and unaffected soprano of Rose-Marie Mézac and the chastely white chorus sopranos in the In Paradisum are the best things about this soft, smooth and impactless reading, in which the baritone soloist, Michel Piquemal, also doubles as choirmaster and has obviously taught his singers all his own bland habits. Boy trebles are used in the Sanctus only, for some reason; they are placed a long way away in a large acoustic.

It is a great relief to turn to Louis Frémaux, who has recorded the work twice, both times with distinction. His basically Francophone performance for Erato has the advantages of a nasal but touchingly tiny-voiced and very young-sounding treble, Denis Thilliez, one of the best of the French choirs (the Chorale Philippe Caillard, sopranos and tenors both having an attractively edged purity of timbre − and they sing full-throatedly when required), and a fine sense of both pace and drama. The baritone is again Bernard Kruysen: sincere and earnest, still rather reedy, but less nagging than he was for Fournet. Until very recently this was among the most generally recommendable for all recordings of the Requiem, along with Frémaux's other performance using British singers. This is a slightly more reflective reading, with firm and clear-detailed choral singing. Norma Burrowes is the serenely tranquil soprano soloist, Brian Rayner Cook the soberly thoughtful baritone, and the orchestral playing is if anything even better and more aware of the essentially chamber textures of the score than in Frémaux's Erato version.

Ideally one wants French voices in this work, and perhaps the coloration given to the lines by French-inflected Latin. With the low recent standard of French choral singing demonstrated in most of the above recordings, however (one wonders what it was like in Fauré's day), it is not surprising that British choirs have in recent years recorded the Requiem with increasing frequency. Many British performances use cathedral or university chapel choirs, which ensures a professionalism, subtlety and precision sadly lacking from most French performances, while at the same time inevitably translating Fauré's choral style into a language that is foreign to it.

A classic among these 'Anglicanised' readings is that by David Willcocks with the choir of King's College, Cambridge. John Carol Case has the ideal vocal quality, restrained expressiveness and immaculate diction for the baritone solos, while Robert Chilcott is an effectively pure-voiced treble; Willcocks's rather somnolent tempo in the Pie Jesu causes him no problems at all. Tempi are otherwise good, as is the balance between choir and orchestra, but the placing of the trebles well in front of the rest of the choir is eccentric, and the suave beauty of the 'King's sound' goes with a certain lack of urgency and eloquence. George Guest's reading, using the neighbouring choir of St John's College, Cambridge, is not free of this flaw, but he counteracts it with tempi that are on the whole more alert than Willcocks's (save in the sleepy In Paradisum) and by a greater emphasis on the graininess of the orchestral sound. Both his soloists are excellent: Benjamin Luxon, just a touch of unsteadiness marring the exceptional beauty of his voice and line, and Jonathan Bond, a treble who is touchingly moved by the Pie Jesu while in the act of singing it. A later King's College recording under Philip Ledger is in many respects better still, dramatic as well as beautiful, and with a genuinely chamber orchestral texture, with fibre and urgency to it. It is perhaps ungrateful to complain of the whitish tenors and of the comfortably etherealised trebles (just the sort of qualities many people value the King's choir for, after all), but in the context of Ledger's otherwise idiomatic reading they dress Fauré in the incongruous robes of an eminent Church of England divine. The soprano soloist, Arleen Augér, is quite acceptable but sounds like a guest star in this company; Benjamin Luxon is in slightly less steady voice than he was for Willcocks.

Richard Hickox has many of Ledger's qualities, not least his sense of urgent pace. He uses a fair-sized mixed choir and a full orchestra (the big moments are very big), but takes great care to clarify orchestral detail throughout, and the organ is as clearly audible as in most of the Cambridge performances. Stephen Roberts, light-voiced and gravely eloquent, is another first-class baritone soloist; not everyone will admire the soprano-ish flutter of Aled Jones's treble as much as whoever it was that decreed that his name should dominate all else on the record sleeve, but he sings with sincerity; both soloists are placed too close.

A special case among British performances, and to my mind one of the very best of them, is that conducted by David Hill using the individual, incisive and inspiritingly open sound (very far from the 'Anglican hoot') of the Westminster Cathedral Choir. The trebles (and sopranos: Westminster uses both) have a pleasantly throaty edge, the tenors are more forthright than most of their compatriots and combined with the firm grip of Hill's direction this makes for powerful drama in the Libera me, grand exultation in the 'Hosanna' and forceful urgency alongside the devout plangency elsewhere. The baritone, David Wilson-Johnson, is a trifle unsteady, though his voice has the right quality; Aidan Oliver, the treble, pipes reedily and expressively.

The ever-increasing popularity of the Requiem has led to a third style of performing the work, alongside the Gallic and the Anglican. It might be termed the 'international', and usually involves soloists who are better known in the opera house than as interpreters of Fauré. Sometimes an outstandingly imaginative conductor is in charge, and his vision of the work may convince, even though it seems worlds removed from Fauré's conception. This is certainly the case with Sir Colin Davis's reading, which sees the work as a lofty and solemnly hieratic ceremonial: the large (and superb) German choir is placed at a distance in a splendidly spacious acoustic, sounding like acolytes around the Judgement Seat, the orchestra (also large) has a gravely burnished radiance – Fauré would have recognised it, I suspect, as rather more like *Parsifal* than his 'petit Requiem d'un caractère DOUX' but he might well have been impressed by its reverent, mystical remoteness. Lucia Popp has the right purity of line to sustain a rather slow Pie Jesu, but the melodramatic barking and the Teutonic Latin of Simon Estes in the baritone's music are intolerable.

The 'star' soloists in Frederic Waldman's recording are Martina Arroyo (unsuitably vibrant and *spinto*, Aida in the organ-loft) and Hermann Prey: his voice at its most beautiful in the range exploited by this music, the tone lightened very effectively. Waldman has none of Davis's visionary quality, and some of his tempi are on the slow side, but the scale of his reading is good (an excellent balance between his accomplished chorus and the not over-large orchestra); its main faults are inadequate dynamic contrast and an organ that seems to move from foreground to middle ground at the whim of the recording engineer.

Carlo Maria Giulini treats the Requiem as a great masterpiece of devotional literature. His tempi are reverently slow throughout, the choral and orchestral sound is gravely rich, opulently sober, and although both soloists are excellent (Kathleen Battle, touchingly simple in expression despite a fast vibrato, and Andreas Schmidt, an exceptionally beautiful baritone voice, most subtly used) the overwhelming impression of black velvet and swirling incense smoke is remote from Fauré. Daniel Barenboim's reading, although not without its moments of urgency, is on an even larger scale; its frequent slow pages almost grind to a halt at times (the Offertoire, for example, goes at less than half the marked tempo). The extremely fine but huge Edinburgh Festival Chorus sometimes obscures the orchestra, the recorded sound is sumptuously rich, and even the excellent soloists (Sheila Armstrong and Dietrich Fischer-Dieskau) are tempted by their surroundings to overstate the scale of their music.

Charles Dutoit, finally, offers a demonstration that the 1901 score need not obscure the intimacy and quiet gravity of Fauré's conception, even when quite large forces are used. He takes careful note of the dynamic markings, and his tempi are about right; if they seem a shade on the slow side it is because the weight of choral tone softens his articulation a little. His choir can sing with purity (a silvery In Paradisum) as well as attack (a jubilant, properly horn-dominated 'Hosanna') and the careful balance of the orchestra concentrates, as it should, on the graininess of divided lower strings. The choir is occasionally lazy with its Latin ('Libera may, Dominay') and Sherrill Milnes's voice is worn and strenuous, but Kiri Te Kanawa's sincere and carefully phrased Pie Jesu is beautifully done.

There remain four recordings of Rutter's edition and (so far) one of Nectoux's to put all the others into context. Robert Shaw's account of the Rutter edition is, alas, a lesson in how not to do it. Despite Rutter's careful specification of the appropriate size of forces to be used, Shaw deploys a fairly large and glumly opaque choir and a rich, even beefy string group. A clue to his conception of the work is provided by his casting of James Morris, a Wotan and a King Philip, in music for which Fauré specified 'a tranquil bass-baritone, something of a cantor'. The voice is simply too big, as is the sound of the performance as a whole, with its heavy bass and dense textures. Shaw's tempi are sometimes ill-judged: a jog-trot of a 'Dies irae', sentimental slackenings in the Pie Jesu (Judith Blegen, not quite secure) and the In Paradisum, and the two string solos, which should add a luminous edge to the tone of the main string force, are given a concerto-like prominence. Matthew Best's reading has far more appropriate soloists (the treble-like soprano Mary Seers and the fine-grained baritone of Michael George) and exceptionally beautiful choral singing. Slowish tempi, however, a fair-sized string group and a luxuriously spacious acoustic give the work a solemnity and a golden glow that reduce its expressive urgency. It sounds like a compromise between the plainness of Rutter's edition and the rich softness of which the 1901 score is capable, and the bones of the work have been slightly but crucially softened. They turn to jelly in Stephen Cleobury's version with the choir of King's College, Cambridge, where the 'King's sound' itself, with pale trebles and bland tenors, is the principal softening agent. Even fairly swift tempi have a touch of the languid to them in this reading; everything is exquisitely moulded but devoid of attack or urgency. The effect is sweetly soporific, despite one of the best baritones ever to have recorded the work (Olaf Bär) and a clean, pure-voiced treble in the Pie Jesu.

Rutter's own performance of his edition was a revelation when it first appeared: dynamic gradings that seemed difficult for a 'standard' choir and orchestra to achieve suddenly became both natural and easy; the true colour of the work, hinted at by the better recordings of the 1901 score, came effortlessly into focus and the solo singers (Caroline Ashton, boyish and ethereal, the sensitive and light-voiced Stephen Varcoe) could achieve more in this context, by using less vocal weight and histrionics, than many other more opulently gifted soloists. Above all, the fundamental rightness of Fauré's original conception, achieved in 1894 and uneasily tinkered with in 1900, was shiningly demonstrated, not least by the scrupulously 'authentic' yet by no means uninflected performance. Until the appearance of Nectoux's edition the only disadvantages of Rutter's reading were the slightly bland, white sound of his tenors (the choral singing is otherwise pretty well ideal) and the rather unatmospheric (yet admirably clear) recording.

The first recording of Nectoux's edition differs from Rutter's not only in the editorial points already mentioned but in the style of the performance. It is a slight matter set beside the differences of text, but I wish the conductor, Philippe Herreweghe, had found it possible for this first recording of an edition of major importance to adhere pretty strictly to the marked tempi. He is slightly slow in several passages, notably in the Pie Jesu (the accompaniment here a little over-inflected, making the solo line seem almost static) and the Agnus Dei. But in quality of choral and solo singing (Agnès Mellon, almost as boyishly pure as Caroline Ashton; Peter Kooy, steadier than Stephen Varcoe in *forte*, and no less 'cantor-like'), in the grain and expressiveness of the instrumental contribution and in the scale and colour of the performance as a whole Herreweghe's account is fully the equal of Rutter's.

The editorial differences strike me as crucial. Apart from the changed horn rhythm in the 'Dies irae' (the version of 1901 could well be a second thought, and individual taste will determine which is to be preferred; Nectoux's version is indubitably faithful to Fauré's thoughts in 1894), none of the differences is incompatible with the essence of the score as we know it. The sound of the Requiem was conceived with a basis of divided lower strings and organ. Apart from the dramatic use of brass at the 'Hosanna' and 'Dies irae', the additional instruments (solo violin, harp, timpani and horns) are used to colour the basic strings-plus-organ palette. Nectoux's edition represents the composer's own mixing of these colours, Rutter's a sympathetic and conservative guess at what those colours might have been.

The Rutter edition is by no means put out of court by Nectoux's. It is a 'liberal' edition, allowing a variety of scorings to suit circumstances, acoustic and availability of resources (and it is possible to get very close to the spirit of Fauré's score with an ensemble of no more than strings and an imaginatively registered organ). Nectoux provides the closest possible approach to Fauré's own realisation in performance of that spirit. The 1901 score seems at best a practical compromise between that spirit and the perceived exigencies of concert-giving. No future performance of the 1901 score will be able to ignore the issues raised by Rutter and the material discovered by Nectoux. It is not simply a matter of scoring, but of the very nature of Fauré's cradle-song of death as happy deliverance and aspiration towards the joy that lies beyond.

Elgar: *The Dream of Gerontius*

ALAN BLYTH

For many *Gerontius* is Elgar's outright masterpiece. Having completed the work in the summer of 1900, he commented: 'The trees are singing my music. Or have I sung theirs?' So he himself sensed that the work had a special power and beauty, confirmed when he signed off the score 'This is the best of me'. As David Cairns has remarked: 'No other work of his carries so strong a sense, in a good performance, of having been given, of coming from deep and ancient wells of experience.' There is something inevitable in the setting of Cardinal Newman's text that suggests the work has somehow been there since time immemorial, and that setting itself, combining parlando and lyrical outpouring as appropriate, provides a style perfectly attuned to the deeply felt emotions of the words. A devout Catholic, Elgar responded to the mystical sincerity of Newman's vision with his own. At the same time the work is as close as Elgar came to writing opera. In a convincing performance, the dramatic quality of the writing should carry all before it. And all the recorded accounts of the work are convincing because artists seem to respond instinctively to the greatness in the writing and give of their very best.

That is true even of the very early (1924) version on Edison Bell, although this is little more than a curiosity. The work is substantially foreshortened, the choruses are sung by a choir of just eight solo singers, and the orchestra consists of just twenty-four players! The results are, to say the least, not very satisfactory. But these seven 78rpm discs are not without interest. Joseph Batten, the conductor, evidently had the heart of the matter in him, and what we hear of his reading seems in the central tradition of interpreting the piece. In his memoirs, Batten wrote that he loved the music and hated to cut 'a score in which every bar seemed indispensable and impossible to sacrifice. But it had to be done, otherwise my directors would never have been convinced that what I had in mind was a saleable proposition.' Elgar, apparently, was delighted. A contemporary picture shows Batten posing with the composer and the cardinal.

227

ALAN BLYTH

Dan Jones, a Welsh tenor, then in his forties, was obviously an appreciable Gerontius. His straightforward, honest, slightly too extrovert and operatic voice and style have their counterpart — oddly enough — in the performance of Arthur Davies, the most recent tenor to record the part (see p. 235). Edith Furmedge, who sang Fricka and Erda at Covent Garden before the Second World War, is a secure, stalwart Angel, but a shade hooty and not particularly communicative. David Brazell is uninteresting as the Priest and Angel of the Agony.

The dream of a complete *Dream* conducted by the composer was never to be, but we have a precious glimpse of what might have been in the excerpts recorded at two different performances, in the Albert Hall in February, 1927, and in Hereford Cathedral during the Three Choirs Festival the same year. Originally only four sides of the Queen's Hall performance were issued. Then, in the early 1960s, the indefatigable Elgar scholar, Jerrold Northrop Moore, discovered that the composer's daughter, Mrs Elgar Blake, had five of the missing sides. Many years later, further research revealed that the granddaughters of Elgar's brother Frank still had the three unpublished sides comprising the Prelude, so that twelve (of the original thirteen sides), about half the score, could now be collected on one CD by Pearl (Opal 8910). Only the side with the Demons' chorus was lost.

These records disclose a reading of dramatic power, urgent tempi, natural expressiveness, and conveying a sense of awe. The Albert Hall recording is remarkably immediate in sound. The Royal Choral Society sings with firm and beautiful tone for the composer, the sopranos especially commendable in 'Praise to the Holiest', where Elgar persuades his charges to sing with great urgency, conviction and the right dynamic variety. Steuart Wilson makes a dignified, eloquent Gerontius in the few phrases we hear from him: his 'Novissima hora est' is among the most mystical of all (he sounds the 'h', by the way; no other tenor does that) and 'My soul is in my hand' has the right devout resignation. Margaret Balfour's lovely voice is well attuned to the Angel. Herbert Heyner is the upright baritone in the best English tradition, clear in projection and unaffected in diction both as Priest and Angel of Agony (listen to 'Hasten Lord their hour', so directly moving). How sad this evidently great performance wasn't recorded complete (even some of the sides that *were* made were rejected and destroyed).

The Hereford performance, not so arrestingly recorded (World Records SH 175), fills in some, but not enough gaps, and there are annoying repeats of other passages recorded in London. Elgar's wonderfully convinced way with his own score is again self-evident; so is the saturated sound of the LSO. Most unhappily, as in the Albert Hall, the Demons' Chorus record was destroyed — it seems the climaxes overloaded. The chorus isn't quite so well-trained and unanimous as the RCS. As could be predicted Tudor Davies is a much more overtly emotional, subjective Gerontius than Wilson, tending

228

to the lacrymose, but I hear more clearly than on his studio records the appeal of Davies's singing – most affecting at 'Mary, pray for me' and 'Novissima hora est'. Horace Stevens is also more involving than Heyner: from 'Jesu! by that shuddering dread', which Elgar here takes more freely, one can appreciate his considerable reputation in oratorio. Balfour, heard only in the finale, is as before in 'Softly and gently', that is near-ideal, but here she is rudely chopped off in mid-phrase.

A link with Elgar comes in the first complete recording, made in April, 1945, just as the war was ending, with the classic interpretation of Gerontius by Heddle Nash. Elgar wrote to the tenor in 1930 suggesting that he should sing the part. The wish was father to the deed. Nash sang Gerontius for the first time at Croydon in 1931 with the composer conducting, after which Elgar inscribed the singer's copy with the words 'Many thanks to Heddle Nash'. The same copy has Nash's additional words 'First performance from memory, Sept. 24, 1936'. By 1945 he was the most famous interpreter of the day, and perhaps any day. Of a performance in 1939, Neville Cardus wrote that Nash 'penetrated to the heart of his music as passionately as any of his great fore-runners ... He brought intelligence and feeling to his singing: the tone acquired the spiritual stress and pain for Part One, and more remarkable still, it acquired the right rapt simplicity, the note of release and faith, which is absolutely right for Part Two. His platform manner was moving in its dignity and the sense of utter absorption in a searching, sudden swelling of the heart; it was so expressive in an unselfconscious way ... No living singer, I am certain, can challenge Mr Nash's realisation of one of the most difficult, because one of the most spiritually intense, parts in all music.'

I have quoted Cardus at length because he is a contemporary witness of a live performance. By the time I heard Nash in the role in person, he was, though still remarkable, past his best. My experience of the records since they first appeared amply confirms Cardus's views. His spiritual commitment to the part, expressed in fervent, unstinting tone and flawless diction is exemplary, a model that others have attempted to follow. There is a wonderful variety of feeling from the overt, beseeching passion of 'Sanctus fortis' through the serene calm of 'I went to sleep' to the searing emotion of 'Take me away'. Particularly lovely is the *dolce* quality of the voice, as at 'Mary, pray for me', following the *plintivo* mark. What wonder fills the phrase 'Oh, what a heart subduing melody' as the Angel appears, what a lyrical outpouring he gives to 'there will I sing' in his final solo, with the strings of the Liverpool Philharmonic equally lyrical in support. This is all inspired music-making, historical now too. A similar fervour informs Sargent's interpretation, which follows the flame lit by Elgar himself. It is a forward-moving performance, never lingering too long over detail but encompassing the drama and intensity of every passage. The wartime Huddersfield Choral Society was a legendary body, which sings with steady, sturdy Northern strength and sincerity, finely supported by the Liverpool Philharmonic, who, however, aren't always obedient to all Elgar's *piano* marks.

The Angel is Gladys Ripley, whose flexible mezzo and appealing tone go to the heart of the matter, indeed to Gerontius's soul: the duet for her and Gerontius has its equal only in the performance of Minton and Pears on Decca. She is particularly communicative in describing the 'great Angel of the Agony', and is appropriately confident in 'Softly and gently'. This is the only set that indulges in the luxury of different soloists for the Priest and Angel of the Agony. Typically Walter Legge, the producer, noted that the first solo lies happily for a high baritone, the second for a *basso cantante*. Accordingly he assigned the one to Dennis Noble, whose keen projection of words is marred just once or twice by a loosening of vibrato, the other to Norman Walker, whose soft-grained yet imposing bass and beseeching manner are exactly right for the Angel of the Agony: the final 'Jesu!' is given a properly urgent attack, the word 'gaze' is intoned with appropriate awe.

So a standard was set in 1945 that has proved difficult to equal, let alone surpass except in terms of recorded sound. The second Sargent set, with the same chorus and orchestra, is in many ways admirable. Sargent again showed himself a remarkable enthuser of choristers, and the Huddersfield Choral Society once more responded in kind. The Liverpool Philharmonic again plays for him with verve and feeling, not least in a finely proportioned, never lingering Prelude. Richard Lewis, in the first of his two recordings, proved a worthy successor to Nash, though without quite the special minstrel-like quality of Nash's voice or his predecessor's fervour. Lewis, always involved and involving, identifies at all points with the troubled soul of Gerontius. He and Sargent make the whole solo passage from 'Sanctus fortis' to 'Thine own agony' a true picture of a soul *in extremis*. Then 'Novissima hora est' has a most refined beauty of tone. In the second part, Lewis's singing is at once sweet and urgent. As in Nash's case, this is the tenor's most important contribution to the gramophone.

EMI almost had a house team for oratorio in the 1950s and it included Marjorie Thomas, who projects the concerned side of the character as much as its consoling aspect. The tone isn't always quite as steady as one might wish, but it is expressively used throughout, nowhere more so than at the beginning of the duet with Gerontius, 'A presage falls upon thee' — lovely singing. Then she and Sargent make the section starting 'There was a mortal who is now above' as solemn and moving as any. John Cameron is an upright Priest: with the chorus he creates that sense of a communal act of goodness at 'Go forth upon thy journey'. He is also a troubled Angel of the Agony, though this part lies low for him, proving Legge's point in his choice of two singers for the 1945 version.

EMI seemed, fortuitously or by design, to have recorded the work at about ten-year intervals. The company next called on Barbirolli in 1965, a conductor

230

long associated with the oratorio, who gave many memorable performances of it in Manchester and London. I have never quite shared the high esteem in which this reading is held by some Elgarians. The Prelude immediately shows Barbirolli's penchant for pulling the music out of shape. Tempi tend to be slower than Elgar wanted, and certain sections drag badly. On the other hand, we hear at once in the Prelude the force of Barbirolli's commitment to this score. Few others, Britten perhaps, give the major themes such richness and intensity of utterance. Still, I do feel that the many unmarked *ritardandi* are debilitating. Is this justified licence or self-indulgence? How you view them may depend on your mood. What is never in question is Barbirolli's penetration to the core of the work's spirituality.

The Sheffield Choir begins tentatively but rises splendidly to the ferocity of the Demons (hardly equalled elsewhere) and to the ecstasy of 'Praise to the Holiest', though Sargent is better at controlling the latter's many changes of tempo. The orchestra, in this first stereo recording, gives us a true picture of Elgar's wonderful instrumental effects — the shimmering of strings at 'Pray for me my friends' in Gerontius's first solo. Note too the soft chord on the organ at 'I go before my judge', and all concerned realise thrillingly the mounting climax before 'Take me away'. Lewis, in his second recording, declaims this with the proper terror. Elsewhere he shows himself less communicative than ten years earlier. The cold from which he was suffering does sometimes affect his singing, as at the start of 'Sanctus fortis' and 'I can no more', but the climax just after on 'thine own agony' is successfully accomplished and Barbirolli demonstrates his operatic impulse at the words 'Rescue him' just after. Lewis's dreamy tone at 'Novissima hora est' and 'Into thy hands' is again exactly right. Even so I feel more spontaneity and urgency in his performance for Sargent.

Janet Baker, in her first recording of the work, sings with all the tenderness and beauty one expects from an Angel, suggesting an otherworldly aura and, where needed, the right kind of radiance. Her skill with words comes to the fore in describing St Francis's stigmata, and the farewell is a marvel of serene consolation. Kim Borg, who often sang in this work with Barbirolli, has all the authority for his first role, the supple expression for the second; his less-than-perfect English troubles some more than it does me. No, my chief reservation about this set lies in Barbirolli sometimes killing the score with too much kindness.

Inbetween Barbirolli's and EMI's next effort came the unique Britten version for Decca, recorded in 1972 at the Maltings, Snape, and now available on CD. Several young and sceptical listeners have, I know, been converted to the work by Britten's electrifying interpretation. There is no better example on record of one composer illuminating the music of a noted and beloved predecessor. CD only enhances the immediacy of the experience. In the Prelude, Britten at once achieves a sense of forward movement, urgency and dramatic tension:

we divine that this will be a reading to convey Elgar's own sense of awe and mystery and one that will give vital energy to all aspects of the orchestral writing – listen, at fig. 12, to the depth and concentration of the string tone when the 'Go forth' theme is first enunciated. Then Britten brings out arrestingly what William Alwyn in his notes to the LP set called so appropriately the 'ejaculatory, fragmented, thrusting' music after 'I can no more', and boldly underlines the furious, fantastic lead-in to the Demons' Chorus, and much later the *sforzando* chord before the Angel of the Agony's repeat of 'Jesu! Spare these souls'. At all times Britten observes Elgar's scrupulous markings, such as the hairpin crescendos and decrescendos in the Demons' Chorus and the *animato* in 'Praise to the Holiest' (fig. 89). There is not a trace of the lingering that can suggest sentimentality.

As in all his choral conducting, Britten insisted on precise articulation of words. Thus the dotted notes and verbal emphasis at 'Lord deliver him' are exactly right. Yet none of this attention to minutiae precludes Britten from presenting a longer view of the work, which is obviously viewed as a music-drama in all but name. Britten and his singers respond eagerly to the peculiar beauty and accent of Newman's text, however foreign they may have felt to the beliefs being expressed. In a sense all this makes Britten's interpretation *hors concours*. Britten's main chorus is smaller and therefore more incisive than any of its rivals, and on CD, as opposed to LP, the voices seem well caught in the Maltings' generous acoustics. It was also a good idea to have the Choir of King's College to sing the semi-chorus.

Peter Pears's response to the text is memorable, not merely a question of clear diction but also of the subtle inflection of such phrases as 'How still it is!' and 'My soul is in my hands'. 'Novissima hora est' has just the mystical feeling Elgar intended, and as I have already implied the whole colloquy with the Angel is finely achieved. When Pears's tone comes under pressure, the beat is disturbing, but that is a small price to pay for so many insights.

The young Yvonne Minton sings the Angel's music with a warmer, more opulent tone than any other mezzo. Her high A on the ultimate 'Alleluia' is quite thrilling and 'Softly and gently' is positively radiant. She doesn't always put as much into the text as have singers more experienced in the part, but her slightly distanced approach isn't inappropriate for a visitor from another world and she is never less than sympathetic. John Shirley-Quirk's two contributions are deeply expressive and securely sung. In the second, Britten emphasises the affinity between the Angel of the Agony's music and that of Amfortas. In the CD of this performance you have a bonus in Boult's 1962 recording of Holst's *The Hymn of Jesus*.

And it was to Boult that EMI turned in 1976 for its next recording. At the age of eighty-seven he was still a notable advocate of the score, still equal to controlling every facet of the great choruses, in which the London Phil-harmonic Choir sing, and are recorded (by Christopher Bishop), as well as any, though the voices aren't always quite unanimous in attack, especially where sibilants are concerned. Nor does Boult make Barbirolli's mistake of slowing down for passages such as 'O generous love' in 'Praise to the Holiest'. The orchestral playing is vital. Listen, for instance, to the timpani before 'Triumphant still'. As a whole the reading is straightforward and lovingly prepared.

It has one serious drawback. Nicolai Gedda's Gerontius is too extrovert, too carefully studied – his English is almost too precise – to sound convincing. He learnt the part quickly for this recording, and the want of experience of its idiom shows. At its worst his style is intolerably effusive and 'operatic' in the wrong sense. In compensation he provides as strong and secure a tone as any tenor for 'thine own agony' and 'Take me away', the first phrase of which is taken superbly in a single breath. Helen Watts gives a deeply felt, clearly articulated account of the Angel's music, with a specially grave utterance for 'Thy judgement now is near'. She is in the central tradition of the work's performance. So is Robert Lloyd's contribution, differentiating his two 'characters' and following Elgar's markings scrupulously.

The CRD recording conducted by Alexander Gibson, which appeared a year later, isn't in the same class as its predecessors. By the side of Sargent, Britten and Boult, Gibson sounds matter of fact and uninvolved, though – at faster speeds – Gibson's reading does not lack histrionic force. He is also closer to Elgar's metronome marks than Boult or Barbirolli, nearer Sargent and Britten (most faithful of all) in that respect. Quaver = 92 requests the composer for 'Softly and gently', and Gibson gives us something near that. Gibson is well served by his choir and orchestra, who are obviously familiar with his reading. Attack is clean, detail vivid – or as far as the less than clear recording allows.

Robert Tear's Gerontius is more inward, less extrovert than that of his immediate predecessor, and is sung with an intelligent management of tone and text, but it is management rather than commitment that I sense in Tear's singing, and he isn't always obedient to Elgar's *piano* markings. His entry in the duet with the Angel, 'Now is the hour', is a case in point. That part is taken with fresh tone, natural diction and eager participation by Alfreda Hodgson. Benjamin Luxon makes a suitably incisive Priest, a lightweight Angel of the Agony. His vibrato is sometimes too prominent. Though never less than well considered, this performance is the most dispensable of the complete sets because it misses individuality of utterance.

Simon Rattle's 1987 set is boldly histrionic. Using his own Birmingham forces, Rattle dares and achieves much in terms of making the piece a *dramatic* cantata. He is insistent on observing Elgar's markings. Rests and silences have their full due; expressive indications are scrupulously followed. Rattle also uses the extra trumpet asked for by Elgar at the moment where Gerontius has his blinding vision of his God. This is probably the most precise performance to date, but also a reading that shows total sympathy with the sentiments being expressed. The orchestral playing is splendidly vital but the chorus, at least as recorded in an over-resonant hall, isn't as incisive as one might wish — the Demons are a mite tame.

Don't expect to hear a great deal of beautiful singing *qua* singing from the three soloists on this version, rather look for interpretative insights and a sense of identity with their roles from the three experienced, mature artists taking part. Janet Baker crowns a long and distinguished career with her utterly sympathetic and verbally detailed portrait of the Angel. Every passage has been carefully considered and then weighted with the appropriate meaning, yet happily the spontaneity encountered on the Barbirolli set hasn't been lost. Maintaining a balance between grave other-worldliness and spiritual consolation, she covers every facet of the part. The tone may not be as sappy and resonant as twenty years earlier but it remains lovely. She courageously opts for the higher alternatives and shows little strain.

John Mitchinson is a thoughtful, imaginative Gerontius, who learnt much from Heddle Nash, his teacher, but he has his own individual strengths. Being in the heroic mould, his tenor is able to give an urgent power to the climaxes even when pressure on his tone tends to increase the vibrato. (Indeed if vibrato is a problem for the listener he or she may find Mitchinson a bit of a trial. They will miss many moments of interpretative intelligence.) But he is no less successful at achieving the inner mystery of 'Novissima hora est'. The plaintive note often requested by Elgar is perfectly adumbrated by Mitchinson.

Shirley-Quirk doesn't seem in best voice, his tone sounding grey and sometimes insecure, but again we are consoled by his knowledge of what he is singing about: he's deeply moving, as on the Decca set, as the Angel of the Agony.

The most recent set is yet another to bring out the best in its performers. Richard Hickox has been a fervent advocate of the work and trained the chorus for the first Soviet performance. The tone of the reading is set by the Prelude: Hickox conveys the utmost urgency and interior strength foretelling a peculiarly immediate interpretation. His speeds tend to be quick — he is within seconds of Rattle's swift reading — but only in 'Sanctus fortis' does he hurry unduly. As with Rattle and Britten, he makes the closing pages of 'Praise to the Holiest' as fast as the chorus can manage them. His own chorus is familiar with his methods and he persuades his charges to sing with an impressive unanimity of purpose and with as wide a range of dynamics as any conductor has achieved — you need go only as far as the opening 'Kyrie' to hear how quietly they can sing. Perhaps an element of dignity and grandeur achieved by Boult or Barbirolli, in their more measured readings, is missing, little else. The recorded sound of the chorus is much more amenable than that on the Rattle version. Indeed it is as spacious and immediate as that on any set, including the Boult, and the orchestra is simply tremendous at Gerontius's moment of revelation.

Arthur Davies has a stronger, more secure voice than any other tenor who has recorded Gerontius; unlike several of them he was in his prime at the time of recording. At first his reading is too overtly operatic: 'Sanctus fortis' is even matter of fact. But he soon gets the measure of the role. 'Mary, pray for me' and 'Novissima hora est' are sung appropriately with sweet sadness, 'I went to sleep' with mystery, the duet with the Angel tenderly, and 'Take me away' with terrified vigour. He doesn't match Nash or Pears in verbal acuity at such points as 'How still it is!' nor does he manage − quite − Mitchinson's agony of the soul, but it is an appreciable performance, firmly projected.

Felicity Palmer's understanding of the Angel's part is vitiated by the deterioration in tone when it comes under pressure. We have to be consoled by the depth of feeling in such reflective moments as 'into the veiléd presence of our God'. On the other hand Gwynne Howell's Priest and Angel of the Agony are as exemplary as any other. His warm, firm bass-baritone easily encompasses the different tessituras of the two roles. His deep commitment is moving to hear. All in all, of stereo versions, I would place this one alongside the Britten as a recommendation.

In the heaven to which Gerontius may have ascended I would want to hear Janet Baker as the Angel, Nash as Gerontius, Gwynne Howell or Norman Walker in the bass-baritone parts, the LSO Chorus and Orchestra under Britten's baton.

Walton: *Belshazzar's Feast*
Tippett: *A Child of Our Time*
Britten: *War Requiem*

MICHAEL KENNEDY

After the injection of post-Wagnerian Romanticism administered to English choral music by Elgar through *The Dream of Gerontius* in 1900, four major works appeared during the subsequent sixty-two years which showed how powerful a stimulant it had been to composers' imaginations. The first, Vaughan Williams's *A Sea Symphony*, was heard at the Leeds Festival in 1910 and most obviously betrays the Elgar influence while at the same time proclaiming a new and powerful individual voice. Of the other three, Walton's *Belshazzar's Feast* was composed between the wars in 1931; Tippett's *A Child of Our Time* appeared during the Second World War, in 1944; and Britten's *War Requiem* was first performed in 1962, seventeen years after the end of the Second World War, although it is the First World War that it commemorates. Of these four works, only one, Britten's, may be said to be religious, although its use of the Latin text of the Requiem Mass is almost secularised by the interpolation of nine poems by Wilfred Owen. It is true that *Belshazzar's Feast* has a text compiled from the Old Testament by Osbert Sitwell, but it is not religious music in any spiritual sense, while Tippett's oratorio *A Child of Our Time* has a libretto by the composer which is interspersed, in the manner of the chorales in Bach's Passions, by Negro spirituals. Vaughan Williams selected passages from Whitman for his *Sea Symphony*, some of which have a religious connotation.

Belshazzar's Feast is the most frequently recorded of these works, and probably the most frequently performed too. It has the economic advantage that it requires only one soloist and lasts only thirty-five minutes, which means it can be accommodated as half a concert-programme. It is more at home in a concert-hall than anywhere else. In fact, it was not until 1957 that the authorities at the Three Choirs Festival allowed it to be performed in one of their cathedrals. They regarded it as barbaric music, not fit to be heard by cathedral audiences. Only the establishment of the Church of England would have perpetuated an inconsistency of this kind, for presumably the words Walton set to music have been read as lessons within the sacred walls of Worcester, Hereford and Gloucester at many services.

Following the sensational impact of the first performance, conducted by Malcolm Sargent at the Leeds Festival in 1931, there was talk of Sir Hamilton Harty recording *Belshazzar's Feast*. Nothing came of the plan; one can only presume that someone decided (rightly) that the recording technique of the time would not be able to cope with the brassy and percussive din of the orchestra, let alone the exultant yells of the choir. So it was not until two wartime Sundays in January 1943 in the Philharmonic Hall, Liverpool, that the first recording was made. Walton conducted the Huddersfield Choral Society and Liverpool Philharmonic Orchestra, with Dennis Noble, who had been the baritone in the first performance, as soloist. Walter Legge was the producer. The recording was issued on ten sides of plum-label HMV 78s and was the second in the series of British Council-sponsored recordings of British music which were issued during the Second World War when there was a tremendous surge of interest in the native product. I remember buying them all as soon as they were in the shops, and rushing home to explore Moeran's Symphony in G minor and Bliss's piano concerto, territory unknown to me then. *Belshazzar's Feast* was the most exciting of them all and seemed to mark a new era in recording technique. As I sharpened an Imhof top-hat box of fibre needles and settled down, while on leave from naval training, to wallow in Walton's barbarities, the war seemed far away, despite the music's appropriate ferocity.

Sweet days of youth! Listening to this recording now, in its mono reissue on LP, I wonder how one can ever have been satisfied by its sound. The trombone fanfare with which the work begins is more like the hooting of a Parisian taxi's horn. And it soon becomes clear that the choir was seriously depleted by a wartime lack of young voices and that the orchestra, although it contained several fine individual players (such as the leader Henry Holst, the principal cellist Anthony Pini and the clarinettist Reginald Kell, with Rex Mortimer of Foden's Band in the extra brass), was not yet the splendid body it was to become. Yet of course the recording has historical interest and some virtues. For one thing, it preserves the original scoring; in 1948 Walton revised two sections of the final chorus (they are those between rehearsal-cue numbers 62 and 65 and between 74 and 77) and reduced the percussion and adjusted the scoring elsewhere. Later still, he re-scored the last fourteen bars, extending them to eighteen. The recording also allows us to hear Noble as soloist only just over a decade after he first sang the part. He is notably more lyrical than many of his successors in the opening section, reserving a sterner, more declamatory manner for Belshazzar's own words. Most significantly of all, we have here the first of the two performances Walton himself conducted. Although he was not technically a good conductor and it is said that whenever he was making 78rpm recordings Legge always had Constant Lambert or someone else on hand (Ernest Irving at Liverpool), in fact Walton was an excellent interpreter of his own music. He had strong views about *Belshaz- zar's Feast*, insisting that it should be kept on a tight rein and that too many other conductors made a shambles of it by trying to add to the excitement by accelerating the tempo. In two places in the score, he indicates that there should be a gradual *più mosso* and he gives the metronome readings and indicates exactly where the acceleration begins and ends. He observes his own instructions, and the performance is consequently ideally paced, with excite- ment mounting towards the work's final exultant chorus.

Belshazzar's Feast is a cleverly, almost cunningly, constructed work. Walton calls it neither cantata nor oratorio, and in his later years encouraged the view that it was a choral symphony. This is feasible, for it can be divided sectionally into an opening slow movement, an *allegro*, a *scherzo* (the 'Praise ye' episode) with march trio, and a *finale* ('Then sing aloud'). Although composed in emulation of Lambert's *The Rio Grande*, its forerunner closest in shape, length and content was Vaughan Williams's *Sancta Civitas* of 1925, which also has a baritone soloist, uses a semi-chorus and has a passage about the Fall of Babylon. Whether Walton had heard it before he wrote *Belshazzar's Feast* is not known. If he had not, then the similarities between the two are remarkable coincidences.

Walton packs an extraordinary range of expression into thirty-five minutes. Because of the electric impact of the last five minutes, when the choir's shouts of 'Alleluia' mix with the jazzy rhythms of the brass and the battery of percussion, audiences leave a performance of *Belshazzar's Feast* convinced that they have heard an exciting, noisy, barbaric and modernistic masterpiece. Up to a point they have; but if they think back, they have also heard long serene stretches of nineteenth-century harmony, belonging in the choral ambience of Parry and Elgar. They have heard, in the orchestral interlude in the 'Praise ye' movement, the first of Walton's *Crown Imperial*-style marches in which he laid claim to Elgar's ceremonial mantle. The baritone's operatic declamation and the equally operatic string *tremolandi*, together with the Berliozian use of two optional extra brass 'bands' (each comprising three trumpets, three trombones and tuba), contribute to the intensely dramatic illustration of Sitwell's brilliantly assembled text.

Because of the flashpoints in *Belshazzar's Feast* and the danger, which Walton saw so clearly, that conductors would pile excitement on excitement and blunt its striking-power, the dividing-line between success and failure is thin indeed. And it is a composition, now the shock of novelty and surprise has long since worn off, that needs a really splendid performance if its original impact is to be renewed and re-created. When it receives one, then there is no doubting that this is a masterpiece, original despite its essential un- originality, unconventional despite its trappings of conventionality. But if the performance fails fully to deliver the goods, then *Belshazzar's Feast* can seem dated, rather noisy and a too obviously contrived series of climaxes. The danger of its falling into the latter category is increased in a recording, where there is no atmosphere of a 'live' performance and where it is difficult to sustain the impression of a brief, explosive crescendo over several sessions during which a number of 'takes' may be made of certain sections and the work may be performed piecemeal and out of sequence.

So it is not surprising that many of the recordings are no more than adequate. The majority are technically acceptable, but few of them one would want to play often, or at all, as a substitute for the real thing, a live performance. Solti (1977), for example, whom one might have expected to give the most dynamic performance of all, is if anything slightly too respectful of the score. If it had been by Bartók, one surmises, he might have felt less inhibited. As it is, while there is much to admire in his performance – a dark and menacing introduction, with particularly rich low strings, good choral diction and Benjamin Luxon an expressive and dramatic soloist – the final impression is of a misfire. One plus-point is that Solti has taken the trouble to find a decent anvil for the illustrative section of 'Praise ye the god of iron'. On most recordings, the stroke on the anvil sounds feeble and tinny; on Solti's it is more Wagnerian.

Nor are the Hallé Choir and Orchestra, on a 1973 Classics for Pleasure disc, in a mood to do full justice to their fellow-Lancastrian's music. The rich, clean, sonorous sound of the trombones at the start raises hopes of special insights to follow, but the choir's glum enunciation of Isaiah's prophecy swiftly lowers the temperature and James Loughran's slowish tempi do nothing to retrieve the situation. The Hallé brass is in far from its best form in the 'Praise ye' section and the recording quality generally is only average. The baritone, Michael Rippon, gives a splendid recital of what Walton called 'the shopping-list', the unaccompanied recitative-like description of the riches of Babylon. He alone among recorded soloists pronounces 'brass' with a northern short 'a' and he puts plenty of expression into the punch-line, 'the souls of men'. (Later in the work he gives less pleasure by singing '*dee*-vided'.)

Sargent, surprisingly, made only one recording of *Belshazzar's Feast*, in 1958. His tempo for the introduction is faster than Walton's but he still creates real atmosphere. His *allegro giocoso* to begin the final section is more convincing than most in its buoyancy of rhythm, and in the beautiful quiet episode in this section, where the semi-chorus describes how the kings and merchants wept and wailed over the destruction of Babylon – a passage which reminds us that the boy Walton had a thorough grounding in the masterpieces of religious choral music while he was a chorister in Christ Church Cathedral, Oxford – Sargent obtains lovely *piano* singing from the choir that enables him to bring out the detail in the writing for woodwind. The baritone is James Milligan, a Canadian who sang Wotan at Bayreuth in 1961, the year before his untimely death. His performance is a poignant reminder of what a fine singer we lost. He imparts more drama than anyone else to his first solo, 'If I forget thee, O Jerusalem', and Sargent follows up by magnificently emphasising the choral and orchestral dissonance of the forecast that Babylon shall 'be thrown down'.

Two American performances were made for LP, one conducted by Eugene Ormandy, the other by Maurice Abravanel. What a shame that Walton's most sympathetic and dynamic transatlantic interpreter, Georg Szell, did not record it. One can imagine the intensity he would have imparted to the opening chorus, 'By the waters of Babylon', the most affecting part of the work, with its echoing wails of 'we wept', and the brazen splendour with which he would have praised the gods of iron, wood, silver, gold, stone and brass. Ormandy rather draws out the opening; throughout, we hear plenty of orchestral detail, mainly because the choir is placed too far back. Walter Cassel is a strong, clear, open-throated baritone, with exemplary diction. So is Robert Peterson for Abravanel and his Utah forces, though this is an enthusiastic rather than a disciplined performance.

Sir Alexander Gibson's 1977 recording with the Scottish National Orchestra and Chorus has many good points, the choral singing in particular being alert and sensitive, every word expressively sung. His is one of the few performances where the complex rhythms and counterpoint of 'Blow the trumpet' are surely and successfully negotiated. Sherrill Milnes is a somewhat over-dramatic soloist, even when it comes to the Writing on the Wall. But Gibson is highly successful in creating the necessary tension at this point, and he highlights the use of castanets here better than anyone else.

Besides the composer, the only conductor to record *Belshazzar's Feast* twice is André Previn. Both recordings are available on compact disc. The first (1972) was made for EMI to celebrate the composer's seventieth birthday. (Incidentally, the *Penguin Guide* errs in saying Walton attended the sessions.) It is in many respects a stunning achievement, with the London Symphony Chorus in overwhelming form and John Shirley-Quirk an admired soloist. The recording is spacious, but so are some of the tempi, too spacious, and there follows a mad scramble in the exciting choruses. It is then that one appreciates the virtues of Walton's second recording, made for Columbia in 1959 with the Philharmonia Orchestra and Chorus, both at their zenith. The growl of the cellos and basses when they first enter is vividly recorded; the fanfares at 'Blow the trumpet' are incisive; and the elegiac unaccompanied choral singing of the 'trumpeters and pipers' passage underlines the rightness of Walton's judgement in placing this reflective episode in the midst of the finale's jazzy rejoicing. But, above all, it is the composer's sure command of the structure of his work that makes this performance the definitive one on record: how well he generates a high-voltage charge even when the music is apparently relaxed and reflective, and all without extremes of pace or sudden dynamic vagaries. As a result, the final pages have a frenzied exaltation that, in many performances, emerges merely as excitable loud singing. Donald Bell is, beside Noble, a pallid soloist.

The one other recording that allows of no doubts that *Belshazzar's Feast* is a masterpiece was made in 1953 and is conducted by Sir Adrian Boult with the London Philharmonic Orchestra and Chorus. It was originally issued as a Nixa LP, and its transfer thirty-five years later to CD shows how good the master tapes were. It is an odd performance in that the choir has been reduced to a handful of voices for certain passages, presumably so that the words will be distinct. The semi-chorus at times sounds like a vocal quartet, and is recorded at close quarters. A small choir in *Belshazzar's Feast* sounds like a contradiction in terms, but there can be no doubt that Boult made this decision with recording in mind, and in the hectic passages enough choral sound is forthcoming. But the curious recording hardly matters in view of the quite extraordinary fierceness of the performance. Even more than Walton, Boult treats the work as an Old Testament drama of blood-and-thunder. He differentiates more than other conductors between the chorus as the children of Israel and as the licentious inhabitants of Babylon. A rasp enters the voices at 'O daughter of Babylon, who art to be destroyed', and the closing chorus is a gloating paean. Like Walton, Boult appreciates that the cumulative excitement is there in the score, written in the notes, and all he needs to do is to bring the score to expressive life. It is sometimes forgotten that he conducted the first London performance, so had a long association with the work. He chose Dennis Noble as the baritone for the recording, with the happy result that we have a much clearer impression than from the 1943 recording of how magnificent he was in the part. His cry of 'slain' is truly savage. When one hears this performance, one realises how woolly is Benjamin Luxon's singing in Previn's second (1986) recording. This RPO Records issue has generally been regarded as inferior to Previn's 1972 version, but I prefer it. The Brighton Festival Chorus makes a good clean incisive sound and the RPO plays excellently. But the superiority lies in Previn's interpretation, which, though occasionally too relaxed, is on the whole better structured, releasing pent-up tension on a slow-burning fuse.

Belshazzar's Feast, with its wide range of dynamics, is music which clearly benefits from the advantages of CD, especially where clarity of the orchestral part is concerned. Walton's dramatic use of silences, too, is obviously more impressive when there is no danger of hearing disc surface-noise or clicks. Previn's second version was made for CD and three more appeared in 1989. Richard Hickox's interpretation with the London Symphony Chorus and Orchestra is straightforward and well recorded. The performance of the march in the 'Praise ye' section is ponderous, though, and David Wilson-Johnson's singing of the baritone solos is disappointingly constricted and wobbly.

On Telarc the American choral conductor Robert Shaw obtains virtuoso singing and playing from the Atlanta Symphony Orchestra and Chorus, with

William Stone as a sturdy and vigorous exponent of the solo part. But what is in many respects as good a performance as any on record is rendered artistically unacceptable by the conductor's extraordinary decision to reinforce the final chord of the work with the choir! Or if that's not what he does, then it's some peculiar acoustic effect that sounds exactly like human voices. In either case, it's a pity. No such eccentricity mars Sir David Willcocks's conducting of the Bach Choir and Philharmonia Orchestra. This is an electrifying performance, speeds perfectly judged and with the CD recording allowing us to hear all the barbaric splendour of Walton's scoring in the great 'Praise' chorus. Willcocks is scrupulous in observance of the score's instructions and the result is a memorably exciting interpretation with Gwynne Howell much the best soloist on record since Milligan.

There is another recording which deserves a special commendation. This was made in 1977 by the Senior Choir of Chetham's School of Music, Manchester, with Chetham's Senior Orchestra and members of the orchestra of the junior school of the Royal Northern College of Music, conducted by Michael Brewer, and with Howard Briggs as a light-voiced but accurate baritone soloist (his 'shopping-list' is the only one on record enunciated exactly as the score prescribes). The recording is of a public performance and therefore has an extra immediacy and excitement. This also means, though, that the strains of the occasion are preserved: the young voices cannot sustain the strident jubilant mood and the orchestra's string players come to grief in the feast itself. Brewer is a very considerate conductor – the march is too slow, however – and such points as the impressively accurate *fp* on 'wept' are a lesson to more illustrious interpreters. In conclusion, and for the sake of completeness, one should perhaps mention the shortest *Belshazzar's Feast* on record – the chorus's shout of 'slain', conducted by the composer with a fly-swat, at a Hoffnung Music Festival in the Royal Festival Hall on 28 November 1961!

Tippett's *A Child of Our Time* was a work of its time and seems likely to remain topical at any time, given the state of the world. At any rate for English-speaking audiences, it has, since its first performance in 1944, become part of the documentary fabric of the cruel twentieth century, on a par with Joyce's *Ulysses* and T. S. Eliot's *The Waste Land*. Tippett unerringly struck a chord in listeners' hearts and consciences which will vibrate as long as persecution and pogroms are part of what is called civilisation. But the oratorio works in its political and sociological context only because the music is so emotionally charged and expertly crafted. Tippett's use of five Negro spirituals as the equivalents of Lutheran chorales in Bach's Passions is often cited as the prime reason for the work's popularity and success. It is a marvellous dramatic coup, but it is by no means the sole cause of success. The spirituals are effective precisely because they fit naturally into the framework of Tippett's own music as its inevitable outcome. It is not the spirituals which 'make' *A Child of Our Time*; it is *A Child of Our Time* which lifts the spirituals to a higher plane.

It is, viewed objectively, a less mature score than *Belshazzar's Feast*. At twenty-seven Walton had already found his own voice and style, and although one may trace the tributaries which flowed into his mainstream, he shows in *Belshazzar's Feast* a sureness of touch that comes from total artistic confidence. Tippett was thirty-four when he began to compose *A Child of Our Time* on 5 September 1939, and his style was by no means as settled as Walton's. One may even hear a trace of Walton's influence in the Chorus of the Oppressed in Part I, where 'By the waters of Babylon' seems to have been a model. But whereas *Belshazzar's Feast* may have been designed in a symphonic format, *A Child of Our Time* took Handel's *Messiah* and the Bach Passions as its models, being laid out in three parts, with recitatives, arias, ensembles and chorales. The libretto is Tippett's own: he had first asked Eliot to provide it, but after the poet had studied the outline scenario he advised the composer to write his own text because he felt that his (Eliot's) words might overwhelm the music. Nevertheless, Tippett's glosses on lines from Eliot (and other poets) remain at the heart of the work. Much of the text is movingly eloquent and generally less abstruse than parts of Tippett's opera libretti. Only at the passage 'The words of wisdom are these: winter's cold means inner warmth' is there a suggestion of something like an advertisement for Bournvita.

A Child of Our Time was inspired by the shooting in Paris in November 1938 of Ernst von Rath, Third Secretary at the German Embassy, by a 17-year-old Polish Jew, Herschel Feibel Grynspan, who was being illegally sheltered by his uncle and aunt and was driven to his deed because of the persecution of his mother. The shooting led directly to the terrible 'Crystal Night' of 9 November, so called because the windows of Jews' shops and houses in Central Europe were smashed during an outbreak of violence, looting and killing. Tippett took his title from a novel, *Ein Kind unserer Zeit*, by the anti-Nazi author Odon von Horvath. His libretto is not a dramatisation of the Paris events, but a reflection on them. Part I deals with oppression generally, Part II with the boy's attempt to seek justice by violence (here the soloists are named as Boy, Mother, Aunt and Uncle) and Part III attempts to draw a moral. Like many a later Tippett work, it is also a progress from dark to light; specifically in this case from winter to spring.

In Tippett's own words, *A Child of Our Time* is about 'a man whose god has left the light of the heavens for the dark of the collective unconscious. The work asks the question: what happens to this man as the confusion deepens and the collective forces become ever more undiscriminating and unjust? Indeed, what happens when individual actions of apparently righteous protest produce colossal ensuing catastrophes? As the text says somewhere: "God overpowers him — the child of our time".'

243

One cannot imagine Walton having written like that about his music. *Belshazzar's Feast*, for all its moving laments, is essentially a physical sensation. *A Child of Our Time* strikes at our emotions and our conscience, and does so through music of surprising simplicity. The so-called complexity of a Tippett score is absent here. Every point is made concisely and the scoring is both clear and light, with some memorable orchestral passages, such as the Bach-like woodwind and cellos which precede the contralto's first entry in The Argument, the exquisite solo flutes in the Interludium and the high strings and flutes which introduce the Boy's song in prison.

The three recordings date from 1958, 1975 and 1986. It is surprising that there have been so few. The first was a British Council sponsorship and was conducted by John Pritchard, a keen and sensitive interpreter of Tippett, who conducted the premieres of the first two operas, *The Midsummer Marriage* in 1955 and *King Priam* in 1962. As an interpretation on record, his *A Child of Our Time* remains for my taste the best of the trio, even though as a recording it now shows its age. The big choral climaxes are constricted and lack spaciousness – generally, there is insufficient dynamic range.

But what a lovely performance it is nevertheless. The four soloists are easily the best matched; even if one finds Richard Standen's bass too ecclesiastical for present taste, he sings with controlled fervour. Richard Lewis is throughout ideal as the Boy, light and lyrical, with deep poetic feeling, and strength too. His first solo, 'I have no money for my bread', with its *allegro agitato* introduction that recalls the syncopated rhythms of the Double String Concerto, is sung with a pathos wholly devoid of self-pity. Pamela Bowden's alto arias are models of dignity and warmth. Elsie Morison's sweet, pure and firm soprano floats gloriously over the chorus's first spiritual, 'Steal away', and she is touching in the Mother's arias. Pritchard does not attempt to disguise the work's borrowings – a touch of Walton here and there, as already noted, and a Vaughan Williams feel in the final general ensemble – 'Then courage, brother, dare the great passage' echoes *A Sea Symphony*, albeit subconsciously. There are anticipations, too, of *The Midsummer Marriage*, particularly the 'It is spring' duet for the soprano and tenor soloists and the four soloists' wordless ecstasies at the end of this same ensemble. Pritchard's affectionate treatment, sincere, never too heavy-handed, allows the great work to emerge as wholly typical of its creator.

Colin Davis's performance, made with BBC forces when he was the symphony orchestra's chief conductor, is a tougher proposition, almost as if he were scared of letting the work topple over into sentimentality. He is a confirmed Tippettian, but I'm not sure that this particular work benefits from his astringent approach. I suspect that today he might record it differently. From the urgency of the chorus's 'We are lost' right through to 'Deep River', the performance has tremendous drive. The violins in their upper register before the Boy's song in prison are here given a cutting-edge which prompts

244

the belief that, hearing the first performance in 1944 while he was at work on *Peter Grimes*, Britten must have taken a strong hint from this passage had it not already been suggested to him in Shostakovich.

Davis's four soloists are almost too individualistic for the work. Janet Baker comes nearest to the spirit of the music, but Jessye Norman, besides showing scant regard for dynamics, is too aggressive. John Shirley-Quirk is himself, as always reliable but here not especially imaginative. The tenor Richard Cassilly is no more ingratiating than he is as Walton's Troilus in the EMI recording of the opera made not long after this set. This Boy is not Siegfried, after all.

Previn's recording, made with the excellent Brighton Festival Chorus and the Royal Philharmonic Orchestra, is so far the only CD version – the advantage can be heard at once in the power of 'We are lost'. His interpretation is neither so moving as Pritchard's nor so compelling as Davis's, but it is filled with understanding and compassion. Some of his tempi are slower than one has come to expect – there is almost a liturgical feel to 'Go down, Moses' – but the Terror chorus is swift-moving in its fugal bewilderment. The soloists are Philip Langridge, a little dry-toned as the Boy, Felicity Palmer, very much the recording angel, John Shirley-Quirk, much as before, and Sheila Armstrong, who is emotionally the most involved, but cannot disguise that the top of her voice is under strain.

Britten's *War Requiem* attracted more publicity, probably, than any other work of its kind has ever done. It was written to mark the consecration of the new cathedral at Coventry which Sir Basil Spence designed to replace the old cathedral destroyed in a German air raid in the Second World War. The completion of the new cathedral was widely seen as an occasion for reconciliation. Britten, a lifelong pacifist, jumped at the chance to expound his views in a large-scale work that would combine an expression of international bridge-building with his personal feelings about war. By a stroke of genius, he took the Latin Requiem Mass as the public utterance, set for soprano, large orchestra and chorus, into which he threaded nine poems by Wilfred Owen, set for tenor, baritone and chamber orchestra.

Even before the work was performed on 30 May 1962, it was declared to be Britten's masterpiece by the music critic of *The Times*, much to the chagrin of Igor Stravinsky, who complained that the 'Battle-of-Britten sentiment' was 'so thick and the tide of applause so loud that I, for one, was not always able to hear the music'. He would not have heard much of it if he had been in Coventry Cathedral on that historic evening. The acoustic was totally unsuitable for a work of this kind, and the large-scale episodes reached me, sitting two-thirds of the way back in the nave, as a muddle of sound. Only the Owen settings made much impression. Yet I left the cathedral deeply moved, unlike the late John Culshaw, the record producer, who felt that the audience was ill-at-ease with the work and 'sent out waves which the performers could not define but most certainly felt. It was not a happy occasion.' (*Putting the Record Straight* by John Culshaw, London, 1981, p. 292).

The fact remains that *War Requiem* was the right work at the right time. It caught the anti-war mood of the 1960s and it appeared two years before the 50th anniversary of the outbreak of the First World War, with which, because of the Owen poems, it seemed to have much more connection. Choral societies everywhere rushed to perform it, and it was taken up in Europe and the United States.

Britten's plan to consolidate international understanding by having a Russian soprano, German baritone and English tenor as the soloists at Coventry was frustrated by the Soviet Union, which made various unconvincing excuses not to release Galina Vishnevskaya for the first performance. Her place with Peter Pears and Dietrich Fischer-Dieskau was taken by Heather Harper. Culshaw was anxious to record the work for Decca as soon as possible, with the soloists for whom it was intended, and the sessions began in the Kingsway Hall in January 1963, with Britten conducting. As she had not been at Coventry, Vishnevskaya had no idea that the soprano was intentionally set apart, placed with the main choir, and when she found herself in the dress circle of the hall while Pears and Fischer-Dieskau were on the stage near the conductor, she thought she had been snubbed. All efforts to explain to her, through an interpreter, why this had to be only made matters worse and, as Culshaw has entertainingly described in his book, she eventually lost her head and lay on the floor shrieking at the top of her voice for some considerable time. Next day, when she arrived at the hall, she appeared to have mastered the situation and took her place with the chorus, working hard and causing no fuss. Culshaw had had much difficulty persuading Decca to record the work anyway. When the recording was ready, insufficient copies were pressed to meet the demand. Although over 200,000 sets were sold within the first five months of issue, Culshaw was convinced that even more would have been sold if the sets had been available when demand was at its height. Taxing the individual who was responsible for deciding to press an initial few hundred sets only, Culshaw received the reply: 'Daren't take the risk, old boy. First thing of Britten's that ever sold at all.'

Nearly thirty years later, the recording, now available on CD, remains a monument to Culshaw's enterprise and skill. He took endless trouble to convey the 'spatial' aspects of the music, with the acoustic sensitively adjusted between the big choral setpieces and the more intimate Owen settings. Britten's interpretation must be regarded as definitive, as are the contributions by Pears and Fischer-Dieskau, culminating in their profoundly moving singing of 'Strange Meeting'. About Vishnevskaya, there will always be individual reservations. Britten wanted her voice because he wanted what he called a 'wild animal sound' and that is certainly what he gets, though it may not be clear to all why he wanted it. The soprano represents the voice of suffering humanity speaking in impersonal Latin, but Vishnevskaya sometimes sounds more like an avenging angel. Nevertheless, these are the voices for which the music was written, and one cannot imagine the general effect ever being surpassed.

Such was the success of the recording at every level that there was no room for a rival. Since everyone who admired the work seemed to possess the Decca set, none of the other companies thought it worthwhile to produce an alternative. It is a powerful tribute to the authenticity of the Britten performance. Yet there may have been another reason. After the first flush of enthusiasm, doubts about the quality of the work itself began to be expressed and performances became fewer. There are still divisions of opinion about an alleged disparity between the level of invention in the Latin sections and the inspired Owen settings. So not until 1983 did a second recording emerge in Britain, when HMV recorded Simon Rattle's interpretation with the City of Birmingham Symphony Orchestra and Chorus. Rattle appears determined to reinstate confidence in the Latin portions of the work. His choice of soprano was Elisabeth Söderström, who brings more warmth and personal expressiveness to the music, humanising it to a degree more than perhaps the composer wished. Compare Vishnevskaya and Söderström in the Sanctus. The former's opening cries are hieratic, the latter's appealing. When it comes to the lulling, gentle Benedictus Söderström is all feminine consolation, Vishnevskaya is a kind of deified compassion. Both sing the movement with extraordinary beauty of tone and phrasing, and to say that one prefers one to the other is scarcely possible. One may feel that the Russian approaches nearer the composer's original vision, whereas the Swedish soprano brings another dimension to the music which the composer may not have realised was there. One must be grateful for two wonderful performances, while at the same time regretting that Heather Harper's authoritative and beautiful interpretation has never been recorded.

Nor is it any easier, or more sensible, to make comparisons between the male soloists. There is something about Fischer-Dieskau's German accent as he sings Owen's poetry that gives his performance almost an unfair authority, but Thomas Allen's equally intense and dark-toned singing is on an exalted level. Tear is possibly too near to Pears in timbre and style for any comparison to be other than invidious, the master being, as it were, the music's co-creator. Tear is more convincing in the jaunty duet 'Out there' — neither Pears nor Fischer-Dieskau is wholly at ease here — but cannot rise to the astonishing heights of vocal artistry scaled by Pears in the Agnus Dei, possibly the sublime feature of the whole work. There are differences of tempo and emphasis between Britten and Rattle, but none that matters — both are conductors who bring out the very best from everyone under their baton and both make the trumpets blaze and shine in the Hosanna in the most remarkable way.

There have been three other recordings of *War Requiem*, two American and one German. The first American performance (1975) was conducted – more than adequately – by William D. Hall, associate professor of music at Chapman College, Southern California, and also a pacifist and Methodist minister of music. The sleeve-note and general presentation of the album are so redolent of the post-Vietnam atmosphere of 'make love not war' that one half expects to find that the soprano part is sung by Jane Fonda. As it happened, the recording was made in a Vienna beer hall while the William Hall Chorale was on toûr. The Vienna Festival Symphony Orchestra has a hard time of it with Britten's brilliant brass writing, but it is a creditable performance, with the Chorale's singing and that of the Columbus Boychoir the best feature. The tenor Michael Sells and the baritone Douglas Lawrence are sympathetic performers, with good voices, and the soprano is none other than Jeannine Altmeyer, Bayreuth's memorable Sieglinde, here at the beginning of her rise to stardom and with a marked tendency, which becomes irritating, to attack her high notes from below.

Robert Shaw's 1989 performance with the Atlanta Symphony Orchestra, Chorus and Boys' Choir is magnificently recorded and is outstandingly successful in the big choral episodes. The Dies irae and Libera me emerge as powerfully, if not quite as dramatically, as in Rattle's recording. Shaw, like Rattle, exonerates Britten from a failure of inspiration at these points: indeed, the inspiration sounds white-hot. The Atlanta chorus is superb and the three soloists are well chosen. Lorna Haywood has something of Vishnevskaya's 'wild animal' quality, not always beautiful but thrilling. Anthony Rolfe Johnson brings security and poise to the tenor songs. Benjamin Luxon is both forceful and eloquent (and relatively wobble-free) in the baritone part.

The East German performance was recorded in a translation by Fischer-Dieskau and Ludwig Landgraf (Britten's friend, the late Prince Ludwig of Hesse and the Rhine) in 1968 and conducted by Herbert Kegel, with the Leipzig Radio Symphony Orchestra, Choir and Children's Choir. The records were made in a reverberant acoustic – the boys seem to be miles away – but the impression of the three planes of sound is well conveyed and so is the spirit of the music. The baritone, Günther Leib, has a lightish voice but is marvellous in 'Strange Meeting', and the soprano, Hanne-Lore Kuhse, is nearer to the Vishnevskaya style than either Söderström or Altmeyer. The choir's performance of the Recordare is especially well recorded; it is well sung, too. I would question whether the start of the Offertorium is *largamente*. The recording is worth seeking out above all for Peter Schreier's singing of the tenor role. As singing, it is superior to Pears's and not far short of his consummate artistry in the expressiveness of the Agnus Dei and in many other places.

Stravinsky: *The Wedding*
Symphony of Psalms

PAUL GRIFFITHS

Both of Stravinsky's largest choral works, *Oedipus Rex* (1926–7) and *Perséphone* (1933–4), fall outside the scope of this book, the one because, as an 'opera-oratorio', it has already been covered in *Opera on Record 2* (Hutchinson, 1983), the other more mundanely because there have been too few recordings to form a basis for comparison. The same reason of neglect disqualifies other pieces, including the great sequence of late choral monuments: the *Canticum sacrum* (1955), *Threni* (1957–8), *A Sermon, a Narrative and a Prayer* (1960–1) and the *Requiem Canticles* (1965–6), of which the last was one of the few works for large forces that the composer himself did not record. But there is a typicalness too in *Oedipus Rex* in its straddling of worlds, its being at once a drama, a concert item and a ritual. *The Wedding* (1914–23), for example, was composed as a ballet of a ceremonial nature, but can work in the concert hall as a ritual cantata. And the more straightforwardly sacred pieces, beginning with the *Symphony of Psalms* (1930), are liturgies transposed on to the concert platform: apart from small unaccompanied prayers, only the Mass (1944–7) sets a standard liturgical text, and here the accompaniment for ten wind instruments makes concert performance more likely. All Stravinsky's choral works are at once sacred and secular, theatrical and purely musical. So it is entirely suitable that his two most frequently recorded compositions of this kind should be a ballet of wedding songs and a symphony of psalms.

The Wedding (Svadebka; Les noces) had a more protracted genesis than was at all usual for Stravinsky. He appears to have begun selecting the texts and composing the music in the second half of 1914,[1] but other works intervened, and the sketch score was not completed until October 1917, at which stage the work was envisaged as being for four soloists, chorus and

---

1 See Vera Stravinsky and Robert Craft: *Stravinsky in Pictures and Documents* (London, Hutchinson, 1979), p. 150. This volume provides the most comprehensive published documentation of the work's composition.

an ensemble of orchestral wind, solo strings, harp, harpsichord, piano, cimbalom and percussion. Much of the fourth scene was orchestrated thus, and an entire '1917 version' was posthumously edited by Robert Craft and others. Stravinsky himself did not continue with it because he changed his mind about the accompanying ensemble, and did so twice: in 1919 he scored the first two scenes for pianola, harmonium, two cimbaloms and percussion; then in 1923 he made the definitive version, for four pianos and percussion. This is the edition that most performances follow, though Craft in 1973 recorded both the premature scores, and Eötvös's 1988 recording puts the 1917 and 1923 versions side by side.

There is also a choice in the matter of language. The French version was made in 1917 by C.F. Ramuz, working closely with the composer while the music was being written.[2] Quite possibly (the sources are silent on this point) it was used at the first performance; certainly it has more claim to authenticity than most translations, in acknowledgement of which the title 'Les Noces' remains current long after other Stravinskyan Gallicisms (*Le Sacre du printemps, Symphonie de psaumes*) have generally been put into English. So the four recordings in French, including one from the 1970s (Dutoit), need not be dismissed on that count alone. Yet against that view there stands Stravinsky's own judgement in a letter of 1930 that 'the French translation ... does not render the character of the rhythmic accentuation which constitutes the basis of the Russian chant of this work'.[3] And his own note on the piece, published with his second recording, makes much of the work's Russian character and the importance of the sounds of the Russian words.

This would be stronger evidence, though, if that second recording were not, like the composer's first, sung in English. Perhaps he had little choice for the first recording, made in London on 10 July 1934:[4] English singers were then not so used to working outside their own language. But Craft informs us that before the second recording (New York, 21 December 1959), Stravinsky laboured on and then abandoned an English translation (what he used instead, as in 1934, was the standard version by D. Millar Craig), which must suggest that he wished, rather than was obliged, to record the work in English. If he had made a third recording, then perhaps he would have used the Russian text: all his Russian-language recordings date from the 1960s. However, his 1962 recording of *Renard*, the work closest to *The Wedding*, is in English, so the point remains moot, and the various recordings, seen as a body,

---

2 See Charles F. Ramuz: *Souvenirs sur Igor Strawinsky* (Lausanne, Mermod, 1929).
3 Quoted in Stravinsky and Craft, *Stravinsky in Pictures and Documents*, p.145.
4 All information concerning the places and dates of Stravinsky's recordings is taken from David Hamilton: 'Igor Stravinsky: a Discography of the Composer's Performances', *Perspectives of New Music*, IX/2–X/1 (1971), p.169 for *The Wedding* and p.172 for the *Symphony of Psalms*.

accurately reflect the nature of the work in favouring Russian while keeping French and English (and American) open as options.

There is much more agreement among the recordings in matters of tempo, and this too is in accord with the essence of the music, nearly all of which is geared to one of two pulse rates (80 and 120) with very little invitation to rubato: most conductors find this results in a total duration close to twenty-three minutes, the outstanding exception being Stravinsky himself in his later recording, which extends the length to twenty-five minutes (it is markedly below the written tempo at fig. 2, for example). This seems just plain wrong – though hardly as wrong as the bizarre estimated duration given in the score of 'approx. thirty-five minutes': one feels inclined to trust Stravinsky's pen rather than his baton or his stopwatch.

So it is with other aspects of his recordings. His use of perhaps three singers for the basso profundo line at fig. 50 in 1934 was probably a practical necessity, though it may also have been a reversion to an earlier plan: Eötvös's recording of the 1917 score (though not Craft's) has both parts of the duet sung chorally. There is also a quaintness in this recording that comes partly from the evident difficulty experienced by the instrumentalists, partly from the English style of the singers. Parry Jones, who sang in the first English *Wozzeck* the same year, is better than many of his later colleagues in coping with the high, Slavonic tessitura of the solo tenor part, and Roy Henderson's suggestion of a pantomime dame in his falsetto is not wholly inappropriate, but the plummy calls of 'Come to the wedding' are not quite right for an icon of peasant marriage. Stravinsky's ensemble of 1959 is much more in control, even if the presence of four composers at the pianos is only a charming gesture of homage. This later recording also benefits from the splendid choral training of Margaret Hillis.

But her own recording of the early 1950s is so much superior: exuberantly lively but also neatly controlled in rhythm, and with all the detail clear despite the dullness of the sound. She has a good team of soloists: a bright soprano, properly sultry mezzo, youthful tenor and warm bass (though Arthur Burrows is billed as a baritone, and his low register is indeed weak). Her recording also, uniquely, includes the clap at fig. 100 that somehow got into the English text: it is a minor and dubiously authentic point, but here it speaks for the vividness of the performance. This is certainly the best *Wedding* in English, and one of the best altogether, along with those of Craft and Eötvös.

Nearer to it in time are the recordings conducted by Felix de Nobel at the Holland Festival in 1954, and by Mario Rossi in Vienna. The former has a fragile soprano and a weak bass (curiously, his line at fig. 23 is sung chorally), but a fine tenor in Ernst Haefliger: his entry at fig. 10 is a keenly vivid new beginning, marking the point at which a male voice is heard for the first time in the work, and his downward glissando on the spoken 'tous' before fig. 114 initiates a tradition followed in the other French-language recordings.

In general the recording is forward and clear; its main deficiencies are in rhythm, which in this music is a fairly crucial domain. There are problems of ensemble (notably at fig. 59), and the turn of speed between figs. 41 and 44 is another, more regrettable feature imitated in later performances (those of Ančerl, Dutoit and Bernstein for instance).

There are moments of shaky ensemble too in the Rossi recording, which was the first in Russian, and remained alone until the Ančerl version appeared in 1965. That must be its principal distinction. The soloists are again variable, with a soprano uncertain in rhythm and intonation, a good mezzo, a beefy tenor and, in Eberhard Waechter, a bass who is likable but perhaps excessively modest in his falsetto singing.

Ansermet's recording, published in 1961, might be thought to have a claim to authenticity, since thirty-eight years earlier he had conducted the first performance; it is, however, as dubious a witness as either of the composer's own versions. The percussion instrumentation is occasionally enriched (in the two bars before fig. 49, for instance), and the line 'Ah! les jolis sourcils noirs!' before fig. 125 is done as a solo. There begins to seem some justice in Stravinsky's remark, at the time of his rift with the conductor over *Jeu de cartes* in 1937, about Ansermet wanting 'to do his Bach–Busoni'.[5] But even if these are judged to be minor retouchings, there remain the problems of muddy texture (e.g. at fig. 62) and, most seriously, of an un-Stravinskyan pathos (notably at fig. 35 and in the bass bicinium at fig. 50). There are, though, isolated moments of surprise: the soprano Basia Retchitzka takes an effective jazzy swing at the syncopation after fig. 122, and the bass Heinz Rehfuss is excellent, being full of character in his early falsetto lines and then producing pure harmonics for the high Fs at fig. 109.

The Boulez recording, associated with performances he conducted at the Paris Opera in 1965 with choreography by Béjart, also boasts a good bass in the young José van Dam, but the other soloists (especially the mezzo) are poor, and the instrumental sound is confused: partly because it is not very well played, partly because the recording favours the voices. Also, there is quite extraordinary lack of momentum, so that pauses (at fig. 55, for example) almost stop the music in its tracks: one misses the achievement here that Boulez might have picked up from observing Roger Désormière rehearse the score,[6] and one misses too the 'unusual synthesis of violence and irony' he has remarked in it.[7] Perhaps it is significant that he has not made a second recording of the piece, and has returned to it in the concert hall only very rarely. But there are a couple of interesting points in this 1965 recording. One is the

5 Quoted in *Stravinsky: Selected Correspondence*, ed. Robert Craft, vol. 1 (London, Faber, 1982), p. 227.
6 See Pierre Boulez: *Orientations* (London, Faber, 1986), p. 508.
7 Ibid., p. 351.

occasional alteration of the French words to fit the Russian rhythms better; the other is the omission of one of the silent bars before fig. 135, so that the bell strokes fall at regular intervals of eight crotchets (apparently there exists a film of Boulez pointing out this 'error' to the composer, and obtaining sanction for an amendment, though all other conductors follow the printed score).

From the same period, Ančerl's recording is enlivened by a dark, cutting sound to the Russian that perhaps comes from the use, for the first time, of a wholly Slav ensemble of singers. The soprano's yelps at the opening also add character, though later her vibrato is worrying. However, what thoroughly mars this version is the fierce compression and at times (just before fig. 71, for instance) the poor balance.

Robert Craft's recording, published in 1973, raises the level considerably. The soprano Mildred Allen, who had sung for the composer, returns in Russian with a new brightness (her bell tones for the Es after fig. 21 are superb, and very much to the point in this bell-blown score). Also nicely judged is the dark but detached, objective singing of the mezzo Adrienne Albert, while the men soloists, Jack Litten and William Metcalf, bring the dialogue of the fourth scene to life as in no other recording. The starry pianists of the composer's 1959 recording have gone, but their replacements excel them in tone and ensemble (at fig. 82, for instance). Moreover, Craft clearly marks the dynamic contrasts (notably after fig. 46), relishes the chromatic spice (at fig. 52 and elsewhere), and achieves the crescendo after fig. 42 without any acceleration.

Craft also stands out among those who recorded the work in the 1970s. Dutoit's version is clearly recorded, and brightened by the singing of Basia Retchitzka, Ansermet's soprano, but much is exaggerated: the hypertension towards fig. 24, for instance, or the shock of the opening of the final scene, where the bass's falsetto becomes silly and the tenor's glissando on 'tous' ridiculous. The cost of punch is vulgarisation. And though Bernstein obtains his dynamism more innocently, here too there are problems of unwanted rubato and weak ensemble (especially in the third scene), and of wonky singing of the bass duet at fig. 50 (though the soprano and tenor are both good). Against these, Craft's 1973 recording provides the only version of the wholly extraordinary, jangling 1919 instrumentation, and a performance of the 1917 score which has been dimmed only by the appearance of the Eötvös recording (though it was always disfigured by crude stereo placement).

After Bernstein's 1977 recording there was a gap of almost a decade before a strangely laid-back performance was recorded under Roland Hayrabedian in 1986, interesting only for its fresh-toned soprano. Then came the Eötvös, which offers the 1917 orchestration in a later state of reconstruction than was available to Craft (the scoring at fig. 49, for instance, is more convincing, and as already mentioned, the ensuing bass duo is choral in both parts). Both here and in the definitive score, Eötvös has no rival in realising both the zest and the automatic motion of the work: it says much for his metronomic sense that the timings of the two versions correspond almost exactly. The singing and playing is crisply alert throughout, and for the first time the work is heard on record sung by Russian soloists. That alone is a great benefit, even if *The Wedding* still remains to be celebrated by an entirely Russian team of performers.

Unlike *The Wedding*, the *Symphony of Psalms* was written in a single stretch, between January and August 1930, leaving no failed versions. There are, however, two editions of the full score, of which the second, published in 1948, differs most crucially in giving a slower tempo for the coda (the passage beginning at fig. 22). In the original version this continues at the tempo of minim = 48 established at fig. 20, but in the revision there is a new instruction: 'Molto meno mosso, ♩ = 72 rigorosamente'. As one might expect, Stravinsky's first recording, made only a couple of months after the first performance on 17–18 February 1931 in Paris,[8] follows the original score, but neither his second (19 December 1946, New York) nor his third recording (30 March 1963, Toronto) observes the sudden slowing of the revision. Indeed, no conductor does quite what the 1948 score requires at this point: Sixten Ehrling is the only one to mark the deceleration in roughly the right proportion, and his speeds are slow. The usual solution, endorsed by the composer in his 1963 recording, is to adopt the slower tempo right from fig. 20 (cf. Ančerl, Ansermet's London recording, Bernstein, Chailly, Foss, Fricsay, Karajan, both Markevitch performances, Preston). Ansermet's Swiss recording follows the 1930 version; Bertini reduces the scope of the slowing, from around minim = 40 to the correct crotchet = 72; Barenboim and Shaw follow the extraordinary example of the composer's 1946 recording, where the coda goes at crotchet = 56 and the preceding music is also considerably slowed down.

The other great crux in the work is the matter of vocal scoring. On this point the 1948 edition is clear: 'The choir should contain children's voices, which may be replaced by female voices (soprano and alto) if a children's choir is not available.' Again, though, Stravinsky's recordings all depart from his own instruction, all having women on the top two lines. And again his example has been followed by most of his successors. The only recordings with boy trebles are those made by Markevitch in Russia and by Preston. In the former case, the richly dark Russian quality of the singing (this is the only Russian recording) is a huge advantage in a work which, though the language is Latin, looks more to the Orthodox than to the Catholic tradition. By the same token, the Anglican character of Preston's choir is less helpful, the men altos sounding woefully out of place (in the *a cappella* section after fig. 10 in the second movement, for example).

8 See *Stravinsky: Selected Correspondence*, vol. 1, p. 220.

Stravinsky

The choir of Stravinsky's 1931 recording bears a Russian name, but the singing here is lamentable, especially where the wobbly sopranos are exposed (at fig. 20 in the finale, for instance). Not much better is the playing of the unnamed orchestra, who experience difficulties of ensemble and include such oddities as an almost trumpet-like third flute. Altogether the recording conveys the difficulty of a work only six months finished — though the sopranos of the composer's 1946 and 1963 recordings do not sound so very much happier. The 1946 performance is further spoiled by sour woodwind tone, while the spotlit 1963 recording exaggerates textual niceties (the cello solo after fig. 2 in the first movement), embarrassingly brings forward the problems of individuals (the trumpeter at the end of the second movement, the horns in the fast climaxes of the finale) and also underlines places where ensemble is at risk (after fig. 9 in the middle movement, a passage that often causes problems). The main achievements of these later Stravinsky recordings are in details of articulation, such as the staccatos after fig. 8 in the finale (1946) or the echo effect of the *poco sfp* in the coda (1963). Perhaps, though, one should be wary of taking such things as evidence of the composer's intentions: the first oboist's magnification of his commas at the start of the second movement seems more questionable, as does the second oboist's mellow vibrato, making the instrument sound more like a cor anglais (both from the 1963 recording).

As with *The Wedding*, Ansermet's view may merit some notice, since he was the conductor of the first performance. However, his London recording is so dim as to offer a guide to little except the tempi and his Swiss performance, though clearer, has weakness among the performers. The youthfulness of the sopranos is appealing at fig. 20 in the finale, but the choral fugue in the second movement is confused, and there are also orchestral problems (notably in the transition from fig. 12 to fig. 14 in the second movement), quite apart from the fast tempo already mentioned. Curiously, Ansermet came much nearer the work in writing about it: 'As Stravinsky, in response to some form of inner compulsion, does not make of his music an act of self-expression, his religious music can reveal only a kind of "made-up" religiosity. The Symphony of Psalms, for instance, expresses the religiosity of others — of the imaginary choir of which the actual singing choir is an *analogon*; but it must be agreed that the expression of this religiosity is itself absolutely authentic.'[9] Here the conductor provides a fitting extension to the composer's own formula: 'It is not a symphony -in which I have included psalms to be sung. On the contrary, it is the singing of the psalms that I am symphonizing.'[10]

9 *Les Fondements de la musique dans la conscience humaine*, quoted in Eric Walter White: *Stravinsky* (London, Faber, 2nd edn 1979), p. 366.
10 Letter of 12 August 1930 to André Schaeffner, quoted in Stravinsky and Craft, *Stravinsky in Pictures and Documents*, p. 297.

Apart from Stravinsky and Ansermet, the only other conductor to record the work before the 1960s was Ferenc Fricsay, whose choir ostensibly included children's voices, though they are completely outweighed by the women sopranos and altos. His tempi in the first two movements are slow, in the latter case much too slow. However, the rhythmic control of the rushing passages in the finale is secure, and there is a nice distinction of the various choral accent markings.

In the 1960s came Ančerl's recording and both of Markevitch's. Ančerl is much too fast in the first movement and suffers a loss of control in the second (after fig. 6), though the orchestra is punchy and vital in the finale. Markevitch's Russian recording, published in 1963, is the strongest the work has received, and not only on account of the singing. The first movement is distinguished by sharp attacks on the staccato chords and an implacability, a deep sense of importance and weight. In the second movement the instrumental fugue is too fast, but there is enormous character in the orchestral passage after fig. 12 (especially in the bass trombone playing), and the clamour of the dotted rhythm after fig. 14 is another product of Markevitch's unrivalled intensity in this score. One hears this clearly too in the great climaxes of the third movement, where again the Russian voices seem to bring the work, for the only time on record, its correct colour (a tiny but telling example, even if it slightly contravenes the 'non cresc.' of the score, is the contribution of the tenors in the high fourth bar after fig. 27). Markevitch's later recording, made at a concert in Paris in 1967, has many of the same features (the fast instrumental fugue and the vigorous dotted rhythm in the central movement, for instance), along with others of comparable drama, like the grand curtain-parting at the start of the finale. But the choir is inferior: they are in trouble in the unaccompanied passage in the second movement, and they smudge the alleluias of the finale.

From the 1970s there are again three recordings, by Bernstein (1972), Karajan (1975) and Preston (1975). The Bernstein version achieves massiveness in the first movement, but in the second its slowness is hard to take, especially when the tempo sags still further for the orchestral interlude at fig. 12: Bernstein's timing for this movement (8'10") is two minutes beyond the general run (Stravinsky's 1963 recording, for instance, gets there in 6'15"). What distinguishes this performance is the singing of the English Bach Festival Chorus. In the last movement, for instance, they produce a hushed expectancy at the start, and the women are fresh-toned in the passage beginning at fig. 6; Bernstein also brings an apt jazz spirit to the galloping climaxes. However, the coda is made sentimental, and brought to an exaggerated crescendo.

Karajan provides almost the diametric alternative. His climaxes in the finale are unexciting, and his women singers are weak (at fig. 5 in the second movement, for example). On the other hand, this is a beautifully controlled and beautifully recorded orchestral performance. The chords in the first movement are real points of punctuation, and the first oboist manages, like none of his colleagues, to make the high line after fig. 7 in this movement sound *espressivo*, as marked. Karajan also scores a rare point in letting the trumpet be heard, and advantageously, at the end of the middle movement. There are, too, some good things in the singing, such as the whispering intimacy of the tenors at fig. 8 in the finale. Altogether this is a performance of impressive solidity, joining Markevitch's Russian recording among the choicest.

Of the six recordings 'added in the 1980s, only the Bertini (1982) and the Shaw (1983) are quite on that level. Shaw's distinction as a choral conductor is evident as soon as the singing begins, and his Atlanta Symphony Chorus excels at many points. At the start of the last movement, for instance, they produce a soft, sure *piano*, and the crescendos on the middle syllable of 'Laudate', if unmarked, make the music move effectively in wave upon wave. But there is fine orchestral playing, too, particularly from the woodwind in the central movement, and the numinous coda justifies the composer's 1946 choice within a much richer sound world.

Sixten Ehrling (1988) also comes to the work as an outstanding choirmaster, but his orchestra is less admirable, especially in the first movement and at the start of the instrumental fugue: this is a pity when the singing is so strong, and when, as mentioned above, Ehrling comes closer than anyone else to following the notated tempo changes at the end of the piece.

Among the rest, the Foss recording (1983) has little to recommend it: the second movement, for instance, is directionless, diffuse in texture, and further disfigured by an unmarked, unnecessary *rallentando* to fig. 17. Barenboim's 1987 recording has a wandering, forwardly recorded chorus and a dull orchestra, as well as a coda even slower than Stravinsky's in 1946 and Shaw's without anything like the same strength of glow. Chailly (1983) has fresh-voiced women in his chorus but weak basses (after fig. 8 in the second movement, for example), and his recording is too fast at the start. His singers also pronounce the Latin even more Germanically than do Karajan's.

Bertini has a German chorus too, but he takes the trouble to have them singing Italian soft c's, besides drilling them excellently in other respects. Helped by a fresh, clear recording, this performance captures a lean energy that suits the fast passages in the finale and the very beginning of the work (though here Bertini's tempo is dangerously fast). Since there is a vocal immediacy to the wind playing (notably in the instrumental fugue), one hears more of the psalmody than the symphonising – quite by contrast with Karajan, for example – and ultimately this seems the better way.

Janáček: *Glagolitic Mass*

DAVID MURRAY

Janáček was entering his seventy-third year when he composed the *Mša Glagolskaja* in 1926. Long before, he had composed one Mass, now lost, and begun another which he left incomplete. The 'Glagolitic' is one of the fruits of his famous Indian summer, warmed by his passionate affection for Kamila Stösslová, thirty-eight years his junior. He had just finished his Sinfonietta, an instant success, and more music was still to come from his remaining two years: the Second String Quartet, the *Říkadla* ('Nursery rhymes') settings, the Capriccio for one-armed pianist and ensemble, and the opera *From the House of the Dead*.

By Janáček's advanced standards of quirkiness, the Mass is rather straight-forward − wholly idiosyncratic, of course, but nothing like so odd as the Capriccio or the last opera or quartet. There is an obscure quirk in its title: having chosen to set the Mass not in Latin but in an Old Slavonic version from the ninth century, he seems to have got the idea that the word 'Glagolitic' applied to that language. In fact it means the script in which it was originally written down, with which of course he had no concern. Certain sections of the Latin text are shortened in this Slavonic Mass; the Sanctus and the Benedictus are run together. To the choral movements, which include all the solo singing as well, Janáček added not only an Introduction but a final *Intrada* for orchestra, and between the Agnus Dei and the latter a churning Postlude for organ alone.

Among several purely instrumental episodes in the other movements, there is a tripartite one − extended and dramatic − in the middle of the Credo, with a strenuous organ cadenza before the chorus returns for the Crucifixus. The canonical text mentions nothing between the Incarnation and the Crucifixion; it seems that the composer intended to fill in that gap, though we do not know whether the successive parts of this interlude are attached to specific events in the gospel story. At any rate, the music here is more like symphonic drama than anything else in the score, and it needs judicious appreciation by the conductor.

258

Janáček composed the work not out of orthodox piety — he repudiated any notion that old age might be nudging him into the ranks of the faithful, and he hated visiting churches — but to celebrate the national spirit of which he took the old Mass to be a natural expression. (Furthermore, in a letter to Mrs Stösslová he described his Mass in pantheistic terms: sanctification within homely Nature, in the spirit of his opera *The Cunning Little Vixen*.) He had declared himself pleased with his Sinfonietta because, he thought, he had managed there to get 'as close as possible to the mind of the simple man', the 'ordinary Czech man'; and his Mass shares the same animating intention. That alone would be a reason for singing this work always in its original language; but in any case no plausibly ecclesiastical translation of Janáček's pithy word-setting into, say, German or English can avoid spoiling the sharp rhythmic profile of his phrases — altering rhythms and even pitches, adding and subtracting notes. (Compare the German version in the published score.) All the recordings I have found, wherever they come from, employ the original text, though with varying degrees of linguistic conviction.

For the earliest one — monaural, of course, though the record-sleeve indicates stereo — the conductor was Janáček's devoted pupil Břetislav Bakala, who died in 1958. Not only was he the pianist for the first performance of the song cycle *Diary of One who Disappeared*, but he also led the posthumous premieres of two Janáček operas, the early *Osud* and the last, *From the House of the Dead*. Some authority naturally attaches to his readings (the LP includes the Sinfonietta as well as the Mass). Here he had the Brno Radio Symphony at his disposal, with the Vsmu and Moravian Choruses and a quartet of nameless soloists, among them a fresh, cultivated soprano and a good tenor, less than ideally fervent in the *Věruju* (the Credo). His organist, sound and unhysterical, is dully recorded. It has to be admitted that this Mass, like the Requiems of Berlioz and Verdi, is designed at many points for sheer physical impact, grand public thrills; for any recorded version, audible depth and a generous range of dynamic contrasts are vital desiderata.

As the 'Glagolitic' has become almost a repertory piece in the West not least because it can generate such direct excitement, Bakala's insistence — like most other Czech conductors — upon lyrical breadth and warmth is worth remarking. Just those virtues distinguish his fine provincial choruses, dignified in the *Slava* (Gloria) and pleading urgently in the *Věruju*. His Introduction is uncommonly spacious, the Sanctus (*Svet*) sweet and fragile, the Agnus Dei a touch too smoothly poised to admit mystery. Janáček's scrubby, repetitive string-figures — nervily effective when the strings can bear to keep them up — begin to plod here in the *Slava*. After the organ explosion in the *Věruju* there is no shuddering suspense; and the end of the movement, like that of the *Svet*, is underwhelming, with mild, unemphatic tolling on brass and drums. One misses any frank relish for the barbaric pomp which those climaxes surely invite.

In Leonard Bernstein's recording with the New York Philharmonic, The Westminster Choir and multi-national soloists, some ruffled moments suggest a concert performance. Bernstein's reading is loyally intense at its best (notably in the jubilant *Věruju* peroration), but neither flashy nor heart-on-sleeve, though solos – from harp and violin as well as voices – are often miked excessively close up. All in all, the breadth and warmth which every Czech account displays are decidedly attenuated here.

Though there is sober feeling in Bernstein's Introduction, the arrival of the choir in the Kyrie (*Gospodi pomiluj*) is neutrally polite. Helga Pilarczyk's committed soprano helps later, as does Nicolai Gedda's vehement tenor in the *Slava*; and the choir rises to the conclusion of the *Věruju* with imposing gravity. Thereafter things decline. From the Sanctus, in which the prominent pulse has a leaden tread, the solo voices seem to lose heart – especially at Bernstein's discouraging tempo for the Agnus Dei. The big organ solo, well sustained, remains temperate for too long; after that, Bernstein's deliberate *Intrada* (with decidedly frayed strings) makes a decent but unremarkable end.

The net effect of Rafael Kubelik's performance is deeper by some way, despite the soft-grained Czech pronunciation and occasionally fallible pitch of his Bavarian chorus. From Ernst Haefliger's tenor entry in the *Slava* the music springs to life, with a brisk, tautly constructed *Věruju* and a gripping Sanctus and Agnus Dei to come. At the organ Bedřich Janáček (any relation?) contributes mightily: a wild cadenza for the *Věruju*, and a properly shrill, even baleful Postlude which leads to Kubelik's resonant final *Intrada*, barely smudged by the over-taxed Bavarian brass. The wealth of controlled feeling in the whole performance has made it revered among Janáček devotees these many years.

Rudolf Kempe's 1973 recording, also with non-native forces (mostly British this time), is a fair match for Kubelik's. There is more intensity in the Kempe Introduction and Kyrie, the latter enhanced by Teresa Kubiak's plangent soprano in the central 'Christe eleison', and the recorded sound is riper. The tenor Robert Tear's lusty utterances in the *Svet* and in the *Věruju* – where the consonants of Kempe's keen Brighton chorus suddenly become more articulate – seize one's attention. (Though Janáček often prefers to keep his soloists on the margins of the music, even their florid marginalia must tell strongly: they represent imploring individuals amid the acts of collective worship.) A ringing *Intrada* rounds the performance off. It is a pity, however, that the organist John Birch should have had to deliver his part on such a heavy, lacklustre instrument. The longer one's familiarity with the *Mša Glagolskaja*, the plainer it becomes that the solo-organ interventions are crucial to Janáček's conception of the whole dramatic structure, and they cannot be too vivid.

On the remaining recordings the long-experienced Czech Philharmonic Chorus figures often – even in Jílek's Brno performance, and I imagine that the Prague Philharmonic Chorus (Mackerras) and the Czech Singers' Chorus (Ančerl and the same chorus-master, Veselka) may be pretty much the same people too. The Ančerl recording favours them less than their parent orchestra: there is good acoustic depth for his broad-tempo Introduction, but the choral sound in the Kyrie is slightly blotty.

Libuše Domanínská's excited soprano solo in the 'Christe eleison' is a compensating bonus. The bright, alert Gloria does better justice to everybody, and so does the Credo (though it is unfortunately split between the two sides of the LP). Each anxious cry of 'Věruju!' – never, in Janáček's setting, a round affirmation of faith, but something more like an unconfident plea for belief – captures an essential nuance, a sharp dynamic hairpin to which non-Czech choirs are often shy about giving full value. Beno Blachut is a fine solo tenor. The organist's cadenza is effortful; he is firmer in his Postlude, but then he conveys little sense of desperate thrust. Perhaps Ančerl did not want that, for he takes the *tutti* movements that flank the Postlude with impersonal dignity. At a slowish pace the Sanctus is impressively forceful, with Eduard Haken a grand, albeit wobbly, solo bass and assured singing from Soukupová. There is no great theatrical blaze in the closing *Intrada*, but it swings with majestic conviction – which may quite possibly be nearer to what Janáček imagined.

Václav Neumann's performance was recorded with the Czech Philharmonic and its Chorus at a concert – there are moments of shaky ensemble – in 1978. It shares its solo contralto with the Ančerl account, its soprano (Gabriela Beňačková) with the Jílek, its tenor (František Livora) with the Mackerras and its organist (Jan Hora) with both the latter. Livora wields a virile heroic tenor each time. Beňačková is particularly lovely in Neumann's Sanctus, where the bass Průša is as wobbly as Ančerl's Haken. He improves in the Agnus Dei; and there, the close-up recording of the soloists gives striking emphasis to their individual characters. The fervent chorus sounds almost equally close throughout, and survives the test with distinction.

With Neumann the prevailing tone is lyrical and reflective – even pious, in the Introduction and the Kyrie. The tempo of the Gloria seems relaxed until the last pages, but everything tells, not least the clear, well-tuned timpani. (Why are ill-tuned ones so often passed for recording? Are sound-engineers prey to loss of hearing in the bass register? Are timpanists?) The cries of 'Věruju!' are justly nuanced; though the middle of that movement is unusually slow, it picks up urgently for the approach to the Crucifixus, and the rest of the Credo is measured with authority. There is a strict, insistent rhythm for the Sanctus, which nevertheless concludes a little lamely; the Agnus Dei winds down in leisurely fashion too, though the suppressed, mysterious quality of its orchestral opening is potent. Jan Hora's organ here carries less brightly than his Brno instrument in Jílek's recording; his Postlude begins and ends with the proper roar, but for a minute or so in the middle his bland treble-stops

261

make a flat, churchy effect. In the *Intrada*, the hard-working band is audibly tiring.

Recorded just eighteen months later, the Jílek reading sounds dramatically bigger from the start, with excellently clean playing. The later portion of the Gloria is unduly stately, however, with an under-powered final *accelerando* (like the middle one in his Sanctus) and a disappointing end: earlier, the ringing attack of Vilem Přibyl's tenor is a much-needed asset. Unfortunately his contribution to the *Věruju* is gauche and loudly inexpressive, and again the movement is divided between the LP sides. In the slow interlude Jílek captures a sense of Berliozian recitative: that, I think, is a penetrating insight. This time Hora's organ-cadenza feels tentative; the *tutti* close of the movement finds the right energy, rather too late. The solo quartet sounds merely dogged in the Sanctus, despite the alert chorus, and the net impression is slightly dull; so too with the Agnus Dei, gracefully turned though it is. Jílek's *Intrada* — much more crisply executed than Neumann's, if not quite fault-free — recovers at last the grand scale of his Introduction.

The two most up-to-date recordings, by Rattle and by Mackerras, expand magnificently on compact disc. Though the Birmingham chorus is kept well up front, the Rattle performance boasts remarkable aural depth, due no less to the extreme finesse of his orchestral shadings than to the engineers. The fine breadth of his Introduction is sustained by heavy-brass legato playing of a high order. By contrast — much more contrast than usual — the *Intrada* epilogue is muscular and incisive. The Gloria has a thrilling climax; that of the Credo is powerful too, but less cannily prepared than in the tighter, sometimes brittler Mackerras version. If the string episode around 'Et incarnatus' is prosaically forthright, the Sanctus that follows has a lovely opening, all bated-breath mystery. After the Agnus Dei the organ crashes in with the Postlude to brave effect, and rises to some grandeur.

Whether or not the Czech pronunciation of Rattle's singers would pass muster among natives, the choral consonants — especially in the Gloria — lack the ideal bite. Otherwise the chorus acquits itself with sterling credit, granted the odd patch of imperfect synchronisation with the orchestra in passages where Rattle is unconventionally quick. The soloists are more controversial, and different listeners will react strongly to them in different directions. Felicity Palmer is strikingly personal in the Kyrie, uncommonly keen and forward-running in the Gloria. At the time of recording she was already becoming a mezzo, however, and in later movements one misses a true, bright soprano colour in places where Janáček surely expected it — not to mention a proper contrast with Ameral Gunson's dusky tone. John Mitchinson, a hefty tenor, offers a recklessly exciting bleat which becomes downright woofly in the Credo and in the Sanctus. There and in the Agnus Dei too, the solo voices make an oddly assorted quartet: unfair to the mezzo and bass, who have little enough chance to make themselves noticed anyway.

Janáček: *Glagolitic Mass*

The Mackerras quartet is safer, led by Elisabeth Söderström, who adopts a good, piercing Slav-soprano timbre for the occasion. Livora's confident way with the tenor part will please more tastes than Mitchinson's idiosyncratic delivery for Rattle. The singers here collaborate much more smoothly in the quartet of the Agnus Dei. Alike in the Gloria, the Credo and the Sanctus, the sound of the Prague chorus is rich and full-blooded, and at the organ Hora outdoes himself in a brilliantly urgent Postlude. Mackerras makes the closing *Intrada* sharp, swift and keen.

As usual he has striven assiduously to establish the best reading of Janáček's literal score − a daunting business, given that composer's chaotic manuscripts. He has even restored a few bars inadvertently omitted from the published music: nothing of great moment, just a repetition of an earlier passage, though it fits convincingly. Some tingling detail elsewhere in the Mackerras recording has surely gained from the improved text. The imperious thrust of the whole performance is nonetheless pure Mackerras, like the deceptively no-nonsense manner which is nearly at an opposite pole from Rattle's imaginative subtlety. With the latter, the *Mass* almost becomes a series of artistic vistas. Mackerras's tough, direct approach − knowingly calculated, of course! − probably answers better to the ideal of lusty collective outcry.

In considering this whole roster of performances on record, the technical proficiency of the latest ones is unbrookable, and so is the dazzling clarity of the modern digital masterings. The inspired economy of Janáček's score − a very few elements stretched, compressed and revolved with extraordinary resource − needs no special pleading: it reveals itself in any version that doesn't smudge details, but obviously state-of-the-art engineering can capture those more vividly. In any case there can be no real substitute for the experience of hearing the *Mša Glagolskaja* live, amid a large audience − or even better, maybe, actually singing in the chorus.

What I miss slightly in the Rattle and Mackerras versions (just occasionally, and their virtues make splendid compensation) is broad warmth and easy naturalness in some choral passages. In each of these newest accounts there is plainly total control from the top; the choruses do sedulously, if also enthusiastically, just what their conductors require. It is salutary to be reminded in some of the older Czech recordings − Neumann's live performance, for example − that the communal celebration can roll forward with a sturdy, unforced momentum of its own. That might be a clever illusion, but I suspect it is a native Czech gift.

Discographies

Compiled by Alan Blyth, John T. Hughes, and Teri Noel Towe (Bach and Handel)

These discographies list issues in chronological order, with the dates of release given as far as they can be ascertained, except in the case of Bach and Handel, where the numbers attached accord with those in the relevant chapter. Numbers given are the most recent in the current catalogues, with CD numbers preferred to LP numbers. Where discs were first issues in 78 rpm form, the 78 numbers are given first followed by the LP or CD number. Soloists' names appear first in the order soprano, mezzo, tenor, bass, followed by choir, chorus and conductor. Every effort has been made to ensure accuracy, but it has not always been possible to find date and/or details of often very obscure discs. Not every performance listed in the discographies is necessarily mentioned in the relevant chapter.

Monteverdi: Vespers (1610)

1953 The Swabian Choral Singers, The Stuttgart Bach Orchestra Vox PL 7902
1953 The London Singers, L'Ensemble Orchestral de L'Oiseau-Lyre/Lewis
L'Oiseau-Lyre OLS 107/8
1967 The Gregg Smith Singers, The Texas Boys Choir, The Columbia Baroque Ensemble/Craft CBS 77212
1967 Ambrosian Singers, Orchestra of the Accademia Monteverdiana/Stevens
Vanguard VSL 11000/1
1967 Monteverdi-Chor Hamburg, Concentus Musicus Wien/Jürgens
Teldec 6.35045
1968 Choir, Children's Choir and Orchestra of the French National Radio/Le Roux
Concert Hall SMSC 2518A/B
c. 1968 Ensemble Vocal et Instrumental de Lausanne/Corboz
Erato STU 70325/6/7
1974 Monteverdi Choir and Orchestra/Gardiner Decca 414 572–2
1975 Regensburger Domspatzen/Schneidt Archiv 2723 043
1976 King's College Choir, Cambridge, Early Music Consort of London/Ledger
EMI ASD 3256/7
1976 Escolania de Montserrat, Pro Cantione Antiqua, Collegium Aureum/Segarra
Harmonia Mundi HM 1C 165-99681/2

Bach: *St John Passion*

The numbers found in parentheses in the following listings refer to the Bach Gesellschaft Edition.

11 Grümmer (s) [Arias], Otto (s) [Maid], Ludwig (a), Wunderlich (t) [Evangelist], Traxel (t) [Arias], Schafertons (t) [Servant], Fischer-Dieskau (bar) [Jesus], Kohn (bs) [Arias, Peter, Pilate]; Choir of St Hedwig's Cathedral, Berlin, Berlin Symphony Orchestra/Forster   HMV ASD 526/8

12 Harwood (s) [Arias, Maid], Watts (a), Pears (t) [Evangelist], Young (t) [Arias], Tear (t) [Servant], Alan (bs-bar) [Arias], Ward (bs) [Jesus], Etheridge (bs) [Peter], Heather (bs) [Pilate]; The Choir of King's College, Cambridge and the Philomusica of London/Willcocks   Argo ZRG 5270/2

13 Harper (s) [Arias], Hill (s) [Maid], Hodgson (a), Pears (t) [Evangelist], Tear (t) [Arias], Howell (bs) [Jesus], Shirley-Quirk (bs) [Pilate, Arias], Burgess (bs) [Peter], Tobin, Thompson (t) [Servants]; Wandsworth School Boys' Choir, The English Chamber Orchestra/Britten   Decca SET 531/3

14 Anonymous boy soloists (s), (a), Equiluz [Evangelist], van t'Hoff (t) [Arias, Servant], van Egmond (bs) [Jesus; Nos 31, 60], Villisech (bs) [Pilate; No. 48], Schneeweiss (bs) [Peter]; Wiener Sängerknaben, Chorus Viennensis, Concentus Musicus Wien/Gillesberger   Teldec 8.35018 ZA

15 Raskin (s) [Arias, Maid], Forrester (a), Lewis (t) [Evangelist], Shirley (t) [Arias, Servant], Treigle (bs-bar) [Jesus], Paul (bs) [Peter, Pilate, Arias]; Singing City Chorale, Philadelphia Orchestra/Ormandy

Columbia Masterworks M3 30517

16 Giebel (s) Höffgen (a), Haefliger (t) [Evangelist], Young (t) [Arias], Berry (bs-bar) [Jesus], Crass (bs) [Arias]; Netherlands Radio Choir, Concertgebouw Orchestra/ Jochum   Philips 412 415–1

17 Harvey (s), Dieleman (a), van Altena (t) [Evangelist], Bufkens (t) [Arias], Kruysen (bs) [Jesus, Arias], Withag (bs) [Peter, Pilate]; Residentie Bachkoor, Residentie Bachorkest/Akkerhuis   Mirasound KS 7007/09

18 Kalmár (s), Hamari (a), Réti (t) [Evangelist, Arias], Fülöp (t) [Servant], Melis (bar) [Jesus], Abel (bs) [Pilate, Arias], Kovats (bs) [Peter]; Chamber Chorus of the Ferenc Liszt Music Academy, Ferenc Liszt Chamber Orchestra/Lehel

Hungaroton SLPX 11580/82

19 Palmer (s), Finnilä (a), Equiluz (t) [Evangelist], Krenn (t) [Arias], van der Meer (bs) [Jesus], Huttenlocher (bar) [Peter, Pilate, Arias]; Ensemble Vocal de Lausanne, Orchestre de Chambre de Lausanne/Corboz   Erato ECD 88208

20 Sahesch-Pur (s) [Arias, Maid], Hankeln (a), Hopfner (t) [Evangelist], Baldin (t) [Arias, Servant], Hillebrand (bs) [Jesus], Ahrens (bs) [Peter, Pilate, Arias]; Regensburger Domspatzen, Collegium St Emmeran/Schneidt

Deutsche Grammophon Archiv 2723 060

21 Frühaber (s), Helling (a), Harder (t) [Evangelist, Arias], Brodard (bar) [Pilate, Arias], Porter (bs) [Jesus]; Kölner Kammerchor, Kölner Bach-Collegium/Neumann

Motette-Live M 5005

22 Hagner (s) [Maid, Arias], Russ (a), Ramírez (t) [Evangelist], Keönch (t) [Arias], Brodard (bs) [Jesus], Volz (bs) [Peter, Pilate, Arias]; Amadeus Chor, Amadeus Orchester/Beringer   Bellaphon 794–05–301

23 Augér (s), Soffel (a), Kraus (t) [Evangelist], Harder (t) [Arias], Loosli (bs) [Jesus], Widmer (bs) [Pilate, Arias]; Berner Bach-Chor, Kammerensemble Bern/Loosli

EMI Electrola 1C 157–99 860/62

24 Resick (s) [Arias], Mane (s) [Maid], Kuhlmann (a), Vandersteene (t) [Evangelist], Baldin (t) [Arias], Straka (t) [Servant], Schöne (bs) [Jesus], Salomaa (bs) [Arias], Hartmann (bs) [Peter], Franzen (bs) [Pilate]; Chorus and Chamber Orchestra of the Schweizer Fernsehen DRS/Brunner   Relief CH–852 001
25 Kozyreva (s), Filatova (a), Nikitin (t), Zarins (t), Pankratov (bar), Antipov (bs); Leningrad Philharmonic Chamber Orchestra and Chorus/Steinlucht
Melodiya S10–06773/78
26 Belobragina (s), Romanova (a), Martynov (t), Safiulin (bs) [Jesus, Arias], Saveliev (bs) [Peter, Pilate]; Boys' Choir of the Moscow Choral School, Leningrad Chamber Orchestra of Old and Modern Music/Serov   Melodiya S10 17943
27 Stamenkovic (s) [Aria No. 13, Maid], Madunic (s) [Aria No. 63], Car (m-s), Robinsak (t) [Evangelist, Arias], Fatovic (t) [Servant], Lesaja (bar) [Jesus], Belemaric (bar) [Peter, Pilate]; Choir and Orchestra of the Yugoslav Music Academies and Faculties/Gjadrov
Jugoton LSY 65067/68 (Omits Nos. 9–11, 23–7, 31, 32, 40, 48, 60, 64 and 65.)
28 Argenta (s) [No. 63], Holton (s) [No. 13], Ross (s) [Maid], Chance (a), Rolfe Johnson (t) [Evangelist], Archer (t) [Nos. 19, 62], Murgatroyd (t) [Servant], Robertson (t) [Servant], Varcoe (bs) [Jesus], Hauptmann (bs) [Pilate, Arias], Birchall (bs) [Peter]; The Monteverdi Choir, The English Baroque Soloists/Gardiner
Deutsche Grammophon Archiv 419 324–2
29 Schlick (s), Jacobs (a), Prégardien (t) [Evangelist], van der Meel (t) [Arias], van der Kamp (bs) [Jesus], van Egmond (bs) [Arias]; La Petite Bande/Kuijken
Deutsche Harmonia Mundi GD 77041
30 Schlick (s), Patriasz (a), Crook (t) [Evangelist], Kendall (t) [Arias], Lika (bs) [Jesus], Kooy (bs) [Pilate, Arias]; Collegium Vocale, Gent, Orchestre de La Chapelle Royale, Paris/Herreweghe   Harmonia Mundi France 901264/5
31 Baird (s) [Arias], Corssin (s) [Maid], Dooley (ct), Thomas (t) [Evangelist], Pincus (t) [Arias], Sharp (bs) [Jesus], Ostendorf (bs) [Pilate, Arias], Negron (bs) [Servant]; Brandenburg Collegium Chorus and Orchestra/Newman
Newport Classics NC 60015–2
32 Ameling (s) [Arias], Dürr (s) [Maid], Fassbaender (a), Altmeyer (t) [Evangelist], Equiluz (t) [Arias], Crass (bs) [Jesus], Nimsgern (bs) [Arias], Kühnle (bs) [Peter], Moll (bs) [Pilate]; South German Madrigal Choir, Consortium Musicum/Gönnenwein   HMV SLS 949
33 Ameling (s) [Arias], Koehnlein-Goebel (s) [Maid], Hamari (a), Ellenbeck (t) [Evangelist], Hollweg (t) [Arias], Isenhardt (t) [Servant], Berry (bs-bar) [Jesus], Prey (bar) [Arias], Ackermann (bs) [Peter], Ahrans (bs) [Pilate]; Stuttgart Hymnus Boys' Choir, Stuttgart Chamber Orchestra/Münchinger   Decca 414 068–2
34 Augér (s) [Arias], Hoffmann (s) [Maid], Hamari (a), Schreier (t), Müller (t) [Servant], Huttenlocher (bar) [Jesus], Fischer-Dieskau (bar) [Arias], Keitz (bs) [Peter], Schmidt (bar) [Pilate]; Gächinger Kantorei Stuttgart, Bach Collegium Stuttgart/Rilling   CBS M2K 39694
35 Schlick (s) [Arias], Meppelink (s) [Maid], Helling (a), Meens (t), Bartels (t), van Egmond (bs) [Jesus, Peter], Polster (bs) [Arias]; Holland Bach Choir, Amsterdam Chamber Orchestra/de Wolff   Fidelio 8804/5

36 Baird (s) [No. 63], Bryden (s) [No. 13], Lane (a) [No. 58], Loverde (a) [Maid], Rickards (c-t) [No. 11], Boutt (t) [Servant, No. 32], Romano (t) [No. 19], Thomas (t) [Evangelist, No. 62, BWV 245 b, c], Ripley (bs) [Peter, Pilate, No. 48], Rowe (bs) [No. 31, BWV 245 c], Weaver (bs) [Jesus, No. 60]; The Smithsonian Chamber Chorus, The Smithsonian Chamber Orchestra/Slowik, Smithsonian Collection of Recordings ND 0381, N. B.: the five alternative numbers from the 1725 version are not included on the LP or audio cassette formats of the recording.

37 Forbes (s) [Maid], Kwella (s) [Arias], James (a) [Arias], Kendall (t) [Arias], Mackenzie (t) [Servant], Roy (t) [Servant], Partridge (t) [Evangelist], George (bs) [Arias], Wilson-Johnson (bs) [Jesus]; The Sixteen Choir and Orchestra/Christophers
Chandos CHAN 0507/8

Bach: *St Matthew Passion*

1 Helton (s) [Soprano in ripieno, First Maid, Second Maid, Pilate's wife], Jensen (s) [Chorus Two], Monoyios (s) [Chorus One], Fast (a) [Chorus Two], Rickards (a) [Chorus One], Kelley (t) [Chorus One], Romano (t) [Chorus Two], Finson (bs) [Judas, First Priest], Honeycutt (bs) [Peter, Pilate, High Priest, Second priest], Sharp (bs) [Chorus One], Moses (bs) [Chorus Two]; The Bach Ensemble/Rifkin
Private Recording

2 Two anonymous boy soprano soloists from the Wiener Sängerknaben [Arias – Chorus One and Chorus Two], Esswood (a) [Arias – Chorus One], Bowman (a) [Arias – Chorus Two], Sutcliffe (a) [Arias – Chorus Two: Nos. 33, 77], Equiluz (t) [Evangelist, Arias – Chorus One], Rogers [Arias – Chorus Two], Ridderbusch (bs) [Jesus], van Egmond (bs) [Arias – Chorus One], Schopper (bs) [Arias – Chorus Two]: Boy Soprano Voices of the Regensburg Cathedral Choir, Men's Voices of the King's College Choir, Cambridge, Concentus Musicus Wien/ Harnoncourt
Teldec 8.35047

3 Augér (s) [Arias – Chorus One, First Maid, Pilate's Wife], Greenawald (s) [Arias – Chorus Two], Rappe (a) [Arias – Chorus One, Second Maid], van Nes (a) [Arias – Chorus Two, First Witness], Equiluz (t) [Evangelist], Rosenshein (t) [Arias, Second Witness], Holl (bs) [Jesus], van der Meer (bs) [Arias – Chorus One, Peter, Judas, High Priest, Pilate, First Priest], Scharinger (bs) [Arias – Chorus Two, Second priest]; Boys' Choir Orchestra and Chorus/Harnoncourt
Teldec 8.35668

4 Fliegner (s) [Arias – Chorus One], Kiener (s) [Arias – Chorus Two], Cordier (a) [Arias – Chorus Two], Jacobs (a) [Arias – Chorus One], Elwes (t) [Arias – Chorus Two], Schäfer (t) [Arias – Chorus One], Prégardien (t), van Egmond (bs), Lika (bs) [Chorus Two], Mertens (bs) [Chorus One], Tölzer Knabenchor, La Petite Bande/Leonhardt
Deutsche Harmonia Mundi RD 77848

5 Schlick (s) [Arias, Pilate's Wife, First Maid], Bignalet (s) [Second Maid], Jacobs (a) [Arias, First Witness], Blochwitz (t) [Arias, Second Witness], Crook (t) [Evangelist], Machart (bar) [Judas], Cold (bs) [Jesus], Kooy (bs) [Arias, Pilate, High Priest, Second Priest], Meersman (bs) [First Priest]; Ensemble Vocale de la Chapelle Royale [Chorus One], Collegium Vocale de Gent [Chorus Two], Choeur d'Enfants 'in Dulci Jubilo', Orchestra/Herreweghe
Harmonia Mundi France HMC 901155/57

6 Bonney (s) [Nos. 18, 19, 33, 77; Pilate's Wife], Holton (s) [First Maid], Monoyios (s) [Nos. 12, 57, 58], von Otter (a) [Nos. 10, 11, 36, 60, 61, 77], Chance (c-t) [Nos. 33, 47, 69, 70, First Witness], Crook (t) [Arias, No. 77, Second Witness], Rolfe Johnson (t) [Evangelist], Bär (bar) [Nos. 28, 29, 65, 66, 77; Peter, Pilate, High Priest, First Priest], Schmidt (bar) [Jesus], Hauptmann (bs) [Nos. 51, 74, 75; Judas]; Monteverdi Choir/English Baroque Soloists/Gardiner
DG Archiv 427 648–2

7 László (s) [Arias], Molden (s) [First Maid], Glöckner (s) [Second Maid], Monsberger (s) [Pilate's Wife], Hofstätter (s) [First Witness], Rössl-Majdan (a), Cuénod (t) [Evangelist], Munteanu (t) [Arias], Equiluz (t) [Second Witness], Rehfuss (bs) [Jesus], Standen (bs) [Arias], Wächter (bar) [Judas, Pilate], Lagger (bs) [Peter, First Priest], Heppe (bs) [Second Priest]; Vienna Academy Chorus, Vienna State Opera Chorus/Scherchen
Nixa WLP 6401

8 Feuge (s), Klose (a), von Pataky (t), Schoeffler (bs-bar) [Jesus], Böhme (bs) [Arias]; Leipziger Universitätskantorei und Madrigalkreis, Knabenchor der Petri-Schule, Leipziger Symphonieorchester/Weissbach
Acanta FA 23076

9 Briem (s), Hammer (a), Ludwig (t), Nissen (bar), Drissen (bs); Bruno Kittel Choir, Berlin Philharmonic/Kittel
Polydor 67951/68
(Omits 19, 23, 28, 29, 38, 40, 41, 48–51, 55, 61, 64–6, 70, 75; abridges 10, 12, 34, 35, 37, 39, 52, 54, 59, 63, 67, 73, 76, 78.)

10 Trötschel (s), Eustrati (a), Krebs (t), Fischer-Dieskau (bar) [Jesus], Haertel (bs) [Arias]; Boys' Choir of St Hedwig's Cathedral, Chorus and Orchestra of Berlin Radio/Lehmann
Vox DL 6070

11 Lemnitz (s), Beckmann (a), Erb (t), Hüsch (bar) [Jesus], Schulze (bs) [Arias]; Thomanerchor Leipzig, Leipzig Gewandhaus Orchestra/Ramin
EMI Da Capo 1C 147–29 121/23 M
(Omits 18, 19, 28–31, 34, 37, 38, 41, 56, 61, 65, 66, 70, 75.)

12 Vreeland (s), Meisle (a), Priebe (b), Falkner (bs) [Arias], Lechner (bs) [Jesus]; Harvard Glee Club, Radcliffe Choral Society, Boston Symphony Orchestra/Koussevitzky
RCA Victor 14635/61

13 Campenhausen (s), Haentschel (a), Viguhr (t), Herfeld (bar); Berlin Cathedral Choir, The Berlin Symphony Orchestra/Balzer
Royale 1290/93
(Pseudonymous; really the Fritz Lehmann commercial recording.)

14 Anonymous [really the Fritz Lehmann]. The Cathedral Choir and Symphony Orchestra
Gramophone 20167/70

15 Chorus of St Hedwig's Cathedral, Berlin, Berlin Symphony/Forster.
In 'In Memoriam Karl Forster', Eurodisc S 70 663 XK
(Nos. 1, 3, 16, 21, 23, 31, 35, 38, 44, 48, 53, 55, 63, 72, 78.)

16 Giebel (s), Fischer (a), Kretschmar (t), Günter (bs); Kantorei der Dreikönigskirche, Frankfurt, Collegium Musicum Orchestra/Thomas
Oiseau-Lyre OL 50113/16

17 Gröschke (s), Wenkel (a), Ellenbeck (t) [Arias], Juhani (t) [Evangelist], Abel (bar) [Arias], König (bs) [Jesus]; Palatinate Youth Kantorei, Kaiserslautern Boys' Choir, Heidelberg Chamber Orchestra/Göttsche
Orpheus OR 275/78

18 Stolte (s) [Arias], Hassbecker (s) [Pilate's Wife], Wustmann (s) [First Maid], Burmeister (a) [Arias], Schreier (a) [First Witness, Second Maid], Schreier (t) [Evangelist], Rotzsch (t) [Arias, First Priest, Second Witness], Adam (bs) [Jesus],

Leib (bar) [Arias], Vogel (bs) [Peter], Künzel (bs) [Judas], Polster (bs) [Pilate], Nau (bs) [High Priest, Second Priest]; Thomanerchor Leipzig, Dresdner Kreuzchor, Leipzig Gewandhaus Orchestra/Mauersberger   Eurodisc 80 613 XK

19 Te Kanawa (s) [Arias, Pilate's Wife], Michaels (s) [First Maid], Austin (a) [Second Maid], von Otter (a) [Arias, First Witness], Blochwitz (t) [Evangelist], Rolfe Johnson (t) [Arias], Watson (t) [Second Witness], Bär (bar) [Jesus], Cohn (bs) [Peter], Krause (bs) [Arias, Judas, Pilate, High Priest]; Chicago Symphony Orchestra and Chorus, The Glen Ellyn Children's Chorus/Solti   Decca 421 177−2

20 Schwarzkopf (s) [Arias, First Maid, Pilate's Wife], Baker (a) [Second Maid], Ludwig (a) [Arias], Watts (a) [First Witness], Brown (t) [Second Witness], Gedda (t) [Arias], Pears (t) [Evangelist], Berry (bar) [Arias, Peter], Carol Case (bar) [Judas], Fischer-Kieskau (bar [Jesus], Kraus (bar) [High Priest, First Priest, Pilate], Evans (bar) [Second Priest]; Philharmonia Orchestra and Choir, Boys of the Hampstead Parish Church Choir/Klemperer   EMI Angel CMS7 63058−2

21 Addison (s) [Arias], Washington (s) [First Maid], Allen (m-s) [Arias], Skouras (a) [Second Maid], Bressler (t) [Arias], Lloyd (t) [Evangelist], Bell (bs-bar) [Arias, Judas, Peter, Pilate], Wildermann (bs) [Jesus]; the Collegiate Chorale, Boys' Choir of the Church of the Transfiguration, New York Philharmonic/Bernstein
          Columbia Masterworks M3S 692

22 Connor (s), Watson (a), Hain (t), Harrell (bar), Janssen (bar), Alvary (bs); The Westminster Choir, Junior Choirs of the Pius X School of Liturgical Music, New York Philharmonic-Symphony Orchestra/Walter   Bruno Walter Society WSA 702/03 (Part One only; abridges Nos. 10, 12, 19, and 29.)

23 Vincent (s), Durigo (a), Erb (t) [Evangelist], van Tulder (t) [Arias], Ravelli (bs) [Jesus], Schey (bs) [Arias]; Amsterdam Toonkunst Choir, 'Zanglust' Boys' Choir, Concertgebouw Orchestra/Mengelberg   Philips 416 206−2 (Omits 23, 29, 38, 41, 48, 50−2, 55, 61, 65, 66, 70, 75; abridges 9, 12, 37, 39, 49, 54, 63, 64, 67, 75, 76, 78.)

24 Bijster (s), Delorie (a), van Hese (t), Willink (bs); Amsterdam Oratorio Chorus, Vredescholen Boys' Chorus, Rotterdam Chamber Orchestra/van Egmond
          Concert Hall Society CHS−1255

25 Spoorenberg (s), Hermes (a), Brand (t) [Evangelist], Blanken (t) [Arias], van Egmond (bs) [Arias − Chorus Two], Bogtman (bs) [Jesus], Hollestelle (bs) [Arias − Chorus One]; Chorus of the Nederlandse Bach-Vereinigung, Het Residentie-Orkest, Boys' Choir of the Amsterdam Vredesscholen/van der Horst
          Telefunken LT 6598/6601

26 Grümmer (s), Höffgen (a), Dermota (t), Fischer-Dieskau (bar) [Jesus], Edelmann (bs) [Arias, Peter, Pilate, High Priest]; Wiener Singverein, Wiener Sängerknaben, Vienna Philharmonic/Furtwängler   Movimento Musica 051−005 (Omits 19, 23, 29, 38, 40, 41, 48−51, 55, 61, 64, 70, 75; abridges 32, 34, 39, 52, 63, 67, 73, 76.)

27 Seefried (s) [Arias], Felbermeyer (s) [Pilate's Wife], Rathauscher (s) [First Maid], Sterba (s) [Second Maid], Ferrier (a) [Arias], Stowasser (a) [First Witness], Ludwig (t) [Evangelist, Arias], Uhl (t) [Second Witness], Schoeffler (bs) [Jesus], Edelmann (bs) [Arias], Kaufmann (bs) [Peter], Pröglhöf (bs) [Judas], Wiener (bs) [Pilate], Berry (bs) [High Priest]; Wiener Singverein, Vienna Symphony/Karajan
          Foyer 3−CF 2013

28 Janowitz (s) [Arias, Pilate's Wife, First Maid], Ludwig (a) [Arias, First Witness, Second Maid], Laubenthal (t) [Arias, Second Witness], Schreier (t) [Evangelist], Fischer-Dieskau (bar) [Jesus], Berry (bs) [Arias], Diakov (bs) [Peter, Pilate, High Priest, Judas]; Wiener Singverein, Chorus of the Deutschen Oper Berlin, Boys' Choir of the Staats- und Domchores Berlin, Berlin Philharmonic/Karajan
Deutsche Grammophon 419 789–2
29 Giebel (s), Höffgen (a), Haefliger (t) [Evangelist], van Kesteren (t) [Arias], Berry (bs) [Jesus], Crass (bs) [Arias], Ketelaars (bs) [Peter, Pilate, High Priest, Judas], Netherlands Radio Choir, Boys' Choir of St Willibrordskerk, Amsterdam, Concertgebouw Orchestra/Jochum
Philips 420 900–2
30 Iglesias (s), Forrester (a), Haefliger (t), Warfield (bs) [Jesus], Berberian (bs) [Arias]; Cleveland Orchestra Chorus, Festival Casals de Puerto Rico Orchestra/Casals
[Number unknown]
31 Brockless (s), Evans (a), Greene (t) [Evangelist], Brown (t), Clinton (bs) [Jesus], Carol Case (bar); Leith Hill Festival Choir and Orchestra/Vaughan Williams
Caviar CH–104
(Omits 9, 10.)
32 Suddaby (s), Ferrier (a), Greene (t), Cummings (bar) [Jesus], Parsons (bs) [Arias], Clinton (bs) [Judas, Peter]; The Bach Choir, The Jacques Orchestra/Jacques
Decca D42D3
(Omits 11, 21, 65, 66; abridges 10, 12.)
33 Unidentified soloists, Westminster Abbey Special Choir, unidentified organist/ Bullock HMV C 2252 (nos. 54, 71, 72 only); HMV D 1084 (no. 78 only)
34 Schaffner (s), Benedict Jones (a), Jones (t), Pirnie (bar), Cuthberg (bs); Choir of St Bartholomew's Church, New York City/Williams
Victor 11285/96
(Omits 6–10, 19, 20, 22, 25, 27–9, 34–6, 38–9, 46, 48, 49, 51, 57, 58, 60, 61, 64–8, 70, 74–6; abridges 37, 47, 50, 52, 59, 73, 78.)
35 Stover (s), Pierce (a), W. Young (t) [Evangelist, Aria], Adkins (bs) [Jesus, Arias], Kincs (bs) [Judas, Pilate]; Handel Oratorio Society, Snyder and Lundholm, organists/Veld
Key LS–501
36 Marshall (s) [Arias], Morrison (s), Newton (s), Stillwell (a), Johnson (t) [Evangelist], Lamond (t) [Arias], Brown (bar), Tredwell (bar), Milligan (bs) [Jesus]; Bloor Street United Church Choir, Toronto, Toronto Mendelssohn Choir, Orchestra/Macmillan
Beaver LPS 002
(Omits 10, 23, 41, 50, 51, 55, 61, 70, 75, 76; abridges 12.)
37 Dovenman (t) [Evangelist], Dashkov (bs) [Jesus]; Latvian State Academic Choir, Moscow State Philharmonic Orchestra/Dumins
Melodiya M10–42551
(Nos. 1, 3, 15, 43, 67, 78 only.)
38 Seefried (s) [Arias], Fahberg (s) [First Maid, Pilate's Wife], Töpper (a) [Arias, Second Maid], Haefliger (t) [Evangelist, Arias], Engen (bs) [Jesus], Fischer-Dieskau (bs) [Arias], Proebstl (bs) [Judas, Peter, Pilate, High Priest]; Munich Bach Choir and Orchestra/Richter
Deutsche Grammophon Archiv 2712 001.
39 Buckel (s) [Arias, First Maid, Pilate's Wife], Höffgen (a) [Arias, Second Maid], Haefliger (t) [Evangelist, Arias], Engen (bs) [Jesus], van der Bilt (bs) [Arias, Judas, Peter, Pilate, High Priest]; Munich Bach Choir and Orchestra/Richter
Polydor Japan Archiv 96MA 0113/6

271

40 Mathis (s) [Arias, First Maid, Pilate's Wife], Baker (a) [Arias, Second Maid], Schreier (t) [Evangelist, Arias], Fischer-Dieskau (bar) [Jesus], Salminen (bs) [Arias, Judas, Peter, Pilate, High Priest]; Munich Bach Choir and Orchestra/Richter

Deutsche Grammophon Archiv 427 704–2

41 Augér (s) [Arias], Hofmann (s) [First Maid], Bollen (m-s) [Second Maid], Murray (m-s) [Pilate's Wife], Hamari (a) [Arias], Schnaut (a) [First Witness], Baldin (t) [Arias], Kraus (t) [Evangelist], Lang (t) [Second Witness], Frohnmayer (bs) [High Priest], Heldwein (bs) [Peter], Hillebrand (bs) [Pilate], Huttenlocher (bar) [Arias], Kosters (bs) [First Priest], Nimsgern (bs) [Jesus], Thomas (bs) [Judas], Volz (bs) [Second Priest]; Gächinger Kantorei Stuttgart, Bach-Collegium Stuttgart/Rilling

CBS Masterworks M4 39715

42 Ameling (s) [Arias, First Maid, Pilate's Wife], Höffgen (a) [Arias, Second Maid], Pears (t) [Evangelist], Wunderlich (t) [Arias], Blankenburg (bar) [Peter, High Priest, Pilate], Krause (bar) [Arias], Messthaler (bs) [Judas], Prey (bar) [Jesus]; Stuttgarter Hymnus-Chorknaben, Stuttgart Orchestra/Münchinger   Decca 414 057–2

43 Dutoit (s), Nussbaumer (a), Majkut (t) [Evangelist], Kreuzberger (t) [Arias], Buchsbaum (bs) [Jesus], Wiener (bs) [Arias]; Vienna Academy Chorus, Vienna Chamber Orchestra/Grossmann   Vox PL 8283

44 Dürr (s) [Second Maid], Leertouwer (s) [Pilate's Wife], Renner (s) [First Maid], Scherr (s) [First Witness], Zylis-Gara (s) [Arias], Hamari (a) [Arias], Altmeyer (t) [Evangelist, Second Witness], Gedda (t) [Arias], Crass (bs) [Jesus], Haertel (bs) [Judas], Prey (bar) [Arias], Sotin (bs) [Peter, Pilate, High Priest]; South German Madrigal Choir and Boys' Choir, Consortium Musicum/Gönnenwein

HMV SAN 228/31

45 Buckel (s) [Arias], Gentele (s) [First Maid], Sundberg (s) [Pilate's Wife], Lehane (a) [Arias], Mellnäs (a), Sirén (a) [First Witness], Forslöw (t) [Second Witness], van Kesteren (t) [Evangelist, Arias], Borg (bs) [Jesus], Gunneflo (bs) [Second Priest], Hellström (bs) [Peter], Leandersson (bs) [High Priest, First Priest], Nilsson (bs) [Judas]; Swedish Radio Chorus and Orchestra/Ericson

Swedish EMI 354/57

46 Kalmár (s) [Arias, First Maid], Hamari (a) [Arias, Second Maid, Pilate's Wife], Vandersteene (t) [Evangelist, Arias], Gáti (bar) [Jesus], Schramm (bs) [Arias, Judas, High Priest, Peter, Pilate]; Chorus 'Jeunesses Musicales', Ferenc Liszt Chamber Orchestra/Sándor   Hungaroton SLPX 12069/72

47 De Crousaz (s) [First Maid, Pilate's Wife], Marshall (s) [Arias], Martin-Fiaux (a) [First Witness], Schuwey (a) [Second Maid], Watkinson (a) [Arias], Bolay (t) [Second Witness], Equiluz (t) [Evangelist], Rolfe Johnson (t) [Arias], Estoppey (bs) [Second Priest], Faulstich (bs) [Jesus], Huttenlocher (bar) [Arias, Judas, Peter, Pilate], Koechlin (bs) [High Priest]; Schola des Petits Chanteurs de Notre-Dame de Sion, Ensemble Vocal de Lausanne, Orchestre de Chambre de Lausanne/Corboz

Erato ECD 88063

48 Dutoit (s) [Pilate's Wife, First Maid], Stich-Randall (s) [Arias], Rössl-Majdan (a) [Arias], Zottl-Holmstaedt (a) [Second Maid], Ebrelius (t) [Evangelist], Kmentt (t) [Arias], Vogel (t) [Second Witness], Berry (bs) [Arias], Braun (bs) [Jesus], Kummer (bs) [Judas], Welrich (bs) [Peter]; Vienna Chamber Choir, Boys' Choir of the Schoffenstift, Vienna State Opera Orchestra/Wöldike

Vanguard Everyman Classics SRV 269/72 SD

49 Ameling (s) [Arias], Clark (s) [First Maid]. Kennard (s) [Pilate's Wife], Finnilä (a) [Arias], Minty (a) [Second Maid, First Witness], Haefliger (t) [Evangelist], McCoy (t) [Arias], Midgley (t) [Second Witness], Luxon (bar) [Arias, Pilate], McDaniel (bar) [Jesus], Noble (bar) [High Priest, First Priest], Fyson (bs-bar) [Judas, Second Priest], Taylor (bs-bar) [Peter]; Ambrosian Singers, Desbrough School Boys' Choir, English Chamber Orchestra/Somary   Vanguard VSD 71231/34

50 Popp (s) [Arias], Ihle (s) [First Maid], Termer (s) [Pilate's Wife], Lipovšek (a) [Arias], Schneiderheinze (a) [First Witness], Wilke (a) [Second Maid], Büchner (t) [Arias], Schreier (t) [Evangelist], Wegner (t) [Second Witness], Bär (bar) [High Priest], Scheibner (bar) [Peter], Adam (bs) [Jesus], Holl (bs) [Arias], Polster (bs) [Pilate], Wlaschiha (bs) [Judas], Ribbe (bs) [First Priest], Henkel (bs) [Second Priest]; Rundfunkchor Leipzig, Dresdner Kapellknaben, Staatskapelle Dresden/ Schreier   Philips 412 527−2

51 Denman (s) [First Maid], Laki (s) [Arias], Jacobeit (s) [Pilate's Wife], Riedel-Pax (s) [Second Maid], Murray (a) [Arias], Uphagen (a) [First Witness], Britton (t) [Arias], Garrison (t) [Evangelist], Ahrens (bs) [Jesus], Biebach (bs) [Pilate, Second Priest], Brühl (bs) [Judas], Bülow (bs) [High Priest, First Priest], Gebhardt (bs) [Peter], Luxon (bar) (nos. 28, 29, 74, 75), Stamm (bs) [Nos. 51, 65, 66]; Knabenchor Hannover, Chorus and Orchestra of the North German Radio/Leppard   EMI SLS 5257

Bach: Mass in B Minor

1 Marshall (s), Alberts (a), McCollum (t), Smith (bs); The Bach Choir of Bethlehem, The Bach Festival Orchestra/Jones   Classics Record Library SRL

2 Schumann (s), Balfour (a), Widdop (t), Schorr (bs); Royal Choral Society, London Symphony Orchestra/Coates   HMV set G−87 (C 1710/26)

3 McKnight (s), Gardner (s), Summers (a), Metz (t), Matthen (bs); RCA Victor Chorale and Orchestra/Shaw   RCA Victor LM 6100

4 Endich (s), Addison (s), Kopleff (a), Walker (t), Berberian (bs); Robert Shaw Chorale and Orchestra/Shaw   RCA Victor LSC 6157

5 Schwarzkopf (s), Ferrier (a), Ludwig (t), Poell (bar) [No. 18], Paul Schoeffler (bs) [No. 10]; Vienna Singverein, Vienna Symphony Orchestra/Karajan   Foyer 2−CF 2022

6 Schwarzkopf (s), Höffgen (a), Gedda (t), Rehfuss (bs); Vienna Musikfreunde Chorus and Orchestra/Karajan   Col. 33CX 1121/3

7 Price (s), Ludwig (a), Gedda (t), Souzay (bar) [No. 18], Berry (bs) [No. 10]; Vienna Philharmonic Orchestra/Karajan   Movimento Musica 03.012

8 Janowitz (s), Ludwig (a), Schreier (t), Kerns (bar) [No. 18], Berry (bs) [No. 10]; Vienna Singverein, Berlin Philharmonic Orchestra/Karajan   DG 415 622−1

9 Birmele (s), Wolf-Matthäus (a); Thomanerchor Leipzig, Dresdner Kreuzchor, Leipzig Gewandhaus Orchestra/Ramin   Cantate 675 604 (Nos. 1−3, 11, 19, 20, 24, 25.)

10 Graf (s), Töpper (a), Lutze (t), Proebstl (bs); Chorus of the Lehrergesangverein of Munich, the Orchestra of Bavaria/Ramin   Musical Masterpiece Society MMS 2021

11 Schwarzweller (s), Fischer (s), Kretschmar (t), Müller (bs); Choir of the Dreikönigskirche, Frankfurt, Collegium Musicum Orchestra/Thomas
Oiseau-Lyre OL 50094/96
12 Stader (s), Wagner (a), Haefliger (t), Adam (bs); Dresdner Kreuzchor, Dresden
Staatskapelle Dresden/Mauersberger   Eterna 8 20 074/76
13 Stader (s), Töpper (a), Haefliger (t), Fischer-Dieskau (bar), Engen (bs); Munich
Bach Choir, Munich Bach Orchestra/Richter

DG Archiv 413 946–1
14 Buckel (s), Höffgen (a), Haefliger (t), Schramm (bs); Munich Bach Choir, Munich
Bach Orchestra/Richter   DG Archiv 72MA 0117/19
15 Augér (s), Hamari (a), Kraus (t), Schöne (bar), Nimsgern (bs); Gächinger Kantorei
Stuttgart, Bach Collegium Stuttgart/Rilling   CBS Masterworks 79 307
16 Sonntag (s), Lipovšek (a), Crook (t), Schmidt (bar); Gächinger Kantorei Stuttgart,
Stuttgart Chamber Orchestra/Rilling   Intercord INT 885.855
17 Ameling (s), Minton (m-s), Watts (a), Krenn (t), Krause (bar); Vienna Singakademie,
Stuttgart Chamber Orchestra/Münchinger   Decca 414 251–2
18 Popp (s), Watkinson (a), Büchner (t), Lorenz (bar) [No. 18], Adam (bs) [No. 10];
Leipzig Radio Chorus, Neues Bachisches Collegium Musicum Leipzig/Schreier
Eurodisc 610 089
19 Loose (s), Česka (s), Burgsthaler-Schuster (a), Dermota (t), Poell (bar); Vienna
Singakademie, Vienna Symphony Orchestra/Scherchen   Nixa WLP 6301
20 Weber (s), Di Landi (a), Krebs (t), Wolfram (bar); Chorus and Orchestra of Radio
Berlin/Lehmann. Saga XID 5280/82 [3 LPs]; Berlin Chamber Choirs, Berlin
Symphony Orchestra/Lehmann Bach Guild BG 527/28; Vienna Festival Orchestra
and Chorus/Lehmann   Music Treasures of the World MT 38
21 Anonymous Conductor and Soloists, The Cathedral Choir and Symphony Orchestra
Gramophone 20164/66
22 Defraiteur (s), Fischer (a), Kretschmar (t), Vessières (bs); Choeur de l'Eglise Saint-
Guillaume, Orchestre Municipale de Strasbourg/F. Munch

Decca 173.863/65
23 Marshall (s), Töpper (a), Pears (t), Borg (bs), Braun (bs); Bavarian Radio Symphony
Orchestra and Chorus/Jochum   Philips 6768 214
24 Donath (s), Fassbaender (a), Ahnsjö (t), Hermann (bar) [No. 10], Holl (bs) [No.
18]; Bavarian Radio Symphony Orchestra and Chorus/Jochum
EMI 1C 157–43 205/07
25 de la Bije (s), Matthes (a), Brand (t), Hollestelle (bs); Chorus and Orchestra of the
Niederlandische Bach-Vereinigung/van der Horst
Telefunken Das Alte Werk SAWT 9416/18–B
26 Lehmann (s), Kirchner (a), Gilvan (t), Illerhaus (bs); Tübingen Cantata Choir,
Heidelberg Chamber Orchestra/Achenbach

La Camera Magna 94 026/28
27 Alarie (s), Delfosse (s), Hofmann (a), Simoneau (t), Rehfuss (bs); Choir and
Orchestra of the Philharmonic Society of Amsterdam/Goehr
Vanguard SRV–216/17 SD
28 Steber (s), Elias (a), Verreau (t), Cross (bs-bar); The Temple Univesity Choirs,
The Philadelphia Orchestra/Ormandy   Columbia M3S 680

Discographies

29 Stich-Randall (s), Reynolds (a), Haefliger (t), Shirley-Quirk (bar); RIAS-Kammer-chor, Berlin Radio Symphony Orchestra/Maazel   Philips 6747 438
30 Yakar (s), Smith (s), Finnilä (a), Rolfe Johnson (t), Huttenlocher (bar) [No. 18], van Dam (bs); Ensemble Vocal de Lausanne, Lausanne Chamber Orchestra/Corboz
Erato STU 71314
31 Perrin (s), Staempfli (s), Schwartz (m-s), Perret (a), Dufour (t), Huttenlocher (bar), Tüller (bs); Ensemble Vocal et Instrumental de Lausanne/Corboz
Erato STU 70715/17
32 Giebel (s), Baker (a), Gedda (t), Prey (bar) [No. 18], Crass (bs) [No. 10]; BBC Chorus, New Philharmonia Orchestra/Klemperer   HMV CMS 63364–2
33 Marshall (s), Baker (a), Tear (t), Ramey (bs); Academy and Chorus of St Martin-in-the-Fields/Marriner   Philips 416 415–2
34 Hansmann (s), Iiyama (s), Watts (a), Equiluz (t), van Egmond (bs); Vienna Sänger-knaben, Chorus Viennensis, Concentus Musicus Wien/Harnoncourt
Teldec 8.35019 ZA
35 Blasi (s), Ziegler (s), Rappé (a), Equiluz (t), Holl (bs); Arnold Schoenberg Choir, Concentus Musicus Wien/Harnoncourt   Teldec 8.35716 ZA
36 Nelson (s), Baird (s), Dooley (c-t), Minter (c-t), Hoffmeister (t), Brownless (t), Opalach (bs), Schultze (bs); The Bach Ensemble/Rifkin   Nonesuch 9 79036–2
37 Kirkby (s), van Evera (s), Iconomou (a), Immler (a), Killian (a), Covey-Crump (t), Thomas (bs); Taverner Consort, Taverner Players/Parrott   EMI 7 47293 8
38 Poulenard (s), Laurens (m-s), Jacobs (a), Elwes (t), van Egmond (bs) [No. 18], van der Kamp (bs) [No. 10]; Collegium Musicum van de Nederlandse Bachvereiniging, La Petite Bande/Leonhardt   Deutsche Harmonia Mundi GD 77040
39 Schlick (s), Helling (a), Elwes (t), van der Kamp (bs); Junge Kantorei, Florilegium Musicum Rotterdam/Martini   MD + G L 3146/47
40 Schlick (s), Patriasz (s), Brett (a), Crook (t), Kooy (bs); Chorus and Orchestra of Collegium Vocale, Ghent/Herreweghe   Virgin Classics VCD 7 90757–2
41 Argenta (s), Dawson (s), Kwella (s), Hall (m-s), Nichols (m-s), Chance (a), Milner (t), Evans (t), Lloyd Morgan (bs), Varcoe (bs); The Monteverdi Choir, The English Baroque Soloists/Gardiner   DG 415 514–2
42 Sailer (s), Bence (a), Wunderlich (t), Wenk (bs); Swabian Choral Society, Stuttgart Pro Musica/Grischkat   Vox VBX 7
43 Palmer (s), Watts (a), Tear (t), Rippon (bs); Amor Artis Chorale, English Chamber Orchestra/Somary   Vanguard VSD 71190
44 Smith (s), Chance (ct), van der Meel (t), van der Kamp (bs), Netherlands Chamber Choir, Orchestra of the 18th Century/Brüggen   Philips 426 238–2
45 Kopleff (c), McCoy (t), Robert Shaw Chorale and Orchestra/Shaw
Melodiya S10 26061

Handel: *Messiah*

In the following discography, all the numbers in the parentheses following some, but not all, of the listings refer to the Prout Edition numbering of the components of *Messiah*. 6* indicates that the Guadagni version of 'But who may abide the day of His coming' is sung by a bass; + after either 23 or 48 indicates that the central section and reprise have been omitted.

Complete and excerpts

1 Smith (s), King (tr), Brett (ct), Hill (t), Cold (bs); Worcester Cathedral Choir, La Grand Ecurie et la Chambre du Roy/Malgoire   CBS 79336

2 Ameling (s), Reynolds (c), Langridge (t), Howell (bs); The Academy of St Martin-in-the-Fields and Chorus/Marriner   Argo 421 234−2

3 Popp (s), Fassbaender (a), Gambill (t), Holl (bs); South German Radio Chorus, Stuttgart Radio Symphony Orchestra/Marriner

German EMI 270 080−3

4 Raskin (s), Kopleff (a), Lewis (t), Paul (bs); Robert Shaw Chorale and Orchestra/Shaw   RCA LSC 6175

5 Cable (s), Pelton (s), Ringholz (s), Baldwin (ms), DeGaetani (a), McCoy (t), Courtney (bs-bar), Paul (bs); Eastman Chorale and Philharmonia/Neuen

Word SPCN 7−01−8929

6 Hoagland (s), Wallace (s), Gore (a), Livings (t), Evitts (bs); Handel and Haydn Society Chorus and Orchestra/Dunn   Sine Qua Non Superba SA 2015

7 Kirkby (s), van Evera (s), Cable (c), Bowman (ct), Cornwell (t), Thomas (bs); Taverner Choir, Taverner Players/Parrott   EMI Reflexe CDS 7 49801−2

8 Nelson (s), Kirkby (s), Watkinson (a), Elliott (t), Thomas (bs); Choir of Christ Church Cathedral, Oxford, The Academy of Ancient Music/Hogwood

Oiseau-Lyre 411 858−2

9 Graf (s), Haasemann (a), Bossow (t), Pommerien (bs); Westfalische Kantorei, Het Kunstmaandorkest Amsterdam/Ehmann   Cantate 658 213
(Includes only 4, 10, 12, 16, 17, 23, 25, 26, 31, 32, 40, 44, 45, 53.)

10 Erickson (s), McNair (s), Hodgson (ms), Humphrey (t), Stilwell (bs); Atlanta Symphony Orchestra and Chamber Chorus/Shaw   Telarc 80093−2

11 Dawson (s), Denley (a), James (ct), Davies (t), George (bs); The Sixteen/Christophers   Hyperion CDA 66251/2

12 Augér (s), von Otter (a), Chance (ct), Crook (t), Tomlinson (bs); The English Concert and Choir/Pinnock   DG Archiv 423 260−2

13 Kirkby (s), Jacobs (ct), van Altena (t), van Egmond (bs); University of Michigan Early Music Ensemble Chorus, Ars Musica/Parmentier.

University of Michigan School of Music Recordings SM 0017
(Includes only 1−7, 12−17, 19−21.)

14 Kwella (s), Drew (tr), Cable (a), Kendall (t), Jackson (bs); Winchester Cathedral Choir, London Handel Orchestra/Neary   ASV CD 525
(Includes only 2−4, 12−17, 23, 44, 45, 47, 48, 53.)

15 Mathis (s), Bowman (ct), Ahnsjö (t), Krause (bs); Cathedral Choral Society, University of Maryland Chorus, Smithsonian Concerto Grosso/Dorati

Intersound Pro Arte CDD 232

16 Kupper (s), Anday (a), Fehenberger (t), Greindl (bs); Salzburg Cathedral Choir, Salzburg Mozarteum Orchestra/Messner   Remington R199−69
(68, omits 7, 9 [solo section], 21, 23 [da capo reprise], 26−8, 31, 32, 34−6, 39−52.)

17 Cole (s), Krap (a), Larsen (t), Hoekman (bs); Handel Society Chorus and Orchestra [Netherlands Philharmonic Orchestra]/Goehr

Musical Masterpiece Society MMS 2019
(68, 23 +, 48 +, omits 7, 21, 25, 34−9, 49−52.)

18 Dobbs (s), Hoffman (a), Simoneau (t), Rehfuss (bs); London Handel Society Chorus and Orchestra/Goehr   Concert Hall SMSC 2153

19 Mathis (s), Finnilä (a) Schreier (t), Adam (bs); Austrian Radio Chorus and Symphony Orchestra/Mackerras   DG Archiv 2710 016
(Authentic Mozart arrangement complete: 68, 48 +, omits 35, 36.)

20 Lott (s), Palmer (a), Langridge (t), Lloyd (bs); Huddersfield Choral Society, Royal Philharmonic Orchestra/Mackerras   RPO CDR PD 001
(48 +, omits 35, 36, 39, 49–52.)

21 Crystal Palace Handel Festival Choir and Orchestra/Wood
                                        Columbia 78:L 1768, L 1769 and D 1555
(Includes only 4, 22, 28, 33, 41 [22 and 33 on Pearl GEMM 161.]

22 Addison (s), Sydney (a), Lloyd (t), Gramm (bs); Handel and Haydn Society Chorus and Orchestra, Zimbler Sinfonietta/Stone   Unicorn UNS 1
(68, 23 +, 48 + [Mozart Revision], omits 7, 25, 34–7, 39, 46, 49–52.)

23 Allen (s), Dews (a), Harrison (t), Knowle (bs); London Welsh Choir, Queen's Hall Players/Anon.   25 10″ and 12″ G&T 78s

24 Suddaby (s); Orchestra/Scott   HMV C 1742
(Includes only 12 and 14–16.)

25 Labbette (s), Brunskill (a), Eisdell (t), Williams (bs); BBC Chorus, London Symphony Orchestra/Beecham   Columbia 9320/9337; Pearl GEMM CD 9456
(68, 23 +, 48 +, omits 13, 34–7, 39, 49–52, 53 [Amen].)

26 Suddaby (s), Thomas (a), Nash (t), Anthony (bs); Luton Choral Society, Royal Philharmonic Orchestra/Beecham   HMV ALP 1077/80
(68)

27 Vyvyan (s), Sinclair (a), Vickers (t), Tozzi (bs); Royal Philharmonic Orchestra and Chorus/Beecham   RCA SER 4501/4
(68, 23 +, 48 +)

28 Baillie (s), Ripley (a), Johnston (t), Walker (bs); Huddersfield Choral Society, Liverpool Philharmonic Orchestra/Sargent   Columbia DX 1283/1301
(68, 23 +, 48 +, omits 34–6, 49–52.)

29 Morison (s), Thomas (a), Lewis (t), Walker (bs); Huddersfield Choral Society, Liverpool Philharmonic Orchestra/Sargent   HMV XLP 30050/2
(68, 23 +, 48 +, omits 34–6, 49–52.)

30 Morison (s), Thomas (a), Lewis (t), Milligan (bs); Huddersfield Choral Society, Royal Liverpool Philharmonic Orchestra/Sargent   Columbia SAX 2308/10
(68, 23 +, 48 +, omits 34–6, 49–52.)

31 Harwood (s), Procter (a), Young (t), Shirley-Quirk (bs); Royal Choral Society, Royal Philharmonic Orchestra/Sargent   Quintessence P3C 2701
(68, 23 +, 48 +, omits 34–6, 49–52.)

32 Marshall (s), Palmateer (a), Vickers (t), Milligan (bs); Toronto Mendelssohn Choir, Toronto Symphony Orchestra/MacMillan   World Records T 216/8
(68, 48 +, omits 7, 34–6, 49–52.)

33 Lott (s), Hodgson (a), Langridge (t), Cold (bs); London Philharmonic Orchestra and Choir/Alldis   Birdwing BWR 2011
(68, 23 +, 48 +, omits 34–7.)

34 Burrowes (s), Caley (t); London Philharmonic Orchestra and Choir/Gamley
                                        Gold Award Classics
(Includes only 1, 2, 3, 4, 12, 44, 45, 53.)

35 Allister (a), Robinson (bs); Black Dyke Mills Band, Bradford Choral Society/Brand
Pye GSGL 10475
(Includes only 1, 4, 8, 9, 13, 23*, 33, 40 [with *da capo*] 44, 47, 48*.)

36 Anonymous soloists; Pro Musica Antiqua Chorus and Chamber Orchestra/Jones
CMS/Summit SUM 1014
(Includes only 2, 3, 9, 12, 28, 38, 40, 44, 45, 48 +, 53 ['Amen' only].)

37 Anonymous conductor and soloists   Spinorama XMK 4011
(Includes only 2, 3, 9, 12, 28, 38, 40, 44, 45, 48 +, 53 ['Amen' only].)

38 Anonymous soloists; Homburg Symphony/von Baum   Premier SM/S 1 37
(Includes only 2, 3, 9, 12, 28, 38, 40, 44, 45, 48 +, 53 ['Amen' only].)

39 Harwood (s), Procter (a), Lewis (t), Holmes (bs); London Philharmonic Orchestra
and Choir/Pritchard   Durium Concertato DCS 48014
(Includes only 2, 3, 4, 7, 12, 13, 20, 22, 23 +, 44, 45, 48 +.)

40 One Experience Choir, Revelation Philharmonic Orchestra/Belling
AmCol KC 31713
(Includes only 4, 12, 17, 24, 26, 28, 44, 45, 46, 48 +.)

41 Elmer Iseler Singes, Synthescope Digital Synthesizer Ensemble/Iseler
MMG 113
(Includes only 1, 4, 12, 13, 17, 22, 24–6, 44, 53.)

42 Troxell (s), Sanders (a), Fredericks (t), Darwin (bs); unidentified chorus, John
Cartwright, organ and conductor   Allegro Royale 1539/1541
(6*, 23 +, 48 +, abridges 20, omits 21, 27, 28, 34–9, 49–52.)

43 Summers (a), Haugh (t), Edkins (bs); Handel Oratorio Society of Augustana
College, Lundhon; Snyder organ/Veld   Bibletone
(Includes only 2, 3, 8, 9, 14, 15, 16, 17, 20, 23 +, 24, 44, 45, 47, 48 +.)

44 Ritchie (s), Shacklock (a), Herbert (t), Standen (bs); London Philharmonic Choir,
London Symphony Orchestra/Scherchen   Precision PVCDBS 9101

45 Vyvyan (s), Procter (a), Maran (t), Brannigan (bs); London Philharmonic Choir
and Orchestra/Boult   Decca ECS 613/5
(6*)

46 Alarie (s), Merriman (a), Simoneau (t), Standen (bs); Vienna Academy Chorus,
Vienna State Opera Orchestra/Scherchen   Westminster WST 306

47 Sutherland (s), Bumbry (a), McKellar (t), Ward (bs); London Symphony Orchestra
and Chorus/Boult   Decca SET 218/220
(6*)

48 Farrell (s), Lipton (a), Cunningham (t), Warfield (bs); Mormon Tabernacle Choir,
Philadelphia Orchestra/Ormandy   CBS M2S 607
(6*, 23 +, abridges 20, 48, omits, 27–32, 34–9, 41, 49–52.)

49 Addison (s), Oberlin (ct), Lloyd (t), Warfield (bs); Westminster Choir, New York
Philharmonic Orchestra/Bernstein   CBS M2S 603
(6*, 23 +, 48 +, omits 10, 11, 21, 24, 32, 34–9, 49–52.)

50 Armstrong (s), Procter (c), Bowen (t), Cameron (bs); London Symphony Orchestra
and Chorus/Stokowski   Decca SPA 284
(Includes only 1, 4, 13, 19, 20, 29–32, 40 [with *da capo*], 44–6, 53 ['Amen' only].)

51 Sutherland (s), Coleman (tr), Tourangeau (a), Krenn (t), Krause (bs); Ambrosian
Singers, English Chamber Orchestra/Bonynge   Decca SET 465/7
(Abridges 48.)

52 Harper (s), Watts (a), Wakefield (t), Shirley-Quirk (bs); London Symphony Orchestra and Chorus/Davis   Philips 420 865 – 2

53 Harwood (s), Baker (a), Esswood (ct), Tear (t), Herincx (bs); Ambrosian Singers, English Chamber Orchestra/Mackerras   HMV CDS7 62748 – 2

54 Price (s), Schwarz (a), Burrows (t), Estes (bs); Bavarian Radio Symphony Orchestra and Chorus/Davis   Philips 412 538 – 2

55 Janowitz (s), Höffgen (a), Haefliger (t), Crass (bs); Munich Bach Orchestra and Choir/Richter   DG 2721 076

56 Donath (s), Reynolds (a), Burrows (t), McIntyre (bs); John Alldis Choir, London Philharmonic Orchestra/Richter   DG 417 797 – 2
(6*)

57 Schwarzkopf (s), Hoffman (a), Gedda (t), Hines (bs); Philharmonia Orchestra and Chorus/Klemperer   HMV CDM7 636212
(6*, omits 34 – 6, 39 – 52.)

58 Palmer (s), Watts (a), Davies (t), Shirley-Quirk (bs); English Chamber Orchestra and Chorus/Leppard   Erato STU 70921

59 Boy soprano, Bowman (ct), Tear (t), Luxon (bs); King's College Choir, Cambridge, Academy of St Martin-in-the-Fields/Willcocks   HMV SLS 845

60 Price (s), Minton (a), Young (t), Diaz (bs); Amor Artis Chorale, English Chamber Orchestra/Somary   Vanguard Cardinal VCS 10090/2
(6*)

61 Harper (s), Watts (a), Robertson (t), Stalman (bs); London Philharmonic Orchestra and Chorus/Jackson   Saga STXID 5111/3
(6*)

62 Cantelo (s), Watts (a), Brown (t), Stalman (bs); London Philharmonic Orchestra and Chorus/Susskind   Pye GSGL 10062
(6*, omits 34 – 7, 39, 49 – 52.)

63 Unidentified soloists; The Masterwork Chorus, J. Clifford Welsh, organ/Randolph   Realistic 50 – 1967
(6*, 23 + , 48 + ; omits 27, 28, 31, 32, 34 – 9, 49 – 52.)

64 Bjoner (s), Töpper (a), Traxel (t), Engen (bs); St Hedwig's Cathedral Choir, Berlin Symphony Orchestra/Forster   Eurodisc GD 69088
(6*, 23 + , 48 + , omits 7, 26.)

65 Wenglor (s), Prenzlow (a), Unger (t), Adam (bs); Berlin Radio Symphony Orchestra and Chorus/Koch   Eterna 8 20 51/54

66 Werner (s), Riess (a), Schreier (t), Adam (bs); Berlin Radio Symphony Orchestra and Chorus/Koch   Eterna 092 087/9

67 Le Sage (s), Greevy (a), Morton (t), Knapp (bs); Warsaw National Philharmonic Orchestra and Choir/Kord   Muza SX 1691/4

68 Kenny (s), Esswood (ct), Hill (t), Linden (bs); Stockholm Bach Choir; Members of the Swedish Radio Symphony Orchestra/Öhrwall   Proprius 7871/3
(48 + ; omits 39 and 50 – 2.)

69 Gale (s), Lipovšek (a), Hollweg (t), Kennedy (bs); Stockholm Chamber Choir, Concentus Musicus Wien/Harnoncourt   Teldec 8.35617

70 Marshall (s), Quirke (tr), Robbin (a), Brett (ct), Rolfe Johnson (t), Hale (bs); Monteverdi Choir, English Baroque Soloists/Gardiner

           Philips 411 041 – 2

71 Te Kanawa (s), Gjevang (a), Lewis (t), Howell (bs); Chicago Symphony Orchestra and Chorus/Solti   Decca 414 396–2
72 Battle (s), Quivar (ms), Aler (t), Ramey (bs); Toronto Mendelssohn Choir, Toronto Symphony Orchestra/A. Davis   EMI CDS7 49027 2
   (6*)
73 Bogard (s), Green (a), Gall (ct), Bressler (t), Guinn (bs); American Boychoir, Norman Scribner Chorus, Smithsonian Chamber Players/Weaver
                                                      Smithsonian N 1025
74 Woodland (s), Procter (a), Esswood (ct), Tatnell (ct), Johnston (t), Roberts (bar); London Choral Society, English Symphony Orchestra/Tobin   GFH 1/4
75 Blegen (s), Ciesinski (a), Aler (t), Cheek (bs); Musica Sacra Chorus and Orchestra/ Westenburg   RCA ARC 3–4352
76 Kweksilber (s), Bowman (ct), Elliott (t), Reinhart (bs); The Sixteen, Amsterdam Baroque Orchestra/Koopman   Erato 880503

Mozart: Requiem in D Minor K.626

1937   Schumann, Thorborg, Dermota, Kipnis; Vienna State Opera Chorus, Vienna Philharmonic Orchestra/Walter   HMV EG 290781 1
1940   Anonymous Soloists; Pennsylvania University Choral Society, Philadelphia Orchestra/McDonald   HMV DB 10136/41; Camden CAL 276
1941   Briem, Freimuth, Ludwig, Drissen; Bruno Kittel Choir, Berlin Philharmonic Orchestra/Kittel   Polydor 67731/9(78)
1941   Tassinari, Stignani, Tagliavini, Tajo; EIAR Chorus and Symphony Orchestra/De Sabata   HMV DB 9541/8(78); Heliodor 88005
1951   Gueden, Anday, Patzak, Greindl; Salzburg Cathedral Choir, Salzburg Mozarteum Orchestra/Messner   Remington R 199–96
1951   Pech, Breitschopf, Ludwig, Pröglhöf; Vienna Hofmusikkapelle Chorus and Orchestra/Krips   Decca AX 366/72(78); Eclipse ECS 715
c. 1951 Cianella, Okerson, Carringer, Keast; Robert Shaw Chorale, Victor Symphony Orchestra/Shaw   RCA Victor LM 1712
1954   László, Rössl-Majdan, Munteanu, Standen; Vienna Academy Chorus, Vienna State Opera Orchestra/Scherchen   Ducretet-Thomson DTL 93079
1955   Seefried, Pitzinger, Holm, Borg; Vienna State Opera Chorus, Vienna Symphony Orchestra/Jochum   DG DGM 18284
c. 1955 Grümmer, Höffgen, Krebs, Frick, St Hedwig's Cathedral Choir, Berlin Philharmonic Orchestra/Kempe   HMV ALP 1444
1956   Morison, Sinclair, Young, Nowakowski; BBC Chorus, Royal Philharmonic Orchestra/Beecham   Fontana CFL 1000
1956   Seefried, Tourel, Simoneau, Warfield; Westminster Choir, New York Philharmonic Symphony Orchestra/Walter   CBS CD 45556
1956   Stich-Randall, Malaniuk, Kmentt, Böhme; Vienna State Opera Chorus, Vienna Symphony Orchestra/Böhm   Philips 420 772–2
1957   Lipp, Höngen, Dickie, Weber; Vienna Musikfreunde Chorus, Vienna Pro Musica Symphony Orchestra/Horenstein   Vox DL 270
1959   Jurinac, West, Loeffler, Guthrie; Vienna Academy Chorus, Vienna State Opera Orchestra/Scherchen   Westminster XWN 18766

1961 Lipp, Rössl-Majdan, Dermota, Berry; Vienna Singverein, Berlin Philharmonic Orchestra/Karajan DG 423 213–2

1962 Stader, Töpper, van Kesteren, Kohn; Munich Bach Choir and Orchestra/Richter Teldec 844 264

1964 Endich, Alberts, DiVirgilio, Morgan; Chorus Pro Musica, Harvard Glee Club, Radcliffe Choral Society, New England Conservatory Chorus, Boston Symphony Orchestra/Leinsdorf RCA Victor LM 7030

1964 Equiluz, Buchbauer, boy-soloists from the Vienna Boys' Choir; Vienna Konzerthaus Chamber Orchestra/Grossmann Realm RM 169

1965 Buckel, Bence, Mielsch, Wollitz; Böblingen Bach Choir, Stuttgart Philharmonic Orchestra/Bader Vox STPL 512740

1966 Petrescu, Cortez, Teodorian, Rintzler; Philharmonic Chorus and Orchestra of 'Banatul' of Timisoara/Boboc Electrocord ECE 0259

1966 Ameling, Horne, Benelli, Franc; Vienna State Opera Chorus, Vienna Philharmonic Orchestra/Kertész Decca 417 681–2

1966 Zylis-Gara, Domínguez, Schreier, Crass; South German Madrigal Choir, Consortium Musicum/Gönnenwein German Columbia SMC 91283

1967 Donath, Minton, Davies, Nienstedt; John Alldis Choir, BBC Symphony Orchestra/C. Davis Philips 420 353–2

1968 Mathis, Bumbry, Shirley, Rintzler; New Philharmonic Chorus and Orchestra/Frühbeck de Burgos CFP 4399

1969 Harper, Hesse, Page, Engen; Vienna Academy Chorus, Vienna Opera Orchestra/Colombo Concert Hall SMSC 2593

1971 Kooy, Schelland, Barneveld, Jagtenberg, Veldman, de Groot; Youth Choir of Soest Reformed Church, Netherlands Singers, Orchestra/Kooy Saga 5332

1971 Yegorova, Kozlova, Maslennikov, Reshetin; USSR State Academic Choir, Moscos State Philharmonic Symphony Orchestra/Sveshnikov
Melodiya D 025609/10

1971 Armstrong, Baker, Gedda, Fischer-Dieskau; John Alldis Choir, English Chamber Orchestra/Barenboim HMV CZS 7 62892 2

1971 Mathis, Hamari, Ochman, Ridderbusch; Vienna State Opera Choir; Vienna Philharmonic Orchestra/Böhm DG 413 553–2

1974 Buchhierl, Krämer, Krenn, McDaniel; Tölz Boys' Choir, Collegium Aureum/Schmidt-Gaden EMI (Harmonia Mundi) 1C 065 99694/Q

1975 Tomowa-Sintow, Baltsa, Krenn, van Dam; Vienna Singverein, Berlin Philharmonic Orchestra/Karajan DG 429 821–2

1976 Ameling, Scherler, Devos, Soyer; Gulbenkian Symphony Chorus and Orchestra/Corboz Erato ECD 88157

1976 Equiluz, Eder, boy-soloists from the Vienna Boys' Choir; Vienna Hofmusikkapelle Chorus and Orchestra, male voices of the Vienna State Opera Chorus, Vienna State Opera Orchestra/Gillesberger RCA GD 86535

1977 Cotrubas, Watts, Tear, Shirley-Quirk; Chorus and Orchestra of the Academy of St Martin-in-the-Fields/Marriner Decca 417 746–2

1978 Donath, Ludwig, Tear, Lloyd; Philharmonia Chorus and Orchestra/Giulini
EMI CDZ7 62518 2

1979 Augér, Watkinson, Jerusalem, Nimsgern; Gächinger Singers, Stuttgart Bach Collegium/Rilling CBS 76819

Discographies

1979   Kalmár, Takács, Korondy, Gregor; Hungarian Radio and Television Chorus, Hungarian State Orchestra/Ferencsik   Hungaroton HCD 12038

1980   Kemmer, Bartelloni, Quenez, Martin; Chorale Marc-Antoine Charpentier/ Nuremberg Symphony Orchestra/Muller   Colosseum SM 587

1982   Yakar, Wenkel, Equiluz, Holl; Vienna State Opera Chorus, Concentus Musicus Wien/Harnoncourt   Teldec 8 42756

1983   Price, Schmidt, Araiza, Adam; Leipzig Radio Chorus, Dresden State Orchestra/Schreier   Philips 411 420–2

1983   Kirkby, Watkinson, Rolfe Johnson, Thomas; Westminster Cathedral Boys' Choir, Chorus and Orchestra of Academy of Ancient Music/Hogwood
                Oiseau-Lyre 411 712–2

1984   Battle, Murray, Rendall, Salminen; Paris Chorus and Orchestra/Barenboim
                EMI CDC7 47342 2

1986   Augér, Ziegler, Hadley, Krause; Atlanta Symphony Chorus and Orchestra/ Shaw   Telarc CD 80128

1986   Tomowa-Sintow, Müller-Molinari, Cole, Burchuladze; Vienna Singverein, Vienna Philharmonic Orchestra/Karajan   DG 419 610–2

1986   Bonney, von Otter, Blochwitz, White; Monteverdi Choir, English Baroque Soloists/Gardiner   Philips 420 197–2

1986   Schmithüsen, Patriasz, Mackie, Hölle; Netherlands Chamber Choir, La Petite Bande/Kuijken   Accent ACC 68645

1987   Pace, Meier, Lopardo, Morris; Swedish Radio Chorus, Stockholm Chamber Choir, Berlin Philharmonic Orchestra/Muti   HMV CDC7 49640–2

1987   Kenny, Walker, Kendall, Wilson-Johnson; Choir of St John's College, Cambridge, English Chamber Orchestra/Guest   Chandos CHAN 8574

1988   McLaughlin, Ewing, Hadley, Hauptmann; Bavarian Radio Chorus, Bavarian Radio Symphony Orchestra/Bernstein   DG 427 353–2

Haydn: *The Creation*

1949   Eipperle, Riegler, Patzak, Hann, Pernerstorfer; Vienna State Opera Chorus, Vienna PO/Krauss   Saga Pan 6213/4

1952   Seefried, Ludwig, Hotter; Bavarian Radio Chorus and Orchestra/Jochum
                Melodram MEL 208

1956   Seefried, Holm, Borg; St Hedwig's Cathedral Choir, Berlin PO/Markevitch
                DG LPM 18489/90

1957   Kupper, K. Kraus, Traxel, Greindl, Berry, Cologne Radio Choir and Symphony Orchestra/Keilberth   Melodram MEL 231

1958   Stich-Randall, Felbermayer, Dermota, Guthrie, Schoeffler; Chorus and Orchestra of the Vienna State Opera/Wöldike   Philips GL 5726/7

1960   Coertse, Patzak, Ernster; Vienna Singverein, Vienna Volksoper Orchestra/ Horenstein   Turnabout TV 34184/5S

1961   Grümmer, Traxel, Frick; St Hedwig's Cathedral Choir, Berlin, Berlin SO/ Forster   HMV ASD 409/11

1964   Wenglor, Unger, Adam; Chorus and Orchestra of Berlin State Radio/Koch
                DG 89576/7

282

1965 Giebel, Holm, Rehfuss; Vienna Academy Chorus, Vienna Symphony Orchestra/Goehr   Concert Hall CM–2209

1965 Raskin, Conway, McCollum, Watson; Musica Aeterna Chorus and Orchestra/Waldman   Brunswick SXA 4533/4

1966 Giebel, Kmentt, Frick; Bavarian Radio Chorus and SO/Jochum   Philips 6700 002

1967 Ameling, Spoorenberg, Krenn, Krause, Fairhurst; Vienna State Opera Chorus/Vienna PO/Münchinger   Decca SET 362/3

1969 Raskin, Young, Reardon; Camerata Singers, New York PO/Bernstein   CBS 77221

1969 Janowitz, Ludwig, Wunderlich, Krenn, Berry, Fischer-Dieskau; Vienna Singverein, Berlin PO/Karajan   DG 410 951–1

1974 Werner, Schreier, Adam; Chorus and Symphony Orchestra of Berlin Radio/Koch   Eterna 8 26 746/7

1974 Harper, Tear, Shirley-Quirk; Choir of King's College, Cambridge, Academy of St Martin-in-the-Fields/Willcocks   CMS7 69894–2

c. 1975 van Dijck, Schreier, Adam; Gürzenich Choir and Orchestra/Wand   Musidisc 30 RC 621/3

c. 1975 Donath, Kraus, Widmer; South German Madrigal Choir, Orchestra of the Ludwigsburg Festival/Gönnenwein   Vox QSVBX 5214

1977 Popp, Döse, Hollweg, Moll, Luxon; Brighton Festival Chorus, RPO/Dorati   Decca 421 605–2

1978 Donath, Tear, van Dam; Philharmonia Chorus and Orchestra/Frühbeck de Burgos   CFPD 414444–3

1981 Mathis, Denley, Baldin, Fischer-Dieskau; Chorus and Academy of St Martin-in-the-Fields/Marriner   Philips 416 449–2

1982 Augér, Kraus, Tüller; Gächinger Kantorei, Bach-Collegium, Stuttgart/Rilling   Intercord INT 180–810

1982 Burrowes, Greenberg, Wohlers, Morris, Nimsgern; Chicago Symphony Chorus and Orchestra/Solti   Decca D262D2

1982 Marshall, Branisteanu, Tappy, Rydl, Huttenlocher; Suisse Romande Radio Chorus and Pro Arte Chorus, Lausanne Chamber Orchestra/Jordan   Erato NUM 750202

1982 Mathis, Murray, Araiza, van Dam; Vienna Singverein, Vienna PO/Karajan   DG 410 718–2

1982 Laki, Mackie, Huttenlocher; Collegium Vocale, Ghent, La Petite Bande/Kuijken   Accent ACC 58228/9D

1983 Augér, Sima, Schreier, Berry, Hermann; Arnold Schoenberg Choir, Collegium Aureum/Kuhn   Harmonia Mundi HM 20325/6

1986 Gruberova, Protschka, Holl; Arnold Schoenberg Choir, Vienna Symphony Orchestra/Harnoncourt   Teldec 8.35722

1987 Blegen, Popp, Moser, Ollman, Moll; Bavarian Radio Chorus and Symphony Orchestra/Bernstein   DG 419 765–2

1988 Marshall, Popp, Cole, Weikl, Howell; Bavarian Radio Chorus and Symphony Orchestra/Kubelik   Orfeo C150852H

1989 Dawson, Rosenhein, Cheek; Minnesota Chorale, St Paul Chamber Orchestra/Revzen   Albany AR 005/6

Discographies

Haydn: *The Seasons*

1942   Eipperle, Patzak, Hann; Vienna State Opera Chorus, Vienna Philharmonic
Orchestra/Krauss   Preiser 93053

*c.*1943   Gatti, Albanese, Neroni; Italian Radio Symphony Orchestra/Gui
Cetra LP0 2004

1950s   Stich-Randall, Kretschmar, Wenk; North German Radio Chorus, North
German Symphony Orchestra/Goehr   Concert Hall BM 2078

1956   Trötschel, Ludwig, Greindl; St Hedwig's Cathedral Choir, Berlin RIAS
Symphony Orchestra/Fricsay   DG 2721 170

1958   Morison, Young, Langdon; Beecham Choral Society, Royal Philharmonic
Orchestra/Beecham   HMV SLS 5158

1967   Janowitz, Schreier, Talvela; Vienna Singverein, Vienna Symphony Orchestra/
Böhm   DG 423 922−2

1968   Harper, Davies, Shirley-Quirk; BBC Symphony Orchestra and Chorus/Davis
Philips 6770 035

1972   Janowitz, Hollweg, Berry; Berlin Deutsches Oper Chorus, Berlin Philharmonic Orchestra/Karajan   HMV CMS7 69224−2

1970s   Stolte, Schreier, Adam; Leipzig Radio Chorus and Symphony Orchestra/
Kegel   Ariola XG 85507 K

1970s   Donath, Kraus, Widmer; South German Madrigal Choir, Ludwigsburg
Festival Orchestra/Gönnenwein   FSM 33001/5

1970s   Mathis, Gedda, Crass; South German Madrigal Choir, Bavarian State
Orchestra/Gönnenwein   Electrola 1C 163−28531/3

1978   Cotrubas, Krenn, Sotin; Brighton Festival Chorus, Royal Philharmonic
Orchestra/Dorati   Decca D88D3

1980   Mathis, Jerusalem, Fischer-Dieskau; Academy of St Martin-in-the-Fields/
Marriner   Philips 411 428−2

1987   Blasi, Protschka, Holl; Arnold Schoenberg Choir, Vienna Symphony
Orchestra/Harnoncourt   Teldec 835741

Beethoven: Missa Solemnis

1930s   Leonard Land, Schlosshauer-Reynolds, Topitz, Transky, Guttmann, Schey;
Bruno Kittel Choir, Berlin Philharmonic Orchestra/Kittel
Decca CA 8069/79

1930s   Fornells, Gallao, Brünig, Forges; Orfeó Catalá of Barcelona, Orchestra/
Millet   Victor 9133/44; Spanish HMV AB 239/50

1930s   Vreeland, Kaskas, Priebe, Cordon; Harvard Glee Club, Radcliffe Choral
Society, Boston Symphony Orchestra/Koussevitzky   HMV ED 235/46

1935   Rethberg, Telva, Martinelli, Pinza; New York Schola Cantorum, New York
Philharmonic Orchestra/Toscanini   GRP 1001

1940   Milanov, Castagna, Björling, Kipnis; Westminster Choir, NBC Symphony
Orchestra/Toscanini   Toscanini Recordings CD 259

1952   Steingruber, Schürhoff, Majkut, Wiener; Vienna Academy Choir, Vienna
Symphony Orchestra/Klemperer   Turnabout TV 37073 S

1953   Marshall, Merriman, Conley, Hines; Robert Shaw Chorale, NBC Symphony
Orchestra/Toscanini   RCA AT 200

1955	Stader, Radev, Dermota, Greindl; St Hedwig's Cathedral Choir, Berlin Philharmonic Orchestra/Böhm	DG 89679/80
1958	Schwarzkopf, Ludwig, Gedda, Zaccaria; Vienna Singverein, Philharmonia Orchestra/Karajan	HMV SLS 5198
c.1960	Graf, Hoffman, Kretschmar, Wenk; North German Radio Chorus and Symphony Orchestra/Goehr	Vanguard SRV 214/5
1962	Farrell, Smith, Lewis, Borg; Westminster Choir, New York Philharmonic Orchestra/Bernstein	CBS 77208
1964	Stich-Randall, Casei, Dickie, Guthrie; Vienna Symphony Orchestra and Chorus/Wallberg	Concert Hall SMSC 2422
1965	Söderström, Höffgen, Kmentt, Talvela; New Philharmonia Orchestra and Chorus/Klemperer	HMV CMS7 69538-2
1966	Janowitz, Ludwig, Wunderlich, Berry; Vienna Singverein, Berlin Philharmonic Orchestra/Karajan	DG 423 913-2
1960s	Molnar, Westen, Gilvan, Illerhaus; Landau Oratorio Choir, Pfalz Philharmonic Orchestra/Kloor	Oryx EXP 8/9
1960s	Arroyo, Forrester, Lewis, Siepi; Singing City Chorus, Philadelphia Orchestra/Ormandy	Amer-Columbia 2-30083
1960s	Kirschstein, Deroubaix, Schreier, Morbach; Cologne Symphony Chorus, Gürzenich Orchestra/Wand	Nonesuch HB 3002
1970	Giebel, Höffgen, Haefliger, Ridderbusch; Netherlands Radio Choir, Concertgebouw Orchestra/Jochum	Philips 6799 001
1973	Tomowa-Sintow, Burmeister, Schreier, Polster; Leipzig Radio Choir, Leipzig Gewandhaus Orchestra/Masur	RCA LRL2 5045
1974	Price, Ludwig, Ochman, Talvela; Vienna State Opera Chorus, Vienna Philharmonic Orchestra/Böhm	DG 413 191-1
1974	Janowitz, Baltsa, Schreier, van Dam; Vienna Singverein, Berlin Philharmonic Orchestra/Karajan	HMV CMS7 69246-2
1975	Harper, Baker, Tear, Sotin; New Philharmonia Chorus, London Philharmonic Orchestra/Giulini	HMV SLS 5198
1977	Geszty, Soffel, Rendall, Widmer; South German Madrigal Choir, Collegium Aureum Orchestra/Gönnenwein	EMI 1C 157 99688/9
1977	Tomowa-Sintow, Payne, Tear, Lloyd; London Symphony Orchestra and Chorus/Davis	Philips 6769 001
1977	Popp, Minton, Walker, Howell; Chicago Symphony Orchestra and Chorus/Solti	Decca 411 843-1
1978	Moser, Schwarz, Kollo, Moll; Hilversum Radio Chorus, Concertgebouw Orchestra/Bernstein	DG 413 780-2
1985	Cuberli, Schmidt, Cole, van Dam; Vienna Singverein, Berlin Philharmonic Orchestra/Karajan	DG 419 166-2
1987	McNair, Taylor, Aler, Krause; Atlanta Symphony Orchestra and Chorus/Shaw	Telarc CD 80150
1987	Hirsti, Watkinson, Murgatroyd, George; Oslo Cathedral Choir, The Hanover Band/Kvam	Nimbus NI 5109
1988	Kiberg, Lang, Cochran, Krutikov; University of Maryland Chorus, European Symphony Orchestra/Dorati	BIS CD 406/7

285

1989 Vaness, Meier, Blochwitz, Tschammer; Tallis Chamber Choir, ECO/Tate
EMI CDC 7 49950 2

1989 Coburn, Quivar, Baldin, Schmidt; Stuttgart Gächinger Singers, Stuttgart Bach
Collegium/Rilling   Hänssler 98956

Mendelssohn: *Elijah*

Complete

1930 Baillie, Serena, Jones, Williams, Purvis; BBC National Chorus and
Orchestra/Robinson   Columbia DB 49/63

1947 Baillie, Ripley, Johnston, Williams; Huddersfield Choral Society, Liverpool
Philharmonic Orchestra/Sargent
Columbia DX 1408/23; Am. Col SL 55

1950s Buckel, Bence, Mielsch, Wollitz; Liederkranz Böblingen, Stuttgart Philharmonic Orchestra/Bader   Vox SVBX 5208

1954 Delman, Cunningham, Procter, Maran, Boyce; Hampstead Parish Church
Boys' Choir, London Philharmonic Orchestra and Chorus/Krips
Decca LXT 5000/2

1957 Morison, Thomas, Lewis, Cameron, Huddersfield Choral Society, Royal
Liverpool Philharmonic Orchestra/Sargent   Columbia 33CX 1431/3

1962 Bjoner, Malaniuk, Kmentt, London; West German Radio Chorus and
Orchestra/von Dohnányi   Melodram MEL 227

1968 Jones, Wolff, Baker, Gedda, Fischer-Dieskau; New Philharmonia Chorus
and Orchestra/Frühbeck de Burgos   HMV SLS 935

1968 Ameling, Krahmer, Krug, Trexler, Burmeister, Schröter, Wandelt, Schreier,
Rötzsch, Adam, Polster; Leipzig Radio Choir and Gewandhaus Orchestra/
Sawallisch   Philips 420 106–2

1968 Marsh, Verrett, Lewis, Krause; Columbus Boychoir, Singing City Choirs,
Philadelphia Orchestra/Ormandy   Victor LSC 6190

1981 Augér, Horowitz, Schreckenbach, Graf, Tear, Nimsgern; Stuttgart Gächinger
Singers, Stuttgart Radio Symphony Orchestra/Rilling   CBS 79353

1984 Wiens, Watkinson, Lewis, Luxon; Lisbon Gulbenkian Foundation Chorus
and Orchestra/Corboz   Erato ECD 75147

1990 Plowright, Finnie, A. Davies, White; London Symphony Chorus and
Orchestra/Hickox   Chandos 8774/5

Excerpts

1964 Harwood, Thomas, Lewis, Shirley-Quirk; Royal Choral Society, Royal
Philharmonic Orchestra/Sargent   CFP 40014

Rossini: *Stabat mater*

1949 Seefried, Anday, Fehenberger, Frantz; Salzburg Cathedral Choir, Mozarteum
Orchestra/Messner   Remington R199 111/2

c.1951 Steingruber, Hermann, Dermota, Schoeffler; Vienna Academy Choir, Vienna
State Opera Orchestra/Sternberg   Saga XID 5216

286

1955	Stader, Radev, Haefliger, Borg; RIAS Chamber Choir, St Hedwig's Cathedral Choir, Berlin Radio Symphony Orchestra/Fricsay	DG LPM 18340
c.1960	De Osma, Cossotto, Iaia, Trama; Coro Polifonico, Milan, Orchestra of the Angelicum, Milan/Cillario	Select CC 15044
1960	Lorengar, Allen, Traxel, Greindl; St. Hedwig's Cathedral Choir, Berlin Symphony Orchestra/Forster	HMV ASD 588
1965	Arroyo, Wolff, Del Bianco, Díaz; Camerata Singers, New York Philharmonic Orchestra/Schippers	CBS SBRG 72382
c.1967	Aidinyan, Galachyan, Dovenman, Erkat; Armenian State Academy Choir, State Cinema Studio Orchestra/Chekidzhyan	Melodiya S 1493/4
1971	Lorengar, Minton, Pavarotti, Sotin; London Symphony Chorus, London Symphony Orchestra/Kertész	Decca 417 766–2
1981	Ricciarelli, Valentini Terrani, González, Raimondi; Philharmonia Chorus, Philharmonia Orchestra/Giulini	DG 410 034–2
1982	Malfitano, Baltsa, Gambill, Howell; Chorus and Orchestra of the Maggio Musicale, Florence/Muti	EMI CDC 747402–2
1986	Liani, Jaques, Zamfir, Krause; Ensemble Vocal et Orchestre Elans, Geneva/Crispini	Gallo CD 487
1987	Gasdia, Zimmermann, Merritt, Garcia; Ambrosian Singers, I Solisti Veneti/Scimone	Erato ECD 75493
1989	Field, Jones, Davies, Earle; London Symphony Chorus, City of London Sinfonia/Hickox	Chandos CHAN 8780

Rossini: *Petite messe solenelle*

1954	Tuccari, Salvi, Besma, Catalani; Chorus and Orchestra Sinfonica Romana della Società del Quartetto/Vitalini	Nixa PLP 588
1955	Mancini, Domínguez, Berdini, Petri; Coro Polifonico dell'Accademia di Santa Cecilia, Rome; Gorini, Vidusso (pno); Vignanelli (org)/Fasano	HMV ALP 1278/9
1964	Scotto, Cossotto, Kraus, Vinco; Coro Polifonico, Milan; Verganti, Franz (pno); Bendetti (harmonium)/Bertola	Ricordi MRC 2002/3
1969	Van Bork, Lensky, Maurer, Loomis; Choir of Società Cameristica, Lugano; Sgrizzi, Bernand (pno); Canino (harmonium)/Loehrer	Erato/World Records ST 1016/7
c.1970	De la Cruz, Gilles, Saretzki, Grimm; North West German Philharmonic Choir and Orchestra/Albert	Oryx 1826/7
1972	Lövaas, Fassbaender, Schreier, Fischer-Dieskau; Munich Vokalsolisten; Sawallisch, Hirsch (pno); Raffalt (harmonium)/Sawallisch	Eurodisc 610 263
1977	Marshall, Hodgson, Tear, King; London Chamber Choir; Holford, Constable (pno); Birch (harmonium)/Heltay	Argo ZRG 893/4
1979	Freni, Valentini Terrani, Pavarotti, Raimondi; Coro Polifonico del Teatro alla Scala, Milan; Magiera (pno); Rosetta (harmonium)/Gandolfi	Decca 421 645–2
1984	Ricciarelli, Zimmermann, Carreras, Ramey; Ambrosian Singers; Sheppard, Berkowitz (pno); Nunn (harmonium)/Scimone	Philips 412 548–2

Discographies

1984 Popp, Fassbaender, Gedda, Kavrakos; Choir of King's College, Cambridge; Labèque sisters (pno); Briggs (harmonium)/Cleobury   EMI CDS7 47482–8
1984 Capelle, Patriasz, Cornwell, Draijer; Nederlands Kamerkoor; Immerseel, Jordans (pno); Doeselaar (harmonium)/Immerseel   Accent ACC 68639/40D
1987 Combattimento; Mason, Egarr (pf), Roblou (harmonium)/Mason
Meridian CDE 84133
1989 Gasdia, Fink, La Scola, d'Artegna; Ensemble Vocal, Lausanne; Sgrizzi, Antonioli (pf), P. Corboz (harmonium)/M. Corboz   Erato 2292–45321–2
1989 Genova, Mineva, Mihailov, Pavlov; Bulgarian Television and Radio Mixed Choir; Dimitrova, Popova (pf), Moussev (organ)   Forlane UCD 16576/7

Berlioz: *Grande messe des morts*

1940s Jouatte; Passani Choir, Paris Radio Orchestra/Fournet
Fr.Col. FCX 148/9
1956 de Voll; Rochester Oratorio Society Choir and Orchestra/Hollenbach
Philips NBL 5034/5
1957 Giraudeau; French Radio Chorus, Paris Opéra Orchestra/Scherchen
Vox VUX 2013
1957 Gedda; Cologne Radio Chorus and Orchestra/Mitropoulos
Hunt CD 562
1957 Lloyd; Choir, Hartford Symphony Orchestra/Mahler
Philips GL 5750/1
1959 Simoneau; New England Conservatory Choir, Boston Symphony Orchestra/Munch   RCA RD 86210
1966 Valletti; Temple University Choir, Philadelphia Orchestra/Ormandy
CBS SBRG 72400/1
1966 Schreier; Bavarian Radio Chorus and Symphony Orchestra/Munch
DG 2726 050
1969 Dowd; London Symphony Chorus and Orchestra/Davis
Philips 416 283–2
1975 Tear; City of Birmingham Symphony Orchestra and Chorus/Frémaux
HMV CMS7 69932–2
1975 Burrows; French National Orchestra and Chorus/Bernstein
CBS 79205
1979 Riegel; Cleveland Orchestra and Chorus/Maazel   Decca D137 D2
1979 Tear; London Philharmonic Orchestra and Chorus/Previn
HMV SLS 5209
1980 Domingo; various choruses, Orchestre de Paris/Barenboim
DG 2707 119
1985 Aler; Atlanta Symphony Orchestra and Chorus/Shaw
Telarc CD 80109–2
1987 Lewis; various choruses, Cologne Radio Symphony Orchestra/Bertini
EMI CDS7 47540–8
1988 Lewis; various choruses, Frankfurt Radio Symphony Orchestra/Inbal
Denon CO 73205/6

Berlioz: *Te Deum*

1953	Young; London Philharmonic Choir/Royal Philharmonic Orchestra/ Beecham	CBS 77395
1968	Tagliavini; London Symphony Chorus and Orchestra/Davis	Philips 416 660–2
1977	Dupouy; Orchestre de Paris and Choir/Barenboim	CBS 76578
1981	Araiza; various choruses, European Community Youth Orchestra/Abbado	DG 410 696–2

Berlioz: *L'Enfance du Christ*

1951	Bouvier, Giraudeau, Roux, Médus, Noguéra; Raymond Saint-Paul Chorus, Paris Conservatoire Orchestra/Cluytens	VOX VUX 2009
1953	Davenport, Simoneau, Singher, Gramm; Choral Art Society, Little Orchestra Society/Scherman	Philips NBL 5022/3
1957	Kopleff, Valletti, Souzay, Tozzi, Oliver; New England Conservatory Chorus, Boston Symphony Orchestra/Munch	RCA Victrola VICS 6006
1960	Morison, Pears, Fleet, Cameron, Rouleau, Frost; St Anthony Singers, Goldsborough Orchestra/Davis	Oiseau-Lyre 425 445–2
1966	De los Angeles, Gedda, Corazza, Blanc, Cottret, Soyer, Depraz; Duclos Choir, Paris Conservatoire Orchestra/Cluytens	HMV SLS 928
?	Berbié, Vanzo, Andreozzi, Calès, Brossmann, Soyer, Soumagnas; French National Radio Choir and Orchestra/Martinon	Nonesuch HB 73022
1976	Baker, Tappy, Langridge, Allen, Herincx, Rouleau, Bastin; John Alldis Choir, London Symphony Orchestra/Davis	Philips 416 949–2
1985	Kimm, Rolfe Johnson, Stephenson, Luxon, Shimell, Van Allan, Thomas; John Alldis Choir, English Chamber Orchestra/Ledger	ASV CDDCD 452
1987	von Otter, Rolfe Johnson, Fockenoy, Cachemaille, Schirrer, van Dam, Bastin; Monteverdi Choir, Lyons Opera Orchestra/Gardiner	Erato ECD 75333

Verdi: Requiem Mass

1929	Fanelli, Minghini-Cattaneo, Lo Giudice, Pinza; La Scala Chorus and Orchestra/Sabajno	HMV D1751/60* Pearl GEMM CD 9324
1938	(Live performance – Queen's Hall, London) Milanov, Thorborg, Roswaenge, Moscona; BBC Choral Society, BBC Symphony Orchestra/Toscanini	Olympic ATS 1108/9
1938	(Broadcast performance) Teschemacher, Willer, Roswaenge, Hann; Stuttgart Radio Chorus and Orchestra/Keilberth	Preiser LV 151/2
1939	Caniglia, Stignani, Gigli, Pinza; Rome Opera Chorus and Orchestra/Serafin	EMI CDH7 63341–2
1940	(Live performance – Carnegie Hall, New York) Milanov, Castagna, Björling, Moscona; Westminster Choir, NBC Symphony Orchestra/Toscanini	Atra – 240 (2)

Discographies

1949   (Live performance – Salzburg Festival) Zadek, Klose, Roswaenge, Christoff; Vienna State Opera Chorus, Vienna Philharmonic Orchestra/Karajan
Cetra LO 524 (2)

c. 1950   Anonymous soloists; Berlin Cathedral Choir and Symphony Orchestra/ Balzer   Royale 1377/8

1951   (Live performance – La Scala) Tebaldi, Rankin, Prandelli, Rossi-Lemeni; La Scala Chorus and Orchestra/De Sabata   Nuova Era 6346/7

1951   (Live performance – Carnegie Hall, New York) Nelli, Barbieri, Di Stefano, Siepi; Shaw Chorale, NBC SO/Toscanini   RCA GD 60326

1951   Hunt, Moudry, Knowles, Smith; Calvary Church Choir, Ossewaarde (organ)
Concert Hall CHS 1311

1951   Kaye, Pirazzini, Sinimberghi, Beuf; Rome Opera Chorus and Orchestra/Ricci
Urania URLP 213

1952   Steingruber, Anday, Delorko, Czerwenka; Austrian Symphony Orchestra and Chorus/Koslik   Remington 199–105

1954   (Live performance – Academy of Music, Boston) Nelli, Turner, Conley, Moscona; chorus, Boston Symphony Orchestra/Cantelli
Cetra LO 503 (2)

1954   Stader, Radev, Krebs, Borg; Berlin RIAS Chamber Choir, St Hedwig's Cathedral Choir, Berlin Radio Symphony Orchestra/Fricsay
DG 2721 171

1954   Schwarzkopf, Domínguez, Di Stefano, Siepi; La Scala Chorus and Orchestra/ De Sabata   Columbia 33CX 1195/6

1955   Brouwenstijn, von Ilosvay, Munteanu, Czerwenka; Santa Cecilia Academy Chorus and Orchestra/van Kempen   Philips A 00284/5 L

1956   Bijster, Pritchard, Garen, Wolovsky; Netherlands Philharmonic Choir and Orchestra/Goehr   Concert Hall SMS 2038

1959   Vartenissian, Cossotto, Fernandi, Christoff; Rome Opera Chorus and Orchestra/Serafin   EMI SXDW 3055

1960   Vishnevskaya, Arkhipova, Ivanovsky, Petrov; Leningrad Glinka Academy Choir, Leningrad Philharmonic Orchestra/Melik-Pashayev
Melodiya D 035389/92

1960   Vishnevskaya, Isakova, Ivanovsky, Petrov; RSFSR Academy Choir, Moscow Philharmonic Orchestra/Markevitch   Philips 6768 215

1960   L. Price, Elias, Björling, Tozzi; Vienna Singverein, Vienna Philharmonic Orchestra/Reiner   Decca 421 608–2

1960   Stader, Domínguez, Carelli, Sardi; St Hedwig's Cathedral Choir, Berlin Radio Symphony Orchestra/Fricsay   DG 429 076–2 (issued 1989)

1963–4   Schwarzkopf, Ludwig, Gedda, Ghiaurov/Philharmonic Chorus and Orchestra/Giulini   EMI CDS 7 47257–8

1964   Amara, Forrester, Tucker; London, Westminster Choir, Philadelphia Orchestra/Ormandy   CBS 72297/8

1965   Nilsson, Chookasian, Bergonzi, Flagello; Boston Pro Musica, Boston Symphony Orchestra/Leinsdorf
RCA (UK) SER 5537/8; (US) LSC 7040

1967   Sutherland, Horne, Pavarotti, Talvela; Vienna State Opera Chorus, Vienna Philharmonic Orchestra/Solti   Decca 411 944–2

1967 Davy, Leal, Peterson, Rehfuss; Vienna State Opera Chorus and Orchestra/
Rivoli   Concert Hall SM 2312
1969 Caballé, Cossotto, Vickers, Raimondi; New Philharmonia Chorus and
Orchestra/Barbirolli   EMI C257 62892 2
1970 Arroyo, Veasey, Domingo, Raimondi; LSO Chorus, London Symphony
Orchestra/Bernstein   CBS CD 77231
1972 Freni, Ludwig, Cossutta, Ghiaurov; Vienna Singverein, Berlin Philharmonic
Orchestra/Karajan   DG 413 215–2
1973 Wiener-Chenisheva, Milcheva-Nonova, Bodurov, Ghiuselev; Obretenov
Chorus, Sofia Philharmonic Orchestra/Marinov
                                          Harmonia Mundi HM140
1976 Harper, Veasey, Bini, Sotin; London Philharmonic Choir, Royal Philharmonic Orchestra/Paita   Lodia LO–CD772/3
1976 Barker, Dunn, Mauro, Plishka; Slovak Philharmonic Choir, Strasbourg
Philharmonic Orchestra/Lombard   Erato STU 70965/6
c.1976 Eichner, Schubert, Johns, Ridderbusch; Gutersloh Society Choir, Herford
Philharmonic Orchestra/Buchei   Ariola-Eurodisc 80926XR
1976 L. Price, Baker, Luchetti, van Dam; Chicago Symphony Chorus and
Orchestra/Solti   RCA RL 02476
1978 Scotto, Baltsa, Luchetti, Nesterenko; Ambrosian Chorus, Philharmonia/
Muti   EMI SLS 5185
1970s Molnar-Talajic, Lilova, Ottolini, Giaiotti; Leipzig Radio Chorus and
Orchestra/Patané   Eterna 826694/5
1980 Ricciarelli, Verrett, Domingo, Ghiaurov; La Scala Chorus and Orchestra/
Abbado   DG 415 976–2
1983 Caballé, Berini, Domingo, Plishka; Musica Sacra Chorus, New York Philharmonic Orchestra/Mchta   CBS 36927
1985 Tomowa-Sintow, Baltsa, Carreras, van Dam; Vienna State Opera Chorus,
Sofia National Opera Chorus, Vienna Philharmonic Orchestra/Karajan
                                                  DG 415 091–2
1987 Zylis-Gara, Szostek-Radkowa, Ochman, Mróz; Warsaw Philharmonic
Orchestra and Chorus/Kord   Rodolphe RPC 32470/1
1987 Studer, Zajic, Pavarotti, Ramey; La Scala Chorus and Orchestra/Muti
                                          EMI CDS7 49390–2
1987 Dunn, Curry, Hadley, Plishka; Atlanta Philharmonic Orchestra and Chorus/
Shaw   Telare CD 80152
1989 Sweet, Quivar, Cole, Estes; Ernst Senff Choir, Berlin Philharmonic
Orchestra/Giulini   DG 423 674–2

Brahms: A German Requiem

1940 Vincent, Kloos; Amsterdam Toonkunst Choir, Concertgebouw Orchestra/
Mengelberg   Philips 416 213–2
1947 Schwarzkopf, Hotter; Vienna Singverein, Vienna Philharmonic Orchestra/
Karajan   HMV CDH7 61010–2
1948 Lindberg-Torlind, Sönnerstedt; Stockholm Philharmonic Chorus and
Orchestra/Furtwängler   Unicorn WFS 17/8

Discographies

c.1949	Steber, Pease; Victor Chorus and Orchestra/Shaw	RCA LM 6004
c.1953	Wissmann, Adam; Frankfurt Opera Chorus and Orchestra/Solti	
		Capitol PBR 8300
c.1954	Stader, Wiener; Berlin Motet Choir, Berlin Philharmonic Orchestra/ Lehmann	DG DGM 18258/9
1954	Seefried, London; Westminster Choir, New York Philharmonic Symphony Orchestra/Walter	CBS 61284
1955	Grümmer, Fischer-Dieskau; St Hedwig's Cathedral Choir, Berlin Philharmonic Orchestra/Kempe	HMV XLP 30073/4
1950s	Sailer, Titze; Stuttgart Choir and Orchestra/Couraud	World Records CM 44/5
1960s	Stich-Randall, Pease; Hamburg Singakademie, North German Radio Symphony Orchestra/Bamberger	Concert Hall SMS 2099
1961	Schwarzkopf, Fischer-Dieskau; Philharmonia Chorus and Orchestra/ Klemperer	EMI CDC7 47238-2
1961	Lipp, Crass; Vienna Singverein, Vienna Symphony Orchestra/Sawallisch	Philips 6720 006
1964	Giebel, Prey; Lausanne Pro Arte Choir, Suisse Romande Orchestra/Ansermet	Decca DPA 583/4
1964	Janowitz, Waechter; Vienna Singverein, Berlin Philharmonic Orchestra/ Karajan	DG 427 252-2
1969	Caballé, Milnes; New England Chorus, Boston Symphony Orchestra/ Leinsdorf	RCA GD86800
1972	Mathis, Fischer-Dieskau; Edinburgh Festival Choir, London Philharmonic Orchestra/Barenboim	DG 415 000-1
1976	Cotrubas, Prey; New Philharmonia Chorus and Orchestra/Maazel	CBS CD 45853
1976	Tomowa-Sintow, van Dam; Vienna Singverein, Berlin Philharmonic Orchestra/Karajan	EMI CDM7 69229-2
1978	Te Kanawa, Weikl; Chicago Symphony Chorus and Orchestra/Solti	Decca 414 627-2
1976	Donath, Widmer; South German Madrigal Choir, Ludwigsburg Festival Orchestra/Gönnenwein	Electrola 1C 157 99703/4
1980s	Schlick, Langshaw; Bremen Cathedral Choir, Hannover Radio Symphony Orchestra/Helbich	MD&G J1064/5
1980s	Aruhn, Holl; Danish Radio Philharmonic Chorus and Orchestra/Corboz	Erato ECD 88227
1980s	Tokody, Gáti; Slovak Philharmonic Chorus and Orchestra/Ferencsik	Hungaroton SLPD 12475/6
1983	Janowitz, Krause; Vienna State Opera Chorus, Vienna Philharmonic Orchestra/Haitink	Philips 411 436-2
1984	Augér, Stilwell; Atlanta Symphony Chorus and Orchestra/Shaw	Telarc CD 80092
1984	Norman, Hynninen; London Philharmonic Choir and Orchestra/Tennstedt	EMI EX 270313-3
1985	Hendricks, Van Dam; Vienna Singverein, Vienna Philharmonic Orchestra/ Karajan	DG 410 521-2

1985   Häggander, Lorenz; Leipzig Radio Chorus and Symphony Orchestra/Kegel
Capriccio 10 095

1986   Price, Allen; Bavarian Radio Symphony Chorus and Orchestra/Sawallisch
Orfeo C 039101A

1986   Price, Ramey; Ambrosian Singers, Royal Philharmonic Orchestra/Previn
Teldec 8.43335

1986   Battle, Hagegård; Chicago Symphony Chorus and Orchestra/Levine
RCA RD 85003

1987   Bonney, Schmidt; Vienna State Opera Chorus, Vienna Philharmonic
Orchestra/Giulini   DG 423 574−2

1989   Popp, Brendel; Prague Philharmonic Choir, Czech Philharmonic Orchestra/
Sinopoli   DG 429 486−2

Fauré: Requiem

1930s   Malnory-Marseillac, Morturier; Bach Society Chorus and Orchestra/Bret
HMV.D2101/5

1938   Dupont, Didier; Lyons Chorus and Orchestra/Bourmauck
Col. LX773/7; Helios H80003

1940s   Denya, Harrell; Disciples of Massenet, Montreal Festival Orchestra/
Pelletier   HMV ED 364/8; Canadian Victor LCT 7003

1948   Peyron, Conrad; Chorus and Orchestra/Boulanger
HMV CDH7 61025−2

1950   Sautereau, Demigny; Paris Philharmonic Chorus and Orchestra/Leibowitz
Saga XID 5246

1951   Angelici, Noguéra; St Eustache Singers, Orchestra/Cluytens
Col. CX 1145

1951   Ogéas, Demigny; French Radio Chorus, Théâtre des Champs-Elysées
Orchestra/Inghelbrecht   Ducretet-Thomson DTL 93083

c.1952 Beems, Uppman; Roger Wagner Chorale, Concert Arts Orchestra/Wagner
Capitol CTL 7050

1952   Alarie, Maurane; Elisabeth Brasseur Chorale, Lamoureux Orchestra/Fournet
Philips G 03101 L

1959   Danco, Souzay; Chorale de la Tour de Peilz, Suisse Romande Orchestra/
Ansermet   Decca 421 026 2

1962   de los Angeles, Fischer-Dieskau; Elisabeth Brasseur Chorale, Paris Conservatoire Orchestra/Cluytens   EMI CDC7 47836−2

1967   Chilcott, Case; King's College Choir, New Philharmonic Orchestra/Willcocks
HMV ASD 2358

?   Arroyo, Prey; Musica Aeterna Chorus and Orchestra/Waldman
Am. Decca DL 710169

1972   Clément, Huttenlocher; Chorus, Berne Philharmonic Orchestra/Corboz
Erato 2292−45116−2

1974   Armstrong, Fischer-Dieskau; Edinburgh Festival Chorus, Paris Orchestra/
Barenboim   HMV CDM7 69038−2

293

1975   Bond, Luxon; St John's College Choir, Academy of St Martin-in-the-Fields/
Guest   Argo ZRG 841

1977   Burrowes, Rayner Cook; City of Birmingham Philharmonic Orchestra and
Chorus/Frémaux   HMV CDM7 69841−2

1977   Popp, Nimsgern; Ambrosian Singers, Philharmonic Orchestra/A. Davis
CBS 76734

1981   Augér, Luxon; King's College Choir, English Chamber Orchestra/Ledger
HMV ASD 4234

1981   Aruhn, Shirley-Quirk; Chorus, Belgian National Opera Orchestra/Cambreling
Opéra National 1981 011

1984   Ashton, Varcoe; Cambridge Singers, City of London Sinfonia/Rutter
Conifer COLCD 109

1985   Hendricks, van Dam; Orfeón Donostiarrá, Toulouse Capitole Orchestra/
Plasson   HMV CDC7 47317−2

1985   Popp, Estes; Leipzig Radio Chorus, Dresden Staatskapelle/C. Davis
Philips 412 743−2

1986   Jones, Roberts; London Symphony Chorus, RPO/Hickox
RPO/ASV CDRPO 8004

1986   Battle, Schmidt; Philharmonia Chorus and Orchestra/Giulini
DG 419 243−2

1986   Mézac, Piquemal; Argenteuil Vittoria Choir, Bernard Thomas Chamber
Orchestra/Thomas   Forlane UCD 16536

1986   Blegen, Morris; Atlanta Symphony Orchestra and Chorus/Shaw
Telarc CD 80135

1987   Ameling, Kruysen; Netherlands Radio Chorus; Rotterdam Philharmonic
Orchestra/Fournet   Philips 420 707−2

1987   Oliver, Wilson-Johnson; Westminster Cathedral Choir, City of London
Sinfonia/Hill   IMP PCD 896

1987   Te Kanawa, Milnes; Montreal Symphony Orchestra and Chorus/Dutoit
Decca 421 440−2

1988   Mellon, Kooy; Paris Chapelle Royale Chorus, Musique Oblique Ensemble/
Herreweghe   Harmonia Mundi HMC90 1292

1988   Seers, George; Corydon Singers, English Chamber Orchestra/Best
Hyperion CDA 66292

?   Mathis, Widmer; Lucerne Festival Chorus, Swiss Festival Orchestra/Fournet
Schwann AMS 3555

198?   Thilliez, Kruysen; Chorale Philippe Caillard, Monte Carlo National Opera
Orchestra/Frémaux   Erato ECD 40006

1989   Eteson, Bär; King's College Choir, Cambridge, English Chamber Orchestra/
S. Cleobury   EMI CDC 7 49880 2

Elgar: *The Dream of Gerontius*

1924   Furmedge, Jones, Brazell; anonymous chorus and orchestra/Batten
                                                 Edison Bell VF 591/8

1945   Ripley, Nash, Noble, Walker; Huddersfield Choral Society, Liverpool Philharmonic Orchestra/Sargent   HMV C 3435/46; RLS 709

1954   Thomas, Lewis, Cameron; Huddersfield Choral Society, Liverpool Philharmonic Orchestra/Sargent   EMI CHS7 63376−2

1965   Baker, Lewis, Borg; Sheffield Philharmonic Choir, Hallé Choir and Orchestra/Barbirolli   EMI CMS 7 63185−2

1972   Minton, Pears, Shirley-Quirk; King's College Choir, London Symphony Chorus and Orchestra/Britten   Decca 421 381−2

1976   Watts, Gedda, Lloyd; John Alldis Choir, LPO Choir, New Philharmonia Orchestra/Boult   EMI CDS 7 47208−8

1976   Hodgson, Tear, Luxon; Scottish National Chorus and Orchestra/Gibson
                                                 CRD CRD 3326/7

1987   Baker, Mitchinson, Shirley-Quirk; City of Birmingham Chorus and Orchestra/Rattle   EMI CDS 7 49549−2

1988   Palmer, Davies, Howell; London Symphony Chorus and Orchestra/Hickox
                                               Chandos CHAN 8641/2

Excerpts

1927   Balfour, Wilson, Heyner; Royal Choral Society, Royal Albert Hall Orchestra/Elgar   Opal 810

Walton: *Belshazzar's Feast*

1943   Noble; Huddersfield Choral Society, Liverpool Philharmonic Orchestra/Walton   HMV C 3330/4; HMV ED 29 0715−1

1953   Noble; London Philharmonic Chorus and Orchestra/Boult
                                                 PRT PVCD 8394

1958   Milligan; Huddersfield Choral Society, Royal Liverpool Philharmonic Orchestra/Sargent   EMI CHS7 63376−2

1959   Bell; Philharmonia Chorus and Orchestra/Walton   Columbia SAX 2319

*c.*1960   Cassel; Rutgers University Choir, Philadelphia Orchestra/Ormandy
                                                 CBS S61264

*c.*1970   Peterson; University of Utah Civic Chorale and Symphony Orchestra/Abravanel   Vox STGBY 658

1972   Shirley-Quirk; London Symphony Chorus and Orchestra/Previn
                                             EMI CDC7 47624 2

1973   Rippon; Hallé Choir and Orchestra/Loughran   Cfp 40063

1977   Milnes; Scottish National Chorus and Orchestra/Gibson
                                             RCA GL 13368

1977   Luxon; London Philharmonic Choir and Orchestra/Solti
                                             Decca 425 154−2

1977   Briggs; Chetham's Senior Choir and Senior Orchestra, Orchestra of the RNCM/Brewer   RNCM 03

1986   Luxon; Brighton Festival Chorus, London Collegium Musicum, Royal
Philharmonic Orchestra/Previn   RPO CD 8001

1988   Wilson-Johnson; London Symphony Chorus and Orchestra/Hickox
                EMI CDC7 49496 2

1989   Stone; Atlanta Symphony Chorus and Orchestra/Shaw
                Telarc CD 80181

1989   Howell; Bach Choir, Philharmonia Orchestra/Willcocks
                Chandos CHAN 8760

Tippett: *A Child of Our Time*

1958   Morison, Bowden, Lewis, Standen; Royal Opera House, Covent Garden,
Chorus and Orchestra/Pritchard   Argo 425 158–2

1975   Norman, Baker, Cassilly, Shirley-Quirk; BBC Singers, Choral Society and
Symphony Orchestra/Davis   Philips 420 075–2

1986   Armstrong, Palmer, Langridge, Shirley-Quirk; Brighton Festival Chorus,
Royal Philharmonic Orchestra/Previn   RPO CD 8005

Britten: *War Requiem*

1962   Vishnevskaya, Pears, Fischer-Dieskau; Bach Choir, Highgate School Choir,
Melos Ensemble, London Symphony Orchestra/Britten

                Decca 414 382–2

1968   Kuhse, Schreier, Leib; Leipzig Radio Choir and Children's Choir and
Symphony Orchestra/Kegel   Eterna 825 906/7

1975   Altmeyer, Sells, Lawrence; William Hall Chorale, Columbus Boychoir,
Vienna Festival Symphony Orchestra/Hall   Klavier KS 44

1983   Söderström, Tear, Allen; Christchurch Cathedral Choir, City of Birmingham
Chorus and Orchestra/Rattle   EMI CDS7 47034 8

1989   Haywood, Rolfe Johnson, Luxon; Atlanta Symphony Chorus and Orchestra/
Shaw   Telarc CD 80157

Stravinsky: *The Wedding*

1940   Winter, Seymour, Jones, Henderson/Stravinsky   Col. LX 326/8

1952   Luz, Meesen; Dresden State Opera Chorus and Ensemble/Schreiber
                Allegro 4010

1953   Addison, Okerson, Price, Burrows; New York Concert Choir and Orchestra/
Hillis   Vox PL 8630

1953   Steingruber, Kenney, Wagner, Waechter; Vienna Chamber Choir, Instru-
mentalists/Rossi   Vanguard PVL 7009

1954   Bijster, Canne-Meijer, Haefliger, Schey; Netherlands Chamber Choir
Instrumentalists/de Nobel   Philips ABL 3124

1959   Allen, Sarfaty, Driscoll, Oliver; American Concert Choir, Instrumentalists/
Stravinsky   CBS 74066

1965   Brumaire, Scharley, Pottier, van Dam; Paris Opera Chorus, Instrumentalists/
Boulez   Concert Hall SMS 2433

1961	Retchitzka, Devallier, Cuénod, Rehfuss; Motet Choir of Geneva, Instrumentalists/Ansermet	Decca ECS 822
1965	Domanínská, Mrázová, Žídek, Jedlička; Czech Philharmonic Chorus Instrumentalists/Ančerl	Supraphon SUAST 50623
1967	Allen, Albert, Litten, Metcalf; Gregg Smith Singers, Instrumentalists/Craft	Am.Col. M33201
1970s	Retchitzka, Chedel, Tappy, Huttenlocher; Lausanne University Chorus, Instrumentalists/Dutoit	Erato STU 70737
1973	Reef, Taylor, Nelson, Fifer; Gregg Smith Singers, Orpheus Chamber Ens./Craft	CBS SBRG 72609
1977	Mory, Parker, Mitchinson, Hudson; English Bach Festival Chorus, Instrumentalists/Bernstein	DG 423 251–2
1986	Quercia, Cooper, Capelle, Marinov; Choeur Contemporain, Les Percussions de Strasbourg/Hayrabedian	Pierre Verany PV 787032
1988	Ablaberdyeva, Ivanova, Martinov, Safiulin; Slovak Philharmonic Chorus, Savaria Symphony Orchestra/Eötvös	Hungaroton SLPD 12989

Stravinsky: *Symphony of Psalms*

c.1931	Alexei Vlassov Choir, Orchestra/Stravinsky	CD LX 147/9
1946	Choir, CBS SO/Stravinsky	Philips ABL 3065
1950	London Philharmonic Chorus and Orchestra/Ansermet	Decca LXT 2916
1954	Berlin RIAS Chamber Choir, St Hedwig's Cathedral Choir; Berlin Radio Symphony Orchestra/Fricsay	DG DGM 19073
1960	Lausanne Radio Chorus, Suisse Romande Orchestra/Ansermet	Decca SXL 2277
1963	Russian State Academy Choir, Russian State Philharmonic Orchestra/Markevitch	Philips SAL 3430
1963	Festival Singers of Toronto, CBC Symphony Orchestra/Stravinsky	CBS CD 42434
1967	Czech Philharmonic Chorus and Orchestra/Ančerl	Supraphon SUAST 50778
1967	French National Chorus and Orchestra/Markevitch	Montaigne TCE 8811
1972	English Bach Festival Chorus, London Symphony Orchestra/Bernstein	CBS CD 44710
1975	Berlin Deutsche Oper Chorus, Berlin Philharmonic Orchestra/Karajan	DG 423 252–2
1975	Choir of Christ Church Cathedral, Oxford, London Sinfonietta/Preston	Decca 417 230–1
1982	Stuttgart Radio Symphony Orchestra and Chorus/Bertini	Orfeo C 015821 A
1983	Berlin Radio Symphony Orchestra and Chorus/Chailly	Decca 414 078–2
1983	Wisconsin Conservatory Symphony Chorus, Milwaukee Symphony Orchestra/Foss	ProArte PAD 169

Discographies

1985 Atlanta Symphony Chorus and Orchestra/Shaw   Telarc CD80105
1987 Paris Orchestra Chorus, Paris Orchestra/Barenboim

Erato ECD 75494
1988 Swedish Radio Choir and Symphony Orchestra/Ehrling

BIS BIS-CD 400

Janáček: *Glagolitic Mass*

1951 Unidentified soloists; Vsmu and Moravan Choruses, Brno Radio Symphony
Orchestra, Michalek (organ)/Bakala   Heritage HCN 8005
1963 Domanínská, Soukupová, Blachut, Haken; Czech Singers' Chorus, Czech
Philharmonic Orchestra, Vodrážka (organ)/Ančerl

Supraphon 11–0609–2
1964 Lear, Rössl-Majdan, Haefliger, Crass; Bavarian Radio Symphony Chorus
and Orchestra, Janáček (organ)/Kubelik   DG 429 182–2
1965 Pilarczyk, Martin, Gedda, Gaynes; Westminster Choir, New York Philharmonic Orchestra, Prince-Joseph (organ)/Bernstein   CBS SBRG 72361
1973 Kubiak, Collins, Tear, Schöne; Brighton Festival Chorus, Royal Philharmonic Orchestra, Birch (organ)/Kempe   Decca SXL 6600
1978 Beňačková, Soukupová, Livora, Průša; Czech Philharmonic Chorus and
Orchestra, Hora (organ)/Neumann   Panton 11 0720
1979 Beňačková, Randová, Přibyl, Kopčák; Czech Philharmonic Chorus, Brno
Philharmonic Orchestra, Hora (organ)/Jílek   Supraphon 1112 26989
1982 Palmer, Gunson, Mitchinson, King; CBSO Chorus, City of Birmingham
Symphony Orchestra, Parker-Smith (organ)/Rattle

EMI CDC7 47054 2
1984 Söderström, Drobková, Livora, Novák; Prague Philharmonic Chorus, Czech
Philharmonic Orchestra, Hora (organ)/Mackerras

Supraphon C37–7448

Index of Conductors and Soloists

Index

Index

302

Index

Index

Index